Methodological Advances
in Cross-National Surveys
of Educational Achievement

Board on International Comparative Studies in Education

Andrew C. Porter and Adam Gamoran, *Editors*

Board on Testing and Assessment
Center for Education
Division of Behavioral and Social Sciences and Education

National Research Council

NATIONAL ACADEMY PRESS
Washington, DC

NATIONAL ACADEMY PRESS • 2101 Constitution Avenue, NW • Washington, D.C. 20418

NOTICE: The project that is the subject of this report was approved by the Governing Board of the National Research Council, whose members are drawn from the councils of the National Academy of Sciences, the National Academy of Engineering, and the Institute of Medicine. The members of the committee responsible for the report were chosen for their special competences and with regard for appropriate balance.

This study was supported by Grant No. REC-9815157 between the National Academy of Sciences and the National Science Foundation, which includes funds from the National Center for Education Statistics of the U.S. Department of Education. Any opinions, findings, conclusions, or recommendations expressed in this publication are those of the author(s) and do not necessarily reflect the views of the organizations or agencies that provided support for the project.

Library of Congress Cataloging-in-Publication Data

Methodological advances in cross-national surveys of educational
achievement / Board on International Comparative Studies in Education ;
Andrew C. Porter and Adam Gamoran, editors.
    p. cm.
"Board on Testing and Assessment, Center for Education, Division of
Behavioral and Social Sciences and Education, National Research
Council."
Papers and discussions from a public symposium held by the Board on
International Comparative Studies in Education (BICSE) of the National
Research Council in November 2000.
Includes bibliographical references and index.
  ISBN 0-309-08333-8 (pbk.)
  1. Education—Research—Methodology—Congresses. 2. Academic
achievement—Congresses. 3. Comparative education—Congresses. I.
Porter, Andrew C. II. Gamoran, Adam, 1957- III. National Research
Council (U.S.). Board on International Comparative Studies in Education.
IV. National Research Council (U.S.). Division of Behavioral and Social
Sciences and Education. Board on Testing and Assessment. V. National
Research Council (U.S.). Center for Education.
  LB1028 .M419 2002
  370'.7'2—dc21

2002002602

Suggested citation: National Research Council. (2002). *Methodological advances in cross-national surveys of educational achievement*. Board on International Comparative Studies in Education. A.C. Porter and A. Gamoran, Editors. Board on Testing and Assessment, Center for Education, Division of Behavioral and Social Sciences and Education. Washington, DC: National Academy Press.

Additional copies of this report are available from National Academy Press, 2101 Constitution Avenue, N.W., Lockbox 285, Washington, DC 20055; (800) 624-6242 or (202) 334-3313 (in the Washington metropolitan area); Internet, http://www.nap.edu/.

THE NATIONAL ACADEMIES

National Academy of Sciences
National Academy of Engineering
Institute of Medicine
National Research Council

The **National Academy of Sciences** is a private, nonprofit, self-perpetuating society of distinguished scholars engaged in scientific and engineering research, dedicated to the furtherance of science and technology and to their use for the general welfare. Upon the authority of the charter granted to it by the Congress in 1863, the Academy has a mandate that requires it to advise the federal government on scientific and technical matters. Dr. Bruce M. Alberts is president of the National Academy of Sciences.

The **National Academy of Engineering** was established in 1964, under the charter of the National Academy of Sciences, as a parallel organization of outstanding engineers. It is autonomous in its administration and in the selection of its members, sharing with the National Academy of Sciences the responsibility for advising the federal government. The National Academy of Engineering also sponsors engineering programs aimed at meeting national needs, encourages education and research, and recognizes the superior achievements of engineers. Dr. Wm. A. Wulf is president of the National Academy of Engineering.

The **Institute of Medicine** was established in 1970 by the National Academy of Sciences to secure the services of eminent members of appropriate professions in the examination of policy matters pertaining to the health of the public. The Institute acts under the responsibility given to the National Academy of Sciences by its congressional charter to be an adviser to the federal government and, upon its own initiative, to identify issues of medical care, research, and education. Dr. Kenneth I. Shine is president of the Institute of Medicine.

The **National Research Council** was organized by the National Academy of Sciences in 1916 to associate the broad community of science and technology with the Academy's purposes of furthering knowledge and advising the federal government. Functioning in accordance with general policies determined by the Academy, the Council has become the principal operating agency of both the National Academy of Sciences and the National Academy of Engineering in providing services to the government, the public, and the scientific and engineering communities. The Council is administered jointly by both Academies and the Institute of Medicine. Dr. Bruce M. Alberts and Dr. Wm. A. Wulf are chairman and vice chairman, respectively, of the National Research Council.

v

Reviewers

This report has been reviewed in draft form by individuals chosen for their diverse perspectives and technical expertise, in accordance with procedures approved by the Report Review Committee of the National Research Council (NRC). The purpose of this independent review is to provide candid and critical comments that will assist the institution in making the published report as sound as possible and to ensure that the report meets institutional standards for objectivity, evidence, and responsiveness to the study charge. The review comments and draft manuscript remain confidential to protect the integrity of the deliberative process. We thank the following individuals for their participation in the review of this report:

Stephen P. Heyneman, Vanderbilt University
Susan Holloway, University of California, Berkeley
Neville Postlethwaite, Hamburg University, Germany (retired)
Laura H. Salganik, American Institutes for Research

Although the reviewers listed above have provided many constructive comments and suggestions, they were not asked to endorse the conclusions or recommendations nor did they see the final draft of the report before its release. The review of this report was overseen by Judith Torney-Purta, University of Maryland. Appointed by the NRC, she was responsible for making certain that an independent examination of this report was carried out in accordance with institutional procedures and that all review comments were carefully considered. Responsibility for the final content of this report rests entirely with the authoring committee and the institution.

Preface

In November 2000, the Board on International Comparative Studies in Education (BICSE) of the National Research Council held a public symposium titled "Methodological Advances in Large-Scale Cross-National Education Surveys" (see Appendix A for the symposium agenda and list of participants). The purpose was to draw on the wealth of experience gathered over a four-decade period, to evaluate improvement in the methodology, and to identify the most pressing methodological issues that remain to be solved. The papers prepared for that symposium and the discussions of those papers make up this volume. Collectively, they represent the most up-to-date and comprehensive assessment of methodological strengths and weaknesses of international comparative studies of student achievement.

BICSE has a long and distinguished history of monitoring the quality of large-scale international studies of student achievement; this was the primary purpose for which it was originally established. In the late 1980s, in response to growing public interest in using international comparisons to inform U.S. education reform, the National Science Foundation (NSF) and the National Center for Education Statistics (NCES) sought assistance from the National Academy of Sciences. BICSE's two principal objectives were (1) to help improve the quality of international comparative studies in education generally, and (2) to aid U.S. policy makers in ensuring the high quality of the data collected by the United States for those studies. During its first nine years, BICSE served in an oversight role regarding U.S. participation in international education studies—guiding and enhancing the collection, interpretation, and use of international education data that can inform policy making.

In 1998, BICSE was reconfigured to take on an expanded agenda, seeking to provide the locus for conceptual leadership in the field of international education studies and comparative analyses of education systems. Keeping its original charge, BICSE sought to become more pro-active, conducting syntheses of comparative work, documenting lessons learned from previous work, and documenting advances in the method-ology of comparative surveys (the purpose of this volume). The reconfig-uration of BICSE was endorsed enthusiastically by its sponsors, NSF and NCES. In November 1999, BICSE held a workshop on the uses of video in international education studies as its first public initiative under its expanded agenda. The November 2000 symposium on methodological advances in large-scale cross-national education surveys represented BICSE's second initiative.

Although we had the privilege of leading BICSE's assessment of meth-odological advances, this volume represents an accomplishment of the entire board. We are fortunate to work with wise and dedicated colleagues on BICSE who contributed to the project at each step of the way—from its initial conception, to selecting symposium participants, to providing feed-back to authors on multiple drafts of the papers contained in this volume (see Appendix B for contributing members' biographical sketches). In addition to current and recent BICSE members, former member John Dossey played a leadership role at an earlier stage of this project. We are also indebted to BICSE's superb staff, including former director Patricia Morison, current director Colette Chabbott, and staff members Monica Ulewicz and Jane Phillips, for their help in moving this project forward. We also thank Laura Penny for her editorial advice, and Kirsten Sampson Snyder and Yvonne Wise for their guidance of the report through the review and production process. We appreciate the support of Larry Suter of NSF and Eugene Owen of NCES, which came not only in the form of funding their agencies provided to BICSE, but also as helpful insights on this project.

Andrew C. Porter and Adam Gamoran, *Editors*

Contents

Introduction

1

Progress and Challenges for Large-Scale Studies

*Andrew C. Porter and Adam Gamoran**

"Poor Scores by U.S. Students Lead to 10-State Math Effort," "U.S. Seniors Near Bottom in World Test," "A World-Class Education Eludes Many in the U.S." Headlines like these have splashed across the pages of major newspapers in the United States with increasing frequency in recent years. Although international studies of student achievement have attracted positive attention, they have also drawn critics. How useful are these international comparisons? A crucial issue in judging the value of international studies is the quality of their methodologies. A symposium of leading experts on the methodology of large-scale international education surveys, organized by the Board on International Comparative Studies in Education (BICSE) in November 2000, addressed the following questions:

- What is the methodological quality of the most recent international surveys of student achievement? How authoritative are their results?
- Has the methodological quality of international achievement studies improved over the past 40 years?
- What are promising opportunities for further improvement?

The chapters in this volume are products of that symposium, and they answer these questions. Readers will learn that, overall, the quality

---

*Andrew C. Porter is the former chair of BICSE. Adam Gamoran is a current member of BICSE. Biographical sketches of both can be found in Appendix B.

of international achievement studies is high, and according to these experts, the results can be taken as authoritative. Four decades of experience with large-scale cross-national surveys have led to substantial improvements in methodology, including better tests, better samples, better documentation, and better statistical analyses. At the same time, substantial challenges remain, including a need to develop a better appreciation of differences in the social and cultural contexts in which education takes place in different nations and the manner in which those contextual differences may be reflected in the results of achievement tests.

The symposium had a considerable body of experience from which to draw. Since 1960, the United States has participated in 15 large-scale cross-national education surveys: 13 conducted by the International Association for the Evaluation of Educational Achievement (IEA) and two by the International Assessment of Education Progress (IAEP). In more recent years, the Organization for Economic Cooperation and Development (OECD) also has become involved, creating a Program for International Student Assessment (PISA) that will survey achievement of 15-year-olds. The most assessed subjects have been science and mathematics, though reading comprehension, geography, nonverbal reasoning, literature, French, English as a foreign language, civic education, history, computers in education, primary education, and second-language acquisition all have been assessed. Several of the international studies have included survey questionnaires that supplemented the achievement tests. Most commonly, the surveys were addressed to students, but teachers and principals also have been queried. A few studies have had case study components, and most recently, one study (the Third International Mathematics and Science Study [TIMSS] and its repeat, TIMSS-R) had a large-scale classroom video component. The frequency, number, and complexity of these international studies of student achievement have increased in recent years.

PURPOSES OF INTERNATIONAL
COMPARATIVE STUDIES OF ACHIEVEMENT

Before assessing the methodology of international comparative studies, it is important to clarify their purposes. Previous writers have offered a variety of reasons why international comparative studies of student achievement are useful (Beaton, Postlethwaite, Ross, Spearritt, & Wolf, 1999; National Research Council, 1990, 1993; Postlethwaite, 1999). The most powerful and widely agreed upon of these is that education in one country can be better understood in comparison to education in other countries. One piece of this argument could be called benchmarking: For example, how does the achievement of U.S. students compare to the achievement of students in other countries? Do some countries stand as existence proofs for the possibility of higher levels of achievement? Another piece of this argument concerns hypothesis generation: By studying education in other countries, alternative approaches to teaching and learning may be discovered. When alternative practices occur in unusually high-achieving countries, they may suggest hypotheses for how education in low-achieving countries might be improved. Of course, countries differ in so many ways that one cannot simply interpret associations between alternative practices and high student achievement as matters of cause and effect. Furthermore, because cultures differ across countries, sometimes quite sharply, it may be that practices in one country cannot be replicated in another. Still, hypotheses about potentially more effective educational practices have been generated by international studies of student achievement, and they can be tested for their feasibility and effects. For example, an analysis of TIMSS (Schmidt, McKnight, & Raizen, 1996) concluded that U.S. mathematics and science education, in comparison with that of higher achieving countries, is characterized by a "splintered vision" and that the United States must strive to create a curriculum with greater focus and less redundancy across grades. Standards-based reform could be seen as testing that hypothesis.

Another reason why international comparative studies of student achievement are useful is that, at least in the United States, policy makers often view them as more authoritative than within-country research. For example, the highly visible and influential report *A Nation at Risk* (National Commission on Excellence in Education, 1983) used international surveys of student achievement results to argue, "The educational foundations of our society are presently being eroded by a rising tide of mediocrity that threatens our very future as a nation and a people" (p. 5). Unquestionably, the inflammatory language of the report had a great deal to do with its influence. Still, it was largely the international comparative data on student achievement, showing the United States as ranking low among other countries, upon which the report built its case. There was plenty of within-country data on which the report might have built its case, including the declines in National Assessment of Educational Progress (NAEP) and Scholastic Aptitude Test (SAT) scores during the 1970s.

There is at least one more purpose that international comparative studies of student achievement can serve—contributing to the advance of methodology. As is clearly documented in this volume, international comparative studies are complicated and difficult to do well. Over the past 40 years, many methodological advances have been made in the context of this international comparative work, and these advances have strengthened the quality of education research within the United States. The development of video methodologies for TIMSS is one example. The evolution of the concept of *opportunity to learn* and its shift from use as a control variable to a policy output variable is another.

The BICSE Symposium

Nine papers were commissioned by BICSE for the November 2000 symposium. Revised versions of those papers constitute the main body of this volume, and they are grouped into three areas: Study Design, Culture and Context, and Making Inferences.

Study design. Robert Linn wrote on the measurement of cognitive achievement in the design, conduct, and analysis of international studies in education. Ronald Hambleton addressed the translation of achievement tests and other instruments involved in international studies. James Chromy discussed the statistical issues of sampling, excluded populations, and age-versus-grade cohorts.

Culture and context. Janine Bempechat, Norma Jimenez, and Beth Boulay looked at cultural-cognitive issues in academic achievement and the assessment of student achievement beliefs, including attributions for success or failure. Claudia Buchmann addressed the measurement and use of family background variables in international studies of education. Gerald LeTendre identified methodological issues that arise in international comparative studies on education stemming from the varying cultural contexts of schooling in different nations.

Making inferences. Robert Floden addressed the measurement and use of opportunity to learn and other explanatory variables in the design, conduct, and analysis of international studies in education. Stephen Raudenbush and Ji-Soo Kim wrote on the statistical issues surrounding the comparisons of data across countries and between countries over time. Marshall Smith, former U.S. Undersecretary of Education, addressed the use of international comparative studies of education for drawing inferences for national policy.

Each author was asked (1) to describe, with reference to the particular topic, how, if at all, international surveys of student achievement have improved over time; (2) to assess the quality of the most recent work in the area; and (3) to identify ways in which future work might be strengthened.

Criteria for High-Quality International Studies of Student Achievement

How might one assess the quality of international comparative studies of student achievement? In 1990, BICSE identified the following criteria for a quality study (National Research Council, 1990):

- The study has value for better understanding and/or improving U.S. education.
- The study is tied to previous work for purposes of comparison.
- The study takes into account cultural differences between countries.
- The study is characterized by research neutrality (e.g., not just a Western perspective).
- There is adequate capacity to conduct a study, both internationally and within each participating country.
- The study has technical validity, including representative samples; precise estimates of parameters; appropriate achievement tests, with standardized administration; good translations; appropriate background questionnaires; an adequate analysis plan; an adequate reporting plan; dissemination to both technical and lay audiences; and adequate data audit.

These criteria informed the plans for the November 2000 symposium and the feedback to authors for revisions of their papers.

Other Types of International Comparative Work

Although the focus of this volume is on large-scale quantitative studies of student achievement, BICSE recognizes the importance of other forms of international comparative work. Small, focused studies can provide much greater depth in addressing questions of the purposes of schooling, the nature of teaching, and the attitudes and beliefs of students and parents. Reiterating a BICSE statement in *A Collaborative Agenda for Improving International Comparative Studies in Education* (National Research Council, 1993, p. 22):

> In addition to large-scale surveys, there is a need for a wide range of other cross-national research, such as ethnographic studies, case studies, small-scale focused, quantitative and qualitative studies, and historical studies, that would allow us to understand what it means to be educated in diverse settings around the world.

KEY FINDINGS:
METHODOLOGICAL ADVANCES AND LIMITATIONS

The nine research syntheses included in this volume provide a sense of progress over time, indicate current methodological quality, and identify areas in which improvements are needed. The remainder of this chapter highlights the major findings and conclusions of the syntheses. A concluding chapter by Brian Rowan, following the nine syntheses, offers further reflections on what the major findings mean for the future of large-scale comparative international studies of achievement.

Study Design: Achievement Tests, Translation, and Sampling

The chapters by Linn, Hambleton, and Chromy report substantial progress over 40 years of effort in improving the quality of the design and execution of comparative international studies of achievement. Recent and ongoing studies such as TIMSS and PISA exhibit high levels of methodological quality; confidence in the results they provide is justified. Important exceptions to the general high level of quality exist, and these will be noted here (and are spelled out in greater detail in subsequent chapters). However, the overriding conclusion from this volume is that the level of methodological quality is high and therefore the findings of large-scale studies are worth taking seriously.

Progress in test design, translation, and sampling. Tests of student achievement used in international comparative studies have improved markedly over time. The frameworks used to guide test construction have gotten better, delineating not only finer arrays of topics, but also—crossed with topics—cognitive demand (expectations for student achievement). Using the elaborated framework, matrix sampling has allowed achievement tests to achieve greater breadth of coverage. The result has been better attention to testing higher order skills than was previously possible. At the same time, increasingly high-quality country reviews of item pools have helped to determine test alignment with each country's curriculum. This alignment, in turn, has made possible analyses of how well a country does on just those items that it deems appropriate. (Interestingly, the results have not greatly changed between-country rankings.)

Despite having students take different samples of items, more sophisticated uses of item response theory have allowed the creation of common scales. At the same time, there also has been an increase in the use of subscales, an important development because countries can differ in their achievement on subscales. Test designers now use differential item functioning (DIF) to identify items that might be culturally biased. Field testing of items and clearer standards for item statistics represent another improvement. Rigorous translation procedures are used in the most recent international studies, and translation errors involve only a small fraction of the test items. In short, important psychometric advances have made it feasible to accomplish many of the improvements in student achievement testing that early researchers recognized as needed.

Early cross-national analyses of educational achievement often had major shortcomings in both the design and the execution of sampling. Response rates were weak and poorly documented. That is no longer the case. Recent studies have improved dramatically and now meet reasonable standards that justify confidence in statistical inferences. These improvements include much better monitoring of quality and substantial improvement in documentation, supported by increased technological capacity to gauge response rates and sampling error. For example, sampling designs, response rates, and documentation for TIMSS were much improved over the Second International Mathematics Study (SIMS).[1] PISA is at least as strong. Indeed, the execution of samples has improved to the point where the sampling *plans* may be more problematic than the samples that are drawn in some cases.

Important challenges of study design. The chapters on study design provide details about several problems that require attention. In BICSE's view, three problems are paramount. First, the design of international standardized achievement tests reflects an inherent tension between depth and coverage of topic areas, given necessary constraints on test burden. Tests reflect mainly the *intersection* of curricular topics from different countries, rather than their *union*. Testing the content that is common among participating countries is challenging enough. Testing the shared content plus content specific to subsets of countries has not proven feasible. Still, it would be desirable to know not only which countries are most effective in the achievement of common content, but also how achievement is affected by the unique content focuses of specific countries. Moreover, the need to cover a wide range of topics and the emphasis on testing efficiency have led to a reliance on multiple-choice questions and thus have limited the assessment of higher order skills (e.g., through problems whose solutions require multiple steps). We conclude that the tension between depth and coverage probably has no resolution, but it is important to be aware of its source and consequences. Thus far, large-scale international studies of achievement have tilted toward broad coverage of content common across countries.

Second, whereas excellent work has been done to create common scales across studies within grades, more work needs to be done to create common scales across grades within studies. TIMSS-R could not estimate cohort gains from fourth to eighth grade because the tests at fourth and eighth grade were not constructed to be on a common scale, despite the fact that TIMSS-R was sold largely on the ability to do exactly such analyses.

Third, sampling designs for the oldest secondary cohort are unsatisfactory. In TIMSS, the most recent effort to attempt a study of this cohort (known in TIMSS as Population 3), students in the last year of compulsory schooling were surveyed. Because of differential dropout rates across nations, the last year of school is attended by very different fractions of the population in different countries. Moreover, students' exposure to schooling varies dramatically across countries, as some have school-leaving ages as young as 16 and others as old as 21. Consequently, it is not clear what comparison this cohort study really offers. The symposium papers in this volume and other related work lead BICSE to conclude that the type of end-of-school cohort design used in previous studies should not be repeated. A different approach is offered by PISA, which is sampling 15-year-olds regardless of their grade level. This approach offers the best way to obtain a representative sample of an entire age cohort. Of course, it does not address the goal that TIMSS's Population 3 study attempted to meet—namely, an estimate of achievement in the final year of compulsory schooling. Because of differences within and across countries in what *compulsory schooling* means, we conclude that goal is probably impossible to achieve. Still, a sample of 25-year-olds might provide a better estimate of achievement differences after completion of schooling.

Culture and Context

In the early surveys of international achievement, the focus was mainly on describing between-country differences in attainment. It wasn't long, though, before interest spread to understanding differences in approach, context, and explanation of achievement differences. The November 2000 BICSE symposium leads the Board to conclude there are at least three reasons to study culture and context in large-scale studies: (1) to help in applying findings to our own country; (2) to interpret findings about cross-national achievement differences appropriately; and (3) to learn more about designing indicators of context.

The chapters in this volume on culture and context bring together three different views on the different contexts in which large-scale international studies take place. Bempechat, Jimenez, and Boulay write on culture and cognition from a psychological perspective; Buchmann focuses on the concept and measurement of family background from the standpoint of sociology; and LeTendre explores the cultural contexts of cross-national analyses from the viewpoint of anthropology. The different perspectives add richness to our understanding of methodological advances and challenges in the study of the contexts of international achievement studies.

Progress in understanding the contexts of international studies. Each of the three perspectives can identify progress from its own standpoint, but each also sees a need for deeper appreciation of contextual differences. Bempechat, Jimenez, and Boulay's statement (this volume, p. 127) no doubt holds for the other authors as well: "Much of the literature on student achievement across nations has been devoid of the cultural contexts in which learning takes place."

From the psychological perspective, because cognitive processes and sociocultural conditions are interdependent, understanding cognitive performance requires appreciation of cultural conditions. For this reason, no matter how tempting, it may not be effective to simply import the pedagogy of one nation into another, whatever the achievement standing of the first nation. An example is the Japanese study lesson, an approach to professional development in which teachers work together over time and through many iterations to produce highly polished instructional units and to master the teaching of those units. Will study lessons work in the United States, despite our very different norms for the teaching profession? Probably not without at least some modifications and special support (Fernandez, Chokshi, Cannon, & Yoshida, in press). Still, the principles on which Japanese lesson studies are based may be useful in designing and implementing effective professional development in other countries. Furthermore, researchers are just beginning to attend to cross-national variation in the meaning of school achievement. For the most part, however, this approach has not been integrated into large-scale studies.

The sociological perspective offers more evidence of progress. As the conceptualization of family background has become broader and more complex in sociological research, the measurement of family background in international education surveys has developed correspondingly. Family background now refers not only to socioeconomic status (i.e., parents' education, occupation, and income), but also to family structure, parent involvement in schooling, and social and cultural resources. On the whole, recent comparative international studies are doing a better job of taking these conditions into account than did the early studies, although important exceptions to the general trend of progress exist. Moreover, reports of the results of comparative international analyses of achievement are increasingly likely to attend to the association of achievement with students' family background conditions. Nonetheless, international studies fall well short of appreciating differences in the meaning of various family background measures in different national contexts.

An increasingly rich understanding of the cultural contexts of teaching and learning, which has emerged quite apart from large-scale studies, has helped enable us to place findings from large-scale studies in cultural perspective. For example, insights from previous case studies allowed Stevenson and Baker (1992) and Akiba and LeTendre (1999) to understand the importance of extra tutoring, to conceptualize it as a sort of "shadow education," and to test their conception with large-scale data. More recently in TIMSS and the IEA Civic Education Study, case studies have augmented the large-scale data collections. Although the case study reports have been insightful, they have not been analytically linked to the large-scale surveys, so their full potential for providing richer understanding of the context of achievement differences has not been effectively realized.

Important challenges of culture and context. Overall, progress in grappling with issues of cultural context has been modest, and the need for deeper understanding remains great. The three perspectives on context expressed in this volume are intertwined, as each recognizes that differences in cultural *meanings* across context affect the interpretation of cross-national achievement differences. For example, to understand achievement differences it is essential to understand differences in wealth and poverty, among as well as within nations. But what represents wealth in different contexts? Although much progress has been made in measuring family circumstances, such "background" conditions cannot be fully standardized across countries. Consequently, although large-scale international studies need to do a better job of applying comparable indicators across contexts, they also need to expand the range of indicators that are specific to particular contexts. These indicators will not necessarily be comparable across contexts, but they are essential for enabling deeper analysis of differences within countries.

Although TIMSS had many strengths, it took a step backward in measuring family background: Its survey question about family structure was too crude to be fully useful, and it omitted parental occupation entirely from student surveys. By contrast, PISA contains a fuller and more sophisticated array of background questions, including parents' occupation and a question about parents' education that lends itself to standardized categories more easily than the IEA surveys. Despite problems with missing data on questions about parent characteristics, we can find no compelling reason for omitting such questions entirely. Both TIMSS and PISA included questions about family cultural and economic resources, and questions of this sort offer promise for richer indicators of social background in future studies.

One of the most powerful features of TIMSS was its case study and video components along with the achievement surveys. Yet the different components remain largely separate, partly by design and partly, according to LeTendre, because TIMSS has so much information to offer that integration has been difficult to manage: "[The] simple fact of 'data overload' meant that the potential insight to be gained by comparing the [qualitative and quantitative] databases has not yet been achieved. . . ." (this volume, p. 211). LeTendre offers a vision of an iterative, multimethod process in which different methodological approaches and conceptual lenses would be placed in dialogue with one another over time.

Making Inferences from Large-Scale Studies

One might expect that substantial progress in designing studies would bring corresponding developments in the ability to draw inferences from large-scale international achievement studies. On the whole, this is true, especially as this progress was accompanied by developments in the assessment of opportunity to learn and in statistical methods of processing data.

Progress in drawing inferences. International comparative studies of student achievement have popularized the concept of opportunity to learn; over time, opportunity to learn has become an increasingly large part of these international comparative studies. While there is not one universally accepted definition of opportunity to learn, in the international comparative research context, opportunity to learn means students receiving instruction on certain content in an academic subject area. Similarly, international comparative studies have distinguished between the intended curriculum, the implemented curriculum, and the achieved curriculum; these distinctions, in turn, have had a considerable impact on education research in the United States. In this volume, Floden notes that measures of opportunity to learn have changed over time, but, with one exception, not with clear improvement. Initially, questions about opportunity to learn were asked in the context of whether students had received sufficient instruction to answer a particular achievement item correctly. TIMSS shifted the focus away from specific items to topics represented by multiple items. This change in focus should improve the quality of information by clarifying that a particular topic is of interest, not features of a particular achievement item (including, for example, format). However, because TIMSS contains no measure of achievement prior to the reported opportunity to learn (unlike SIMS, which included pretest and posttest achievement data for the U.S. sample), it is not possible to link the TIMSS measures of opportunity to learn to achievement growth or to see whether the new measures perform better than those of previous studies in predicting gains in achievement. Moreover, advances in measuring opportunity to learn outside the large-scale studies, such as work by Porter (1998) and Mayer (1999), have not been incorporated into comparative international research. Instead, large-scale international studies seem to have made more progress in developing new ways to measure the intended rather than the implemented curriculum.

The importance of progress in statistical analyses during the history of comparative international studies cannot be overstated. As Raudenbush and Kim explain (this volume, p. 292), "Over the past several decades, statistical methods have greatly enhanced the capacity of researchers to summarize evidence from large-scale, multilevel surveys such as TIMSS and IALS [the International Adult Literacy Survey]." Developments such as item response models, estimation procedures for multilevel data, and new approaches for handling missing data have greatly enhanced the quality with which international comparative data can be analyzed. Better statistical analyses allow researchers to learn more from the data, and concomitant improvements in other aspects of study design—such as achievement tests, translation, sampling, and measurement of family background and opportunity to learn—make statistical inferences more reliable and meaningful. Despite these advances, great caution is needed in making statistical inferences from cross-national studies.

Since the 1980s, results from international studies have drawn considerable attention from policy makers and their advisors. Yet these results tend to become politicized, used as ammunition to support a position rather than as data to help select among competing alternatives. The decentralized governance structure of U.S. education makes it difficult to identify appropriate inferences from comparative international studies at the national level. At the same time, the increasing salience of state-level decision making in U.S. education, coupled with state- and district-level participation in international studies (TIMSS and TIMSS-R), may mean that the results from international studies have more bearing on decisions about education policy at the state level than at the federal level.

Important challenges in making inferences. Despite improvements in opportunity-to-learn measures and statistical modeling techniques, important challenges remain. In the case of measuring opportunity to learn, it is ironic that international studies, which pioneered and popularized the study of opportunities for learning, have not kept pace with research developments. Moreover, few reports on the results of international studies take advantage of the opportunity-to-learn data that are available. In the future, more sophisticated and fine-grained assessment of opportunities for learning should be considered.

The fact that TIMSS lacks a pretest makes it quite clear that the TIMSS data cannot be used for drawing causal inferences. Interestingly, however, Raudenbush and Kim point out that even with pretest data other sources of bias may be present, and causal inference is problematic. Indeed, Raudenbush and Kim as well as Smith question whether large-scale comparative international studies are the proper arena for assessing causal explanations for achievement differences. In light of the important contextual differences between countries, the value of international studies may lie more in their potential for *generating* hypotheses about causal explanation than in their use as platforms for *testing* hypotheses. After all, it makes little difference for U.S. education policy if, for example, extra tutoring "accounts" for the achievement advantage of Japanese over U.S. students, if tutoring does not enhance achievement in an *internal* assessment of variation among U.S. students. As the international comparative education community has learned from its consideration of context and culture, a policy that works in Japan may not work in the United States; consequently, what can be expected from a comparative study are provocative new hypotheses about what may account for differences in student achievement. Studies of internal U.S. variation are indispensable if one wishes to determine whether a policy change in the United States would make a difference in this context under our cultural conditions.

In some cases, sufficient variation may not exist for an internal assessment of variation. For example, very few U.S. students may receive rigorous academic tutoring, so it may not be possible to assess whether tutoring would make a difference here. But a comparative international study cannot help with this quandary; the solution, as Raudenbush and Kim explain, lies in manipulating the U.S. context in order to create the variation necessary for a test of the hypothesis within the United States.

In short, the symposium papers in this volume lead BICSE to conclude that it is most productive to use international comparative studies to develop hypotheses that are then tested in experimental and quasi-experimental studies within the United States. It is not clear that the hypothesis-testing studies need to be part of the comparative international framework. If they are, however, then it is absolutely essential that pretest data be gathered from study participants.

Although statistical analyses in current international studies are competent, they could do much more to describe national systems of education. In particular, indicators of central tendency (means) garner more attention than they deserve, and more attention should be paid to two additional elements: the overall *dispersion* of achievement around the central tendency, and the relationship of achievement to important social categories such as family background. Raudenbush and Kim commend the use of confidence intervals to mark the degree of uncertainty around particular means. Finally, Raudenbush and Kim as well as Smith recognize that more could be done to enhance readers' understanding of the possibilities and limitations of statistical analyses of large-scale comparative databases. A sort of "consumer's guide" might be helpful to policy makers, journalists, educators, and the general public—in short, the entire potential audience of consumers of international comparative education studies.

CONCLUSIONS

The chapters in this volume and the discussions at the symposium where they were originally presented lead the Board to conclude that the methodology of large-scale international comparative studies of student achievement has improved markedly over the past 40 years. Methodological work in these studies is sounder today than ever, and in absolute terms very good. Although progress has been made on virtually all fronts —achievement testing, translations, sampling, sensitivity to culture and context, and statistical analysis—more progress has been made in some areas (e.g., sampling and testing) than in others (e.g., accounting for culture and context).

Benefits of Large-Scale International Studies

These increasingly rigorous studies of international student achievement have produced basic knowledge, generated ideas for improved practice in the United States, and contributed to methodological advances. Not only has this body of work made clear that U.S. student achievement in mathematics and science at the eighth grade is not ideal, it also has made clear that this deficiency is not a new development. The international standing of the United States in mathematics and science achievement in eighth grade has remained relatively stable over all of the international assessments addressing those subjects. Large-scale international surveys of student achievement also have made clear that U.S. achievement is among the best in the world in mathematics and science at the fourth-grade level and also in reading achievement in the early grades. Not only does such international benchmarking of U.S. achievement help U.S. citizens, policy makers, and educators better understand our system's productivity, but it also helps to set a context for interpreting achievement standards recently adopted in the United States. For example, the finding that progressively fewer U.S. students achieve at high levels on NAEP standards as one goes from elementary to middle to high school is consistent with the finding that U.S. achievement falls progressively further behind that of other countries at increasing grade levels. In contrast, the high performance of the United States relative to other countries in reading and science in the elementary grades is not consistent with U.S. students' performance against NAEP standards.

Large-scale international assessments of student achievement also have generated important new hypotheses about how U.S. education might be strengthened. TIMSS curriculum analyses, as well as earlier results from SIMS, revealed that the U.S. curriculum puts a premium on breadth of content coverage, whereas curricula in some other countries are much more focused, emphasizing depth over breadth. This finding has led researchers to the hypothesis that a more highly focused U.S. curriculum might result in improved student achievement. Although the current U.S. standards reform movement was not stimulated by this hypothesis, it represents a massive attempt to bring greater focus and depth to the U.S. curriculum. This reform may provide an opportunity to test the importance of depth over breadth. The Japanese lesson study is yet another example of an approach to education from another country that might prove useful in the United States. Still, whether the lesson study can actually be implemented in our culture and, if so, what its effects might be on student achievement are questions that remain to be answered. Fortunately, work is under way to test the hypothesis that lesson studies could improve the quality of U.S. education (Fernandez et al., in press).

The TIMSS video studies provided powerful new insights into how U.S. teachers share certain tendencies in their pedagogical practices and style, and how those practices and style stand in sharp contrast to those of teachers in Japan. Stigler and Hiebert (1999) conclude that Japanese teachers teach in ways more consistent with the vision of today's U.S. education reformers than do our own teachers.

Methodologically, large-scale international studies of student achievement have been influential as well. The powerful concept of opportunity to learn, conceptualized originally as a control variable but more recently as an explanatory variable in studies of student achievement, has had an enormous impact on education research in the United States. Increasingly, studies attempting to explain differences in student achievement in the United States are including opportunity-to-learn variables as well as pedagogical strategy variables. In some cases, opportunity-to-learn variables are being used as education system output measures in their own right. Clearly, opportunity to learn has established itself as the legal requirement for use of high-stakes testing (National Research Council, 1999). Another example of a methodological advance is the use of video as a research tool. Although video has been used in U.S. education research for some time, its use was relatively limited prior to TIMSS. The surge in enthusiasm for video as an education research tool, although undoubtedly influenced by the TIMSS results, also surely has been fueled by rapid advances in video technology, especially digital video.

In addition to improvements in methodology and in understanding of U.S. education, large-scale international studies of student achievement have led to a third accomplishment—the building of an international infrastructure for conducting comparative research in education. Thirty-five years ago, most countries lacked the capacity to participate in an international study of student achievement. Today, perhaps as many as 60 countries have that capacity. This increased capacity makes it likely that future studies will be of higher quality. However, it also represents an accomplishment in and of itself because the increased capacity of those 60 countries undoubtedly will be used not only for international studies of student achievement, but also for within-country education research.

Thoughts on the Future

The chapters in this volume lead BICSE to conclude that the United States should continue to participate in and encourage the regular conduct of large-scale international studies of student achievement. The Board has not reached consensus on how frequently such studies are needed or how comprehensive each study needs to be in collecting data beyond student achievement (e.g., video; case studies; surveys of principals, students, and teachers). Rowan, in his chapter, suggests that once a decade may be enough for each subject, but that, as with NAEP, there should be a cycle of subjects, so that an international comparative study of student achievement is conducted every two or three years in one subject or another. He points out that this approach should help to maintain the within-country capacity to do such work.

BICSE is also unclear about what age or grade span should be surveyed, though we are inclined to believe that some preschool studies should be attempted, generating baselines for education system productivity, and that some post-school-age cohorts should be studied to get at system yield. On these specifics, the chapters in this volume raise more questions than they answer.

A number of issues are central in thinking about the design of future work and interpretations of past work. The chapters that follow identify these issues; we outline them here as a partial road map to thinking about that work.

1. *Adjustments for between-country differences in background conditions.* One issue concerns whether to adjust for background conditions when

comparing the achievement in one nation to the achievement in another. On the one hand, we know that the student populations being served by one country at a particular age or grade level are not comparable to the student populations being served by another country. They differ on dimensions such as socioeconomic status (SES), age, ethnicity, and urbanicity. As Raudenbush and Kim point out, countries might differ dramatically in average student achievement. Yet if comparisons were made between countries by subgroups, such as within levels of SES, no differences might be found. On the other hand, the chapters in this volume lead to the conclusion that attempting to draw causal inferences from between-country comparisons is not possible. In short, it is not possible to include in analyses sufficient controls to appropriately conclude that between-country differences in student achievement are due to the differences in educational practices between those countries. When adjustments should be made and what kinds of adjustments are appropriate when creating indicators of between-country differences in student achievement remain unclear. Nevertheless, continuing to rely solely on unadjusted differences in student achievement seems certain to be misleading.

2. *Age cohorts versus grade cohorts.* Some international studies of student achievement use age cohorts, and others use grade cohorts. Which approach is more useful remains an issue. There are advantages and disadvantages to each. Age-based samples make studying education effects more difficult because students are spread across a number of grades, making a curriculum-based achievement test problematic. Age-based samples are also more expensive to survey because cluster sampling is more difficult to achieve. Still, when a grade-based sample is taken, countries can differ dramatically in the ages of the students included. An age-based cohort controls for such confounding. Furthermore, an age-based cohort, using household sampling to draw a probability sample of all people of a specific age in a specific country, controls for differential dropout rates between countries. Grade-based cohorts have been the dominant mode in international studies of student achievement, but that pattern may not continue. For example, PISA will sample 15-year-olds. An interesting argument taken from chapters in this volume by Raudenbush and Kim and Rowan suggests that important new insights might result from studies of age-based cohorts at (1) an age prior to entry into schooling for most countries and (2) an age after the completion of most schooling (say, age 25). The preschool age cohort would establish a baseline for theories about the effects of schooling. The 25-year-old cohort, as a household survey, would provide information on whether U.S. students catch up with their international comparison groups during the postsecondary school years.

3. *Assessment of common versus unique content.* A third issue concerns

the construction of student achievement tests used in international comparative studies. Linn makes a distinction between (1) testing only content common to the curricula of all participating countries (the *intersection*) and (2) testing not only that common content, but also all of the unique content across all participating countries (the *union*). The intersection is clearly the more feasible and does represent common ground for comparison. Nevertheless, although testing the union of content across countries may not be feasible, moving in that direction might produce a more ambitious test of student achievement and in that sense might provide a different kind of international benchmarking than we currently have. Until now, achievement tests used in international comparative studies of student achievement have been said to have a U.S. bias. That is, the tests have been similar to tests commonly used in the United States, including a multiple-choice format, and presumably fairly well aligned with current U.S. practice. But today's education reforms in the United States call for a much more ambitious curriculum and much more ambitious student achievement. Are other countries teaching the type of curriculum we seek, and if so, how are their students achieving relative to our own? Perhaps some component of the achievement test used in international comparative studies should test the content we seek, rather than the content we are providing.

4. *Analysis of within-country variance versus central tendency.* A theme across many of the chapters in this volume is the need to look at variance in student achievement within countries, as well as central tendency. Analyzing within-country variance as well as central tendency would represent a change in the practice of large-scale international studies of student achievement, and so we list it here as an issue. In the TIMSS-R benchmarking study in the United States, more than 30 states and large districts participated in the student achievement study as though they were nations (Martin et al., 2001; Mullis et al., 2001). The results from that work reveal—as did the First in the World Consortium from TIMSS (http://www.1stintheworld.org/)—that there exists enormous variance in student achievement within the United States, and that some states and districts achieve at levels comparable to the highest achieving countries in the world. The emphasis on state and district participation in international studies of student achievement ensures that within-country variance, at least in the United States, will be addressed in the future. Designs and analyses that produce valid estimates of between-school, between-class, and within-class variance also are needed. Other approaches also should be utilized. LeTendre points out in his chapter that qualitative studies of achievement contexts also need to focus more on within-country differences than they have in the past. For the United States, where variance in student achievement is enormous, an examination of distribu-

tions will represent a huge improvement in the information yield of international studies of student achievement.

5. *Integration of qualitative and quantitative data.* Over the last 35 years, quantitative results on student achievement from surveys of teachers and students have been augmented by qualitative data from case studies and video. The chapters on culture and context in this volume argue forcefully for the need for such qualitative data to help understand the effects of context and culture on student achievement. Nevertheless, those chapters make clear that progress thus far has been limited, especially in integrating qualitative data with quantitative data. New designs and new analysis strategies will need to be created if the desired integration of quantitative and qualitative data is to be achieved. Qualitative data from small-scale focused studies within and comparatively between countries hold promise for informing the direction and character of the large-scale survey work. Qualitative data might profitably be included as an integral component of large-scale comparative studies as well, although not all efforts to date have resulted in integrated analyses and interpretations.

6. *Use and impact of results.* The international comparative education field needs to think more about the uses of results from international studies of student achievement. Do the results have a positive influence on education policy and practice? Do they contribute to our understanding of the quality of education and how it might be improved in the United States? Are the results used at the local level by districts and states, as well as by the federal government? What are the effects on the international infrastructure for conducting comparative research? Recently, BICSE attempted to determine what was being learned about the uses of TIMSS data by states and districts. Although many anecdotes were offered about important uses, no systematic studies could be found. Smith speculates about how, more generally, the international comparative results have been used, suggesting that they are most influential when used to support reforms already under way (although he acknowledges that results such as those from the early surveys also have been used to generate new education reform). The chapters in this volume lead the Board to conclude that it is worth considering how the impact of international surveys of student achievement on U.S. policy and practice may best be documented and studied. Perhaps a greater investment should be made in documenting this impact.

This collection of methodological analyses is intended to guide three audiences: governmental agencies in the United States and elsewhere that support international studies; nongovernmental agencies such as the IEA and OECD that carry out international studies; and the many researchers who both benefit from and contribute to the findings and methods of large-scale international studies of student achievement. Taken as a whole, the chapters also show how BICSE can contribute to informed decisions about the nature of and participation in these studies. In the future, BICSE may take up some of the key challenges identified in this volume, such as integrating culture and context more effectively in future surveys and encouraging studies about the uses and impact of such work.

NOTE

1. See, for example, the technical standards developed for the International Association for the Evaluation of Educational Achievement (IEA) studies (Martin, Rust, & Adams, 1999).

REFERENCES

Akiba, M., & LeTendre, G. (1999). Remedial, mixed, and enhancement systems: An analysis of math achievement and extra-lessons. Paper presented at the meeting of the Comparative International Education Society, Toronto, Canada.

Beaton, A. E., Postlethwaite, T. N., Ross, K. N., Spearritt, D., & Wolf, R. M. (on behalf of the International Academy of Education). (1999). *The benefits and limitations of international educational achievement studies.* Paris: International Institute for Educational Planning/ UNESCO.

Fernandez, C., Chokshi, S., Cannon, J., & Yoshida, M. (in press). Learning about lesson study in the United States. In E. Beauchamp (Ed.), *New and old voices on Japanese education.* Armonk, NY: M. E. Sharpe.

Martin, M. O., Mullis, I. V. S., Gonzalez, E. J., O'Connor, K. M., Chrostowski, S. J., Gregory, K. D., Smith, T. A., & Garden, R. A. (2001). *Science benchmarking report: TIMSS 1999— Eighth grade: Achievement for U.S. states and districts in an international context.* Chestnut Hill, MA: Boston College, Lynch School of Education, International Study Center.

Martin, M. O., Rust, K., & Adams, R. J. (Eds.). (1999). *Technical standards for IEA studies.* Amsterdam: IEA.

Mayer, D. P. (1999). Measuring instructional practice: Can policymakers trust survey data? *Educational Evaluation and Policy Analysis, 21,* 29-45.

Mullis, I. V. S., Martin, M. O., Gonzalez, E. J., O'Connor, K. M., Chrostowski, S. J., Gregory, K. D., Garden, R. A., & Smith, T. A. (2001). *Mathematics benchmarking report: TIMSS 1999—Eighth grade: Achievement for U.S. states and districts in an international context.* Chestnut Hill, MA: Boston College, Lynch School of Education, International Study Center.

National Commission on Excellence in Education. (1983). *A nation at risk: The imperative for educational reform.* Washington, DC: U.S. Department of Education.

National Research Council. (1990). *A framework and principles for international comparative studies in education.* Board on International Comparative Studies in Education, N. M. Bradburn and D. M. Gilford, Eds. Commission on Behavioral and Social Sciences and Education. Washington, DC: National Academy Press.

National Research Council. (1993). *A collaborative agenda for improving international comparative studies in education.* Board on International Comparative Studies in Education, D. M. Gilford, Ed. Commission on Behavioral and Social Sciences and Education. Washington, DC: National Academy Press.

National Research Council. (1999). *High stakes testing for tracking, promotion, and graduation.* Board on Testing and Assessment, J. P. Heubert and R. M. Hauser, Eds. Commission on Behavioral and Social Sciences and Education. Washington, DC: National Academy Press.

Porter, A. C. (1998). The effects of upgrading policies on high school mathematics and science. In D. Ravitch (Ed.), *Brookings papers on education policy 1998* (pp. 123-167). Washington, DC: Brookings Institution Press.

Postlethwaite, T. N. (1999). *International studies of educational achievement: Methodological issues.* Hong Kong: University of Hong Kong, Comparative Education Research Center.

Schmidt, W. H., McKnight, C. C., & Raizen, S. A. (1996). *A splintered vision: An investigation of U.S. science and mathematics education.* Dordrecht, Netherlands: Kluwer Academic.

Stevenson, D. L., & Baker, D. K. (1992). Shadow education and allocation in formal schooling: Transition to university in Japan. *American Journal of Sociology, 97*, 1639-1657.

Stigler, J. W., & Hiebert, J. (1999). *The teaching gap: Best ideas from the world's teachers for improving education in the classroom.* New York: Free Press.

Part I

Study Design

2

The Measurement of Student Achievement in International Studies

*Robert L. Linn**

The measurement of student achievement is a challenging undertaking regardless of the scope of the domain of measurement, the student population to be assessed, or the purposes of the assessment. The more specific the purpose, the more homogeneous the population of students, and the narrower the domain of measurement, however, the easier is the task of developing measures that will yield results that support valid interpretations and uses.

A teacher who prepares an end-of-unit test in algebra faces a task with a fairly clearly defined content domain and knows a great deal about the common experiences of the students who will take the test. There are still variations in purpose (e.g., grade assignment, formative feedback to students, feedback to the teacher) that need to be considered, but the purposes are reasonably circumscribed. There are also issues of the item types (e.g., multiple-choice, short-answer, extended-response problems) to be used and the cognitive demands of the items. For example, how much emphasis should be given to routine application of algorithms, how much to conceptual understanding, how much to solving new problems that require students to make generalizations, how much to communication, and how much to making connections to earlier concepts and assign-

*Robert Linn is a distinguished professor in the School of Education at the University of Colorado. He is co-director of the National Center for Research on Evaluation, Standards, and Student Testing.

ments? In the individual classroom setting, however, much is known about the familiarity that students have with different item formats, and that familiarity is relatively homogeneous for all students taking the test. Moreover, instructional goals can be used to guide decisions about emphasis given to different cognitive processes.

Large-scale assessments, be they a norm-referenced test designed for use nationally, a state assessment, or an assessment such as the National Assessment of Educational Progress (NAEP), face many of the issues involved in an end-of-unit test for use in a single classroom. Issues of item types and the cognitive demands of the items, for example, remain important, but there is greater diversity in the familiarity that students have with different formats and with items that make different levels of cognitive demands. The delineation of purpose and scope of the content domain are considerably more complicated for the large-scale assessment development than for the classroom test. Moreover, the definition of the target population is no longer a given, and even when defined will be more heterogeneous in background in curriculum exposure and in instruction directed to the content of the assessment. These complications exacerbate the challenges of developing assessments that yield results that support valid interpretations and uses.

Not surprisingly, the challenges are greater still for international assessments of student achievement. An immediately apparent complication is that assessments have to be translated into the multiple languages of participating countries. Variations among countries in educational systems, cultures, and traditions of assessment add to the complexity of the problems of international assessments.

PURPOSES

Consideration of measurement issues for any assessment should start with the identification of the purpose of the assessment. Millman and Greene (1989, p. 335) note that "The first and most important step in educational test development is to delineate the purpose of the test or the nature of the inferences intended from test scores." They justify this claim by noting that "A clear statement of purpose provides the test developer with an overall framework for test specification and for item development, tryout and review" (Millman & Greene, 1989, p. 335). Most assessments, of course, serve multiple purposes, only some of which are intended and clearly specified in advance. Nonetheless, the delineation of purpose(s) is an important undertaking that provides not only a logical starting point, but also the touchstone for evaluating the other measurement decisions throughout the process of assessment development, administration, and interpretation of results.

The purposes of international assessments are manifold. The purpose that attracts the most attention in the press is the horse race aspect of the studies, that is, the tendency to report the relative standing of country average total test scores. Although it is recognized that international competition inevitably draws "attention of policymakers and the general public to what has been referred to as the 'Olympic Games' aspect of the research" (Husen, 1987, p. 131), researchers associated with the conduct of studies under the auspices of the International Association for the Evaluation of Educational Achievement (IEA) have consistently argued that there are many other purposes that are more important than the horse race comparisons.

Mislevy (1995) began his discussion of purposes of international assessments as follows: "In the broadest sense, international assessment is meant to gather information about schooling in a number of countries and somehow use it to improve students learning" (p. 419). In keeping with this broad purpose, the introduction to the report of middle school mathematics results for the Third International Mathematics and Science Study (TIMSS) gives the following statement of purpose: "The main purpose of TIMSS was to focus on educational policies, practices, and outcomes in order to enhance mathematics and science learning within and across systems of education" (Beaton et al., 1996b, p. 7). An implicit assumption is that comparisons of student performances for different countries will contribute toward this end in some way. Otherwise, there would be no need for the involvement of countries other than one's own in the assessment. Thus, it is not surprising that comparing achievement in a specified subject or subjects across countries is a purpose that is common to all of the international studies of achievement.

The objective of comparing relative achievement of students at a target age or grade level by country and subject immediately raises a host of measurement questions. At the most general level, there is the question of whether to limit the measurement domain to the intersection of the content coverage intended by the curricula of participating countries or having it encompass the union of content covered. Or should the domain boundaries fall somewhere between those extremes (Linn, 1988; Porter, 1991)? The union is almost surely too expansive to be practical, while the intersection would restrict the coverage to an unreasonable degree. Hence, the domains defined for international assessments have negotiated limits that fall between the extremes. Once the boundaries have been agreed on, questions remain about the relative emphasis to be given to topics within the domain, about the relative importance of different levels of cognitive demands of the assessment tasks within each topic, about the length of the assessment, and about the mix of item types.

The comparative results obtained on an assessment depend on the degree to which the assessment reflects the curriculum and instruction of the groups of students whose performance is being compared (Linn, 1988; Linn & Baker, 1995; Porter, 1991). In any evaluation of educational programs, "if a test does not correspond to important program goals, the evaluation will be considered unfair" (Linn, 1987, p. 6). This is true for assessments within a nation, but becomes critically important in considering comparisons of performance of nations because there are such large differences between countries in curriculum and instructional emphases. For individual countries the fairness of the assessment necessarily varies as a function of the degree of correspondence between each country's curriculum and the content boundaries and the relative emphasis given to covered topics of the assessment.

SPECIFICATIONS

The particulars of the definition of the domain can have a significant impact on the relative position of nations on the assessment. Heavy weight given to one subdomain can advantage some nations and disadvantage others. Multiple-choice formats familiar to students in some nations may be less so to students in others. Conversely, extended-answer problems are standard fare for students in some nations, but not for students in all nations participating in the study. As Mislevy (1995, p. 423) has noted, "The validity of comparing students' capabilities from their performance on standard tasks erodes when the tasks are less related to the experience of some of the students." Because of the sensitivity of the relative performance of nations to the details of the specification of the assessments, considerable effort must go into negotiating the details of the specifications and to review and signoff on the actual items administered.

Messick (1989, p. 65) has noted that

> [I]ssues of content relevance and representativeness arise in connection with both the construction and the application of tests. In the former instance, content relevance and representativeness are central to the delineation of test specifications as a blueprint to guide test development. In the latter instance, they are critical to the evaluation of a test for its appropriateness for a specific applied purpose.

Details of the approaches used to develop specifications for the assessments have varied somewhat in previous international assessments, but the general nature of the approaches have had a great deal in common. Generally, the approach has been to define a two-way table of specifications, beginning with one dimension defined by content. The topic and subtopic grain size has varied considerably, due in part to the subject matter of the assessment and the grade level; it also has varied from one assessment to the next within the same subject area. The First International Mathematics Study (FIMS) placed the 174 items used across the different age populations assessed into one of 14 topics, ranging from basic arithmetic to calculus (Thorndike, 1967, p. 105). The content dimension was primary, and considerable effort went into defining the topics and obtaining items for them. Despite the emphasis on content, some reviewers of the FIMS results (e.g., Freudenthal, 1975) were sharply critical of the assessments for what was seen as an overemphasis on psychometrics and a lack of involvement of subject-matter experts who were familiar with curricula and teaching practices in the participating countries.

In the Second International Mathematics Study (SIMS), the main emphasis continued to be placed on content categories, but there was substantially greater involvement of mathematics educators and much greater salience was given to the mathematics curricula of the participating countries. SIMS maintained links to FIMS by including a sizable fraction of items from FIMS, but used a different set of topical categories. SIMS had 133 content categories under five broad topics (arithmetic, algebra, geometry, probability and statistics, and measurement) for the eighth-grade population and 150 content categories under nine broad topics for the twelfth-grade population (Romberg, 1985, p. 9). Other international studies have divided the content domain using fewer broad topic areas.

A rather different approach was taken in the International Assessment of Educational Progress (IAEP) studies conducted by the Educational Testing Service (Lapointe, Askew, & Mead, 1992; Lapointe, Mead, & Askew 1992), using frameworks more in keeping with the ones developed for NAEP. In mathematics for 9- and 13-year-olds, the IAEP framework had five broad content categories. Those content categories were crossed with three cognitive process categories to yield a framework with the 15 cells shown in Table 2-1. The broad categories used by IAEP stand in sharp contrast to the fine-grained breakdown in SIMS.

The TIMSS assessments also were based on tables of specifications with characteristics that had some similarity to the frameworks used in the IAEP studies, but had greater specificity of content. For example, the eighth-grade science assessment had eight broad content areas (earth sciences; life sciences; physical sciences; science; technology and mathematics; environmental issues; nature of science; and science and other disciplines). Those categories were crossed with five cognitive process categories called performance expectations in the TIMSS reports (understanding; theorizing, analyzing, and solving problems; using tools, routine procedures, and science processes; investigating the natural world; and communicating) (Beaton et al., 1996a, p. A-6). Finer breakdowns of

TABLE 2-1   IAEP Mathematics Framework for 9- and 13-Year-Olds

	Numbers and Operations	Measurement	Geometry	Data Analysis, Statistics, and Probability	Algebra and Functions
Conceptual understanding					
Procedural knowledge					
Problem solving					

SOURCE: Based on Educational Testing Service (1991, p. 13).

content also were available and used for some analyses. For example, Schmidt, Raizen, Britton, Bianchi, and Wolfe (1997) reported results for 17 science content areas.

In contrast to the relatively fine breakdown of content categories in mathematics and science, the IEA study of reading literacy identified three major domains or types of reading literacy materials: narrative prose ("texts in which the writer's aim is to tell a story—whether fact or fiction"), expository prose ("texts designed to describe, explain, or otherwise convey factual information or opinion to the reader"), and documents ("structured displays presented in the form of charts, tables, maps, graphs, lists or sets of instructions") (Elley, 1992, p. 4).

In addition to variation from one international study to another in the grain size used in the specification of content, there is variation among content categories within a single study. Mesa and Kilpatrick (1998) commented on the lack of uniformity across topics. The lack of uniformity was acknowledged for TIMSS by Schmidt, McKnight, and Raizen (1997, p. 128) as follows: "No claim is made that the 'grain size'—the level of specificity for each aspect's categories—is the same throughout the framework." Mesa and Kilpatrick (1998, p. 8) argue that the lack of uniformity of grain size is problematic, noting, for example, that this means "[s]mall-grained topics such as properties of whole number operations are counted on a par with large-grained topics such as patterns, relations, and functions. Such variation in grain size can result in disproportionate numbers of items for some clusters of topics relative to the intended emphasis in relation to the whole content domain."

The content domains for the international studies have been defined in practice to be somewhere between the intersection and the union of the content domains covered by the curricula of the participating countries, but are closer to the intersection than the union. Because of the prominence of English-speaking countries, especially the United States, in contributing items to the pools of items contributed or developed to make up assessments in line with the specifications, there appears to be a better match to the curricula of English-speaking countries than to the curricula of countries with different languages.

COGNITIVE PROCESSES

As noted, the content dimension of test specification tables has been primary in international assessments. The second dimension of the framework or table of specifications for the assessments generally has focused on the cognitive processes those items or assessment tasks are intended to measure. The well-known breakdown of tasks into six major categories of performance (knowledge, comprehension, application, analysis, synthesis, and evaluation) in Bloom's (1956) taxonomy of educational objectives illustrates one approach to specifying distinct categories of cognitive processes that have been applied to a variety of content domains. The rows of Table 2-1 illustrate another formulation of process categories. For FIMS a table of specifications crossed mathematical topics (e.g., basic arithmetic and elementary algebra) with the following five intellectual process categories:

1. Knowledge and information: definitions, notation, concepts.
2. Techniques and skills: solutions.
3. Translation of data into symbols or schema and vice versa.
4. Comprehension: capacity to analyze problems to follow reasoning.
5. Inventiveness: reasoning creatively with mathematics (Thorndike, 1967, p. 94).

In a similar vein, the First International Science Study (FISS) crossed a content dimension with a "behavioral objectives dimension consisting of four categories: information, comprehension, application, higher processes" (Comber & Keeves, 1973). The Second International Science Study (SISS) used a substantial number of items (nearly half the total) from FISS and supplemented those items with new items for SISS that were categorized into just three of the four behavioral objectives used in FISS (the higher order process category was not used for the new items) (Keeves, 1992). As was true of the contrast of the first and second mathematics studies, the second science study placed greater emphasis on the curricula of the participating countries than had been done in the first science study. Items for the test were selected not from the most common topics, but rather based on the emphasis of topics in each country as defined in the country's intended curriculum.

For SIMS the second dimension was called the "behaviors dimension" and distinguished "four levels of cognitive complexity expected of students—computation, comprehension, application, and analysis" (Romberg, 1985, p. 9). As Romberg notes, the four levels used in SIMS mapped partially, albeit imperfectly, into the Bloom categories. The second dimension for TIMSS made similar distinctions, but was referred to as the "expectations" dimension. As is true of the IAEP process categories in Table 2-1, more recent specification tables have moved farther away from the Bloom taxonomic categories. In the TIMSS mathematics assessment, for example, four categories of expectations or cognitive processes were distinguished: knowing, performing routine procedures, using complex procedures, and solving problems (Beaton et al., 1996b, p. A-7). In science the TIMSS performance expectations dimension consisted of five categories: understanding simple information; understanding complex information; theorizing, analyzing, and solving problems; using tools, routine procedures, and science processes; and investigating the natural world (Beaton et al., 1996a).

The specification of topics of the content domain involves judgments of subject-matter experts that have been informed in international studies by cross-national curriculum analysis. Agreements require negotiated compromises between desires to be comprehensive in coverage, the goal of fairly assessing the achieved curriculum of all participating countries, and issues of feasibility. Determining whether an item fits a content topic area is relatively straightforward once the topics have been defined. Determining the types of cognitive processes required to answer an item is far less straightforward. There is widespread agreement that assessments should tap more than simple knowledge of facts and procedures. The assessment also should measure a student's ability to apply knowledge, skills, and concepts to solve problems and communicate in academic and nonacademic problem settings. Furthermore, it should measure the ability to communicate concepts, make connections, provide explanations appropriate for the subject matter, interpret findings, and evaluate problem solutions and arguments (Glaser, Linn, & Bohrnstedt, 1997). Measuring such higher order cognitive processes and achievement outcomes is more challenging than measuring factual knowledge and skills at applying routine algorithms. The fact that nearly any test development effort that solicits items from a broad range of subject-matter experts, as has been done in the IEA studies, will find an overabundance of items is symptomatic of the greater difficulty in writing items that will tap the higher level problem solving, analysis, explanation, and interpretation skills sought for the assessments.

Although, as will be described, considerable effort has gone into the development of items that do more than measure factual knowledge and low-level skills, critics continue to fault international assessments for falling short of the goal of measuring more complex understanding and problem-solving skills. For example, "Jan de Lange. . . argued that the TIMSS items are primarily useful for testing low-level knowledge and do not necessarily represent anyone's idea of a desirable curriculum" (National Research Council [NRC], 1997, p. 17). The criticism by de Lange is due, at least in part, to a preference for assessments that present students with substantial problems requiring multiple steps to solve and that allow for a variety of solution paths and, sometimes, multiple solutions that would be judged to be of high quality. It is also based on a belief that the multiple-choice and short-answer formats used in the international assessments can only measure factual knowledge and low-level skills. More will be said about that in the following section, but here it is worth recalling an observation made by Thorndike (1967, p. 96) in his chapter describing the FIMS tests.

> Time limitations together with the need to sample widely from the content of mathematics dictated another decision. It was agreed, somewhat reluctantly, that it would be necessary to keep the single problems brief. Much as one might like to explore the students' ability to work through an involved sequence of steps, or develop a complex proof, this seemed impossible. Such a task would exhaust too large (and too variable) a fraction of the limited time that was available.

ITEM FORMATS

The criticism of international assessment on the grounds that they assess only relatively low-level cognitive processes reflects, in part, the difficulty of writing items that tap higher level skills and understanding. Many, like de Lange, would argue that the multiple-choice item formats that are most used in international assessments make it infeasible to assess some of the more complex cognitive processes that correspond to ambitious curriculum aspirations. Multiple-choice and short-answer items are obviously efficient and make it possible to assess a wide range of content in a relatively short period of time. Such items are quite effective at measuring knowledge of fact, procedures, and concepts. Skilled item writers also can and do use these formats effectively to measure understanding and the ability to apply concepts and procedures to solve problems, provide explanations, interpret, and evaluate findings or arguments. There are limits to these formats, however. Nonetheless, for the reasons articulated by Thorndike, multiple-choice has been the dominant item format, supplemented by some short-answer and a smaller number of extended-response items because of considerations of efficiency and feasibility.

The reliance on multiple-choice items was a target of criticism of several of the international studies prior to TIMSS. Stedman (1994), for example, provided the following critique of the earlier science assessments. "In most assessments science has been tested solely with multiple-choice items (Keeves, 1992, p. 59; Lapointe, Mead, & Phillips, 1989, p. 83). This seems particularly inappropriate given how essential experimentation is in science, although it may measure how well students have learned basic curricular facts" (p. 26).

Considerable effort went into expanding the types of items used in TIMSS, the most recent of the IEA studies. Roughly 300 constructed-response items were included across the subject areas and populations assessed in TIMSS. Approximately one-third of the assessment administration time was allocated for responding to the constructed-response items (Mullis & Smith, 1996). In terms of number of items, multiple-choice items were still dominant in TIMSS. TIMSS assessed three populations of students, 9-year-olds, 13-year-olds, and students in the last year of secondary school. Students in the two grades where most students of the target age were enrolled were assessed for the two younger populations. Students in the last year of secondary school were broken down into a mathematics and science literacy subpopulation and subpopulations of students taking advanced mathematics and taking an advanced physics course. Table 2-2 displays the number of items on the TIMSS assessments by item type for each population and subject.

The preponderance of multiple-choice items is evident in Table 2-2. The short-answer and extended-response items had more than the two score points of a multiple-choice item. Even if the score points of short-answer and extended-response items are taken into account, the multiple-

TABLE 2-2   TIMSS Number of Items by Item Type

Population	Subject	Multiple Choice	Short Answer	Extended Response	Total
9-year-olds	Mathematics	79	15	8	102
	Science	74	13	10	97
13-year-olds	Mathematics	125	19	7	151
	Science	102	22	11	135
Last year literacy	Math and science	52	17	7	76
Advanced	Mathematics	47	10	8	65
Advanced	Physics	42	15	8	65

SOURCE: Based on Adams and Gonzalez (1996).

choice items still dominate the assessments. For example, for the 9-year-olds in mathematics, the total number of possible points was 116, 79 of which were based on the multiple-choice items. Only the physics and advanced mathematics assessments for the last year of secondary school population had close to half their points from short-answer and extended-response items. The total points for physics was 81, 39 of which came from the 23 short-answer and extended-response items. The corresponding numbers for advanced mathematics were 82 and 35.

Efficiency of the assessment is enhanced not only by the fact that multiple-choice items can be machine scored, but also by the allocation of time for these items. For all but the advanced students in the oldest population, one minute per item was assumed for the multiple-choice items (three minutes per item was assumed for advanced students). The short-answer items were not much more time consuming, with one minute per item again assumed for the 9-year-olds, two minutes per item for the 13-year-olds and the oldest population in the mathematics and science literacy subpopulation, and three minutes per item for the advanced subpopulations. Even the extended-response items were restricted in amount of testing time assumed—three minutes per item for the 9-year-olds and five minutes per item for all others.

The international study of reading literacy (Elley, 1992) also had tests that were dominated by multiple-choice items. Of the 66 items on the 9-year-olds' test, there were four short-answer items and two items requiring a paragraph-length answer. The test for the 14-year-olds had 20 short-answer items and two items requiring a paragraph-length answer out of the 89 items on that test (Elley, 1992, p. 5).

Measuring some of the higher order cognitive processes that the IEA studies have aspired to measure is exceedingly difficult given the amount of time allowed per item. Measuring some of the aspects of understanding and problem solving—such as problem identification and representation, the use of comprehension and problem-solving strategies, and the development of coherent explanations and interpretations (Glaser, Linn, & Bohrnstedt, 1997)—requires the use of a wider array of extended-answer items and performance assessment tasks. Finding a good balance between the needs for efficiency and the desire to measure a full range of cognitive processes poses a continuing challenge for international assessments.

CURRICULUM AND INSTRUCTIONAL MATERIALS AND DEFINITION OF TEST CONTENT

One of the prominent features of international studies of achievement conducted under the auspices of the IEA has been the emphasis on both the intended and the implemented curricula in participating countries. Emphasis on the curricula of participating countries was present, albeit only to a modest degree, in the earliest IEA studies. This emphasis on the match to what is taught in participating countries was behind the effort made in FIMS, that is, to get countries to identify the topics that the assessment was expected to cover that were taught to students in the populations to be assessed.

> National centers rated items as to universality of inclusion in its education system using the following categories:

> U Universal, i.e., the topic is taught or assumed by all types of schools at this level.

> R Restricted, i.e., the topic is taught only in certain types of schools or courses.

> E Experimental, i.e., the topic is not normally taught in any part of the system up to this level, but occurs sporadically in an experimental program.

> N Nil, i.e., the topic is not taught at all in the educational system at this level, and is not assumed as known from previous teaching (Thorndike, 1967, p. 95).

Using this system of ratings for universality of topic coverage for ten countries that provided ratings, it was found, for example, that all ten countries returned a rating of "U" for a 13-year-old's "ability to carry out simple operations involving simple vulgar fractions." "Notions of square roots," on the other hand, received a rating of "U" from four countries, an "R" from one country, and an "N" from the remaining five countries. "The theorem of Pythagoras for solving simple practical problems" had three "U" ratings, one "R" rating, and six "N" ratings (Husen, 1967, pp. 284-286).

The emphasis on relevance to the curricula of participating countries is also apparent in the SISS report, where the basis for the test development is described by Postlethwaite and Wiley (1992, p. 49) as follows:

> The tests were constructed on the basis of the common intended curriculum in all of the participating countries. The intended curriculum is that content which is included in national or state syllabi, the major science textbooks used by students and—where applicable—national examinations. A first analysis was conducted in the late 1960s for the First IEA Science Study. This was repeated for the second science study. Sufficient items had to be the same for the first and second studies to allow comparisons between the two times of testing.

The centrality of curriculum has, if anything, increased in the more recent studies, culminating in the highly elaborate data collections and analyses conducted as part of TIMSS (Schmidt, McKnight, & Raizen, 1997; Schmidt, McKnight, Valverde, Houang, & Wiley, 1997; Schmidt, Raizen, Britton, Bianchi & Wolfe, 1997). The TIMSS curriculum studies included analyses of textbooks and curriculum guides for approximately 50 countries. These analyses revealed considerable between-country variation in topic coverage and relative emphasis. Although the curriculum analyses were used in developing the TIMSS assessment, the wide range in topics and great variation in coverage and emphasis precluded the development of an assessment that would provide comprehensive coverage of the union of topics found in the curricula of all the countries. An assessment with reasonable depth covering all the topics of the union would have required collections of items several times as large as the ones administered by TIMSS. Feasibility considerations forced a more limited scope. Preliminary results of the curriculum analyses were used to guide the development of the initial frameworks used to classify items and to specify the content domain to be assessed in TIMSS. Considerable effort was required to negotiate refinements in the framework, where it could be used as a detailed table of specifications for the assessment, giving topics and intended cognitive processes to be measured as well as numbers of items in different categories to reflect negotiated agreements of coverage and emphasis.

Important distinctions have been made in the IEA studies between the explicit and implicit goals of a nation's curriculum, known as the "intended curriculum," and the content that is actually taught, known as the "implemented curriculum" (e.g., Schmidt & McKnight, 1995). The distinction between intended and implemented curriculum is relevant to specifications of the content for an assessment to be used in international studies and the valid interpretation of between-country differences in student achievement.

The intended curriculum can be characterized by review of official curriculum guides, analysis of widely used textbooks, and reviews by subject-matter experts from each country, all of which can be used in developing test specifications and in writing and selecting items. The implemented curriculum cannot be defined with as much specificity prior to test development and collection of data because it is defined by teacher ratings of topics taught and student ratings of opportunity to learn (OTL) generally obtained at the time the achievement test data are collected. The distinction between the intended and the implemented curriculum has been a prominent feature of the IEA studies. The implemented curriculum has been determined by using teacher estimates of the percentage of their students who would answer an item correctly without guessing. Teachers also have been asked to provide OTL ratings, which identified whether their students had been taught the material needed to answer each item correctly, or whether that material had been reviewed, was taught in prior years, would be taught in subsequent years, or would not be taught. OTL ratings have been found to be a strong predictor of student achievement on the assessments (the attained curriculum). One might question, however, the degree to which OTL ratings are pure measures of the implemented curriculum, or are contaminated to some degree as reflections of informal predictions of teachers of how students will respond to particular items. Nonetheless, the IEA studies have had an important influence on the development of the concept of opportunity to learn and approaches to measuring it (see Floden, this volume).

CONSENSUS AND SIGNOFF BY PARTICIPATING NATIONS

An international consensus needs to be developed among participating nations for any international assessment. Consensus is needed about the tables of specifications, including agreements about item types, and relative emphasis to be given to categories in each of the dimensions of the table of specifications. Consensus is also needed about the acceptability of individual items that are the instantiation of the cells of the table of specifications. Although relatively large pools of items can be assembled drawing on previous international assessments and on items contributed by participating nations based on their own national assessments or written specifically for the international assessment, the quality of the items and the distribution relative to the requirements of the specifications are more problematic.

SISS sent a matrix of science topics by teaching objectives to national centers with a request for items to measure the cells of the matrix. Although approximately 2,000 items were returned, the quality and appropriateness of the items were quite uneven, many items could not be scored objectively, and relatively few items were judged to be applicable as measures of the higher order cognitive processes (Comber & Keeves, 1973, p. 20). Contributions of potential items were also far from uniform across countries.

The uneven distribution has been characteristic of all the international assessments. FIMS, for example, initially obtained items for the item pool from only five countries, Japan, the Netherlands, Scotland, Sweden, and the United States. Moreover, the assembly of the pool of items that were field tested depended to a very great extent on items from only one country, the United States. "Relying heavily on the stock of items made available by the Educational Testing Service and items from test files at the University of Chicago Examiner's Office and items written specifically for the test a pool of 640 items was assembled" (Thorndike, 1967, p. 98).

The influential role of the United States in contributing items for the assessments is a feature of most of the international assessments. As noted earlier, the IAEP studies used the framework from NAEP to categorize items. Although more than half of the countries participating submitted some items, the IAEP studies also made use of items from NAEP. The reliance on the United States for a disproportionate share of the items in international assessments is undoubtedly expedient. Indeed, such reliance may be the only way to meet the challenges of the creation of an item pool from which the items for the assessments could be selected and assembled into viable tests. This is so, in part, because the United States has a much larger national infrastructure for the development and refinement of tests at the national level than any other country. It is also the case that the United States is relatively unique in the extent of its use of multiple-choice test items, and as will be discussed, this is the format that has been used most in international assessments due to considerations of cost, breadth of coverage, and efficiency.

The dominant role of the United States and, to a lesser extent, Canada in the contribution of items to the assessments raises a question about the degree to which this introduces a North American or U.S. bias into the assessments. There is reason to believe that some bias exists in favor of North America in general, and the United States in particular, because of the disproportionate impact on the item pools used to construct the assessment. The bias is likely to be exaggerated by the heavy reliance on multiple-choice items, a format that is more familiar to students in North America than in many other countries. Although these considerations may have enhanced the relative performance of students in North America, it is impossible to know how much, if any, difference this potential bias had on the actual results of any of the international assessments. Certainly the review and approval of the content domains and the assessment specifications by participating countries were intended to minimize any such bias.

The following description by Garden and Orpwood (1996, pp. 2-3) illustrates the difficulties encountered at the item assembly and identification stage:

> Although large pools of items had been assembled, a disproportionate number were found to assess computation, recall, or simple application in limited content areas. For some content areas an adequate number of potentially good items were available, but for others there were too few items of good quality. Also, because most items had been written for use within particular countries, the panel had to reject many for use in TIMSS because of cultural bias, or because translation was likely to lead to ambiguity or misunderstanding.

Extensive reviews of items by international panels of subject-matter and measurement experts as well as by designated panels within each participating country are needed to assure proper coverage of all cells of the table of specifications and to identify potential shortcomings due to lack of appropriateness for different cultures or likely difficulties in translation. Systematic reviews by panels of experts from participating nations can provide much-needed information to international committees making the final selection. Procedures used in TIMSS, for example, included obtaining ratings from national committees of each item on 1-to-4 scales for each of four characteristics: the extent to which the content of the item was taught and emphasized in the country, the familiarity of the implied approach to teaching by the item, the proportion of students in the country who would answer the item correctly, and overall quality independent of the appropriateness for the country's curriculum (Garden & Orpwood, 1996).

Selection of items for field testing can be guided by ratings from national committees. For example, a criterion might be established that the item was considered appropriate for the curriculum of at least X percent of the countries and that fewer than Y percent of the countries recommend deletion of the item. Once a tentative pool of items is agreed on, they can be assembled into booklets for field testing, a stage that is critical in the evaluation of item quality for any assessment.

TRANSLATION

Before test items for an international assessment can be evaluated by representatives of participating countries, much less be field tested, they must be translated from the language in which the item was originally written into all the languages needed for use of the assessment in the participating countries. Test translation is a demanding enterprise. It is well known that student performance on an item can vary greatly as the result of seemingly minor edits within the language in which the item was originally written. This problem of sensitivity of results to subtle changes in items is compounded when items have to be translated from one language to another. Consideration of the many issues that arise in test translation, particularly where direct comparisons of achievement are desired across versions of the test in different languages, as is required for international studies of achievement, is beyond the scope of this paper. Fortunately, a separate chapter has been prepared by Hambleton (this volume) on the complex issues of translating and adapting tests of comparative international studies of educational achievement, and the reader interested in this topic is referred to that chapter.

FIELD TESTING

Although careful editing by subject matter and measurement experts can detect many problems with items, there is no substitute for actual tryout of the items with students from the populations that will take the operational assessments. Ambiguities in the items, or problems with answer keys or with incorrect options on multiple-choice questions, often defy detection despite numerous rounds of editing and review by measurement and subject-matter experts. For short-answer and extended-response items, the scoring rubric is an essential aspect of the item, one that can be best evaluated and refined in the context of a field trial. Only after student performance on items is obtained during field testing do some item flaws or problems with scoring rubrics become apparent. Field-test data also provide estimates of item statistics that can be useful in the final selection of items for the operational test forms. Even if one takes a criterion-referenced view of test construction that would not rely on item discrimination and item difficulty statistics, item analyses can be quite useful in identifying flawed items and items that display differential item functioning for students from different countries or for male and female students. Although other characteristics such as socioeconomic status or community characteristics also might have been of interest, they are difficult to define in a uniform way across countries. Item difficulty and item discrimination statistics are arguably useful even from a criterion-referenced perspective, if for no other reason than one of efficiency. It is simply not very informative to administer items that almost no one can answer correctly or that are so easy that essentially everyone answers them correctly. In a similar vein, items that do not discriminate or that have negative discrimination will not make useful contributions to the measurement on the main dimensions used for reporting results.

Consequently, the more recent international studies generally have established certain guidelines for field-test item statistics. Items that do not meet the guidelines may be flagged as a caution to those constructing the assessments to use those items only if necessary to fulfill the requirements of the test specifications. If the item pool is large enough, items that do not meet the guidelines may be eliminated from further consideration. The earliest IEA studies also made use of item difficulty and discrimination statistics, but the detailed guidelines on the use to be made of the statistics apparently were not used. Rather, item difficulties and discrimination indices for each country participating in the field tests were presented to the committee responsible for assembling the operational forms, but it is unclear what use the committee made of those statistics, if any, in selecting items for the operational forms (see, for example, Thorndike, 1967, pp. 101-103).

The role of item statistics was more explicit for TIMSS. TIMSS set the criteria that the items have a proportion correct on multiple-choice items of at least 0.25 for four-choice items and 0.20 for five-choice items. Items were also required to have positive point-biserial correlations with the total score for the correct answer and negative point-biserial correlations with the incorrect options (Garden & Orpwood, 1996). "With few exceptions, the selected items had mean field trial p-values between 0.3 and 0.8, discrimination indices (point-biserial correlation between item and booklet scores) above 0.3, and mean review ratings above 2.5 in each of the four review categories" (coverage, the extent the item was taught and emphasized in each country; familiarity; difficulty; and appeal—each rated on a 1-to-4 score by the national committees) (Garden & Orpwood, 1996, pp. 2-16).

Field testing and the extensive review of items by measurement and subject-matter experts have resulted in collections of items that are of relatively high quality and free of major faults. Of course, as has been noted previously, the item sets have been criticized for not doing a better job of measuring higher cognitive processes, and for limitations of coverage of the curricula of participating countries. A few problematic items also have been identified that count as correct responses that are either incorrect or not as good as an alternative response that is treated as incorrect. An extreme example of the former problem is a mathematics items on TIMSS that was identified by Wang (1998b). The item is "Find x if $10x - 15 = x + 20$" (Lie, Taylor, & Harmon, 1996, p. 10). The answer clearly is that $x = 35/9$, but the response that is keyed according to Wang (1998b), who relied on the report of Lie et al. as correct, is 7. An error like this on such a simple problem could only be a misprint. Indeed, a check of the grades 7 and 8 released mathematics items show that item L-16 is: "$10x - 15 = 5x + 20$." And, the correct answer is indeed 7. The multiplicative constant of 5 was mistakenly left off on the right-hand side of the equation in Lie et al., but the actual item was correctly scored. Some other problems identified by Wang (1998a, 1998b), however, are not so easily explained. They reveal the difficulty in assuring the answers keyed to receive full credit are in fact correct for students who know more than the typical student or who think deeply about the problem. One such problem identified by Wang (1998b) is the following: "A glass of water with ice cubes in it has a mass of 300 grams. What will the mass be immediately after the ice has melted? Explain your answer" (Lie et al., 1996, p. 11). The keyed answer is 300 grams, supported by an explanation such as "The ice changes into the same amount of water." As Wang notes, this answer and explanation is correct if evaporation is ignored, but if a student takes evaporation into account, an answer of "Less than 300 grams" is clearly defensible, but would not receive credit.

Another problematic item asks 9-year-old students to explain how the sun and the moon can appear to be about the same size when the sun is much larger than the moon. The keyed response is that the sun is farther away. The response that the sun is higher than the moon is not credited, even though, as Wang (1998a) argues, higher and farther may be used interchangeably by 9-year-olds to convey the same level of understanding of the scientific principle in question. For a few additional examples of problematic items, see Wang (1998a, 1998b). Although questionable items such as the ones identified by Wang represent only a tiny fraction of all the items—not enough to seriously affect the overall validity of the assessment—they illustrate the difficulty of developing items and associated scoring rubrics that are unambiguous and unassailable.

CULTURAL BIAS AND DIFFERENTIAL ITEM FUNCTIONING

All of the international studies have attempted to address problems created by items that put members of one country at a disadvantage as the result of cultural differences in the ways in which particular items might be interpreted. Distinguishing between factors that are the result of cultural differences across countries and those that are due to differences in instructional practices or student opportunity to learn the content of the item is, of course, a difficult and imperfect undertaking. The primary way in which the IEA studies have approached the question of cultural bias in items is through the expert judgment of national committees that reviewed the items. Procedures used to ensure the quality of translations and adaptations needed for items to make them appropriate in different language and cultural contexts were also an important part of the way in which issues of potential cultural bias were addressed.

The most recent studies conducted by IAEP and IEA also have included some statistical analyses of the item responses as a means of flagging items that might be judged to be problematic. The IAEP studies included differential item functioning (DIF) analyses using an omnibus statistic based on Mantel-Haenzel statistics that was developed by Johnson (1992). As Johnson describes, DIF statistics were computed for each item using the United States as the reference group separately for each other participating country, then results were combined into the omnibus statistic. The latter statistic was then used to identify items that were outliers and therefore likely to be problematic. Using this approach, only three items—one age nine mathematics item, one age 13 mathematics item, and one age 13 science item—were identified as outliers with very high DIF (Bertrand, Dupuis, Johnson, Blais, & Jones, 1992). Although the statistical sophistication and magnitude of the analysis are quite impressive, the return for the effort appears quite meager if one expects the approach to be a valuable tool in the identification of items that should be discarded from consideration because of cultural bias. On the other hand, the analyses provide some reassurance that the items generally function in a similar fashion for students from different countries.

TIMSS computed within-country item statistics of various kinds and used them to identify items that might be problematic for particular countries. In addition to the usual within-country difficulty and discrimination statistics, multiple-choice items were flagged if an incorrect option had positive point-biserial correlations with the total score, or if an item had a poor Rasch fit statistic. Item-by-country interaction statistics indicating that an item was easier or harder than would be expected based on the cross-country item difficulty and the overall performance of students from the country were computed. Items with statistically significant item-by-country interactions were flagged (Mullis & Martin, 1998).

The use of item flags as was done in either IAEP or TIMSS is useful for calling special attention to items. However, the flag by itself does not necessarily mean that the item is a biased indicator of student achievement in the country in question. Judgmental review is still needed to determine whether it is reasonable to discount the item for a given country or whether the unusual difficulty may simply reflect differences in instruction. Flagged items were reviewed and judged to be satisfactory. They did not play any further role in the analyses or presentation of results.

TEST DESIGN

Traditional tests are designed to provide information about the performance of individual students. For such tests there are substantial advantages in having all students take the same set of items. International assessments, however, are not designed to report scores for individual students. Instead all that is needed is to obtain estimates of performance for large groups of students (e.g., all students at a grade level in the country, or all students within a broad category defined by other variables such as gender, community type, curriculum strand, or race/ethnicity). For such assessments there are great advantages to administering different subsets of items to different subsamples of students. There is always an interest in administering more items than can be administered in a single sitting to any one student. By administering different subsets of items to different subsamples of students, broad coverage can be achieved with a reasonable amount of testing time for each student in the sample.

A number of designs are available for this purpose. Collectively the designs are referred to as matrix sampling designs to denote the simultaneous sampling of both items and students. Designs used in past international assessments include the administration of different test forms to subsamples of students from each population, as was done in FIMS, and the administration of a common core of items to all students together with one of several unique subsets of items, sometimes referred to as rotated forms, to different subsamples, as was done in SIMS and SISS. Yet another variation is to administer two or more blocks of items to students, with blocks administered together in various combinations. The IAEP studies used blocks of items to make up test booklets or forms, albeit only two booklets were used per subject at age nine and just a single booklet was used at age 13. The limited number of items used in IAEP made it unnecessary to have a larger number of booklets in which blocks of items would be placed. However, experience with NAEP has shown that the use of balanced-incomplete-block designs for the allocation of items can be an effective approach to administering larger numbers of items to students while limiting the administration time for any given student.

The use of a common core together with rotated forms is illustrated by SISS (Postlethwaite & Wiley, 1992). Three student populations—10-year-olds, 14-year-olds, and students in the final year of secondary education—were studied in SISS. Variations of a common core and rotated forms were used for each of the three populations. A core test of 24 items and four rotated forms of eight items each were used for the 10-year-olds. The 70 items for the 14-year-olds were divided into a core of 30 items administered to all students and four rotated forms of ten items each. For students in the last year of secondary school, the items were distinguished by subject area (biology, chemistry, or physics). Three rotated forms of 30 items each, consisting of items in one of the three content areas, were administered to subsamples of approximately one-third of the students together with a 26-core form consisting of nine biology items, nine chemistry items, and eight physics items (Postlethwaite & Wiley, 1992, p. 49).

A more complicated matrix sampling design was used in TIMSS. This can be illustrated by a brief description of the overall assessment design for 199 items administered to the 9-year-old population. Each item was placed into one of 26 item clusters. Cluster A was designated the core cluster. It contained a total of five mathematics and five science multiple-choice items. A total of eight separate test booklets, each consisting of cluster A and six of the remaining 25 clusters of items, were administered. Seven of the noncore clusters of items were designated focus clusters. Focus clusters were included in either three or four of the eight booklets, thereby assuring substantial numbers of students for those items. Ten of the remaining clusters were labeled either mathematics breadth or science breadth. Breadth clusters were included in only a single booklet, and hence were administered to only about one-eighth of the sampled students. The remaining eight clusters consisted of either mathematics or science free-response items. Each of those clusters was included in two of the eight booklets (Adams & Gonzalez, 1996). The IEA and IAEP studies have made effective use of matrix sampling designs to allow for a broader coverage of content domains than otherwise would have been possible.

SUMMARY SCORES

Results of early international assessments were commonly reported in terms of total number of correct scores or average percentage of correct scores. Such scores are reasonable as long as they are based on a common set of items. With a core and two rotated forms used, for example in SISS, total scores for the core and for the core plus the two rotated forms are readily produced, and with proper sampling weights can be used to produce various descriptive statistics. Though not essential to produce results, the more complicated assessment designs of the more recent IAEP studies (e.g., Educational Testing Service, 1991) and TIMSS have relied on scaling based on item response theory (IRT) in addition to percentage correct scores for summarizing results. The IAEP studies used a three-parameter logistic IRT model (Blais et al., 1992). The one-parameter Rasch IRT model was used in TIMSS (Martin & Kelly, 1996).

IRT models the probability that a given student will answer an item correctly based on a single latent proficiency dimension along which both items and persons are placed by person and item parameters. In the case of the Rasch model, the probability of a correct response is determined by the difference of the location of the person on the dimension (the person's proficiency) and the location of the item on the same dimension (the item's difficulty). The dimension or proficiency scale summarizes the achievement level of students and the relative difficulty of items. The three-parameter IRT also has a single-person parameter to locate the person on the proficiency scale, but uses three parameters to characterize items: one for the relative difficulty, one for the discriminating power of the item, and one (the pseudoguessing parameter) to account for the fact that the probability of a correct response on a multiple-choice item is always greater than zero, no matter how low the person's level of proficiency is.

IRT provides a basis for estimating performance on a common scale even when students are given different subsets of items. This is a great advantage over simple number-right scoring for assessments such as those used in international studies where different students are administered different subsets of items. It means, for example, that performance on rotated forms can be compared on a common scale. Thus, when the assumptions of IRT are met to a reasonable approximation by the item response data obtained for a sample of test takers, proficiency estimates for test takers can be defined in relation to the pool of items administered, but do not depend on the particular subset of items taken by a given individual. Moreover, the item statistics do not depend on the particular subsample of test takers who responded to a given item. These two properties often are referred to as "item free ability estimates" and "sample-free or person-free item parameter estimates" (Hambleton, 1989, p. 148).

The assumptions of IRT about the dimensionality of the assessment, local independence (i.e., that test-taker responses to items are statistically independent after proficiency level is taken into account), and the specific mathematical form of the item response function (e.g., the one-parameter Rasch model) are, of course, only approximated in practice. Hence, the properties of item-free proficiency estimates and sample-free item parameter estimates hold only approximately. Nonetheless, IRT, even when a unidimensional model is used, has been found to be relatively robust as long as there is a strong dominant factor or underlying dimension for the set of items.

The TIMSS reports summarized the preference for IRT scaling as follows:

> The IRT methodology was preferred for developing comparable estimates of performance for all students since students answered different test items depending upon which of the eight test booklets they received. The IRT analysis provides a common scale in which performance can be compared across countries. In addition to providing a basis for estimating mean achievement, scale scores permit estimates of how students within countries vary and provide information on percentiles of performance. (Beaton et al., 1996a, p. A-27; the quoted summary statement is also included in other TIMSS reports)

There are considerable advantages provided by a scale for which percentiles and variability can be computed. Clearly there is much more to characterizing the achievement of students in a country even if one is satisfied with a single summary dimension than reporting the mean. Earlier treatments of international assessment results could, of course, report information on variability and percentile points for the core set of items taken by all students simply using number-right scores. Reporting results for the full assessment, including rotated forms, was more complicated and involved forms of linking rotated forms that were less theory based (see, for example, Miller & Linn, 1989) and somewhat problematic because the forms were not comparable in difficulty or content coverage.

A single scale provides an overall summary of student achievement within the subject-matter domain of the assessment. Such summary information is useful for making overall comparisons. Policy makers, the media, and the public like the apparent simplicity that is provided by reports of results on a single scale. The rank order of the average performance of a nation's students can be seen at a glance, and comparisons of the highest or lowest performing 5 or 10 percent of a nation's students to other nations is not much more complicated. For those concerned about curriculum issues, however, the single scale leaves too many questions unanswered. As Mislevy (1995, p. 427) notes, "Because no single index of achievement can tell the full story and each suffers its own limitations, we increase our understanding of how nations compare by increasing the breadth of vision—as *Consumers Reports* informs us more fully by rating scores of attributes of automobiles."

As Black (1996, p. 19) argues, with international summary score comparisons of test performance,

> . . . like most statistics, what they conceal is as important as what they reveal. This is because pupils' performances on a particular question depend strongly on the extent to which its demands are familiar to the pupil and on the opportunities the pupil has had to learn about responding to such demands. Thus, the effectiveness of teaching or the commitment of the pupils are only two of several important determinants of test outcomes. The curricula and the inter-related practices of teaching, learning, and testing to which the pupils are accustomed are of equal, arguably greater, importance.

MULTIPLE SCORES

As has been discussed, the international studies of achievement conducted by IEA traditionally have placed considerable emphasis on issues of curriculum differences and student opportunity to learn. Consistent with this emphasis, reports of results generally have included more than reports of performance on a single global score scale. For example, SISS reported results for 10-year-olds for collections of items under the headings of biology, chemistry, earth science, physics, information, comprehension, and application in addition to an overall score (Postlethwaite & Wiley, 1992). Similarly, SIMS reported topic scores for sets and relations, number systems, algebra, geometry, elementary functions/calculus, and probability/statistics (McKnight et al., 1987). Similar breakdowns by content area were given in both the mathematics and science reports for TIMSS.

The relative standing of a country is often quite different when subscores are used than when rankings are based on total scores. This is apparent in TIMSS, for example, where the eighth-grade results for subscores and total were summarized as follows: "In math, the number of countries outperforming the U.S. in the total score is 17. In the subscales, this ranges from 9 in data representation and analysis to 30 in measurement. In science, the number of countries outperforming the U.S. on the total score is nine. In the subscales this ranges from 1 in environment to 13 in physics" (Jakwerth et al., 1997, p. 11).

The TIMSS reports also allowed national research coordinators to specify subsets of items that were judged to be appropriate for the country's curriculum. Each national research coordinator was asked to indicate whether items were or were not part of the country's intended curriculum. Items that were judged to be in the intended curriculum for 50 percent or more of the students in a country were considered appropriate for that country. Such items were then included in the score derived to match that country's curriculum. Scores were then produced based only on those items. Scores were obtained and summarized not only for the items appropriate for a particular country, but for those appropriate for each of the other countries as well. The number of items judged appropriate by national research coordinators varied substantially by country. For example, on the eighth-grade science test, the number of possible score points for the set of items judged appropriate for an individual country's curriculum ranged from a low of 58 for Belgium to a high of 146 for Spain (Beaton et al., 1996a, p. B-3).

Even with some wide variability in the number of science items judged to be appropriate for the different countries, the impact on the relative performance of countries was only modest. "[T]he selection of items for the participating countries varied somewhat in average difficulty, ranging from 55–59 percent correct at the eighth grade and from 49–56 percent at the seventh grade. Despite these differences, the overall picture provided . . . reveals that different item selections do not make a major difference in how well countries do relative to each other" (Beaton et al., 1996a, p. B-5). The results for mathematics when items were selected to match the curriculum of each country were quite similar to those for science. The fact that the country-selected item sets did not show greater variability in results is not surprising because all countries selected a sizable fraction of the total set of items and the country-specific sets of items all spanned multiple content areas.

When separate scores are produced for each content area (e.g., algebra and geometry within mathematics or earth science and physics within science), some potentially useful distinctions in relative performance of countries are revealed. For example, in eighth grade, the student average percentage correct in overall mathematics was the same for England and the United States (53 percent correct). England outperformed the United States in geometry (54 versus 48 percent correct) and measurement (50 versus 40 percent correct) whereas the United States did relatively better than England in fractions and number sense (59 versus 54 percent correct) (Beaton et al., 1996b, p. 41). Comparable variations in patterns across content areas also occur for other pairs of countries with the same overall performance, and for other grades and for science as well as mathematics. For people concerned with curriculum and instruction, the variations in patterns are more revealing than the comparisons of countries in terms of overall scores.

Still greater variation is obtained in country score patterns when topic scores within content areas are used. Schmidt, McKnight, and Raizen (1997) divided the TIMSS mathematics items into 20 topics using content framework categories. The science items were divided into 17 topics. The range of differences in the topic average percentage-correct scores between the topic with the highest and the one with the lowest average within a country was from 20–55 percent. The relative standing of a country varied greatly across topics. For example, 17 of the 42 countries had an average score among the highest five countries on at least one of the 20 mathematics topics, and 31 of the countries had ranks that fell in at least three quartiles. In science, 30 of the countries had topic area scores that fell in at least three quartiles. The average difference between a country's maximum and minimum ranks across topic areas was 18 for mathematics and 23 for science (Schmidt, McKnight, & Raizen, 1997). Although there are far too few items to support reliable scores for individual students at the level of 17 or 20 topics, such a fine breakdown does yield useful information at the level of aggregation of countries. Some caution is nonetheless needed in interpreting the results for individual topics, however, because the generalization to other potential items within a topic is questionable due to the small number of items per topic. Hence, the results are probably best thought of as illustrating the degree to which the ranking of a country would be subject to change if much greater emphasis were given to some topics than to others.

SUMMARY AND CONCLUSIONS

The international studies of educational achievement sponsored by the IEA have faced great challenges in producing tests that yield a valid basis of comparing the achievement of students from a wide array of nations. Over the course of more than three decades, the studies have shown great promise and produced better measures with each successive study. Starting from scratch, the FIMS and FISS accomplished remarkable feats to assemble a pool of items that passed muster with national committees of reviewers, and produced reliable measures covering relatively broad content domains. Certainly, those studies were subjected to considerable criticism, mostly about issues other than the quality of the measures, such as the comparability of populations of students in different countries that retained widely variable fractions of the age cohorts, and about the quality of the samples of students. There were also, however, some criticisms of the quality of the tests, particularly their relevance to the curricula of different countries and the heavy reliance on multiple-choice items.

The second round of studies made substantial strides to improve the alignment of the tests to the curricula of the participating countries, and went to great lengths to get information about the intended curriculum in each country and to develop measures of opportunity to learn so that the implemented curriculum could be related to the attained curriculum as measured by the SIMS and SISS assessments. Between the second and third round of studies, the IAEP studies were undertaken. Those studies contributed to advances in analytical techniques, using IRT models and conditioning procedures that had proven useful in the context of NAEP. The IAEP studies also introduced differential item functioning techniques as an approach to flagging items deserving closer scrutiny.

TIMSS benefitted from the experience and advances made in the earlier studies. It also moved ahead substantially on several measurement fronts. The analysis of the intended curriculum of participating countries was more sophisticated and complete than anything that came before it. That analysis provided a solid basis for the construction of assessments with a high likelihood of being relevant, valid, and fair to the countries involved in the study. Greater use of short-answer and extended-response items was made. The use of more sophisticated matrix sampling procedures made it possible to achieve broader coverage of the content domains within the constraints of the administration time allowed for each student. Item response theory provided an effective way of producing scores across the whole set of items within a content area. Analyses of subscores for broad topics such as geometry as well as for narrower subsets of items allowed researchers to convey the idea that achievement is more than an overall total score and is better understood in terms of the peaks and valleys that are found for every country. Those patterns of performance and their relationships to curricular emphasis are more likely to suggest educational policy to improve achievement than simple comparisons in terms of total scores.

Another innovation of TIMSS was the provision of an opportunity for countries to choose the items that were most appropriate for their particular curriculum. Results based on the country-specific selections of items, while not greatly different from those for the total scores, provided a basis for testing how different the results would be if the assessment were more closely tailored to fit the curriculum of a particular country. Finally, the within-country item analyses and item-by-country interaction analyses resulted in an effective means of flagging items in need of more careful consideration for individual countries.

Mathematics assessments have been used to illustrate many of the points in this chapter. Although the details vary from subject to subject in considerations such as the relative reliability of results and the details of topic coverage within a domain, the major points apply to subjects other than mathematics.

All in all, the quality of the measurement of achievement is one of the greatest strengths of the IEA studies. Certainly there is room for improvement, but the assessments bear up well under close scrutiny. Improvements that can be anticipated for future international studies are likely to depend on advances in the technology of testing. Computer-based test administration may be too futuristic to consider in the short run for an international study. However, the use of computers has considerable appeal as a means of enabling the administration of problems that are not feasible to administer or score efficiently in a paper-and-pencil mode (see, for example, Duran, 2000; NRC, 1999).

Other suggested improvements are more incremental in nature. The curriculum analyses that were conducted for TIMSS represent a valuable, albeit aging, resource. Those analyses might be put to good use to review, and possibly revise, the specifications for the assessments. Even in the face of changes in the curricula of participating countries between the time of TIMSS and the time of a new study, the curriculum frameworks provide a broad representation of the topics in the domains of mathematics and science that could be an empirical basis for structuring a table of specifications.

REFERENCES

Adams, R. J., & Gonzalez, E. J. (1996). The TIMSS test design. In M. O. Martin & D. L. Kelly (Eds.), *Third International Mathematics and Science Study (TIMSS) technical report, Vol. I: Design and development* (Chapter 3, pp. 1-36). Chestnut Hill, MA: Boston College.

Beaton, A. E., Martin, M. O., Mullis, I. V. S., Gonzalez, E. J., Smith, T. A., & Kelly, D. L. (1996a). *Science achievement in the middle school years: IEA's Third International Mathematics and Science Study (TIMSS).* Chestnut Hill, MA: Boston College.

Beaton, A. E., Mullis, I. V. S., Martin, M. O., Gonzalez, E. J., Kelly, D. L., & Smith, T. A. (1996b). *Mathematics achievement in the middle school years: IEA's Third International Mathematics and Science Study (TIMSS).* Chestnut Hill, MA: Boston College.

Bertrand, R., Dupuis, F. A., Johnson, E. G., Blais, J. G., & Jones, R. (Eds.). (1992). *A world of differences: An international assessment of mathematics and science technical report.* Princeton, NJ: Educational Testing Service.

Black, P. (1996). Commentary. In E. D. Britton & S. A Raizen (Eds.), *Examining the examinations: An international comparison of science and mathematics examinations for college-bound students* (pp. 19-21). Boston: Kluwer Academic.

Blais, J. G., Johnson, E. G., Mislevy, R. J., Pashley, P. J., Sheehan, K. M., & Zwick, R. J. (1992). *IAEP technical report, Vol. two: Part IV. IRT analysis.* Princeton, NJ: Educational Testing Service.

Bloom, B. S. (1956). *Taxonomy of educational objectives: Handbook I, cognitive domain*. New York: David McKay.

Comber, L. V., & Keeves, J. P. (1973). *Science education in nineteen countries: An empirical study*. Stockholm: International Association for the Evaluation of Educational Achievement.

Duran, R. P. (2000). *Implications of electronic technology for the NAEP assessment* (NVS Validity Studies Rep.). Palo Alto, CA: American Institutes for Research.

Educational Testing Service. (1991). *The IAEP assessment: Objectives for mathematics, science, and geography*. Princeton, NJ: Educational Testing Service.

Elley, W. B. (1992). *How in the world do students read? IEA study of reading literacy*. Hamburg, Germany: The International Association for the Evaluation of Educational Achievement.

Freudenthal, H. (1975). Pupils' achievement internationally compared – The IEA. *Educational Studies in Mathematics, 6*, 127-186.

Garden, R. A., & Orpwood, G. (1996). Development of the TIMSS achievement tests. In M. O. Martin & D. L. Kelly (Eds.), *Third International Mathematics and Science Study (TIMSS) technical report, Vol. I: Design and development* (Chapter 2, pp. 1-19). Chestnut Hill, MA: Boston College.

Glaser, R., Linn, R., & Bohrnstedt, G. (1997). *Assessment in transition: Monitoring the nation's educational progress*. Stanford, CA: Stanford University, The National Academy of Education.

Hambleton, R. K. (1989). Principles and selected applications of item response theory. In R. L. Linn (Ed.), *Educational measurement* (3rd ed., pp. 147-200). New York: Macmillan.

Husen, T. (Ed.) (1967). *International study of achievement in mathematics: A comparison of twelve countries (Vol. I.)*. New York: John Wiley & Sons.

Husen, T. (1987). Policy impact of IEA research. *Comparative Education Review, 31*(1), 129-136.

Jakwerth, P., Bianchi, L., Houang, R., Schmidt, W., Valverde, B., Wolfe, R., & Yang, W. (1997, April). Validity in cross-national assessments: Pitfalls and possibilities. Paper presented at the Annual Meeting of the American Educational Research Association. Chicago.

Johnson, E. G. (1992). Theoretical justification for the omnibus measure of differential item functioning. In R. Bertrand, F. A. Dupuis, E. G. Johnson, J. G. Blais, & R. Jones (Eds.). *A world of differences: An international assessment of mathematics and science technical report*. Princeton, NJ: Educational Testing Service.

Keeves, J. P. (1992). The design and conduct of the second science survey. In J. P. Keeves (Ed.), *The IEA study of science II: Change in science education and achievement. 1970 to 1984*. Elmsford, NY: Pergamon Press.

Lapointe, A. E., Askew, J. M., & Mead, N. A. (1992). *Learning science. The International Assessment of Educational Progress* (Rep. No. 22-CAEP-02). Princeton, NJ: Educational Testing Service.

Lapointe, A. E., Mead, N. A., & Askew, J. M. (1992). *Learning mathematics. The International Assessment of Educational Progress.* (Rep. No. 22-CAEP-01). Princeton, NJ: Educational Testing Service.

Lapointe, A. E., Mead, N. A., & Phillips, G. W. (1989). *A world of differences: An international assessment of mathematics and science.* (Rep. No. 19-CAEP-01). Princeton, NJ: Educational Testing Service.

Lie, S., Taylor, A., & Harmon, A. (1996). Scoring techniques and criteria. In M. Martin & D. Kelly (Eds.), *Third International Mathematics and Science Study (TIMSS): Technical report, Vol. I: Design and development* (Chapter 7, pp. 1-16). Chestnut Hill, MA: Boston College.

Linn, R. L. (1987). *State-by-state comparisons of student achievement: The definition of the content domain for assessment* (Technical Rep. No. 275). Los Angeles: UCLA, Center for Research on Evaluation, Standards, and Student Testing.

Linn, R. L. (1988). Accountability: The comparison of educational systems and the quality of test results. *Educational Policy, 1*, 181-198.

Linn, R. L., & Baker, E. L. (1995). What do international assessments imply for world-class standards? *Educational Evaluation and Policy Analysis, 17*, 405-418.

Martin, M. O., & Kelly, D. L. (Eds.). (1996). *Third International Mathematics and Science Study (TIMSS) technical report, Vol. I: Design and development.* Chestnut Hill, MA: Boston College.

McKnight, C. C., Crosswhite, F. J., Dossey, J. A., Kifer, E., Swafford, J. O., Travers, K. J., & Cooney, T. J. (1987). *The underachieving curriculum: Assessing U.S. school mathematics from an international perspective.* Champaign, IL: Stipes.

Mesa, V., & Kilpatrick, J. (1998, September). The content of mathematics education around the world. Paper prepared for the second Mathematics and Science Education Around the World: Continuing to Learn from TIMSS committee meeting, Woods Hole, MA.

Messick, S. (1989). Validity. In R. L. Linn (Ed.), *Educational measurement* (3rd ed., pp. 13-103). New York: Macmillan.

Miller, M. D., & Linn, R. L. (1989). International achievement and retention rates. *Journal of Research in Mathematics Education, 20*, 28-40.

Millman, J., & Greene, J. (1989). The specification and development of tests of achievement and ability. In R. L. Linn (Ed.), *Educational measurement* (3rd ed., pp. 335-366). New York: Macmillan.

Mislevy, R. J. (1995). What can we learn from international assessments? *Educational Evaluation and Policy Analysis, 17*, 410-437.

Mullis, I. V. S., & Martin, M. O. (1998). Item analysis and review. In M. O. Martin & D. L. Kelly (Eds.), *Third International Mathematics and Science Study (TIMSS), Vol. II: Implementation and analysis (primary and middle school years)* (pp. 101-110). Chestnut Hill, MA: Boston College.

Mullis, I. V. S., & Smith, T. (1996). Quality control steps for free-response scoring. In M. O. Martin & D. L. Kelly (Eds.), *Third International Mathematics and Science Study: Quality assurance in data collection* (Chapter 5, pp. 1-32). Chestnut Hill, MA: Boston College.

National Research Council. (1997). *Learning from TIMSS: Results of the Third International Mathematics and Science Study: Summary of a symposium.* A. Beatty (Ed.). Board on International Comparative Studies in Education, Commission on Behavioral and Social Sciences and Education. Washington, DC: National Academy Press.

National Research Council. (1999). *Grading the nation's report card: Evaluating NAEP and transforming the assessment of educational progress.* Committee on the Evaluation of National and State Assessments of Educational Progress. J. W. Pellegrino, L. R. Jones, & K. J. Mitchell (Eds.). Board on Testing and Assessment, Commission on Behavioral and Social Sciences and Education. Washington, DC: National Academy Press.

Porter, A. C. (1991). Assessing national goals: Some measurement dilemmas. In Educational Testing Service, *The assessment of national goals* (pp. 21-43). Princeton, NJ: Educational Testing Service.

Postlethwaite, T. N., & Wiley, D. E. (1992). *The IEA study of science II: Science achievement in twenty-three countries.* Oxford, England: Pergamon Press.

Romberg, R. A. (1985, October). The content validity of the mathematics subscores and items for the Second International Mathematics Study. Paper prepared for Committee on National Statistics, National Research Council of the National Academies.

Schmidt, W. E., & McKnight, C. C. (1995). Surveying educational opportunity in mathematics and science. *Educational Evaluation and Policy Analysis, 17*, 337-353.

Schmidt, W. E., McKnight, C. C., & Raizen, S. A. (1997). *A splintered vision: An investigation of U.S. science and mathematics education*. Dordrecht, Netherlands: Kluwer Academic.

Schmidt, W. E., McKnight, C. C., Valverde, G. A., Houang, R. T., & Wiley, D. E. (1997). *Many visions, many aims: A cross-national investigation of curricular intention in school mathematics*. Dordrecht, Netherlands: Kluwer Academic.

Schmidt, W. E., Raizen, S. A., Britton, E. D., Bianchi, L. J., & Wolfe, R. G. (1997). *Many visions, many aims: A cross-national investigation of curricular intention in science education*. Dordrecht, Netherlands: Kluwer Academic.

Stedman, L. (1994). Incomplete explanations: The case of U.S. performance on international assessments of education. *Educational Researcher, 23*(7), 24-32.

Thorndike, R. L. (1967). The mathematics tests. In T. Husen (Ed.), *International study of achievement in mathematics: A comparison of twelve countries* (Vol. I, pp. 90-108). New York: John Wiley & Sons.

Wang, J. (1998a). A content examination of the TIMSS items. *Phi Delta Kappan, 80*(1), 36-38.

Wang, J. (1998b). International achievement comparison: Interesting debates on inconclusive findings. *School Science and Mathematics, 98*(7), 376-382.

3

Adapting Achievement Tests into Multiple Languages for International Assessments

Ronald K. Hambleton*

International comparative studies of school achievement can provide (1) valuable data for educational policy makers about the quality of education in their countries, (2) possible explanations for the findings, and (3) suggestions for how improvements in achievement might be accomplished. But, as with any research study, valid conclusions and recommendations from a comparative study of educational achievement can only follow when the research methodology for the study is sound, and the data collection design has been implemented correctly.

International studies of achievement such as the Third International Mathematics and Science Study (TIMSS) and the Organization for Economic Cooperation and Development's Program for International Student Assessment (OECD/PISA) are research studies that are particularly difficult to implement well because of special methodological problems. Three of the problem areas are (1) reaching agreement on the variables to measure and the definitions of constructs, (2) choosing nationally representative samples, and (3) standardizing test administration conditions (including matching motivational levels of the students taking the test in participating countries). A fourth methodological problem, which is often given far less attention than it deserves, is the translation and adaptation of test instruments, scoring protocols, and related questionnaires. Unless

*Ronald Hambleton is a Distinguished University Professor and Chair of the Laboratory of Psychometric and Evaluative Research at the University of Massachusetts at Amherst.

the translations (or, more correctly, test adaptations) are carried out well—and this usually means carrying out a combination of careful translations and reviews, conducting field tests of the adapted tests, and compiling validity evidence—the results of an international comparative study such as TIMSS or OECD/PISA may be confounded by the consequences of poorly translated assessment materials. To the extent that a test adaptation changes the psychological meaning and/or test difficulty in the target languages or cultures, comparisons of student performance across language and cultural groups may have limited validity.

Poorly translated assessment materials can have many consequences. Awkward or improper translations may make the test instruments easier or harder for students in some countries. In one recent international assessment, it was learned through self-report that test translators in one country had simplified the language in the mathematics assessment by one grade level to make it more understandable to students. The reading difficulty from the mathematics items had been removed to place the focus of these items on the assessment of mathematics skills only. The consequence was that the test items were easier in this country than they would have been had the reading difficulty of the test items not been removed. Cross-national comparisons of mathematics achievement for the country involved were no longer meaningful.

Also, just plain bad translations may make the test instrument totally invalid. Literal translations are usually problematic. Apparently "out of sight, out of mind" was literally translated as "invisible, insane" in one translation between English and French. This humorous example is cited often among test translators, though the original source is unknown. Poor translations go beyond simply the language aspects of the test and test directions. For example, the multiple-choice format may be less familiar to students in some parts of the world. Africa is one location; China is another. Sometimes the problem of differential familiarity of item formats across countries participating in an international comparative study is handled by using multiple item formats. The idea seems to be that of balancing item format familiarity (or unfamiliarity) across participating countries. Test length also may be a problem. In some countries, tests may be relatively short, so a longer test used in an international comparative study may produce fatigue that can impact test performance. The problem arose in a U.S.–China comparison of mathematics achievement (Hambleton, Yu, & Slater, 1999) and was a potential source of invalidity in the comparison of results. Clearly, then, for international assessments where great importance is given to the results, considerable care must be given to the translation of assessment materials.

The goals of this chapter are (1) to describe some of the major myths about test adaptations, (2) to describe nine steps for adapting tests that follow from the International Test Commission Guidelines for Translating and Adapting Tests, and (3) to provide several examples of good and bad test adaptation practices from the recent TIMSS and OECD/PISA projects. Recommendations for adapting assessments will be offered later in this chapter.

First, two points need to be made. Test adaptation research is not limited to international studies of educational achievement. Popular intelligence, aptitude, and personality tests have been adapted for years, some of the most popular tests into more than 50 languages. Quality of life measures used in medical research are being widely adapted and used around the world (Hambleton & Patsula, 1998). Projects like TIMSS and OECD/PISA are two of many international studies of achievement. Many more studies are underway, including a major study of aging in Europe that is assessing many cognitive variables and involving thousands of participants and more than 10 languages (Schroots, Fernandez-Ballesteros, & Rudinger, 1999). Even in the United States, there are Spanish versions of the Scholastic Aptitude Test (SAT), several state assessments, the GED, and many school district-level achievement tests. Credentialing exams delivered by Microsoft, Novell, and other companies in the information technology field are being given to more than two million candidates a year in over 20 languages, and the numbers of candidates and languages have been increasing exponentially. Clearly the amount of testing in multiple languages is substantial and growing.

Second, the term "test adaptation" is preferred today to the term "test translation" by researchers working in this field (see Hambleton, Merenda, & Spielberger, in press). The former term is more indicative of the process that actually takes place in making a test produced in one language available and validated for use in another. Test translation is only part of the process. Decisions must be made about how to preserve the psychological equivalence of a test in two or more language and cultural groups. Format modifications may be necessary. Directions may need to be revised. For example, in one recent study, it was necessary to ask Chinese students to "check their answers" rather than "fill in the bubbles" that appeared on the American version of the test and to change the placement of the artwork in the Chinese version of the test (Hambleton, Yu, & Slater, 1999). Radical changes may be needed to make the item formats suitable. For example, the incomplete sentence format (with or without answer choices) causes a major problem in countries such as Turkey, where the object of a sentence often appears at the beginning. In this situation, the blank (or answer choices) to be completed (or selected) by candidates appear prior to the portion of the sentence that defines the question for the candidates. One can certainly wonder about the impact of this shift in the order of presentation of test material on the difficulty of the question. Finally, analogy questions almost never work in an adapted version of a test because it is nearly impossible to find words that have exactly the same meaning in two languages and with the same level of familiarity (Allalouf, Hambleton, & Sireci, 1999).

Another example concerns verb tenses. When the passive tense appears in passages, it must be changed in translations because it does not exist in all languages. Here is another example of a translation problem: The word "you" in English is both singular and plural. In some languages, such as Turkish, two possible words can be used in place of "you." The first is singular and informal. The second is formal and polite, and can have either a singular or plural meaning. Michal Beller from Israel (personal communication) talked about the richness of language. In Hebrew, for example, different words are used for the English word "picking" in expressions such as "picking grapes," "picking olives," and so on. Also, there is only one word for "camel" in English and Hebrew. In Arabic, there are numerous words for camel to distinguish different types. Giray Berberoglu from Turkey (personal communication) talked about his difficulty in finding equivalent meanings for words like "cold fish" and "bleeding heart" and translating expressions such as "every cloud has a silver lining." The list of changes that are required to make a test valid in multiple languages and cultures often goes well beyond the already difficult task of translating a test.

FIVE MYTHS ABOUT TEST ADAPTATIONS

Hambleton and Patsula (1999) described five myths about the test adaptation process, as described in the following paragraphs.

Myth 1: The preferable strategy is always to adapt an existing test rather than develop a new test for a second language group.

There are good reasons for adapting a test, but there are also reasons for not proceeding with a test adaptation. Especially when cross-cultural comparisons are not of interest, it may be substantially easier and more relevant to construct a new test for a second language group. This avoids any complications with copyright, ensures that an item format can be chosen that will be suitable for the intended population, and ensures that any desired modifications in the definition of the construct of interest can be made at the outset of the test development process.

Sometimes, too, it may be desirable *not* to adapt a test, but rather to require all examinees to take a test in a single language. For example, in the United States, there has been interest in some states in making high school graduation tests available in both English and Spanish. Technically this is possible, but the question of whether to make two language versions of a test available depends on many factors, including the definition of the construct being measured. Is the language in which performance is to be demonstrated a part of the construct definition or not? In the case of reading, reading in the language of English is nearly always part of the construct of interest. Producing a Spanish-equivalent version of a reading test in English makes very little sense because inferences of English reading proficiency cannot be made from a test administered in Spanish.

The situation with a mathematics test may be different. The construct of interest may be focused on computation skills, concepts, and problem-solving skills. Here, the purpose of the test is to look for a demonstration of the skills, and the language in which the performance is assessed and demonstrated may be of little or no interest. Of course, if the desired inference is the mastery of mathematics skills when the test questions are presented in English, then a Spanish version of the test would be inappropriate in this situation, too.

Myth 2:   Anyone who knows two languages can produce an acceptable translation of a test.

This is one of the most troublesome myths because it results in unqualified persons adapting tests. There is considerable evidence suggesting that test translators need to be (1) familiar with both source and target languages *and* the cultures, (2) generally familiar with the construct being assessed, and (3) familiar with the principles of good test development practices. With the 1995 TIMSS, countries reported that finding qualified translators was one of their biggest problems (Hambleton & Berberoglu, 1997). How, for example, can a mathematics or science test be translated from English to Spanish without some technical knowledge? Would a translator with little knowledge of test development principles know to keep answer choices of approximately the same length, so that length of answer choice does not become a clue to the correct answer? All too often in the cross-cultural literature, there is evidence of unqualified persons being involved in the test adaptation process. Professor Emeritus Ype Poortinga from the University of Tilburg in the Netherlands, who is a past editor of the *Journal of Cross-Cultural Psychology* and an internationally known cross-cultural psychologist, commented (personal communication) that he believed 75 percent of the research in cross-cultural psychology before 1990 was flawed because of the poor quality of test adaptations.

Myth 3:   A well-translated test guarantees that the test scores will be valid in a second language or culture for cross-language comparative purposes.

Van de Vijver and Poortinga (1997) make the point that not only should the meaning of a test be consistent across persons *within* a language group and culture, but that meaning, whatever it is, must be consistent *across* language groups and cultures. For example, if a test is more speeded in a second-language version because of the nature of that language, then the two language versions of the test are not equally valid. We have encountered just such a problem in some German test translations. The German words are longer than English words and take correspondingly longer to read. The result is a slightly more speeded German version of the test. In this instance, the test may be equally valid in each language group and culture, but still will not be suitable for cross-cultural comparisons because the German version with the same time limit as the English version would be administered under slightly more speeded test conditions.

Myth 4:   Constructs are universal, and therefore all tests can be translated into other languages and cultures.

An excellent example of this myth is associated with intelligence tests. This construct is known to exist in nearly all cultures. The Western notion of intelligence places emphasis on speed of response. On the other hand, in some non-Western cultures, speed of response is of minor importance as an operating principle, and members of these cultural groups often score lower on Western intelligence tests because of a failure to perform quickly (Lonner, 1990). But it is only by one of the Western definitions of the construct of intelligence that these cultural groups appear to be of less intelligence. Using a definition that does not place emphasis on speed of response, the results from a cross-cultural comparative study may be very different. See the work of Gardner (1983) and Sternberg (1989) for well-known work on broadening and changing the definition of intelligence. Poortinga and van de Vijver (1991) describe numerous additional examples in which cross-cultural comparisons are flawed because of the nongeneralizability of construct definitions across cultures.

Another example would be the definition, say, of the content to cover on the OECD/PISA 15-year-old assessment of mathematics achievement. The American idea of the relevant content domain is likely to be different from that of other countries. Ultimately, a decision must be made about the breadth and depth of the content domain that is relevant for the assessment; this may place some countries at an advantage, and others at a disadvantage. Content domains for achievement domains such as mathematics, science, and reading are hardly universal. They may not even be equally suitable across states or provinces within the same country.

Myth 5:   Translators are capable of finding flaws in a test adaptation. Field testing is not usually necessary.

The cross-national testing literature includes thousands of examples of poorly adapted test items. The fact is that translators are not able to anticipate all of the problems encountered by examinees taking a test in a second language. Field testing is as important for adapted tests in the target language as it is for tests produced in any language. Field testing should be an integral part of the test adaptation process.

This myth comes from the mistaken belief that a backward translation design is sufficient to justify the use of a test in a second language. In this design, a test is forward translated into the target language, then back translated into the original or source language for the test. The original and back-translated versions of the test are compared, and if found comparable, the assumption is made that the target-language version of the test is acceptable. But many concepts can be translated into another language and back-translated but may not be understood in the target language. For example, passages about snow, ice, and cold weather may not be meaningful in warm-weather countries, and this fact would not be identified in a back-translation design. The material itself may be translated and back translated easily, but the psychological meaning of the material may be very different in the two language versions of the test.

Jeanrie and Bertrand (1999) describe another example of a poor translation that was not caught by the translators; this item has appeared in a French translation of a well-known English personality test for many years. In the English version, the expression was "Generally, I prefer to be by myself." In the French version, the sentence was translated to, "Generally I prefer to be myself." The meaning is quite different, yet candidate responses were scored in exactly the same way with the two very different versions of the statement. This difference may be called a critical error in translation, and it impacts the validity of scores on the scale of the personality test where the item appears.

In summary, all of the myths can seriously compromise the validity of a test in a second language or cultural group, or negatively influence the validity of adapted tests for use in cross-language comparison studies. Fortunately, each myth is straightforward to address in practice. What follows are steps for adapting tests that can eliminate the myths and other shortcomings in test adaptation methodology.

NINE STEPS TO MAXIMIZE SUCCESS IN TEST ADAPTATIONS

The nine steps are based on the International Test Commission guidelines for translating and adapting educational and psychological tests. In 1992 an international committee was formed under the direction of the International Test Commission to prepare guidelines for adapting tests. The committee had 13 representatives from eight countries, with financial support from a number of countries and organizations, including the U.S. Department of Education. The 22 guidelines went through numerous reviews and field tests and have been published (Hambleton, 1994; Hambleton et al., in press; van de Vijver & Hambleton, 1996). They are being adopted by many organizations (see, e.g., Muniz & Hambleton, 1997), and were used in both the TIMSS and OECD/PISA projects. The guidelines appear in the Annex to this chapter. For each of the 22 guidelines, the committee offered a rationale or explanation for including the guideline, described steps that might be taken to meet the guideline, presented several common errors found in practice, and provided numerous references for additional study (see Hambleton et al., in press).

Step 1: Review construct equivalence in the language and cultures of interest.

In international comparative studies, it is important to establish whether construct equivalence exists among participating countries, and if it does not, either considering "decentering" (i.e., revising the definition of the construct to be equivalent in each language and cultural group) or discontinuing the project. The publication by Harkness (1998a) is especially helpful in the study of construct equivalence because she reviews numerous definitions of construct equivalence and approaches for studying it. In the 1995 TIMSS study, for example, initially the mathematics domain that could be agreed on by participating countries was so narrow that the study was nearly discontinued. Later, a decision was made that decentering would be done to redefine the mathematics content domain. Each country was required to be less rigid so that a construct could be defined that would be worthy of an international comparative study of mathematics achievement.

Step 2: Decide whether test adaptation is the best strategy.

Some tests will be more amenable to translation into certain languages than others. The more similar the target language and/or culture are to the source language and/or culture, the easier the adaptation will be (thus, English to Spanish adaptations may make more sense than English to Arabic or English to Chinese adaptations). With tests intended for cross-cultural comparisons, test adaptation (possibly with some decentering) may be the only option. But when cross-cultural comparisons are not of interest, it may be easier to actually produce a new test that meets the cultural parameters in the second-language group than to adapt an existing test that may have a number of shortcomings (e.g., a less than satisfactory definition of the construct, inappropriate item formats, an overly long test, or use of some culturally specific content).

Step 3: Choose well-qualified translators.

Lack of well-qualified translators is often one of the major shortcomings of a test adaptation project. Two points can be made. First, in selecting translators, the search should be for persons who are fluent in both languages, who are very familiar with the cultures under study, and who have some knowledge of test construction and the construct being measured. As knowledge of test construction practices is not common among translators, this may be addressed with some training prior to initiating the test adaptation process. Adding a psychometrician to the mix may be desirable, too.

Second, researchers have found that the double-translation procedure (i.e., two independent translations followed by reconciliation of both versions by a third party) offers advantages over a back-translation procedure or a single forward translation procedure. In the double-translation procedure, multiple individuals judge the equivalence of the source- and target-language versions of the test. In the back-translation design, a single translator may judge the target-language version of the test by comparing the source and back-translated source versions of the test. Another advantage of a double-translation procedure is that any discrepancies in the translation are noted on the all-important target-language version of the test. See, for example, recent work on the OECD/PISA project by Grisay (1998, 1999) for extensive evaluative comments on the double translation with reconciliation design. Idiosyncrasies and misunderstandings of individual translators can be reduced with the use of multiple translators. An unfortunate idiosyncrasy of a translator might be to always make correct answers in multiple-choice items a bit longer than the distractors. A misunderstanding might be when the translator mixes up the meanings of terms and concepts. The use of multiple translators increases the chances that these problems and many others will be identified prior to finalizing a test adaptation.

Step 4: Translate and adapt the test.

One approach to increasing the likelihood of a valid test adaptation is to adopt one of the two (or both) standard designs: forward translation and back translation. Forward-translation designs are the most technically sound because the focus of the review is on both the source- and target-language versions of the test. Backward-translation designs can also reveal poor translations, but without a focus on the target-language version of the test, problems in the adaptation can be missed. For example, concepts like "sales tax" and "hamburger" are hard to translate into Chinese, so these English words may be used in the adapted version. They are very easy to back translate, but they may be quite meaningless in the target-language version of the test (for more examples, see Hambleton, Yu, & Slater, 1999). In practice, both designs could be used to strengthen the methodology of the test adaptation process.

Step 5: Review the adapted version of the test and make any necessary changes.

In a forward-translation design, one set of translators performs the original source-to-target-language translation, while another set of translators examines the adapted version of the test for any errors that may lead to differences in meaning between the two language versions. The focus of the second group of translators would be on the quality of the translation or adaptation of the test. As Geisinger (1994) suggests, this review can be accomplished in a group meeting, individually, or by some combination of individual and group work. Geisinger believes the most effective strategy is first to have the translators review the items and react in writing, then to have the individuals share their comments with one another, reconcile any differences in opinion, and make any changes in the original and/or adapted-language versions as necessary.

The National Institute for Testing and Evaluation in Israel adapts college admissions tests into five languages (Arabic, English, Russian, French, and Spanish) from the original Hebrew-language version. One special feature in their process is that their translators work from the translated version first and attempt to determine the validity of the questions: For example, is the item stem clear? Is there a single correct or best answer? Are there grammatical clues that may lead the test-wise candidate to the correct answer? After the test items are judged to be technically sound, then the equivalence of the adapted version and the original Hebrew version are compared. Translators look at several features of the adapted items: accuracy of the translation as well as clarity of the sentences, level of difficulty of the words, and fluency of the translation.

With a backward-translation design, translators would take the adapted version of the test and back translate to the source language, then judgments would be made about the equivalence of the original and back-translated versions of the test. Where nonequivalence is identified, changes in the adapted version of the test are considered. The idea is that if the adaptation has been effective, the back-adapted version of the test should look very much like the original. Of course, when the adaptation involves format changes, changes in tense, changes in concepts, and other changes, the target-language version of the test may be fine, but a back-translated test may not look at all like the original. In general, a back-translation design seems like an excellent supplement to the forward-translation design, but the design is not likely to be able to stand on its own. The information the design provides about the validity of the adapted test is limited.

Step 6: Conduct a small tryout of the adapted version of the test.

Many studies seem to go wrong at this point. Too often test developers believe a judgmental review is sufficient evidence to establish the validity of a test in a second language. But validity evidence for using a test in a second language depends on stronger evidence than that the test seems to look acceptable to translators and/or reviewers. Not only is empirical evidence needed to support the validity of inferences from an adapted version of a test, but perhaps multiple empirical studies may be needed. A good example of what researchers might learn from a tryout of test items in a second language and culture is highlighted clearly in the papers by Allalouf and Sireci (1998) and Allalouf et al. (1999). Here, it was learned, for example, that verbal analogy items were nearly impossible to translate well. The situation really is no different from validating the scores from any test. Empirical evidence is needed to support the validity of inferences from scores on a test. That a test may function well and produce valid scores in one country is not suitable evidence that similar results will be obtained in a second country or culture with the adapted version of the test.

A pilot test might consist of administering the test as well as interviewing the examinees to obtain their criticisms of the test itself, instructions, time limits, and other factors. These findings form the basis for revising the test. One good suggestion from Ellis and Mead (1998) might be carried out: They suggested that when there are disagreements about the best adaptation of a test item, these variations might be field tested, and the results used to make the final decision about which adaptation is the most suitable.

Step 7: Conduct a validation investigation.

Good translators are often capable of identifying and fixing many shortcomings in adapted tests. But many problems go unidentified until test items are field tested. For example, in a recent study by Hambleton, Yu, and Slater (1999) in which National Assessment of Educational Progress (NAEP) mathematics items were adapted into Chinese, one problem with a NAEP test item went unidentified by the translators. A field test revealed a major problem with the item that could not be identified by the translators because it was a curriculum issue. Chinese students at the eighth grade were unfamiliar with the mathematical concept of estimation. The ability to round off numbers for arriving at approximate or estimated answers was not taught in the Chinese curriculum. As a result, on the estimation items (for example, "find the estimate of the product of 98 and 11"), the eighth-grade Chinese students performed disproportionately more poorly than American students. The validity issue concerned whether or not the estimation items should be retained in the findings from the comparative study.

The adapted test should be field tested using, whenever possible, a large sample of individuals representative of the eventual target population, and preliminary statistical analyses should be carried out, such as a reliability analysis and a classical item analysis. Checking for construct equivalence using factor analysis is desirable if sample sizes are large enough to produce stable factorial structures.

One important analysis is to check that the items function similarly in both the adapted- and source-language versions of the test. This can be accomplished through the use of an item bias study (often called a "differential item functioning" or DIF study) (Holland & Wainer, 1993). If there are items that function differently for each group when the groups are matched on ability, they can be eliminated from the test or they can be retranslated, readministered, and reanalyzed to determine whether they function the same in all adapted versions. This type of analysis has become routine with TIMSS and OECD/PISA. The Muniz, Hambleton, and Xing (2001) study highlights the fact that even small samples (i.e., 50 persons per group) can be useful in detecting flaws in the translation/ adaptation process because the problems of poor translations often are large and therefore easy to detect, even with small samples.

Step 8: Choose and implement a design for placing scores from the source- and target-language versions of the test on a common reporting scale.

This step is necessary when cross-national or cross-cultural comparisons are of interest, or the test score norms or performance standards with the source-language version of the test are of interest with the target-language version of the test. At this step, a linking design is needed to place the test scores from the different versions of the test on a common scale. Three popular linking designs are used in practice: (1) bilingual group design, (2) matched monolingual group design, and (3) monolingual group design. All three designs are popular, though the third design may be the easiest to implement in practice (see, e.g., Angoff & Cook, 1988). For an example based on item response modeling of the data, studies by Angoff and Cook or Woodcock and Munoz-Sandoval (1993) are of special interest.

Step 9: Document the process and prepare a manual for the users of the adapted test.

Documenting the results from steps 1 to 8 and preparing a manual for the users of the adapted test are important activities. The manual might include specifics regarding the administration of the test as well as how to interpret the test scores. This is a very important step, yet it is often overlooked. The OECD/PISA project has done an especially good job of preparing detailed steps for adapting tests and documenting the processes that take place in participating countries (see, e.g., Grisay, 1998, 1999).

TEST ADAPTATION PROCEDURES
FOR TIMSS AND THE OECD/PISA PROJECTS

For the 1995 TIMSS, and at the request of TIMSS project staff, Hambleton and Berberoglu (1997) conducted a survey of 45 participating countries (with 27, or 60 percent, of the surveys being returned). The five main findings of the survey were as follows:

1. The amount of review and revision involved in adapting the tests exceeded the time allocated to do the work. In addition, competent translators were hard to locate in many of the countries. The high cost of translators was also a problem in many countries.

2. The manual laying out the test adaptation process (operations manual) needed to be shorter and more focused. Without specific guidelines, countries were coming up with their own guidelines for translators, but then standardization of translation procedures across participating countries was compromised. For example, one country emphasized the importance of simplicity in translation, while another emphasized detailed rules to be followed by translators. All too often standardization among translators within a country rather than across countries was the focus of attention.

3. Better directives to international writing committees were needed to reduce the number of problems detected during the test adaptation process. For example, one problem arose with long sentences. They were difficult to translate well, and when the sentences were shortened for ease of readability in some countries, language difficulty was not consistent across language versions of the test.

4. Multiple-choice items in the incomplete stem format were difficult to translate. Such items are difficult to translate because the organization of subject, verb, and object in sentences is not consistent across languages. In countries such as Turkey, use of the incomplete stem format meant placing the blanks at the beginning of sentences rather than the end, and revising answer choices to match the format change, and these changes could have influenced the difficulty of test items.

5. The passive tense in passages was a problem because this tense does not exist in all languages. Many countries found themselves translating sentences in the passive tense to the active tense. But such changes probably influenced the structure of the language in the adapted tests and may have affected the difficulty of the test items.

Hambleton and Berberoglu asked national coordinators to comment about the operations manual used in TIMSS. Suggestions for improvement included (1) spell out the qualifications of translators more clearly, (2) offer a process for resolving differences between translators, and (3) emphasize "decentering" in the item writing process. Decentering is the technique of choosing passage topics, expressions, concepts, etc. that are most likely to be understandable or acceptable across languages and cultures. For example, passages about gun control, drugs, or snow may be unacceptable in an international assessment. Even a passage about high school students "getting a job" was rejected in one recent study because several countries worried that the passage may be sending the wrong message to young persons.

The OECD/PISA 2000 study of school achievement in 15-year-olds benefited considerably from the methodology used in TIMSS to adapt the tests. For one, documentation for carrying out the test adaptation process was more directive and concisely written than TIMSS, thus providing more guidance to participating countries. Also, many countries more familiar with French as a second language than English preferred to prepare their adaptations from a French rather than an English version of the test. Therefore, the starting point for the adaptation was the preparation by project staff of equivalent English and French versions of the test. This was a unique feature of the OECD/PISA project and one that was much appreciated by many participating countries. They had the option of starting with either an English or a French version of the test to do their test adaptation work. In fact, countries were encouraged to prepare double translations of the tests if possible—one adaptation from the French and one from the English version of the test. This double-translation, double-source-language design had the advantages of providing participating countries with two standards for evaluating their translations and offering a framework for judging the amount of freedom available to them in doing the translations. A comparison of the English and French versions for many countries, besides providing two sources for doing the translation (especially helpful when problems arose with a translation), offered an indication of the latitude that would be allowed in preparing their translations. In addition, the actual production of the French translation before any of the country translations were carried out identified problems early about difficult-to-translate material, which could then be revised or eliminated in the original English- and French-source-language versions of the test. At the same time, a considerable investment in time and resources was needed to produce formally equivalent English and French versions of the test. But to do otherwise would have made it more difficult for equivalent tests to be produced in participating countries.

In the OECD/PISA project, many important features of an effective test adaptation were learned from the TIMSS experience, but an old problem surfaced again: Too little time was allowed to carry out the test adaptation reviews. In part, this problem was created by the ambitious schedule, but it was also because of some inexperience about the time needed to have committees carry out careful reviews.

Not only do tests need to be adapted, but so do the demographic surveys. Finding cultural and contextual equivalents for questions in the school, teacher, and student questions was sometimes a problem. Terms like "advanced," "special enrichment," and "courses" were not always understood. Entrance exams in one country might be called "oral exams" in another country (e.g., Russia). Questions about school structures and organizations were not always meaningfully adapted because the concepts had no equivalent.

Harkness (1998b) has written about the problems of translating surveys and questionnaires. She notes that an extensive amount of research is reported in the methodology of survey construction literature, but little of it relates to the uses of surveys in multiple languages and cultures. And as she notes, rarely is there an isomorphism of words across languages. With a rating scale, for example, a translation, word for word, may create smaller or larger psychological gaps between points on the rating scale. For example, with a rating scale anchored by the extremes "allow" and "not allow," in one of the language translations the extremes became "allow" and "forbid." But the word "forbid" turned out to be considerably more negative than the extreme "not allow," and this choice appeared to significantly influence the use of the rating scale in the second-language version of the survey. Clearly translating rating scales is more than a word-by-word translation.

Also, in languages such as Hebrew, candidates read from right to left rather than left to right, so the scales need to be reversed. How much might this influence the meaningfulness of the rating scale? Or in Japan, rating scales may be presented vertically rather than horizontally. Will this shift in format influence ratings? Harkness notes that not just the words need to be translated; often the directions may be different (in some languages candidates "tick boxes"; in others they "select boxes" or "choose boxes") and it is not known whether these changes influence candidate responses. She adds that standardizing the administration also may be critical. It may make a big difference in some countries whether the survey is self-administered, administered face to face, or administered in a group.

Clearly the topic of survey/questionnaire adaptation is in its infancy. Future OECD/PISA projects and studies like TIMSS and TIMSS-Repeat (TIMSS-R) will need to focus additional attention on the adaptation of surveys and questionnaires, or risk misinterpreting the data from these instruments.

A number of important points appear to have been learned from the OECD/PISA 2000 project for future test adaptations:

1. Improved methods are being used to locate and train test translators.

2. The test adaptation process is being fully documented and includes important features such as forward and backward translations, double-translation designs from single- and double-source-language versions of the test, national verification, and even international verification. All of these features enhance the quality of test adaptations for international comparative studies.

3. Translators are being given excellent advice. For example, as many as 45 rules are being given to translators in the training documents. These include (a) avoid simplifying language and/or changing the level of abstraction of the testing material, and (b) avoid providing unintentional clues to correct answers by not making the correct answers longer, by eliminating grammatical clues, and so on.

CONCLUSIONS

An increasing number of educational, credentialing, and psychological tests are being adapted for use in multiple languages and cultures. For example, Spielberger's state-trait anxiety measure is now in more than 50 languages; major individually administered intelligence tests such as the *Wechsler Intelligence Scale for Children* are available in over 50 languages; TIMSS in 1995 was administered to students in 32 different languages; and Microsoft is delivering credentialing exams in more than 15 languages. These are but a few of hundreds of tests now available in multiple languages. At the same time, these adapted tests will have limited value unless they are adapted with a high degree of concern for issues of usability, reliability, and validity in participating countries. There is a rapidly emerging psychometric literature on the topic of test adaptation methodology, and more advances can be expected in the coming years as researchers respond to the expanding need for adapted tests of high technical quality (see, for example, Hambleton, Merenda, & Spielberger, in press). Avoiding the five myths and following the nine steps introduced in this chapter for the test adaptation process should go a long way toward improving current practices. In addition, the nine steps provide a framework for incorporating new methodology into the process as it is developed.

Three conclusions follow from the research carried out in completing this paper. First, test adaptation methodology has advanced considerably in the past 20 years. It has moved from the use of a single and possibly unqualified translator and/or limited empirical work with bilinguals to considerably more sophisticated methodologies with focus on establishing construct, method, and item-level equivalence (Hambleton, Merenda, & Spielberger, in press; van de Vijver & Tanzer, 1997). There is an ever-increasing number of papers published on the topic each year; now there is a new journal published by Lawrence Erlbaum Associates under the direction of the International Test Commission called the *International Journal of Testing* that is expected to publish many of the methodological and substantive advances. There has been an emergence of test adaptation guidelines, and more time is being allocated to the process of test adaptations than ever. For example, a comparison of the methodology used for test adaptation in the 1988 and 1991 NCES-ETS studies (see Lapointe, Mead, & Askew, 1992; Lapointe, Mead, & Phillips, 1989) and the TIMSS and OECD/PISA projects in 1995 and 2000, respectively, shows major advances in sophistication and effort. Second, the future of test adaptation seems very positive. The methodology is very much in place, and advances are still being made, but what is needed now are commitments of resources and time to ensure that test adaptation work is carried out well. Finally, the most important areas for improvement in the coming years with international comparative studies of achievement are the following: choosing multiple translators well and training them, aggressively applying current judgmental and statistical designs and methods, and building on experiences and knowledge gained to continually improve the process.

REFERENCES

Allalouf, A., Hambleton, R. K., & Sireci, S. G. (1999). Identifying the causes of DIF in translated verbal items. *Journal of Educational Measurement, 36*(3), 185-198.

Allalouf, A., & Sireci, S. G. (1998, April). Detecting sources of DIF in translated verbal items. Paper presented at the meeting of the American Educational Research Association, San Diego.

Angoff, W. H., & Cook, L. L. (1988). *Equating the scores of the Prueba de Aptitud Academica and the Scholastic Aptitude Test* (Rep. No. 88-2). New York: College Entrance Examination Board.

Ellis, B., & Mead, A. (1998, August). Measurement equivalence of a 16PF Spanish translation: An IRT differential item and test functioning analysis. Paper presented at the 24th meeting of the International Association of Applied Psychology, San Francisco.

Gardner, H. (1983). *Frames of mind: The theory of multiple intelligences.* New York: Basic Books.

Geisinger, K. F. (1994). Cross-cultural normative assessment: Translation and adaptation issues influencing the normative interpretation of assessment instruments. *Psychological Assessment, 6,* 304-312.

Grisay, A. (1998). *Instructions for the translation of the PISA material* (OECD/PISA Rep.). Melbourne: Australian Council for Educational Research.

Grisay, A. (1999). *Report on the development of the French source version of the PISA test material* (OECD/PISA Rep.). Melbourne: Australian Council for Educational Research.

Hambleton, R. K. (1994). Guidelines for adapting educational and psychological tests: A progress report. *European Journal of Psychological Assessment, 10,* 229-244.

Hambleton, R. K., & Berberoglu, G. (1997). *TIMSS instrument adaptation process: A formative evaluation* (Laboratory of Psychometric and Evaluative Research Rep. No. 290). Amherst: University of Massachusetts, School of Education

Hambleton, R. K., Merenda, P., & Spielberger, C. (Eds.). (in press). *Adapting educational and psychological tests for cross-cultural assessment.* Hillsdale, NJ: Lawrence Erlbaum Associates.

Hambleton, R. K., & Patsula, L. (1998). Adapting tests for use in multiple languages and cultures. *Social Indicators Research, 45,* 153-171.

Hambleton, R. K., & Patsula, L. (1999). Increasing the validity of adapted tests: Myths to be avoided and guidelines for improving test adaptation practices. *Journal of Applied Testing Technology, 1,* 1-12.

Hambleton, R. K., Yu, J., & Slater, S. C. (1999). Field-test of the ITC guidelines for adapting psychological tests. *European Journal of Psychological Assessment, 15*(3), 270-276.

Harkness, J. (Ed.). (1998a). *Cross-cultural equivalence.* Mannheim, Germany: ZUMA.

Harkness, J. (1998b, August). Response scales in cross-national survey research. Paper presented at the meeting of the American Psychological Association, Toronto, Canada.

Holland, P. W., & Wainer, H. (1993). *Differential item functioning.* Hillsdale, NJ: Lawrence Erlbaum Associates.

Jeanrie, C., & Bertrand, R. (1999). Translating tests with the International Test Commission Guidelines: Keeping validity in mind. *European Journal of Psychological Assessment, 15*(3), 277-283.

Lapointe, A. E., Mead, N. A., & Askew, J. M. (1992). *Learning mathematics* (Rep. No. 22-CAEP-01). Princeton, NJ: Educational Testing Service.

Lapointe, A. E., Mead, N. A., & Phillips, G. W. (1989). *A world of differences: An international assessment of mathematics and science* (Rep. No. 19-CAEP-01). Princeton, NJ: Educational Testing Service.

Lonner, W. J. (1990). An overview of cross-cultural testing and assessment. In R. W. Brislin (Ed.), *Applied cross-cultural psychology* (pp. 56-76). Newbury Park, CA: Sage.

Muniz, J., & Hambleton, R. K. (1997). Directions for the translation and adaptation of tests. *Papeles del Psicologo*, August, 63-70.

Muniz, J., Hambleton, R. K., & Xing, D. (2001). Small sample studies to detect flaws in item translations. *International Journal of Testing 1*(2), 115-135.

Poortinga, Y. H., & van de Vijver, F. J. R. (1991). Testing across cultures. In R. K. Hambleton & J. Zaal (Eds.), *Advances in educational and psychological testing* (pp. 277-308). Boston: Kluwer Academic.

Schroots, J. J. F., Fernandez-Ballesteros, R., & Rudinger, G. (1999). *Aging in Europe.* Amsterdam, Netherlands: IOS Press.

Sternberg, R. (1989). *The triarchic mind: A new theory of human intelligence.* New York: Viking.

van de Vijver, F. J. R., & Hambleton, R. K. (1996). Translating tests: Some practical guidelines. *European Psychologist, 1*, 89-99.

van de Vijver, F. J. R., & Poortinga, Y. H. (1997). Towards an integrated analysis of bias in cross-cultural assessment. *European Journal of Psychological Assessment, 13*, 29-37.

van de Vijver, F. J. R., & Tanzer, N. (1997). Bias and equivalence in cross-cultural assessment: An overview. *European Review of Applied Psychology, 47*(4), 263-279.

Woodcock, R. W., & Munoz-Sandoval, A. F. (1993). An IRT approach to cross-language test equating and interpretation. *European Journal of Psychological Assessment, 9*, 233-241.

ANNEX TO CHAPTER 3:
INTERNATIONAL TEST COMMISSION
TEST ADAPTATION GUIDELINES

Context

C.1   Effects of cultural differences which are not relevant or important to the main purposes of the study should be minimized to the extent possible.

C.2   The amount of overlap in the constructs in the populations of interest should be assessed.

Test Development and Adaptation

D.1   Test developers/publishers should insure that the adaptation process takes full account of linguistic and cultural differences among the populations for whom adapted versions of the test are intended.

D.2   Test developers/publishers should provide evidence that the language used in the directions, rubrics, and items themselves as well as in the handbook is appropriate for all cultural and language populations for whom the test is intended.

D.3   Test developers/publishers should provide evidence that the choice of testing techniques, item formats, test conventions, and procedures is familiar to all intended populations.

D.4   Test developers/publishers should provide evidence that item content and stimulus materials are familiar to all intended populations.

D.5   Test developers/publishers should implement systematic judgmental evidence, both linguistic and psychological, to improve the accuracy of the adaptation process and compile evidence on the equivalence of all language versions.

D.6   Test developers/publishers should ensure that the data collection design permits the use of appropriate statistical techniques to establish item equivalence between the different language versions of the test.

D.7   Test developers/publishers should apply appropriate statistical techniques to (1) establish the equivalence of the different versions of the test, and (2) identify problematic components or aspects of the test which may be inadequate to one or more of the intended populations.

D.8   Test developers/publishers should provide information on the evaluation of validity in all target populations for whom the adapted versions are intended.

D.9   Test developers/publishers should provide statistical evidence of the equivalence of questions for all intended populations.

D.10   Nonequivalent questions between versions intended for different populations should not be used in preparing a common scale or in comparing these populations. However, they may be useful in enhancing content validity of scores reported for each population separately.

Administration

A.1   Test developers and administrators should try to anticipate the types of problems that can be expected, and take appropriate actions to remedy these problems through the preparation of appropriate materials and instructions.

A.2   Test administrators should be sensitive to a number of factors related to the stimulus materials, administration procedures, and response modes that can moderate the validity of the inferences drawn from the scores.

A.3   Those aspects of the environment that influence the administration of a test should be made as similar as possible across populations for whom the test is intended.

A.4   Test administration instructions should be in the source and target languages to minimize the influence of unwanted sources of variation across populations.

A.5   The test manual should specify all aspects of the test and its administration that require scrutiny in the application of the test in a new cultural context.

A.6   The administrator should be unobtrusive and the administrator-examinee interaction should be minimized. Explicit rules that are described in the manual for the test should be followed.

Documentation/Score Interpretations

I.1   When a test is adapted for use in another population, documentation of the changes should be provided, along with evidence of the equivalence.

I.2   Score differences among samples of populations administered the test should not be taken at face value. The researcher has the responsibility to substantiate the differences with other empirical evidence.

I.3   Comparisons across populations can only be made at the level of invariance that has been established for the scale on which scores are reported.

I.4   The test developer should provide specific information on the ways in which the sociocultural and ecological contexts of the populations might affect performance on the test, and should suggest procedures to account for these effects in the interpretation of results.

4

Sampling Issues in Design, Conduct, and Interpretation of International Comparative Studies of School Achievement

James R. Chromy*

Cochran (1977) outlines eleven steps in the planning of a survey. Good sampling methods must exist in the environment of all of these steps. These steps are (1) a statement of the survey objectives, (2) the definition of the population to be sampled, (3) the data to be collected, (4) the degree of precision required, (5) the methods of measurement, (6) the frame or the partitioning of the population into sampling units, (7) the sample selection methods, (8) the pretest, (9) the fieldwork organization, (10) the summary and analysis of the data, and (11) a review of the entire process to see what can be learned for future surveys. Mathematically, the major concerns for sample design have focused on the sample selection procedures and the associated estimation procedures that yield precise estimates. Optimization of sample designs involves obtaining the best possible precision for a fixed cost or minimizing survey costs subject to one or more constraints on the precision of estimates. Optimized designs sometimes are called efficient designs.

The mathematical presentation of sampling theory often focuses on obtaining efficient sample designs with precision measured in terms of sampling error only, although both Cochran (1977) and many earlier texts (e.g., Deming, 1950, or Hansen, Hurwitz, & Madow, 1953) discuss non-sampling errors in surveys. A more recent text by Lessler and Kalsbeek (1992) is devoted entirely to nonsampling errors in surveys, classified as frame error, nonresponse error, and measurement error.

---

*James R. Chromy is chief scientist at RTI , Research Triangle Park, NC.

Designing surveys that control both sampling errors and nonsampling errors remains a serious challenge. Sample designers also cannot avoid some of the conceptual issues in total survey design, such as defining the survey objectives, defining the target population to be measured, or limiting the resources that can be devoted to data collection. Decisions reached on these issues can lead to serious tradeoffs among sample design options.

The framework and principles document (National Research Council [NRC], 1990) of the Board on International Comparative Studies in Education (BICSE) identifies key sample design issues in the broader context just described. The objective of measuring achievement or performance to permit comparisons across school systems in different countries is clear. Explaining differences is more problematic and may require collection of additional data. Even with these additional data, the approach to analysis and interpretation of differences may be exploratory at best because there are many potential explanatory factors, and only some will be measured. When differences are observed, they properly form the basis for additional studies that would be designed to better understand the differences. The framework makes clear that the objectives of both descriptive and explanatory studies will require rigorous sampling procedures and the capacity to produce national estimates of the variables studied.

Conceptual problems of defining comparable student populations in different countries also are addressed. For students enrolled in school, the problem of defining the study population in terms of age or grade must be resolved. Problems exist with both methods because children start school at different ages, so even first graders may be five, six, or seven years old. Different countries follow different grade progression policies. At the upper grade levels, there may be a much broader representation of ages within a single grade. Different national policies about the legal age of leaving school either to drop out or to enter specialized training may alter the composition of classes completing normal schooling. The guidance document recognizes the difficulty of consistent population definition, but does not recommend one approach over another.

Survey populations also must be defined temporally. The value of national and cross-national data to meet the objectives of trend measurement and trend comparisons requires regular data collection on an established schedule. If too many cross-national studies are carried out simultaneously, both the educational process itself and the success of the surveys can be adversely affected. The administration of surveys disrupts the educational process in the schools involved in the survey. Schools requested to participate in several surveys (national, cross-national, and others) may be less likely to participate in any of them or may have to select among them. Consequently, school response rates will suffer.

The BICSE framework provides several principles for sampling and access to schools for both descriptive and explanatory studies:

- Samples must be drawn from the full population of teachers, administrators, students (at an age or a grade), or policy makers.
- Valid estimation of population parameters requires strict adherence to an explicit sample design.
- Plans should discuss the frame and the approach to selecting the sample.
- Planned exclusions of subgroups (the disabled or persons who do not speak the language in which the test is administered) must be documented. Information should be provided about the size of the population subgroup excluded and the direction of bias due to the exclusion.
- The extent of participation in education may create differences in the student populations in different countries.
- The sample design should support reasonably accurate inferences about an age or grade cohort and capture the existing range of individual, school, and classroom variations.
- Within-country subpopulations may be defined.
- The total population and subpopulations sample must be explicitly delineated.
- An international sampling manual is essential.
- The board encourages the appointment of an experienced and expert sampling consultant to review and approve all country samples before testing takes place.
- The *achieved* sample design is usually different from the *planned* sample design.
- Advance arrangements with school officials should be arranged to ensure high participation rates. A maximum acceptable nonresponse rate should be specified for inclusion of a country's data in the international analyses.
- Subnational units that have separate autonomous school systems may be included in international studies.

The BICSE framework also specifies test administration procedures to control the measurement error component. These include standardized procedures over time and across nations, pilot testing in each participating country, and a meeting with study coordinators between the pilot study and the full-scale study to review procedures and adjust them if necessary. The report also recommends (ideally) that "suitably trained [test administrators] from outside the [school system] be in charge of test administration" and that "people from different countries . . . supervise the implementation of the procedures to be followed (previously agreed on by the countries involved) by being present on site when the field work is conducted" (NRC, 1990, p. 9).

The Board framework also requires that "standard errors be calculated and reported for all reported statistics." It also encourages the use of a single recognized expert consultant for this technically complex process. The Board also recommends audit and evaluation procedures for all aspects of the survey, including participation rates, attrition, and absentee followup.

More recently a technical standards and guidelines document was published by the International Association for the Evaluation of Educational Achievement (IEA) (Martin, Rust, & Adams, 1999). These standards include (among others) standards for drawing a sample, for minimizing burden and nonresponse, for developing sampling weights, and for reporting sampling and nonsampling errors and reinforcing the principles in the BICSE framework. There is a strong emphasis on documentation of all steps of sampling and data collection and the submission of a written record for evaluating each survey.

Sample selection guidelines specify that replacements for nonparticipating schools should be identified when the school sample is drawn. Guidelines for minimizing response burden and nonresponse emphasize simplicity and reasonable approaches to working with respondents. Minimum acceptable response rates are not specified. Weighting guidelines require use of base weights based on the selection probability and adjustments for nonresponse. Nonresponse adjustments should be applied at each stage of sample selection. Procedures for trimming outlier weights are recommended to control the impact of unusually large weights. The guidelines require calculation of standard errors, coefficients of variation, or confidence intervals based on the complexities of the sampling design. Data files and documentation should permit proper calculation of sampling errors. Participation rates at each sampling stage and across all stages should be reported as well as other measures that indicate potential nonsampling error.

This report reviews and comments on selected comparative studies of international education with a focus on the student component. Many of the early studies had serious problems in both the process and the execution. For some, the easily available documentation was not adequate to properly evaluate them. The documentation of quality issues (e.g., documentation of the Second International Study of Mathematics) led to the development of guidelines for future studies, including the BICSE framework. During the 1990s, the processes for conducting international assessments became much better defined, and the execution has continued to improve. The remainder of this report includes sections on selected comparative studies of education completed or planned, a discussion of other general appraisals of sampling issues in international comparative studies, and a section on possible remaining or continuing issues. I will argue that opportunities exist today to refine the specified processes and that execution of designs consistent with established guidelines remains a problem in many countries, including the United States.

REVIEW OF PUBLISHED DESCRIPTIONS AND CRITIQUES

This report section summarizes key points about the sample designs and their execution for 15 studies or sets of international comparative studies in education conducted since the early 1960s. The discussion in this section is mostly descriptive and provides background for the critiques presented in subsequent sections. A theme of this section is that improved documentation of the quality (or lack of quality) of surveys is a prerequisite to achieving any improvement in the quality of future studies. This period of time also coincides with tremendous advances in computational hardware and software. Early in this era, probability sampling, simple weighting procedures, and model-based variance estimation were adequate to define a high-quality sample design by standards of the time. With development of computing power and specialized software, direct estimation of survey sampling errors and the ability to routinely monitor other quality measures, including response rates, became the norm in survey practice. The availability of computers also fostered the execution of more complex sampling plans and the development of comparable sampling approaches through the use of a common set of procedures and sample selection software.

International Comparative Studies Completed Since the 1960s

Table 4-1 summarizes the participation and timeframe of the major studies described by BICSE (NRC, 1995), beginning with the First International Mathematics Study (FIMS) conducted in 1964. The Six Subjects Study was conducted over the period of 1970-71. The general group of IEA science and mathematics studies includes:

- First International Mathematics Study (FIMS);
- Second International Mathematics Study (SIMS);
- First International Science Study (FISS);
- Second International Science Study (SISS); and
- Third International Mathematics and Science Study (TIMSS).

Two international assessments of science and mathematics also were coordinated by the Educational Testing Service, with sponsorship of the coordination and U.S. components by the U.S. Department of Education and the National Science Foundation:

TABLE 4-1   Selected International Comparative Studies in Education: Scope and Timing

Sponsor	Description	Countries	Year(s) Conducted
IEA	First International Mathematics Study (FIMS)	12 countries	1964
IEA	Six Subjects Study:		1970-71
	Science	19 systems	
	Reading comprehension	15 countries	
	Literature	10 countries	
	French as a foreign language	8 countries	
	English as a foreign language	10 countries	
	Civic Education	10 countries	
IEA	First International Science Study (FISS) (part of Six Subjects Study)	19 systems	1970-71
IEA	Second International Mathematics Study (SIMS)	10 countries	1982
IEA	Second International Science Study (SISS)	19 systems	1983-84
ETS	First International Assessment of Educational Progress (IAEP-I, Mathematics and Science)	6 countries (12 systems)	1988
ETS	Second International Assessment of Educational Progress (IAEP-II, Mathematics and Science)	20 countries	1991
IEA	Reading Literacy (RL)	32 countries	1990-91
IEA	Computers in Education	22 countries	1988-89
		12 countries	1991-92
Statistics Canada	International Adult Literacy Survey (IALS)	7 countries	1994
IEA	Preprimary Project		
	Phase I	11 countries	1989-91
	Phase II	15 countries	1991-93
	Phase III (longitudinal followup of Phase II sample)	15 countries	1994-96
IEA	Language Education Study	25 interested countries	1997
IEA	Third International Mathematics and Science Study (TIMSS)		
	Phase I	45 countries	1994-95
	Phase II (TIMSS-R)	About 40	1997-98
IEA	Civic Education Study	28 countries	1999
OECD	Program for International Student Assessment	32 countries	2000 (reading) 2003 (mathematics) 2006 (science)

- First International Assessment of Educational Progress (IAEP-I); and
- Second International Assessment of Educational Progress (IAEP-II).

The IAEP studies were designed to take advantage of the established procedures and instruments from the U.S. National Assessment of Educational Progress (NAEP).

Most of the studies shown in Table 4-1 address enrolled student populations. The Reading Literacy study provides an example outside the science and mathematics arena. The Adult Literacy study provides an example of a study of the general household population, which requires a household sample design as opposed to a school-based sample design. In addition, we examine plans for the Organization for Economic Cooperation and Development (OECD) Program for International Student Assessment (PISA) 2000.

In building Table 4-1, the numbers of participating countries sometimes disagreed among sources because some sources are written at the planning stages and some reflect actual experience; counting of systems, parts of countries, and whole countries also caused confusion. Where possible the actual experience is reflected. The table is provided to give an overview of the wide variety of studies in various stages of completion or planning. Data are sketchy for the early studies due to passage of time and, for the most recent studies, due to the author's inability to locate completed reports.

Medrich and Griffith (1992) described and evaluated five international studies through the late 1980s:

- FIMS;
- FISS;
- SIMS;
- SISS; and
- IAEP-I.

Their work is the primary source used to review sampling issues for three of these studies. For SIMS, the report by Garden (1987) provides the most direct source. The discussion of IAEP-I is supplemented by Lapointe, Mead, and Phillips (1989).

In addition, more recent studies that will be discussed include:

- IAEP-II;
- TIMSS;
- Civic Education Study; and
- PISA.

First International Mathematics Study

FIMS was conducted in the mid-1960s in 12 countries. Two target populations were defined:

- Students at the grade level at which the majority of pupils were age 13 (11 educational systems).
- Students in the last year of secondary education (10 educational systems).

In the United States, these populations corresponded to grades 8 and 12.

Two- or three-stage probability samples were used, with school districts (optional stage used in the United States), schools, and students comprising the sampling stages. Multiple test forms were utilized. Medrich and Griffith (1992, p. 13) note that data on the sample design details and response rates were largely unavailable in published sources, and the total sample was small in some of the countries with the highest means. Individual country reports may have contained this information. Peaker's (1967) discussion on sampling issues makes a persuasive argument for probability sampling and explains the impact of the intraclass correlation and cluster size decisions on the equivalent simple random size (often called effective sample size). Approximation methods are developed for relating the true variance of estimates to variance estimates developed under the assumption of simple random sampling. The use of subsamples to generate a simple measure of sampling error also is discussed. Peaker presents data on achieved sample sizes by population studied, but does not present data on school or student response rates. The concept of an international sampling referee was already in place for FIMS, and Peaker served in this capacity.

First International Science Study

FISS was conducted in 1970-71 as part of the Six Subjects Study in 19 educational systems; not all of them participated in all target populations or reported results in the achievement component of the study. Target populations were:

- Students at age 10.
- Students at age 14.
- Students in the last year of secondary education.

Two test versions were used at ages 10 and 14, and three versions by subject (biology, chemistry, and physics) were used for the third population (Medrich & Griffith, 1992, p. 14).

Sample designs involved either two or three stages of sampling. An international referee approved each country's plan, although no IEA funds were available to monitor the sampling programs. Medrich and Griffith noted a few particular problems:

- At least three countries excluded students who were one or more years behind in grade for their age.
- Two countries excluded states or schools based on language.
- One country excluded students attending vocational schools.
- One country limited the sample to the area around its capital.
- Some countries sampled 10- and 14-year-olds by grade rather than age because of difficulty or cost.

Countries agreed to limit sampling to students enrolled in school. Medrich and Griffith note the controversy that arose over the impact of retention rates on estimates for the "last year of secondary education" population.

Response rates were reported from most countries. For the age 14 sample, 18 systems reported school response rates ranging from 34 to 100 percent and student response rates ranging from 22 to 98 percent. Ten of the 18 had school response rates exceeding 85 percent; only six of 18 had student response rates exceeding 85 percent.[1]

Second International Mathematics Study

SIMS was conducted in 1982 in 10 countries. Two target populations were defined for SIMS:

- Population A: Students in the modal grade for 13-year-olds when age is determined in the middle of the school year.
- Population B: Students in the terminal grade of secondary education who are studying mathematics as a substantial part of their academic program (approximately five hours per week).

Each country had to restate the definition in terms specific to their own situation and to identify any exclusions. Countries could make some judgments about whether the grade tested identified students who had been exposed to the mathematics curriculum covered in the test.

Sample designs generally involved a one- or two-stage PPS sample of schools, with sampling of one or two intact classes per school. Multiple test forms were used. For Population A, all students completed a core set of items and one of four other tests. For Population B, each student was administered two out of a set of eight tests (Medrich & Griffith, 1992,

p. 16). A cross-sectional sample was required for the international study, but individual countries had the option to conduct pretests and posttests during the same school year to measure the impact of the academic program.

An excellent evaluation of sampling procedures for SIMS was prepared by Garden (1987) of the New Zealand Department of Education. Before discussing some of the problems identified in his report, let me quote some remarks from his conclusions:

> Given the administrational challenges involved, both at international and at national level[s], and the difficulties of communication across cultures by correspondence the quality of the data collected is extraordinarily good. Most National Centers had little funding for the project and National Research Coordinators in many cases undertook national supervision of the project with minimal resources and with a minimal time allowance. (p. 138)

This conditional summary, although positive, certainly allows for improvement. He also states:

> There is no simple answer to the question "Is country X's sample so poor that the data cannot be used?" If there was such an answer it would be "No" for all samples in the study. (p. 138)

He points out that the data must be evaluated in conjunction with information about the sample and other aspects of the study.

SIMS had an international sampling manual (copy appended to the Garden report) and an international sampling committee.

Some examples of situations related to the Population A sample that occurred in some countries are cited in the Garden (1987) report:

- An unknown number of schools used judgment rather than random sampling of classes.
- Simple random sampling of students was used rather than selection of intact classes. (Note that this would be an acceptable, perhaps better, alternative, but it does not conform to the international manual.)
- Private schools were excluded.
- Classes were selected directly without an intermediate school sample; this country had a very high sampling rate, making this feasible.
- Vocational education students were excluded, although they sometimes comprise 20 percent or more of the population.
- Logistic and financial constraints forced reduction of the sample geographically within the country, with a coverage reduction exceeding 10 percent.
- Small (fewer than 10 students in grade) schools were excluded (estimated at 2 percent of the population).

- A followup to a previous study was used as the SIMS sample.
- Because of curriculum matching to the test, the country targeted a grade that contained about 10 percent of 13-year-olds and had an average age closer to 15.
- All schools were asked about willingness to participate and about a third agreed. All but two of these were invited to participate, resulting in an essentially self-selected school sample.
- Target populations were limited by the language of instruction in several countries, sometimes amounting to a substantial (but unspecified) portion of the total.

The Population B definition required considerable judgment by each country involved. In many cases, the population defined consisted of less than 10 percent of the age cohort. In many countries, the age cohort coverage was not stated. Most coverage problems were defined away by the population definition.

Garden notes problems in computing response rates. The definition of response rates was problematic, usually computed as the achieved sample compared to the executed sample. Although Garden's summary shows that 12 of 20 systems achieved response rates exceeding 90 percent and only two systems were below a 70-percent response rate, his examination of the country reports leaves some doubt about whether these reports account for the overall response rate when considering both school and student nonresponse or whether the executed student sample size could be determined. In some cases, the achieved sample exceeds the designed sample and no information is provided on the executed student sample size. How substitute schools count in the computation of response rates also is not clear. In the United States, a large sample of districts was drawn in advance in anticipation of a low response rate; 48 percent of districts participated. In addition, only 69 percent of schools selected participated. Finally, 77 percent of students selected (the executed student sample) participated. If substitution were used and masked in the rate computation process, similar results could occur, but be masked in the rate calculation process.

In an attempt to identify sources of bias, Garden examined student sample distributions by gender, student age, father's occupation, teacher judgment about class rank, and other variables where comparisons with official statistics were feasible. Occupation was not coded consistently, and comparisons of fathers of 13-year-olds with all males in the official statistic were not necessarily comparable. The mean age for the selected grade was often much higher than 13.5 (16.7 at time of testing in one country); some increase was expected because the population was defined at midyear and tested late in the year. The use of principal or department head judgment for selecting class samples was identified as a possible source of upward bias for that country.

The tests consisted of a core form plus rotated forms (four for Population A and eight for Population B). Ideally, each student would complete the core form plus two rotated forms, and with an appropriate rotation scheme, the sample of students would be divided equally across all possible pairs of rotated forms. This approach allows for estimation of basic statistics plus the study of relationships among all items (e.g., latent trait analyses). In two countries, rotation schemes did not conform to the desired pattern, but still permitted estimation of population means.

The SIMS samples were designed to be self-weighting under ideal execution and perfect school and student response conditions. All but two countries computed weights for their samples.

Sampling error estimates were computed for the core tests and for one form for Population A and two forms for Population B. Design effects and intraclass correlation coefficients also were estimated. Intact class sampling was thought to contribute to higher than expected intraclass coefficients (median of about .4); wide differences among schools within systems also were identified as possible causes.

Suter and Phillips (1989) examined U.S. components of several international studies, with emphasis on SIMS. They concluded that the "response rate to the U.S. SIMS was lower than would be expected for an important national survey that would be used to draw important policy conclusions" (p. 23). They also noted some departures from the estimated distributions by gender, region, and race when compared to other national estimates. With regard to the estimates, their paper "found no evidence that the results of the IEA Second International Mathematics Study would lead to grossly misleading interpretations about the status of U.S. achievement of eighth grade students when compared with other countries" (p. 23). They also examined design effects for five studies (FIMS, SIMS, FISS, SISS, and IAEP-I) and computed intraclass correlation coefficients, r, at the school level based on equating the design effect to $1 + r(m - 1)$. These estimates of the intraclass correlation coefficient were quite high, ranging from about 0.15 to in excess of 0.50.[2]

Second International Science Study

SISS was conducted in 1983-84 in 17 countries. Target populations were defined as:

- Population 1: Either all 10-year-old students or all students in the grade in which most 10-year-olds are enrolled (typically grades four or five).

- Population 2: Either all 14-year-old students or all students in the grade in which most 14-year-olds are enrolled (typically grades eight or nine).
- Population 3: Students in the last year of secondary education.

Students in the last year of secondary education had additional subpopulations defined as:

- Population 3B: Students studying biology for examination purposes.
- Population 3C: Students studying chemistry for examination purposes.
- Population 3P: Students studying physics for examination purposes.
- Population 3N: Students not studying a science subject in the test year.

Of 15 countries where Population 1 was tested, six tested at grade four, eight at grade five, and one at grades four, five, and six. Of 17 countries where Population 2 was tested, eight tested at grade eight, 10 at grade nine, one at grades nine and 10, and one at grades eight, nine, and 10. For Population 3, which was tested in 13 countries, the mean age ranged from 17 years, 3 months to 19 years. The percentage enrolled in school was reported at between 15 and 90 percent; some of the low-percentage enrollments were associated with students shifting to the vocational track (IEA, 1988).

Populations 1 and 2 received a set of core items plus one of four randomly assigned sets of items. Population 3 students were tested on core items plus subject-specific tests.

Two- or three-stage samples were utilized depending on the need for an initial geographic or district-based stage of sampling in large countries.

Particular problems cited by Medrich and Griffith (1992) included:

- The Population 3 student sample was extremely difficult to draw, and only about half the countries were able to provide complete information on the sampling steps.
- Subject matter subsamples were often extremely small.
- Population exclusions were significant. Less developed countries had high levels of exclusion.
- Enrollment in the sciences varied dramatically.

• The U.S. sample suffered serious nonresponse. A new sample was drawn in 1986 for development of the official U.S. estimates.

The U.S. sample design incorporated the selection of a first-stage sample of districts about twice as large as needed to achieve the required sample. After district nonresponse of about one-half, the target sample sizes were achieved, but the bias associated with selective response (self-selection within a large sample) was not resolved.

Response rates were documented for SISS. Seventeen countries reported response rates ranging from 60 to 100 percent for schools and from 53 to 100 percent for students. Twelve countries achieved school response rates exceeding 85 percent; 11 countries achieved student response rates exceeding 85 percent.[3]

Olkin and Searls (1985) also provide a discussion on statistical aspects of the first two IEA science assessments and note problems with the response rates in these early studies. Their focus is on the U.S. component and their comments on SISS relate to the 1986 U.S. survey.

The more complete documentation of procedures, problems, and quality outcomes for studies completed in the early 1980s (SIMS and SISS) identified the need for better definitions of target populations, for more thorough specification of sampling and other procedures, for consistent measurement of response rates using accepted definitions, and for improved monitoring procedures.

First International Assessment of Educational Progress

IAEP-I was conducted in February 1988 in six countries (12 educational systems) and focused on mathematics and science. The U.S. study was conducted from January through mid-March. This study was modeled on the U.S. NAEP. The study target population was persons born in 1974 (ages 13 years, 1 month to 14 years, 1 month at time of testing). Two test booklets (one in each subject) were administered.

A two- or three-stage sample design was employed consisting of 50 pairs of schools (100 schools), with a sample of 20 students per school. Schools were to be selected with probability proportional to estimated size, and simple random samples of eligible students were selected in sample schools.

School response rates ranged from 70 to 100 percent; student response rates ranged from 73 to 97 percent. Eleven out of 12 systems achieved an 85-percent school response rate and eleven achieved an 85-percent student response rate for the science test (Lapointe et al., 1989).

Second International Assessment of Educational Progress

IAEP-II was conducted in 20 countries, focusing primarily on mathematics and science. The assessment was conducted in March 1991 in most of the countries; in three countries whose school year starts in March, the assessment was conducted in September 1990. Target populations were defined by age (year of birth):

- Population 1: Nine-year-olds (born in 1981).
- Population 2: Thirteen-year-olds (born in 1977).

The core assessment involved a science booklet and a mathematics booklet; selected students were administered one or the other. Countries could supplement the core Population 2 assessment with an additional block of geography questions and with performance-based assessment of ability to use equipment and materials to solve mathematics and science problems.

The sample design called for a representative sample of 3,300 students (1,650 per age group) from about 110 schools. Both public and private elementary and secondary schools were included. A two-stage stratified probability sampling design was used in most cases, with PPS sampling of schools and systematic sampling of students.

Manuals and software were provided for sampling. In addition, countries had the option of having their sample selected by Westat, Inc.; five countries exercised this option and most of the others used the prescribed design and software. Alternatives to the prescribed design were required to be reviewed and approved by Westat. Three-stage sampling was used in two countries; in one country, students were sampled using classrooms as sampling units.

Nine assessments were countrywide, with coverage at age 13 ranging from 93 to 100 percent. Eleven assessments involved parts of countries, with country coverage ranging from 3 to 96 percent at age 13 (one country did not report percentage of coverage).

Response rates were reported for all but one of the 20 countries. For the age 13 sample, the school response rate ranged from 77 to 100 percent, with 16 out of 20 countries exceeding 85 percent. Student response rates ranged from 92 to 99 percent for 19 countries reporting. Overall response rates (which factored in PSU participation in countries using three-stage designs) ranged from 48 to 99 percent, with 17 of 19 reporting countries meeting or exceeding a 75-percent response rate.

This study reported on the grade distribution within each age sample. Of 19 countries reporting these data for Population 2, the modal year of enrollment was 7 for 4 countries, 8 for 13 countries, and 9 for 2 countries. The dispersion across years varied considerably among countries.

Analysis weights were used in reporting. Sampling errors were computed using the jackknife procedure (Lapointe, Askew, & Mead, 1991).

Compliance with the prescribed sample design was fostered with the provision of sampling software and technical assistance. The use of analysis weights and appropriate design-based variance estimation also was enhanced by applying the methods of the U.S. NAEP surveys.

Third International Mathematics and Science Study

TIMSS was conducted in 1994-95 in 45 countries. A longitudinal followup (TIMSS-R) took place in 1997-98 in about 40 countries. The discussion here is limited to the first phase of TIMSS (1994-95). Three target populations and two optional subpopulations were defined for TIMSS:

- Population 1: All students enrolled in the two adjacent grades that contain the largest proportion of 9-year-olds at the time of testing.
- Population 2: All students enrolled in the two adjacent grades that contain the largest proportion of 13-year-olds at the time of testing.
- Population 3: Students enrolled in their final year of secondary education.

Optional subpopulations within Population 3 were:

- Students taking advanced courses in mathematics.
- Students taking advanced courses in physics.

Note that the option of defining the study Populations 1 and 2 by age alone was not offered for TIMSS. Also, the grade coverage was expanded from one grade (as applied in SIMS) to two grades. The age used to identify the target grades was the standardizing factor across countries.

Population 3 definitions were refined to avoid possible double counting due to countries having multiple academic tracks or students completing the final year in more than one track at different times. The Population 3 definition was more particularly defined as "students taking the final year of one track of the secondary system for the first time." Population 3 students would be expected to be between 15 and 19; to assess the coverage by country, the Population 3 enrollment was to be compared with official statistics on the total national population aged 15 to 19 in 1995, divided by 5. Note that students taking the final year in one track (say mathematics) a year later than their final year in the other track (say physics) would be eligible only for the advanced mathematics form because they no longer would be eligible for TIMSS in the year that they complete their final track in physics. This would systematically restrict the sample of students taking advanced courses in physics (or mathematics) to those who include it in their first academic track.

The rules for population exclusions of schools and students within schools were made more specific. Schools could be excluded if they:

- Are located in geographically remote regions.
- Have very small size (few students in target population).
- Offer a curriculum, or school structure, different from the mainstream educational system.
- Provide instruction only to students who meet the student exclusion criteria.

The target population enrollments in excluded schools were to be estimated.

Student exclusions within schools were limited to:

- Educable mentally disabled students.
- Functionally disabled students.
- Nonnative language speakers.

These concepts were specified more fully for operational use. The effective target population was then defined as the defined target population (1, 2, or 3) less allowable exclusions. A criterion of limiting exclusions to 10 percent or less of the defined target populations was specified.

The sampling manual for TIMSS specifies a two-stage sample (schools and intact classes), with options for three-stage or four-stage sampling if a country opts to add geographic primary sampling units prior to selecting schools and/or if selected classes are to be subsampled. The TIMSS analytic requirements include estimates at the school and class level, so these analytic units also must be stages in the sampling process for Populations 1 and 2. The manual specifies standard minimum effective sample sizes for schools (150 schools) and students (400 students) and provides models (tables) for deciding on the nominal sample size given planned (minimum) cluster size and an assumed value of the intracluster correlation coefficient. A value of .3 is to be assumed if no prior data on intracluster correlation coefficient are available.

Options for stratification, handling of small schools and small classes, sampling options for designed self-weighting samples, and general detail are provided in the sample design specifications. Procedures for identifying replacement schools in the context of systematic PPS sampling also are specified.

Consistent formulas for weighted and unweighted response weights at the school and student levels are provided. Standards are specified as

85-percent response for each component and 75-percent response overall (Foy, Rust, & Schleicher, 1996).

Within-school sampling procedures were specified for each population. Populations 1 and 2 were to be sampled by class, with each selected student matched to his or her mathematics and science teacher. In schools where some students were assigned to different class groups for science and mathematics, the mathematics groupings were used for forming the sampling units and special student-to-teacher matching procedures were required to identify all teachers involved in teaching science courses to the selected students. Special tracking forms were used to identify the teacher-student matches.

Because Population 3 involved a general population of all students in the final year of secondary education and two subpopulations based on enrollment in advanced courses in mathematics and science, it was sometimes necessary to partition the eligible students into as many as four groups:

- Those enrolled in both advanced science and advanced mathematics courses.
- Those enrolled in advanced mathematics only.
- Those enrolled in advanced science only.
- Those enrolled in neither advanced mathematics nor advanced science.

Because there was no analytic need to obtain teacher data related to each Population 3 student, simple random sampling from each of the four groups was the preferred sample selection procedure (Schleicher & Siniscalco, 1996).

The survey administration dates for TIMSS were set near the end of the school year. In the northern hemisphere, the prescribed dates were February to May 1995. In the southern hemisphere, Populations 1 and 2 were to be tested from September to November 1994 and Population 3 in August 1995 (Martin, 1996).

One of the major improvements implemented with TIMSS was the systematic collection of quantitative and descriptive information on the implementation of the sample design through a standard set of forms and reporting procedures. Submitted forms were reviewed and archived by Statistics Canada at the various stages of sample implementation. Foy, Martin, and Kelly (1996) use these archived data to evaluate the implementation of TIMSS sampling procedures in the participating countries. They conclude that the reporting and review process had a positive effect on the quality of the sampling enterprise and that most participants did an excellent job of carrying out their sampling tasks. Most countries were able to provide all of the requested information or sufficient information to certify the methods employed. Irregularities and exceptions to specified procedures were identified in a consistent manner and used to flag the data when reported.

TIMSS had an international sampling manual as well as optional sampling software. A TIMSS international referee was appointed. Statistics Canada, working with the TIMSS Technical Advisory Committee and the TIMSS sampling referee, provided advice and support in sampling to participating countries.

Forty-two countries participated in the Population 2 TIMSS. A few comments noted in defining the target Population 2 were:

- Target grades varied by state (one country).
- Students in selected grades were older than expected (four countries).
- Total exclusions exceeded the 10-percent criterion (one country).
- Only one target grade was selected (two countries).

Partial or incomplete reports were obtained from eight countries.

All participants provided data on the design structure and stratification, but 29 countries had partial or incomplete data on at least one item for Population 2. Comments related to sampling Population 2 were:

- Sampled science classrooms (mathematics classrooms were the default).
- Used a school sample for upper grade vocational track.
- Included all schools in the sample (four countries).
- Used stratified simple random sampling of schools (PPS sampling was specified for self-weighting design) (three countries).
- Sampled students rather than classrooms.
- Selected classrooms with PPS (two countries).
- Employed a preliminary sampling stage (two countries).

Most of these items do not invalidate the sample for most purposes, but may create more problems for development of weights or for some special analyses on a comparable basis.

With regard to within-school sample execution, 24 countries provided complete information and all provided some information. Some comments noted included:

- Unapproved school sampling procedures.
- Unapproved classroom sampling procedures (four countries).
- School sampling frame not available.

- Inadequate documentation to compute sampling weights.
- Nonparticipating students not recorded.

Countries reported on their coverage of the *international desired population*. Failure to cover the desired international population involved geographic exclusions (three countries) and exclusion of school systems by language spoken in the schools (three countries). These redefined target populations were called the *national desired populations*. Additional exclusions occurred by school and by students within school. For Population 2, school exclusions ranged as high as 9.6 percent; student exclusions within schools ranged as high as 2.9 percent; and overall exclusions exceeded 10 percent in only one country, at 11.3 percent.

Thirty-one of 42 countries defined their Population 2 in terms of the seventh and eighth years of formal schooling. Two countries used only one grade; the remaining countries had split policies by region or system or other variations (higher or lower years of formal schooling).

All but three countries reported on their target grade coverage of 13-year-olds. Of the remaining 39 countries, 10 had fewer 13-year-olds in the lower grade and 29 had fewer 12-year-olds in the upper grade. The combined coverage of 13-year-olds over the two grades was reported at between 45 and 100 percent of all 13-year-olds, with most countries at the high end of the range.

School participation rates (usually weighted) were reported before and after school replacement. For the upper grade schools in Population 2, before-school replacement rates ranged from 24 to 100 percent; after replacement they ranged from 46 to 100 percent. Most countries were able to increase their participating school sample by using replacements, particularly those with low initial school response rates; one country with a low initial school response rate only increased school participation by one school after replacement sampling.

From the selected student samples, reductions were made to account for students withdrawn from the school or class and those excluded by the student exclusion rules. Weighted participation rates were then computed based on weighted ratios of students assessed to eligible students selected. For the upper grade students in Population 2, weighted student participation rates were generally high, ranging from 83 to 100 percent.

Overall weighted participation rates also were computed for each country. Looking at the upper grade for Population 2 only, 30 out of 42 countries had overall participation rates exceeding 75 percent before replacement of any nonresponding schools. Five additional countries moved above 75 percent after allowing replacements. In the remaining seven countries, overall weighted participation rates remained below 75 percent even after replacement of nonresponding schools.

For reporting purposes, countries were classified into three categories, as shown in Table 4-2. Note that based on the overall response rates alone for the upper grade of Population 2, most countries were in Category 1. This approach allows data to be reported for all participating countries with a warning to users about the quality of the data reported.

The use of standardized forms to record the steps of the sampling process and to provide data on eligibility and response helped to identify additional potential problems. Without this information given freely with no fear of retribution, there would be no basis for future improvement. The information gathered as part of the process of selecting the sample and conducting each country's assessment also helps to identify those issues that need to be resolved in future studies in order to improve comparability. The formal documentation provided for both school and student exclusions is an example of collecting important data for future planning.

Program for International Student Assessment

PISA was conducted in 2000 for reading, and is planned for 2003 for mathematics, and 2006 for science. The study is sponsored by OECD and

TABLE 4-2   Reporting Categories Based on Response Rates

No.	Description	Criteria (Abbreviated and Approximate)	Designation in Reports
1	Acceptable sampling participation rates without replacement schools	Before replacement of schools: School and student response rates each exceed 85 percent, **or** the combined rate exceeds 75 percent	Appear without notation and may be ordered by achievement as appropriate
2	Acceptable sampling participation rates only with replacement schools	Not in Category 1 before replacement, but weighted school response rate before replacement exceeds 50 percent and after replacement the response rates meet the Category 1 requirements	Annotated with a dagger in tables and figures and may be ordered by achievement as appropriate
3	Unacceptable sampling participation rates even with replacement schools	Not in Category 1 or 2	Appear in separate section of reports ordered alphabetically

will focus on measuring the "cumulative yield of education systems at an age where schooling is still largely universal." Because of this focus, the target population is defined as 15-year-olds enrolled in both school-based and work-based educational programs. Between 4,500 and 10,000 students will be assessed in each country (OECD, 1999a, p. 9).

The author reviewed Version 1 of the sampling manual (OECD, 1999b). Comments here are limited to the planned approach outlined in that version; the PISA consortium plans to elaborate on or adjust some of the approaches in subsequent versions of the manual. Each country will have a National Project Manager responsible for the following areas:

- Establishing age definitions.
- Defining exclusions, documenting them, and keeping them to a minimum.
- Developing the school sampling frame.
- Identifying suitable stratification variables.
- Determining school and student sample sizes consistent with PISA requirements.
- Selecting the school sample (or providing the sampling frame to Westat, which will select the sample).
- Maintaining records on school participation and the use of replacements.

The PISA consortium (in particular, Westat) will be responsible for reviewing all sampling procedures and providing assistance.

The target population is defined more fully as 15-year-olds in a country's education system, including:

- Part-time students.
- Students in vocational training.
- Students in foreign schools within the country.

Residents who attend school in a foreign country are not included.

The assessment is to be scheduled over a one-month period, not within the first three months of the academic year. Within reason, the age group should be defined in terms of birth dates so that students are between 15 years, 3 months and 16 years, 2 months at the beginning of the testing period. This facilitates defining 15-year-olds in terms of a calendar year cohort. Forms based on TIMSS and TIMSS-R experience will be used to record the target population definition and to document decisions about testing periods and birth year cohort definitions.

Guidelines are provided for minimizing and justifying all exclusions. School exclusions to control costs (geographically inaccessible, extremely small size, or other nonfeasibility of PISA assessment) are permitted, but limited to .5 percent of enrolled 15-year-olds. Schools enrolling only students who qualify as student exclusions also may be excluded. Student exclusions are limited to educable mentally retarded students, functionally disabled students, and nonnative language speakers. Guidelines for defining these categories are provided. The estimated size of the total excluded population is to be documented and should not exceed 5 percent of the national desired population.

The sampling manual provides specific guidelines for selecting a two- or three-stage sample with at least 150 schools and at least 35 students per school. After allowing for student nonresponse, this should yield in excess of 4,500 students. The estimated or approximated intraclass correlation coefficient and its impact on effective sample may be used to adjust the sample size requirements. If classrooms are used for sampling, allowances for a higher intraclass correlation coefficient are required.

Guidelines and forms for documenting participation at all levels are provided. Decision guidelines for scheduling makeup sessions needed to maintain acceptable student response are provided in a separate manual. Minimum levels of participation at the national level are prescribed as 85 percent for schools and 80 percent for students. Plans are to annotate results of countries that do not meet these minimums.

The PISA sampling manual clearly demonstrates the movement toward more specificity in definitions and procedures as well as some tightening of standards, such as limiting total exclusions.

SOME GENERAL APPRAISALS

This section summarizes some of the critiques provided by other authors. It is helpful to note the date of each critique and to relate it to three broad periods defined as before 1980, the 1980s, and 1990 and later. I believe major shifts occurred in the ways international comparative studies could be and were conducted over these three time periods. Rigor in sample design and execution was a stated goal over the entire period. The collection of detailed information about real or potential problems in sample design and execution began in the early 1980s and helped provide a basis for the BICSE framework and principles document published in 1990. One focus of this framework was the recognition of the need for even more data to help understand and clarify differences across school systems in different countries. The comments of reviewers presented in this section need to be placed in the timeframe of studies completed at the time of each reviewer's comments. Later in this chapter, I present some of my own conclusions, with a focus on current (2000) status of sample design and execution in international comparative studies in education.

Olkin and Searls (1985), in a paper prepared for a National Academy of Sciences conference in October 1985, address the issue of standards related to nonresponse rates. They state:

> We believe that standards need to be set not so much in terms of absolute acceptable non-response rates as on procedures for dealing with non-response—initial approaches, follow-up procedures, analytical approaches for adjusting or weighting the data, and the possible use of adjustments made on the basis of effort required to secure cooperation. (p. 4)

They also note the problem of nonretention in school and the variation among countries. They speculate (p. 4) that "average achievement would appear relatively worse than it would if a smaller proportion of the age group were retained."[4]

The summary report of the conference (NRC, 1985) includes several statements relating to sampling, survey design, and, particularly, response rates. On coordination of survey design, measurement design, and analysis, it states:

> It was recognized that progress toward better statistical standards for international assessments will necessarily involve a more thorough understanding of the interrelationships between the educational measurement aspects of instrument design and testing and of survey sampling design and implementation issues, together with a recognition of the need to make explicit the analytic framework within which the data from the assessments are ultimately to be used. (p. 5)

This comment remains true and, perhaps, provides the opportunity for further improvement in the process. With regard to the age versus grade definition of target population, it states that "consideration should be given in future studies to taking national probability samples of age cohorts of children or of a mixture of such sampling and class level sampling" (p. 11). On improving the overall quality of studies, it states that based on recent experience in science and mathematics studies, "higher quality results are attainable by directing more resources to pre-implementation planning and field arrangements and to vigorous follow up of non-respondents even at the cost of overall sample size" (p. 11). This is a continuing theme from many of the critiques and postsurvey discussions.

It is my understanding that the 1985 National Academy of Sciences conference was instrumental in the establishment of the Board on International Comparative Studies in Education.

The BICSE framework (NRC, 1990) provides general guidelines on sampling and access to schools, as discussed in the introduction.

Horvitz (1992) identifies a broad set of issues in improving the quality of international education surveys and suggests the Deming philosophy for quality improvement, along with cooperative methodological experiments built into ongoing cross-national surveys as a means to determine effective ways of reducing all types of survey error.

Medrich and Griffith (1992) discuss completed mathematics and science studies sponsored by IEA and IAEP. They note:

> The surveys have not achieved the high degrees of statistical reliability across age groups sampled and among all of the participating countries. Thus, from a statistical point of view, there is considerable uncertainty as to the magnitude of measured differences in achievement. Inconsistencies in sample design and sampling procedures, the nature of the samples and their outcomes, and other problems have undermined data quality. (p. viii)

Nevertheless, they believe that these surveys have value and that the challenge is to improve their quality in the future. TIMSS shows improvement in consistent definition of comparable groups across countries, but as documented earlier in this chapter, a small minority of the 42 countries involved in TIMSS still took exception to recommended target population definitions, and some countries provided only partial information.

Goldstein (1995) reviews sampling and other issues in the IEA and IAEP studies conducted prior to TIMSS. He advocates consideration of longitudinal studies beyond those conducted as an option within a single academic year in some countries' science and mathematics studies. He believes that age cohorts might provide a better study definition for longitudinal followup purposes. He also sees age definition as a possible solution to defining a target population near the final year of secondary education among students attending different types of educational institutions. Although sampling procedures for these studies involved standard applications of sample survey methodology, he notes the difficulty of ensuring uniformity across countries. He also notes problems associated with restricted sampling frames and general nonresponse, which both exhibit considerable variation across countries in the studies reviewed. He advocates obtaining characteristics of nonresponding schools and students, and publishing comparisons of these characteristics for respondents and nonrespondents. He discusses the impacts of length of time in school, age, and grade and how they jointly influence achievement under different systems of education due to promotion policies or other factors; he notes that little effort has been devoted to age and grade standardization of results prior to publication.

Postlethwaite (1999) presents an excellent discussion of sampling issues relating to international studies of educational achievement. He reviews population definition issues from both policy and methodological viewpoints, paying particular attention to age versus grade definitions. He also addresses guidelines for setting precision requirements, the sample selection methodology, weighting of data and adjustment for nonresponse, standards for accepting or flagging low-quality surveys, and a general checklist for evaluating the sample design and the resulting data. He also points out that the issue of defining the populations to be tested is an "educational and political" decision. From a sample design perspective, we can leave the question to the education experts and policy makers. Their decisions, however, do impact the sampling and data collection operations. In some countries, students of the same age can be spread across several grades. Postlethwaite cites U.S. data showing 13-year-olds spread across grades 2 through 11, with most in grade eight and nearly 89 percent of enrolled students in grade eight or grade nine; this has serious implications for complete population coverage in the sampling frame when selecting samples defined by age. The grade by age distribution creates a more serious problem for test developers.

Quite specific standards and guidelines are provided by Martin et al. (1999) for IEA studies discussed in the introduction of this chapter. Their heavy focus on documentation is particularly noted because this sets the stage for improvement of current procedures.

REMAINING ISSUES

It is a challenge to add to the critiques already presented and to add any new thoughts. It is also true that lessons learned in the early studies have been applied to the design of more recent studies. Information about what actually occurred is more consistently organized and (currently) accessible for recent studies, particularly SIMS and TIMSS. An understanding of what has happened in prior studies is a fundamental requirement for improving future studies. The documentation and reporting procedures used in TIMSS and planned for PISA are excellent, but still leave room for new ideas. The BICSE framework (NRC, 1990) and the IEA technical standards (Martin et al., 1999) now provide guidance for sample design and survey implementation. What more can be done? Certainly we need to make practice more consistent with plans. In addition, as we get better compliance with the prescribed sampling process, we need to examine the prescribed process itself in light of achievable current practices. I will address issues in the following areas:

- Population definitions.
- Sampling frame completeness.
- Designing the sample.
- Executing the sample design.

- Response rates.
- Other nonsampling errors.
- Annotation of published results.

Population Definitions

The issue of age versus grade definition has been discussed thoroughly by other authors, but remains an issue in recent studies. TIMSS used a two-grade span to define populations close to age nine or age 13 for its Populations 1 and 2, and the final year of secondary education to define Population 3. The plans for PISA call for using age 15 rather than a grade concept to define persons near the end of secondary schooling, but at an age where schooling is still largely universal. So different approaches to the same concept continue to be applied. The plans for PISA are much more thorough in describing what is meant by a person still in the country's education system by including part-time students, students in vocational training, and students in foreign schools within the country as well as students in full-time academic study programs. This is not a sample design decision (as noted by Postlethwaite, 1999), but it has serious implications for defining the sampling frame and selecting the student sample.

The population also can be defined in the time dimension. Allowances have been made for testing at different times in the southern and northern hemispheres in recognition of different starting times for the normal academic year. Recent trends, at least in the United States, include moves to year-round schooling and home schooling. The timing of an assessment during a short period of time could arbitrarily exclude a significant portion of students enrolled in year-round schools who have a break at a nontraditional period. Students schooled at home may be considered in the educational system because they must obtain some exemption from required attendance in a formal school, but no known effort is made to test such students. At a minimum, countries (including the United States) need to quantify the extent of these alternate practices so that the exclusions from the target population defined in two dimensions (type of school enrollment and time of testing) can be better understood. Some allowance for alternate testing times could be effective in covering students in year-round schools; covering students participating in home schooling would be more challenging.

The population definition also includes the definition of exclusions for disability, language, or other reasons. Excellent guidelines have been developed for exclusions of both schools and students within schools and for documenting these exclusions in international studies. Some countries have continued to exclude geographic groups or major language of instruction groups for cost or political reasons. When cost is the only issue, stratification and sampling at a lower rate in the high-cost stratum might provide an alternative to arbitrary exclusion.

Recent U.S. experience in state NAEP has identified potentially serious problems in implementing comparable exclusion rates across states with the development of new guidelines for accommodation (Mazzeo, Carlson, Voelkl, & Lutkus, 2000). The international standards discussed do not address accommodation for disability or language; we might anticipate additional complications in international assessments if similar accommodation policies are more broadly implemented in other countries or applied to the international assessment samples in the United States.

Sampling Frame Completeness

Sampling frame completeness can only be evaluated relative to the target population definition. Exclusion of schools for inappropriate reasons could be viewed as either a population definition issue or a sampling frame incompleteness issue, depending on the intended population of inference for the analysis.

School sampling frames often are developed several months before the actual survey implementation. To the extent that population is defined as of the survey date, procedures may be required to update the sampling frame for newly opened schools or other additions to the eligible school population (changes in grade range taught) occurring since the school sample had been selected. It is not clear that this has been attempted in any of the international studies reviewed. False positives in the sampling frame (schools thought to be eligible at the time of sampling who turn out not to be eligible) can be handled analytically by treating the eligible schools as a subpopulation and are less of a problem. When the target population of schools includes both public and private schools as well as vocational education schools, the development of a complete school frame may become more difficult. Quality controls could be incorporated into advance data collection activities or into the survey process itself to check the completeness of the school sampling frame on a subsample basis, perhaps defined geographically. When sampling by age group, all schools that potentially could have students in the defined age range should be included in the sampling frame. If any arbitrary cutoffs are used to avoid schools with projected very low enrollments for an age group, these also should be checked for excluded schools on at least a sample basis. The feasibility of using arbitrary cutoffs to possibly exclude a small proportion of age-eligible students depends on the dispersion of age-eligible students across grades.

The recent guidelines for developing student sampling frames differ depending on whether the population is defined by grade or age. Age-defined population sampling requires listing all students in the school that meet the age (or birthdate range) definition; generally, the sample is then drawn as a sample of students using simple random sampling. For populations defined by grade, the sampling frame often is developed based on a "complete" list of classrooms. When the focus is on a particular subject (e.g., mathematics or science), classrooms may be limited to the subject matter being studied. There is a potential problem with the classroom approach of excluding students not currently enrolled in the target subject matter class at all or enrolled in a subject matter class at a different grade level. We may need to be more specific in defining what is meant by grade; that is, is it defined based on overall academic progress or only on progress in the subject being tested? After the grade definition is resolved, the ideal approach would be to list all grade-eligible students (just as we list all age-eligible students). Then if direct student sampling is prescribed, a simple random sample of grade-eligible students could be selected. If for logistical reasons a classroom sample is preferred, the list could be partitioned into classrooms and a sample of classrooms would then be selected. Any student not clearly associated with the type of classroom defined for administration purposes could be arbitrarily assigned to one of the classrooms before the classroom sample is selected, then tested with that classroom if it is selected.

Designing the Sample

Other than technical details in constructing complete sampling frames, the sample should be designed to provide the required precision for a minimum cost. Optimizing a sample design to meet precision requirements requires a reasonable model of the variance as function of controllable sample design parameters (typically, the number of schools and the number of students per school). The variance models used in the guidance documents for TIMSS and PISA incorporate the clustering effect into the variance model in terms of an assumed intracluster correlation coefficient. Empirical studies show wide variation in this population parameter; it is correctly noted that a large clustering effect is more likely with classroom sampling than with direct student sampling. Other population and sample characteristics also should be incorporated into the variance model, including stratification effects, unequal weighting effects, and expected cluster size variability. Stratification can be highly effective in reducing the school component of variance; intraclass correlation coefficients computed within strata are likely to be much smaller than those computed ignoring the strata. More data analysis may be required to develop estimates of these values based on prior experience. The correct specification of the variance model is essential to the development of cost-effective sample designs that satisfy the study's precision requirements.

As pointed out by Olkin and Searls (1985), the sample design needs to be consistent with the intended analysis. If two subjects are being assessed in two different samples of students within each school and separate estimates are to be made for each subject, then the average cluster size in the variance model should be based on school-subject sample size and not on total school sample size; the same principle might apply to subtest scores. Procedures that simultaneously control modeled variances for several different estimates for the same defined population also can be implemented.

This is another area where data need to be accumulated in a systematic manner across countries. The availability of microdata with the sample structure for strata, schools, classrooms, and students clearly labeled would make possible the estimation of the required sample design parameters in a consistent manner. These microdata sets also would provide a valuable resource for studying effective sample design consistent with different analytic objectives.

Executing the Sample Design

With development of procedures that include guidance from a respected national statistical organization and the resolution of particular issues by a similarly respected sampling referee, the execution of the sample design has not been and should not be a serious problem. The documentation of procedures following TIMSS or PISA guidelines and forms also helps guarantee correct implementation. These procedures may have room for improvement based on further experience, but must be viewed as quite excellent.

Two areas of the sample design execution relate to dealing with initial nonresponse at the school and student levels. Substitution for non-responding schools has been a practice allowed in most of the international assessments. Although substitution does not eliminate bias due to nonresponse, it does maintain the sample size required to control sampling error. If used with careful matching to the nonrespondent schools, the substitution method also can limit the extent of the potential bias introduced by nonresponding schools. A draft of the PISA sampling manual (OECD, 1999b) provides a reasonable way to implement the substitution by identifying two schools in the ordered school sampling frame as potential replacements for each nonresponding school: the schools immediately preceding and immediately following the selected school (if they are not also selected schools). If the list is ordered by administrative structure of the school system (e.g., by districts), it is likely that near neighbors in the list also might be nonrespondents; close matching or ordering on other school characteristics, however, may be quite effective in supplying replacements with similar characteristics who are not prejudiced by their neighbor's unwillingness to respond.

The practice of selection of substitutes for nonresponding schools needs further review. Different approaches are favored by different applied statisticians. Clearly, no method can totally eliminate the bias due to nonresponse, and all methods just try to maintain the respondent sample size. If possible, empirical studies of alternative approaches should be developed, conducted, and reviewed by a panel of survey experts to determine if current substitution practices are the most appropriate ones for international comparative studies. The empirical research simply might be based on simulation of nonresponse from completed studies in one or more countries.

The practice of routinely scheduling followup sessions for absent or unavailable students whenever response rates fall below set but relatively high levels within schools should be continued and formalized.[5]

Response Rates

The TIMSS response criteria specified 85 percent for schools and students or a combined rate exceeding 75 percent. These criteria were used for flagging the results. The draft PISA sampling manual specified 85-percent response for schools and 80 percent for students. Are these criteria generally achievable?

School response rates appear to be the more serious problem, particularly in the United States. The 1996 main NAEP did not achieve the 85-percent school participation rate for all session types for grades four and eight and did not achieve an 80-percent school participation rate for any session type for grade 12 (Wallace & Rust, 1999). The NAEP survey would be expected to be exemplary among studies undertaken in the United States.

Setting standards is not the solution to the problem of school nonresponse. Studies need to be undertaken in the United States and other countries to better understand why the problem exists. Data on this topic most likely exist, but need to organized and reviewed to formulate better approaches. In the United States, many different surveys compete for testing-schedule time in the schools; assessments are carried out at national, state, and local levels. International assessments just add to the burden. When studies are planned independently and samples are drawn independently, the chance of overburdening some schools is predictable and may contribute to poor participation in all of the studies. Most large school districts are asked to participate in all of these studies. Once we better understand the school perspective in survey participation, we can develop strategies, including possible coordination among studies, to encourage participation while simultaneously limiting the burden on any particular school. Nevertheless, these strategies should be considered as possible options for improving the precision of estimates.

The other theme that has been relatively constant across all the critiques reviewed has been the lack of resources for really thorough study execution. Proper planning and the scheduling of advance contacts required to obtain good study participation from schools require both time and adequate funding. These additional resources should be applied intelligently based on what is learned about the reasons for school nonresponse.

The methods of adjusting analytic weights for nonresponse also should be reviewed. Many noneducation surveys standardize their estimates or poststratify to known population distributions (e.g., age, race, and gender) or to distributions estimated from larger surveys. This is particularly difficult to do with the population of students enrolled in a country's educational system because the population is constantly changing and good enrollment data for the time of testing are difficult to obtain from other sources. If multiple forms are used or if more than one subject is assessed in a given year, the combined sample might provide a better estimate for standardizing the individual estimates developed by subject or by objective within subject. These types of methods add complexity to the weight development process and must be applied with good judgment.

Other Nonsampling Errors

Frame errors and response errors have been discussed. This leaves measurement error. The conditions present at testing, the correlated errors induced by the behavior of test administrators, data processing, and other factors all can contribute to measurement error. Sample and survey design can help control such errors, but monitoring to identify and measure such sources of error is essential in deciding whether the cost of revised procedures is necessary or justified. As noted by Horvitz (1992), cooperative methodological experiments could be extremely valuable in identifying and reducing measurement error.

Annotation of Published Results

As data users become more sophisticated, they expect to be informed about the strengths and weaknesses of the statistical results. The flagging of results depending on participation rates employed by TIMSS is a good example of a way to warn users about data quality based on something other than sampling error. The development of technical reports addressing quality control can be of use to the data professional (e.g., SIMS and TIMSS reports) and is strongly endorsed.

CONCLUSIONS

The sampling and survey design and execution of recent and planned international comparative studies have benefited greatly from the analysis of the results of earlier studies. Challenges remain. We should anticipate that the cutting edge technology of today will not necessarily be viewed favorably 10, 15, or 20 years from now. Our views today about the studies completed prior to 1980 might seem unfair to those who conducted those studies using the cutting edge approaches of those times.

Just as the BICSE guidelines suggest focused studies to interpret differences in educational achievement, we need focused studies to understand and interpret the differences in the background conditions and the feasible survey methodologies that apply to different countries. This applies particularly to the conditions in the educational system and how they should influence the definition of the desired target populations. The concept of final year of secondary education remains vague, especially in countries with alternative academic tracks; procedures designed to avoid double counting in the final year of secondary education population may be creating undercoverage of populations defined by subject matter specialization. These types of problems have solutions that begin with a clear understanding of the study requirements.

Longitudinal studies have not been a major focus of the studies reviewed, but have been a country option in some of them. The value of longitudinal measurements versus repeated cross-sectional measurements needs to be evaluated in terms of educational objectives and the types of country comparisons that are useful in evaluating the achievement of those objectives.

Finally, the focus on meeting tough standards for coverage and response rates should not lead us to solve the problem by defining it away. As an example, there is always a temptation to simply rule that an excluded portion of a study population is not really part of the population of interest. This ruling immediately increases coverage measures in all participating countries, but may totally destroy the comparability of results across countries. It would be better to relax the standards somewhat (and continue to monitor them) than to essentially ignore them by defining them away.

NOTES

1. Table A.7 (p. 55) of Medrich and Griffith (1992), based on data from Peaker (1975).
2. Smaller values might have been obtained if the effects of stratification and unequal weighting had been removed before calculating the intraclass correlation; design effects would remain the same because these factors would need to be put back into the model for total variance.
3. Medrich and Griffith cite data obtained from IEA (1988).
4. The focus here is on populations defined by age group. Retaining fewer students in school leads to excluding the poor performers, which then leads to higher average scores for those remaining in school.
5. For PISA, these procedures are available in the National Project Managers Manual, but they were not reviewed for this chapter.

REFERENCES

Cochran, W. G. (1977). *Sampling techniques.* New York: John Wiley & Sons.

Deming, W. E. (1950). *Some theory of sampling.* New York: Dover.

Foy, P., Martin, M. O., & Kelly, D. L. (1996). Sampling. In M. O. Martin & I. A. Mullis (Eds.), *Third International Mathematics and Science Study: Quality assurance in data collection* (pp. 2-1 to 2-23). Chestnut Hill, MA: Boston College.

Foy, P., Rust, K., & Schleicher, A. (1996). Sample Design. In M. O. Martin and D. L. Kelly (Eds.), *Third International Mathematics and Science Study (TIMSS) technical report, Vol. I: Design and development.* Chestnut Hill, MA: Boston College.

Garden, R. A. (1987). *Second IEA Mathematics Study, sampling report.* Washington, DC: U.S. Department of Education, National Center for Education Statistics.

Goldstein, H. (1995). *Interpreting international comparisons of student achievement.* Paris: UNESCO.

Hansen, M. H., Hurwitz, W. N., & Madow, W. G. (1953). *Sample survey methods and theory.* New York: John Wiley & Sons.

Horvitz, D. (1992). Improving the quality of international education surveys (draft). Prepared for the Board on International Comparative Studies in Education.

International Association for the Evaluation of Educational Achievement (IEA). (1988). *Student achievement in seventeen countries.* Oxford, England: Pergamon Press.

Lapointe, A. F., Askow, J. M., & Mead, N. A. (1991). *Learning science: The Second International Assessment of Educational Progress.* Princeton, NJ: Educational Testing Service.

Lapointe, A. E., Mead, N. A., & Phillips, G. W., (1989). *A world of differences.* Princeton, NJ: Educational Testing Service.

Lessler, J. T., & Kalsbeek, W. D. (1992). *Nonsampling error in surveys.* New York: John Wiley & Sons.

Martin, M. O. (1996). Third International Mathematics and Science Study: An overview. In M. O. Martin and D. L. Kelly (Eds.), *Third International Mathematics and Science Study (TIMSS) technical report, Vol. I: Design and development.* Chestnut Hill, MA: Boston College.

Martin, M. O., Rust, K., & Adams, R. J. (1999). *Technical standards for IEA studies.* Amsterdam: International Association for the Evaluation of Educational Achievement.

Mazzeo, J., Carlson, J. E., Voelkl, K. E., & Lutkus, A. D. (2000). *Increasing the participation of special needs students in NAEP: A report on 1996 NAEP research activities.* Washington, DC: U.S. Department of Education, National Center for Education Statistics.

Medrich, E. A., & Griffith, J. E. (1992). *International mathematics and science assessments: What have we learned?* Washington, DC: U.S. Department of Education, Office of Educational Research and Improvement.

National Research Council. (1985). Summary report of conference on October 16-17, 1985 (Draft). Committee on National Statistics, Commission on Behavioral and Social Sciences and Education. Washington, DC: National Academy Press.

National Research Council. (1990). *A framework and principles for international comparative studies in education.* Board on International Comparative Studies in Education, Norman M. Bradburn & Dorothy M. Gilford, Editors. Commission on Behavioral and Social Sciences and Education. Washington, DC: National Academy Press.

National Research Council. (1995). *International comparative studies in education: Descriptions of selected large-scale assessments and case studies.* Board on International Comparative Studies in Education. Commission on Behavioral and Social Sciences and Education. Washington DC: National Academy Press.

Olkin, I., & Searls, D. T. (1985). Statistical aspects of international assessments of science education. Paper presented at the conference on Statistical Standards for International Assessments in Precollege Science and Mathematics. Washington, DC.

Organization for Economic Cooperation and Development (OECD). (1999a). *Measuring student knowledge and skills, A new framework for assessment.* Paris: Author.

Organization for Economic Cooperation and Development (OECD). (1999b). *PISA sampling manual, main study version 1.* Paris: Author.

Peaker, G. (1975). *An empirical study of education in twenty-one countries: A technical report.* New York: John Wiley & Sons.

Peaker, G. F. (1967). Sampling. In T. Husen (Ed.), *International study of achievement in mathematics, A comparison of twelve countries* (pp. 147-162). New York: John Wiley & Sons.

Postlethwaite, T. N. (1999). *International studies of educational achievement: Methodological issues.* Hong Kong: University of Hong Kong.

Schleicher, A., & Siniscalco, M. T. (1996). Field operations. In M. O. Martin & D. L. Kelly (Eds.), *Third International Mathematics and Science Study (TIMSS) technical report, Vol. I: Design and development.* Chestnut Hill, MA: Boston College.

Suter, L. E., & Phillips, G. (1989). *Comments on sampling procedures for the U.S. sample of the Second International Mathematics Study.* Washington DC: U.S. Department of Education, National Center for Education Statistics.

Wallace, L., & Rust, K. F. (1999). Sample design. In N. L. Allen, D. L. Kline, & C. A. Zelenak (Eds.), *The NAEP 1994 technical report* (pp. 69-86). Washington, DC: National Library of Education.

Part II

Culture and Context

5

Cultural-Cognitive Issues in Academic Achievement: New Directions for Cross-National Research

Janine Bempechat, Norma V. Jimenez, and Beth A. Boulay*

CULTURAL-COGNITIVE ISSUES IN ACADEMIC ACHIEVEMENT: TOWARD AN UNDERSTANDING OF CROSS-NATIONAL DIFFERENCES

The past quarter century has seen a burgeoning interest in cross-national comparisons of student achievement. The fascination with achievement in different nations has been fueled by rapid technological advances that have changed the face of the global economy. Increasingly, nation states are expressing concern with their ability to compete in a world that is becoming ever smaller. Major cross-national investigations of academic achievement have been undertaken systematically by the International Association for the Evaluation of Educational Achievement (IEA) of which the Third International Mathematics and Science Study (TIMSS) and TIMSS-Repeat (TIMSS-R) are the most recent (Beaton et al., 1996; Husen, 1967; McKnight et al., 1987).

In addition to these IEA investigations, a large body of research has compared the achievement outcomes of American students with their peers in other nations. The research programs of Stevenson and Hess are particularly notable in this regard (Hess & Azuma, 1991; Hess, Chih-Miei, & McDevitt, 1987; Stevenson, Chen, & Lee, 1993; Stevenson & Stigler,

*The authors are from the Harvard Graduate School of Education. They wish to acknowledge the generous feedback of Kurt Fischer, Susan Holloway, Julian (Joe) Elliott, and Neil Hufton on earlier drafts of this chapter.

1992). The interpretations brought to the results of this body of research have tended to conclude that American students perform poorly in all aspects of mathematics and science, relative to their peers in other industrialized nations. What can we do with this knowledge? And, having an established database of computational achievement across many nations, what are the next steps that researchers can take to expand our current understanding?

The purpose of this chapter is to take a constructively critical view of what we know about the achievement of children and youth across nations, and to suggest fruitful directions for the next steps in cross-national research. We have organized this chapter around two core themes—culture and methodology—through which we will examine two central domains of study:

- *Social cognitive factors in learning.* In addition to observing and documenting the range of cognitive goals that cultures have for members of their group, it is critical to understand the social and cultural beliefs about learning that give rise to these values. Beliefs and attitudes about learning and achievement form the core of achievement motivation research today. There is a very important benefit to studying how students are motivated. Motivation research has established that achievement beliefs (e.g., implicit beliefs about effort and ability) are critical to school success (Nicholls, 1989). Indeed, in many cases, achievement beliefs appear to be better predictors of school performance than are IQ or achievement tests (see Dweck & Bempechat, 1983). By anchoring our review in achievement motivation theory, we will show the ways in which this body of knowledge can help fill gaps apparent in current cross-national research on achievement.
- *Cognitive psychology.* The assessment focus in cross-national investigations has been on computational skills. However, cognitive psychologists and mathematics educators have been arguing that in order for students to become technologically competent, they need to engage in learning that fosters a deep conceptual understanding of mathematics and science. This argument raises important questions for cross-national investigations—questions that we will explore in this chapter. We will examine the extent to which the available cross-national data shed light on how students come to a deep conceptual understanding of mathematics and science. We will ask: Does this understanding mean the same thing in different countries? Indeed, there may be different pathways to deep conceptual understanding within and between countries. Having considered these issues, we will propose directions that cross-national studies can take to investigate these questions.

Why Study Academic Achievement Across Cultures?

The accumulated work on cross-national achievement generally has been praised for bringing attention to the state of underachievement in the United States, especially as it relates to technical knowledge (Bempechat & Drago-Severson, 1999). The existing research has led educators to take a closer look at factors that may be contributing to the underachievement of American students, such as pedagogical practices (Stigler & Hiebert, 1999), students' and parents' beliefs about learning (Bempechat, 1998), and school structure (Beaton et al., 1996). This kind of comparative self-examination gives us a clearer picture of our own approaches to education. Indeed, examining how other cultures educate their children challenges us to look at our own system with a more critical eye. There is a way in which our own familiar pedagogical beliefs and practices become unfamiliar when set beside those of other nations (Spiro, 1993).

Cross-national research on mathematics and science also has the potential to reveal the rich and varied ways in which students, teachers, and parents conceptualize the meaning and value of learning. In this way, it can help us to understand the cognitive goals that each culture has for its students. Seen in this light, cross-national research on achievement can reveal much more than a simple rank ordering of nations according to technological competence. Comparative studies of achievement provide us with a window through which we can view culture in action. Inasmuch as culture serves as a guide for the socialization of *children*, cross-national research allows us to see how culture guides the socialization of *achievement*.

In addition, cross-national studies of achievement give us some insight into how the logic of individuals' beliefs influences their behavior. For example, Stigler and Perry (1988) note that teachers in Asian cultures (Japan and Taiwan) routinely ask students to display their answers to mathematics problems with which they are experiencing difficulty. In contrast, mistakes and difficulty more often are experienced privately in American classrooms. Indeed, many American teachers and parents would view this Japanese practice as humiliating and cruel. Stigler and Perry (1988) attribute this differential view of a particular pedagogical practice to a cultural difference in beliefs about the nature of mathematics intelligence. On average, Japanese mothers and teachers are less likely than their American counterparts to believe that mathematics ability is innate. Therefore, with the appropriate amount of effort, all children can solve a problem. In this context, mistakes are not something to be ashamed of, but something to work through. The general European-American view of mathematics ability as innate contributes to the notion that mathematics errors are the consequence of low ability, over which students have no control. To send students to the board, then, is to ask them to admit publicly that they have low ability. In the U.S. context, this practice might foster concerns about the potential to erode students' self-esteem.

Theoretical Tensions

One can readily see that each strategy for dealing with struggle may be appropriate, given the *social* and *cultural* context in which it has arisen. Herein lies the key to expanding our knowledge and understanding of cross-national differences in achievement—in realizing that we, as a research community, can move forward only if we situate culture and context at the center of our investigations. At the same time, however, we need to remain cautious about making assumptions about entire nations without considering the variation in beliefs and practices that exist in all cultures. For example, there may very well be a great many students in Japan who **do** experience the public display of their mistakes as humiliating. Similarly, there may be many U.S. students who would experience such a practice as educational and helpful. Yet many of us who study cultural influences in social cognition tend to rely on cultural models that speak of nations as if they were monolithic, when, in fact, there is a great deal of variation in a given society's cultural models.

Shore (1996) has discussed the tension between cultural anthropology and cultural psychology, noting that both disciplines view the construction of meaning as an ongoing, active process that is influenced by culture. He has encouraged scholars to view culture not as one "cultural narrative," but rather as a collection of cultural models which present competing views and interpretations about a society. Shore has argued for the integration of cultural psychology and cognition through his notion of an "ethnographic conception of mind," in which cultural knowledge would be viewed as rich and diverse and shared through various cultural models.

While cultural psychologists do indeed endorse this view, much of the work we discuss in this chapter tends to characterize nations as being at one or the other end of a dichotomy. In this regard, Japan and the United States have come to epitomize the comparisons that are made between "Eastern" and "Western" societies. Japan has been characterized as a culture that fosters interdependence, while U.S. culture fosters independence (White, 1987). Japanese people are said to be oriented around collectivist concerns, in which group loyalty and harmony lead individuals to subjugate their individual needs to those of the group, for the sake of the group's well-being (Mouer & Sugimoto, 1990). In contrast, Americans are characterized as individualistic and concerned with fostering personal goals (Greenfield, 1994).

We view this tension between the disciplines as representing different layers of inquiry. A line of research may reasonably begin with a large-scale survey, through which one might uncover interesting, general differences between groups of individuals. These differences might then be examined in increasingly detailed fashion, through multiple methods, including experiments, targeted questionnaires, indepth interviews, and ethnography. It is thus that research becomes more nuanced and reveals the varied and complex ways in which cultural beliefs are contested in a society.

Social-Cognitive Factors in Learning

As Bruner (1990) argues in *Acts of Meaning*, it is no longer sufficient to explain what children do. It has become imperative to study what children "think they are doing and what their reasons are for doing it" (p. 49). Studying children's achievement beliefs has opened a window into why students engage in behaviors that either promote or inhibit their academic achievement. Any study that measures achievement without concurrently examining the context in which this achievement occurs will yield results that may be limited in their use. The integration of achievement motivation theory with social cognition has resulted in a much deeper understanding of the motivational factors that underlie academic achievement. We have gone from viewing academic achievement as originating from an innate need or drive to the realization that achievement cognitions, such as attitudes, expectancies, and beliefs about ability, mediate the relationship between achievement behavior and achievement outcomes (Bempechat, 1998; Dweck, 1999; Eccles, 1993; Nicholls, Cobb, Wood, Yackel, & Patachnick, 1990; Weiner, Russell, & Lerman, 1979). For example, research has established that students who believe their intelligence is relatively stable (entity theorists) tend to avoid challenging tasks, and have been shown to sacrifice opportunities to learn new material in order to show that they are "smart" (Dweck & Bempechat, 1983). These students tend to succumb to learned helplessness when faced with a difficult task. In contrast, students who believe that intelligence is a malleable quality (incremental theorists) prefer challenging over nonchallenging tasks and tend to display mastery-oriented behavior in the face of difficulty or challenge.

Achievement beliefs include students' attributions for success and failure, their beliefs about the malleability of intelligence, their confidence, expectations and standards for performance, and affect in the face of difficulty or challenge (Ames & Archer, 1987; Bempechat, Graham, & Jimenez, 1999; Eccles, 1993; Marsh & Shavelson, 1985; Nicholls, Cheung, Lauer, & Patachnick, 1989). These motivational factors have been shown to be critical elements in students' achievement-related behavior. For example, Weiner and his colleagues have carefully documented that children and young adults tend to attribute success and failure to three basic categories of *attribution*—effort, ability, and external factors, such as luck or task ease/difficulty. Individuals interpret these attributions along three primary *causal dimensions*—locus (internal/external), stability, and controllability. Weiner has painstakingly shown that each attribution is linked to an emotion (e.g., lack of effort is linked to feelings of embarrassment), and it is the emotion that predicts future achievement behavior (Weiner et al., 1979). In other words, through a process of implicit self-evaluation, a student may decide that he failed a mathematics test because he is not smart (lack of ability). According to Weiner's theory, ability is perceived by the vast majority of students as *internal*, *stable*, and *uncontrollable*. Given that there is little remedy for lack of ability, the student would probably feel ashamed, and this feeling would likely predict maladaptive achievement behavior, such as little or no preparation for the next test.

Weiner's theory views ability as a stable entity that does not change. However, Nicholls (1978, 1989) and Dweck (Bempechat, London, & Dweck, 1991) have demonstrated that under certain circumstances, children can be influenced to perceive intelligence as a malleable quality that changes as a result of disciplined effort. For example, classrooms that are oriented around cooperative learning rather than competition tend to minimize students' concerns about their abilities and foster a greater tendency to take academic risks (Nicholls, 1989). This view of ability as *mastery through effort* focuses children's attentions on the process of learning. However, as Covington has shown, the view of ability as *capacity* fosters the conundrum of effort as the "double-edged sword" (Covington & Omelich, 1979). Many students come to believe that if they *have* to try hard, they must be "dumb." In short, effort becomes an implicit condemnation of ability (Nicholls, 1978).

The Origins of Achievement Beliefs

Students' beliefs about learning do not develop in a vacuum. They are very much influenced by the achievement beliefs of their parents, peers, and teachers, as well as the social and cultural environment in which they are growing (Ames & Archer, 1987; Ogbu, 1986; Peak, 1991). In the context of cross-national comparisons of academic achievement, the issue becomes one of integrating the sociocultural contexts of education with social-cognitive aspects of learning. Although the majority of the research on beliefs about learning has been done at the individual level, these beliefs are indeed culturally and socially constructed, and therefore contribute to a nation's mindset about education (Bruner, 1990; Schurmans & Dasen, 1992). How, then, can we compare the academic achievement of students from different cultures when those cultures differ in their pedagogical goals? The fact that culture guides socialization implies that important influences in academic achievement, such as parent attitudes about learning, teacher expectations, and cultural construals of schooling, will differentially dictate how students understand their educational experiences.

Cross-National Studies of Achievement

Indeed, international studies of achievement are measuring much more than what students have learned (Holloway & Minami, 1996; LeVine, 1977; Markus & Kitayama, 1991; Munroe & Munroe, 1997). In a sense, they are measuring a nation's pedagogical goals. The early IEA cross-national investigations (Husen, 1967; McKnight et al., 1987) were focused primarily on performance and provided us with rank orderings of achievement outcomes in the various domains of mathematics and science. Explanations for these differential outcomes tended to focus on aspects of curriculum, teacher preparation, and system structure, such as the number of days in each nation's school year. Although these factors clearly play a role in student outcomes, these studies left the research community with a gap in our understanding of the extent to which social-cognitive factors may have influenced the academic outcomes that were documented.

The latest investigation, TIMSS (Beaton et al., 1996), represents a major advance in how we study and interpret academic achievement across nations. Through case studies and classroom observations, rich portraits were painted of school systems within countries (Germany, Japan, and the United States). For example, students were asked in individual interviews to speak about the relationship between effort and ability in academic achievement, giving us deeper insights into how they conceptualize achievement within the context of their own cultures. However, less attention was paid to variation within culture. The result is that we know little about how these students' beliefs may differentially influence their achievement.

Achievement Beliefs and Culture

To consider culture in education means that we have to study education in the cultural context in which it takes place (Bruner, 1996). As

Bruner and others have argued, all of us, including teachers, have implicit theories, or "folk theories," of how children's minds work. These folk theories are embedded in cultural construals of what it means to be an educated person; how one understands the role of innate ability, effort, or luck in learning; and the like. Therefore, we need to have a very strong understanding of what these folk theories are as we continue to conduct large-scale cross-cultural comparisons of academic achievement.

Following Bruner, we believe we need to examine what *nations* think they are doing and what their reasons are for doing it. In other words, folk pedagogies drive educational policy and practice, and we need to understand these if we are to be able to draw reasonable and pragmatic conclusions from cross-national comparisons of academic achievement. Indeed, a culture's socialization goals shape its pedagogy. What a culture defines and requires of its citizens shapes what they are taught and the ways in which they are taught (Cole & Scribner, 1973; Spiro, 1993).

Indeed, Bruner (1990) has eloquently argued that we must place culture in a central role in the study of human development. Because each of us develops in a culture, we cannot hope to understand the human psychology at the individual level. Each of us is an active participant in our culture, through which our understandings evolve. In addition, meaning making is negotiated in culture—"By virtue of participation in culture, meaning is rendered public and shared" (p. 12). Finally, a folk theory of mind is a very powerful influence on individual and collective meaning making.

In Japan, for example, some parents identify the ability to *endure hardship* as a quality they wish to foster in their children as they grow (Lee, 1987). The ability to endure hardship is discussed in the national school policy in the following way: "[I]t is desirable that, in the lower grades, one should learn to bear hardship, and in the middle grades, to persist to the end with patience, and in the upper grades, to be steadfast and accomplish goals undaunted by obstacles or failures" (White, 1987, p. 17). This concern with the development of resiliency is ongoing. For example, college entrance requirements in Japan are grueling and arduous. Yet those who succeed are not said to be the "smartest"; they are believed to have the strongest will and character.

According to White and LeVine (1987), a major goal of child rearing in Japan is to encourage children to be "committed to and positively engaged in disciplined effort" (p. 59). The child-rearing beliefs of many Japanese parents illustrate a commitment to fostering strengths of character that are essential for school success. For example, Japanese parents believe that character is molded by ki—the will to live; tamashi—the determination to overcome obstacles; and seishin—the mental attitude that helps a person to embark on a task. Parents also believe that character is shaped by experiences of hardship, endurance, effort, and sustained struggle.

In contrast, the United States is a nation committed to the individual's right to pursue happiness, as stated in the Constitution. Many parents and educators have become concerned with ensuring that children have high self-esteem (Elkind, 1988). Generally speaking, our "ego-ideal" is of a child who is intelligent, athletic, social, musical, and creative—in short, we value the child who is "well-rounded" (Elkind, 1994; Kagan, 1989). The response of many educators and psychologists to the societal and economic upheavals that marked the past three decades has been to place children's salvation in *high self-esteem*. Rich or poor, the new thinking is that if we can get youngsters to feel better about themselves, we can chip away at the problems that threaten their development into healthy and productive citizens. Many parents want their children to develop their skills in many domains, including those outside of school (Bempechat, 2000).

These are but two examples of contrasting cultural models that are by no means characteristic of all parents in Japan and the United States. Indeed, these notions of enduring hardship and fostering self-esteem are contested within each society. Further, we cannot know the extent to which these models play any role in the achievement differences observed between Japanese and American students. At the same time, however, these different models illustrate how culture can guide pedagogical beliefs and goals.

The Differential Meanings of Achievement Beliefs

As mentioned earlier, cultural psychologists and psychological anthropologists agree that culture guides socialization practices, including those related to education (Roopnarine & Carter, 1992; Serpell & Hatano, 1997). An enduring concern for cross-cultural researchers is the differential meaning that students, parents, and teachers bring to the same or similar educational concepts. For example, much has been made of Japanese students' adherence to effort as a means to ensure school success, and American students' beliefs in innate ability as the driving force behind achievement (Stevenson et al., 1993). We do not know, however, what these concepts *mean* to the Japanese and U.S. students who have been studied. Nor do we know how these students, within their *own* cultural group, may vary in the meanings they bring to achievement cognitions such as effort and ability. We have argued elsewhere that this lack of attention to meaning making between and within cultures has led some researchers to draw generalizations about nations' performances in cross-national assessments (Bempechat & Drago-Severson, 1999).

Therefore, the cross-cultural study of academic achievement must begin to integrate both individual meaning making and the social and cultural contexts in which this meaning making takes place. As Sternberg (1990, p. 144) has stated, "To understand perceptions of competence, then, we need to understand the implicit theories that underlie them, where these theories come from, and how they interface with explicit theories of intelligence, intellectual style, and motivation." The implication for cross-national comparisons of achievement is that we need to expand the parameters of the understandings that we bring to the interpretation of cross-national achievement data. In the following section, we discuss models of development in social and cultural contexts.

Sociocultural Models of Development

Kitayama (Kitayama, Markus, Matsumoto, & Noraskkunkit, 1997) has argued that the development of cultural beliefs and practices that are commonly shared and understood takes place at two levels. The first is historical, in the sense that some situations develop over time and are sustained through general consensus. These become retained as part of cultural consciousness. The second level is immediate, in the sense that individuals react on a spontaneous basis to these cultural conventions.

For example, in studying how the behavior of parents is shaped by the culture in which they live, Harkness and Super (1992) have proposed the notion of the "developmental niche, a theoretical framework for understanding the cultural regulation of the child's micro-environment," which they define as the child's physical and social settings, customs of child rearing and child care that are governed by culture, and the psychology of children's caregivers. According to Harkness and Super, these three components operate or function together as a system to mediate children's individual experiences in the larger culture. They believe that developmental trends in day-to-day sociocultural activities are reflective of parents' developmental goals, and that child-care customs are representative of parental ethnotheories (Harkness & Super, 1992). Harkness and Super stress the importance of minimizing the tendency to generalize. They caution that findings should not be assumed to apply to children (or communities) other than those who were the subject of investigation.

The Construction of the Self

More recently, Markus, Kitayama, and their colleagues have attempted to situate the differential psychosocial tendencies of Japanese and American students in cultural context (Kitayama, 2000; Kitayama et al., 1997; Markus & Kitayama, 1991; Markus, Mullally, & Kitayama, 1997). They have proposed a collective constructionist theory of the self, in which psychological tendencies that have to do with the self are constructed collectively in society. For example, these researchers suggest that the tendency towards self-enhancement is common to the United States, while the tendency towards self-criticism is common in Japan. They then argue that these different tendencies enable individuals to function in and adapt to their cultural contexts.

This line of inquiry research has examined the tendency toward self-enhancement in the United States and self-criticism in Japan. In placing the origins of these tendencies in independence and collectivism, respectively, these researchers have proposed that self-enhancement is adaptive in a culture that socializes its members to focus on individual development. In contrast, self-criticism is adaptive in a culture that emphasizes the importance of belonging to a social group and maintaining positive relationships. In other words, self-criticism would not be seen as potentially harmful to self-esteem. In the Japanese cultural context, it would serve to provide feedback for self-improvement, which ultimately reinforces the sense of belonging to the group.

To test this notion, the authors designed experimental situations relevant to self-evaluation. They asked Japanese and American college students to generate situations that they believed would both enhance and decrease their self-esteem (*jison-shin*, or self-respect, in Japanese). A total of 400 scenarios were generated, and the students were asked to indicate whether each one could affect their self-esteem, negatively or positively, and to what extent, on a four-point scale. Results supported the collective constructivist theory of self, in that strong evidence was found for self-enhancement tendencies in the United States and self-critical tendencies in Japan. Specifically, American students reported that their self-esteem would increase more in success situations than it would decrease in failure situations, suggesting that social situations are interpreted in favor of self-enhancement. In contrast, the Japanese students identified more failure than success situations as being important to their self-esteem, and as having an influence on their self-esteem, indicating a bias toward self-criticism.

The researchers argue that, for Japanese students, self-criticism is part and parcel of a cultural context in which interdependence fosters the importance of self-improvement as a way to fit into one's important social units (i.e., family, classroom, workplace). This is captured in the word *hansei*, which means reflection. In Japanese culture, it is considered very important to reflect on one's behavior in order to improve it. Seen in this light, positive self-esteem may not be as important to Japanese individuals, whose engagement in self-criticism is an adaptive means to maintaining self-regard (*jison-shin*). In other words, self-esteem may be more important to sustaining the self in some cultures than others.

Taking this theory further, Markus, Mullally, and Kitayama have proposed that *selfways*, which are typical ways of being and behaving in one's cultural context, are "culturally constructed patterns" (Markus et al., 1997, p. 16). Selfways include critical cultural notions and beliefs, including a shared understanding of what it means to be a good or moral person in the culture in question. The process of selving is qualitatively different in different cultures. Selfways are similar to what Kagan (1989) has called the "ego-ideal" of a culture, and socialization operates in every culture to foster beliefs and attitudes that are conducive to adaptation in that culture—adaptation to events and situations that are common and occur on a regular basis (Kitayama, 2000; Kitayama et al., 1997). In the European-American context, such a person is an independent individual who can see herself in a positive way as having unique qualities or attributes, separate from others. As we have noted, this tendency toward self-enhancement can be seen as adaptive in a culture that socializes its members to focus on individual development (Kitayama, 2000; Kitayama et al., 1997).

In Japan, in contrast, a good person is one who establishes, maintains, and repairs interdependent relationships with others. In this cultural context, socialization operates to foster mutual relations with others and a sense of belonging. To grow and evolve in this society means that individuals will "develop a characteristic set of psychological tendencies—a sense of their connectedness, need to fit in, and tendency to harmonize with others" (Markus et al., 1997, p. 21). Markus and her colleagues argue that the shared nature of understanding characterized by selfways leads to certain cultural universals in members of the same society (Markus et al., 1997).

In its entirety, this work underscores the centrality of culture in self-concept. This, of course, has implications for methods of inquiry. Markus et al. (1997) note that, in cross-cultural research, it has been very common to administer the Twenty Statements Test (TST), in which one is asked to describe oneself by answering the question "Who am I?" This method, designed from a Western perspective where the notion of the self as stable is paramount, is uniquely suited to study the self-conceptions of individuals from Western cultures. In a different cultural context, where self-concepts are perceived as malleable, a method such as the TST is inappropriate because participation in a different culture requires qualitatively different ways of being.

Furthermore, the individualist/collectivist dichotomy does not represent the range of cultural selfways. For example, selfways in the African context can be characterized as neither one or the other. Rather, they are culturally defined in terms of the relationship of the self to others, both living and dead—there is no self without others (Markus et al., 1997). A "good" person must fulfill social obligations not only to those in their group, but especially to elders and ancestors. This is believed to keep one connected to the past. Indeed, an adult is not a "person" without having become a parent. The arrival of children bestows personhood on adults because children represent an important way of becoming connected to the future. In addition, African selfways are distinguished by a belief in the permeability of mind and body. Individuals will not have their pictures taken, or step on another's shadow, because these actions are perceived to threaten or diminish the life of another (Markus et al., 1997).

Again, we recognize that these cultural models are very general, and do not address the ways in which they may vary or be differentially interpreted by members of a society. Fruitful avenues for future research should include the study of how these "selfways" differ as a function of ethnicity or social class. Tudge's recent work addresses the need for cross-cultural studies to consider the heterogeneity that exists *within* a culture (Tudge, Hogan, Snezhkova, Kulakova, & Etz, 2000). He and his colleagues surveyed the parenting beliefs of middle and working class mothers and fathers in Russia and the United States. Mirroring previous research in this area, they found that middle class parents in both cultures shared the view that parents should foster self-direction and that children should experience a relative amount of freedom at home. In contrast, working class parents in both societies were more focused on ensuring that their children adhered to rules.

Tudge's work dovetails nicely with Markus and Kitayama's, in that it highlights the extent to which pathways of development differ, not only between, but within cultures. The overarching message is that, regardless of one's theoretical approach, researchers should not assume universality in beliefs or behaviors. Such an assumption has proved somewhat problematic for a series of cross-national studies on achievement and motivation, which we discuss below.

Applying European-American Concepts to Other Cultures: An Illustration

Much of the literature on student achievement across nations has been devoid of the cultural contexts in which learning takes place. Many researchers have employed methods and constructs drawn from the American research context in order to understand why American students underachieve relative to their peers in other nations. Three problems attach to this approach. The first relates to the assumption of universality, which we have raised. Words, concepts, and phrases commonly used in European-American context have been "exported to study students' conceptions of learning in other cultures." These include concepts such as *intelligence*, and words such as *effort*, *ability*, and *luck*. We cannot assume that European-American conceptions of learning will be understood in the same or similar ways by students educated in other cultures. The second problem is that, in most studies of achievement motivation, these words and phrases have not been articulated by students themselves, but rather have been imposed from the outside by educational researchers. This approach, which is etic in nature, has failed to consider the ways in which students might speak differentially about and understand the meanings of learning, achievement, and motivation in the context of their own educational experiences, an issue we will raise.

Third, this approach assumes that the constructs that American researchers have focused on are the only constructs that are relevant, and fails to leave room for others that are common and important in different cultures. These would be constructs that American researchers would not think to measure, because they have no meaning in European-American culture. For example, Li (in press) has noted that the expression "achievement motivation" has no parallel translation in the Chinese language. Instead, Chinese college students speak about the importance of having "the heart and mind for wanting to learn," and the reality that learning is a lifelong process, regardless of whether one is engaged in formal learning. This research highlights the degree to which any interpretations brought to findings are bound to be inherently flawed, and lead educators to conclusions that may not be well founded.

An example of this problem is found in the cross-national investigations undertaken by Stevenson and his colleagues, the results of which emerged in the early 1980s (Stevenson et al., 1993; Stevenson & Lee, 1990; Stevenson, Lee, & Stigler, 1986; Stevenson & Stigler, 1992; Stigler & Hiebert, 1999). In collaboration with Japanese and Taiwanese colleagues, Stevenson found compelling evidence that by the fifth grade, American children lagged well behind their Asian peers (Stevenson et al., 1986). For example, he showed that American, Japanese, and Taiwanese first graders did not differ in their mathematics proficiency. At the fifth-grade level, however, Stevenson found that the achievement gap had grown, to where there was virtually no overlap between the mathematics achievement of American children and their Asian peers. Foreshadowing findings of two decades of research yet to come, Stevenson documented that the Japanese first graders showed greater mathematics proficiency than the American fifth graders. In later work, the Stevenson team showed that these achievement differences were persistent ten years following the publication of their first investigation (Stevenson et al., 1993; Stevenson & Stigler, 1992).

The Stevenson team drew on attribution theory (Weiner, 1984, 1985) in their attempts to understand the reasons underlying the striking achievement differences they were documenting. As we discussed earlier in this chapter, Weiner (1972) has argued that the "spring of action" that motivates students' achievement behavior is the need to *understand* the reasons that underlie success and failure.

One can readily see the problems inherent in applying a U.S.-based theory to study motivation in Asian students. In a seminal paper, Holloway (1988) showed that effort is a construct that is socially constructed around the notion of obligation to oneself, one's family, and one's community. This is consistent with the notion of selfway raised by Markus, Mullally, and Kitayama, who showed that the process of selving in the Japanese context is closely tied to one's social relationships (Markus et al., 1997). Holloway has demonstrated that effort does not mean simply "trying hard," as it does in the American context. Effort is a multilayered construct in which the performance of students is said to reflect on themselves, their parents, their families, and the communities in which they are being raised. In short, effort is socially oriented, whereas in the United States it is perceived as individually driven.

Ability is a construct that is similarly multifaceted. In adhering strictly to Weiner's theory, Stevenson's work has adhered to its one definition of ability as an internal, stable, and uncontrollable trait. As we discussed earlier, much evidence has accumulated to show that, even in the U.S. context, many students perceive ability as a malleable quality that can grow as a function of effort (Bempechat et al., 1991; Nicholls et al., 1989). We do not know how Japanese and Chinese students vary in their beliefs about the nature of ability. The literature has largely portrayed their views of ability as malleable and unlimited (Stevenson & Stigler, 1992; White, 1987).

Despite the considerable importance of cultural variation in the meanings of words, the Stevenson team presented a compelling, yet incomplete explanation for the high achievement of Asian as compared to American students (Bempechat & Drago-Severson, 1999). Using rank orderings of attributions and Likert-style rankings, Stevenson found that in some, but not all cases, Japanese and Chinese students demonstrate stronger beliefs in the value of effort over innate ability in school performance (Stevenson et al., 1986). He concluded that Asian students outperform American students *because* they believe more in the value of effort than do their U.S. counterparts.

This conclusion is problematic for researchers because correlational data have not been offered for scrutiny. Even with such data in hand, it is well understood that correlation does not imply causality. Furthermore, the apparent link between beliefs and academic outcomes arises from surveys and questionnaires. Student interviews were not quoted in Stevenson's major reports of his cross-cultural investigations. We know nothing, therefore, about the differential meanings that students in these different cultures bring to these achievement-related constructs. The latter have been externally imposed by researchers, with little attention paid to culture and individual meaning making within culture. It behooves us, therefore, to make a concerted effort to understand the meanings that students, parents, and teachers bring to their educational experiences. In other words, we need to develop a deeper understanding of what it means in different nations to be an educated person. A more complete theory of cognitive development should include the broad range of cognitive goals valued across cultures.

Meaning Making in Culture and Context: The Importance of Emic Research

In our more recent work, we have argued that research practices in the field of achievement motivation need to become more integrated with those in psychological anthropology (Bempechat & Drago-Severson, 1999; Quihuis, Bempechat, Jimenez, & Boulay, in press). It is striking that so much research on the motivational underpinnings of academic achievement has taken place without being fully informed by how major players in education think about the enterprise and their experiences within schools. In other words, surveys and experimental procedures abound, but few researchers have taken the time to actually speak to students, parents, or teachers. What would we learn if we began to spend more time seeking the views of those who learn and those who educate? In other words, how can qualitative research advance our understanding of academic achievement across cultures?

To begin, qualitative methods that seek *emic* perspectives—idiosyncratic and contextualized beliefs—are bound to reveal conceptions of learning, achievement, and motivation that are authentic. Instead of identifying categories that we, as researchers, may believe are important in individuals' academic experiences, we allow individuals themselves to set the parameters about which they choose to speak (see Schurmans & Dasen, 1992).

Where cross-national research is concerned, the search for emic perspectives maximizes our chances of uncovering sociocultural beliefs that are unique to a particular culture's common views of being (Markus et al., 1997)—beliefs that we would not have been able to anticipate, because they would hold no meaning for us. In addition, an emic focus allows the variation in beliefs to emerge, thus revealing multiple cultural models of learning and achievement (Shore, 1996). It also minimizes the possibility that we would inappropriately misinterpret educational mores and practices or confer particular cultural beliefs where none exist. Furthermore, the rich and varied understandings that comprise emic beliefs provide us with a context within which we can better understand survey and questionnaire findings. Importantly, insights gleaned from qualitative research have the potential to inform the design of future surveys (see Miller, 1996).

Nicholls et al. (1990) argue that our understanding of children's motivation for learning would be better served if we examined the *meanings* that students see in their work. For example, he stated that the common research tendency to ask children to rate their ability obscured more telling information that could be gleaned from asking them what is ability (Nicholls & Hazzard, 1993).

This example resonates with Shweder's (1990) assertion that:

> [T]he mind ... is content-driven, domain-specific, and constructively stimulus-bound; and it cannot be extracted from the historically variable and cross-culturally diverse intentional worlds in which it plays a co-constituting part. ... It is the aim of cultural psychology to understand the organization and evocative power of all that stuff, to study the major varieties of it, and *to seek mind where it is mindful* [italics added], indissociably embedded in the meaning and resources that are its product, yet also make it up. (p. 13)

We do not advocate that quantitative methods of inquiry should be abandoned altogether. On the contrary, the judicious integration of both methodologies is essential to our continuing efforts to deepen our knowledge and understanding of the social, psychological, and cultural factors that influence approaches to teaching and learning. In this regard, in-depth qualitative studies and ethnographies can provide the rich and contextualized information that we need in order to understand the *meanings* of particular educational beliefs and attitudes in cultural context, defined by criteria from within the culture in question (Schurmans & Dasen, 1992).

To advance our knowledge, qualitative studies need to be (1) derived from existing theory and research, and (2) designed to build grounded theory. As to the first, interview protocols can be developed around those motivational and cultural constructs that make sense in each nation. For example, in the U.S. context, previous research has demonstrated that classroom structure has a profound influence on the extent to which students become focused on the *process* as opposed to the *products* of learning (Nicholls, 1989). When compared to students in cooperative classrooms, those in competitively oriented classrooms tend to be far more preoccupied about their intellectual ability, worried about making mistakes, and concerned about their performance relative to their peers (Ames, Ames, & Felker, 1977). It makes sense, then, to design an in-depth interview that would probe students' beliefs about ability as being stable, malleable, or some combination of those beliefs. Such an interview would reveal *variations* in students' understanding of what it takes to do well in their classroom.

In comparison, theory and research on Japanese schooling has highlighted the central role that mutual interdependence plays in the socialization of academic achievement (White & LeVine, 1987). Doing well in school is but one way that children can uphold their family's honor (White, 1987). In this context, we would want to know how students perceive the role that obligation to parents plays in their achievement behavior. Again, in-depth interviews would put us in a position to glean variations in children's understanding of what obligation means to them.

Elliott, Hufton, and their colleagues found a number of paradoxes emerging from their use of quantitative methods in cross-national studies of achievement motivation in England, Russia, and the United States (Elliott, Hufton, Illushin, & Willis, 2001; Elliott, Hufton, Hildreth, & Illushin, 1999) . For example, although U.S. students appeared to emphasize effort over ability in explaining achievement, their actual levels of engagement appeared far less than that of Russian students, who tended to emphasize ability. Additionally, it has proven difficult to document a relationship within a particular society between an effort orientation and achievement. In Japan, for example, mothers and their children tend to place more emphasis than do their American counterparts on effort as a cause of low achievement in mathematics, but their relative weighting of effort appears unrelated to the studentsí grades in school (Holloway, Kashiwagi, Hess, & Azuma, 1986). Elliott and Hufton found that understanding the complexities behind these and several other such puzzles could best be achieved by means of a combination of classroom observations, in-depth interviews and an analysis of the broader sociocultural context (Elliott et al., 2001; Elliott et al., 1999; Hufton, Elliott, & Illushin, in press; Hufton & Elliott, 2000).

As educational researchers we need to examine our own beliefs about achievement and situate them in our own definitions about effort, ability, and intelligence. Notions about intelligence and "intelligent" behavior vary from one cultural context to another, and it is important to explore such notions to better understand different beliefs about intelligence and achievement. Tobin and his colleagues' comparative study of Japanese, Chinese, and U.S. preschools illustrates important cultural differences related to definitions and attitudes toward intelligence (Tobin, Wu, & Davidson, 1989). Among the Japanese, for example, intelligence is not simply a mastery of the content knowledge, but is tied in with notions of character and behavior (Tobin et al., 1989). Unlike Americans' notions of intelligence, the Japanese stress that children's behaviors, such as helping out in the classroom, which in the U.S. context might never be associated with ability, indeed would be associated with being smart. Japanese teachers, like American teachers, do acknowledge that different children may exhibit different abilities upon entering formal schooling. However, effort and character shape Japanese teachers' definitions of intelligence more than inborn ability, which is in contrast to notions of intelligence among Americans, who see intelligence as a value-free trait (White & LeVine, 1987).

Similarly, Latino parents have expressed a parallel belief regarding notions of intelligence (Reese, Balzano, Gallimore, & Goldenberg, 1995). The concept of being *bien educado*, which directly translates to being well educated, carries very different meanings in the U.S. and Latino contexts. Like the Japanese, a person who is *bien educado* is seen first and foremost as behaving morally and acting appropriately in social situations. Innate ability is of less concern. Furthermore, it is possible that a child is *bien educado* in that she is courteous, respectful, and *acomedido* (helps out without being asked), and displays effort without necessarily displaying innate ability. For Japanese and Latino teachers and parents, respectively, the purpose of formal schooling, then, is not simply to highlight unequal abilities and mastery of content material, but to socialize children toward morality and appropriate social behavior that would have a positive influence on the development of their character.

Unlike Americans, the Japanese reluctance to elevate innate ability to high status is tied to the culture's beliefs about equality (Tobin et al., 1989). Japanese teachers believe that acknowledging different abilities or children with more innate ability might lead to a disproportionate allocation of resources, opportunities, and effort. Teachers are then charged with the responsibility of "leveling out the playing field," or evening out children with different abilities so that a classroom is more homogeneous than heterogeneous with respect to intelligence. In this regard, Japanese pedagogy places an emphasis on working amicably and productively in large and small mixed-ability classrooms so that children do not necessarily highlight their individual skills above others. Unlike American cultural notions that emphasize individual effort and reward individuals for displaying unique characteristics, the Japanese socialize children toward a collective society where members will be sensitive to each others' needs and where they will gain "a sense of security that comes from being a member of a seemingly homogeneous group" (Tobin et al., 1989, p. 26).

It is important to note, however, that research on the motivational underpinnings of achievement in Japan tends to view its curricula, teachers, and pedagogical practices in particularly positive terms. In fact, the conflict and tension around educational policy in Japan is given little attention in much of the cross-national work (Mouer & Sugimoto, 1986). Mouer and Sugimoto (1986) argue that viewing Japanese society as monolithic, through what they term a "holistic" cultural model (*"nihonjinron"*) (see also Holloway, 2000), clouds existing educational conflicts, such as those between the Ministry of Education and the Japanese Teachers Union. For example, the latter has been pushing for more child-directed learning, while the former continues to support teacher-led instruction. A more complete and realistic understanding of Japanese education needs to consider those aspects of learning which are contested within the society.

Building Grounded Theory

Building a grounded theory implies that students', parents', and teachers' own meanings—their *emic* concepts—emerge in interviews and provide insights that have not been described in research that is based on theory and previous findings. The challenge for researchers is to approach interviewees with no preconceived notions of what might constitute their understanding of their educational experiences. According to Shweder (1997), the rich knowledge that results from qualitative research cannot be attained without the "process of discovery" that is inherent in ethnographic research. In building grounded theory, the primary question becomes how do individuals construct meaning about learning and achievement in different cultures and contexts, and how do these meanings vary within culture and context. The use of an unstructured questionnaire to examine this question can be particularly useful in revealing the nuances that exist in any individual's personal construction of meaning. At the same time, unexpected findings can emerge that serve to challenge current theory.

For example, in a mixed-methods study, Quihuis and her colleagues (in press) asked high school students to complete a questionnaire about their theories of intelligence, and then interviewed a subset of students about their beliefs. According to Dweck's theory, students who endorsed an "entity" theory of intelligence were expected to speak about their abilities as being limited, and to express low confidence. Instead, while acknowledging that they had difficulty in some subjects, they spoke with optimism about the ways in which they could improve their performance. In other words, they articulated mastery-oriented beliefs ordinarily associated with "incremental" theorists, who believe that intelligence is unlimited. Both "types" of theorists highlighted notions of *effort, importance,* and *finding the right help*. It could well be that the maladaptive motivational tendencies of entity theorists, such as learned helplessness, may not manifest themselves in the classroom when students are confronted with real assignments that must be completed. It also could be that they do manifest themselves, but in different ways for different students. These are possibilities we are currently studying.

Cross-National Achievement: What Would Cognitive Psychologists Want to Know?

> All psychological functions begin, and to a larger extent remain, cultur-ally, historically, and institutionally situated and context specific. (Cole, 1996, p. 252)

> For researchers to attempt to understand development without consid-ering everyday activities and skills in the context of cultural goals would be like attempting to learn a language without trying to understand the meaning it expresses. (Rogoff, 1990, p. 114)

If cognitive psychologists were setting out to study the mathematical knowledge of students in various countries and cultures, they would likely design a series of investigations that would bear little resemblance to TIMSS. This is because cognitive psychologists, heavily influenced by theorists Piaget and Vygotsky, have placed cultures and contexts at the center of their investigations on cognition. The eminent researchers of our day, including Rogoff, Lave, Haste, Cole, and Scribner, are perhaps best described as comparative cognitive researchers, working in the domains of cultural psychology or cognitive anthropology.

Vygotsky's assertion that knowledge is co-constructed with culture played a major part in his theory of cognitive development (Cole & Wertsch, 1996). According to Vygotsky, we all have a need to mediate our actions through tools, or "artifacts," that are culturally based, including language, symbols, works of art, writings, and the like (Vygotsky, 1978) He argued that the relationship between individuals and their social envi-ronment was dynamic and malleable. Such artifacts, seen in their entirety as having been accumulated and having evolved over generations, form the basis of culture. In short, culture is the medium through which human beings develop (Cole, 1996). Furthermore, in order to gain a meaningful understanding of human behavior, one must examine the daily activities in which individuals take part. This emphasis on practical, everyday be-havior is a central tenet of cultural psychology.

Rogoff has added that a culture's institutions, such as its schools, serve not only to shape thinking, but to communicate shared values for thinking (Rogoff, 1990). According to Rogoff, development is a process in which our social and environmental contexts guide cognition. Therefore, they are integral in the development of meaning making. In her interpretation of Vygotsky's theory, Haste (1994) proposed that meaning making takes place at three levels: "(1) the *intra*personal, which is the personal cognitive process of constructing, reflecting, and consolidating; (2) the *inter*personal, which is an area where the individual participates in social interaction and negotiates meaning; and (3) the social-historical or cultural, where the individual encounters cultural norms and culturally defined expectations, which have a long social history" (Bempechat & Abrahams, 1999, p. 845). Meaning is negotiated and mutually influenced at all levels.

Vygotsky's influential notion of the zone of proximal development (ZPD) arises from the mutual and dynamic relationship between children and adults. The ZPD represents a skill that is just beyond the reach of what a child can complete on her own. Over time, in mutual interactions with an adult, the child gradually learns to complete the task on her own. In other words, knowledge is transferred from expert to novice through the scaffolding of information (Rogoff, 1990).

Investigating Situated Learning

If contemporary cognitive psychologists were asked to contribute to the next international study of mathematics and science, what would they choose to study and how would they go about designing their research? Although there would be variation in areas of focus, all would examine cognition in context, or what has come to be called "mind in action" (Scribner, 1983/1992), "situated learning" (Lave, 1988; Rogoff, 1990), or "distributed cognition" (Cole, 1988; Cole & Wertsch, 1996). Lave's well-known work on Liberian tailors is illustrative of situated learning (Lave, 1977). She studied the influence of apprenticeship training and formal (Western) schooling on the mathematical skills of tailors. After spending time observing their work in shops, Lave devised several tasks that ranged from the familiar (problems derived from their daily work) to the unfamiliar (problems derived from school tasks). She found that years of tailoring experience were more influential to the solution of familiar problems, while formal schooling was more helpful in the solution of school-related problems.

How can this work be applied to cross-national studies in mathematics learning? One goal of large cross-national studies should be to broaden our understanding of cognitive development in cultural context, and to document the varied cognitive outcomes and teaching methods valued in different cultures. Comparative cognitive psychologists would consider studying the tasks that children do on a daily basis—tasks that require mathematical/spatial thinking. By definition, however, these would have to be culturally bound and context specific. They would have to represent goals of development that are valued in different cultures, as well as the varied means used to attain them. For example, it is a common occurrence in some, but not all, cultures for children to accompany an adult to a grocery store, assist in the selection of items from a list, and help put purchases away in cupboards. Such a task emphasizes sorting and categorizing skills and reveals how adults teach children to do an essential household task. It would be inappropriate, however, to conduct this kind of ethnographic study in different nations, given that sorting and categorizing skills may not be scaffolded universally via a grocery shopping trip.

While it is the case that cultural models of learning and achievement are affected by the global adoption of certain structures, such as mass education (Meyer, Ramirez, & Soysal, 1992), implicit in Rogoff's argument is that a culture would not promote a cognitive outcome that had no use in that culture. Just as "necessity is the mother of invention," we train our youth toward the cognitive skills they will need to survive in their culture. Thus, if we continue to focus on only a small portion of the range of cognitive goals for which people around the world strive, we will have an incomplete theory of human cognitive development. Therefore, cognitive psychologists are quite interested in observing both the goals of development and the strategies we use to help children reach those goals. Only then will we have a more complete sense of the cognitive skills we are capable of, and the myriad of ways for attaining proficiency in those skills.

Relatedly, cultural psychologists would want to know how students transfer knowledge of mathematics acquired formally through schooling to contexts in which they have to apply their knowledge. They would also want to understand the extent to which students can be flexible in their application of mathematical principles. In a certain way, this echoes the concern of mathematics educators, who have been distressed over the enduring tendency of many students to view mathematics as a domain that requires no creativity and in which success can be gained through rote memorization (see Cobb et al., 1991). The result is that many students are uncomfortable with mathematics problems when they diverge even slightly from problems they have previously encountered. Researchers in the field have argued that students need to be able to develop a "deep conceptual understanding" of mathematics in order to become comfortably numerate (Lampert, 1990). One way to do this is to teach in ways that foster a more constructive view of the domain (Pirie & Kieren, 1992).

In sum, comparative cognitive psychologists would seek a greater understanding of learning in culture and context than is currently available in cross-national studies, such as TIMSS. We realize this involves conducting a series of smaller ethnographic studies of situated learning in many nations, a task that is formidable indeed. Yet we need to bear in mind that the overall goal in this work is to gain a deeper understanding of thought in action. It is important, therefore, to complement large-scale surveys of mathematics achievement with smaller case-based studies of the practical applications of knowledge in everyday life. This may concern survey researchers, who are accustomed to generating large enough samples for statistical generalizability. Yet, as Robin Alexander, the noted scholar of comparative pedagogy has argued, there is an important distinction between statistical and "cultural" generalizability.

Statistical Versus Cultural Generalizability

Alexander (2000) recently argued that it is possible to derive valid and reliable "cultural" generalizations about national educational thought, practice, and outcomes from qualitative field studies centered in a small number of sites of educational practice. Alexander has contrasted "statistical" and "cultural" generalization, and views the claim for "cultural generalizability" as resting on two conditions. First, he argues that researchers need to accept the "proposition that the culture in which the schools in a country, state or region are located, and which teachers and pupils share, is as powerful a determinant of the character of school and classroom life as are the unique institutional "dynamics, local circumstances and interpersonal chemistries which make one school, or classroom different from another." Alexander adds, "the research methods used [must be] sufficiently searching and sensitive to probe beyond the observable moves and counter-moves of pedagogy to the *values and meanings* which these embody." (Alexander, 2000, p. 266, italics added).

Cross-national research can indeed yield cultural generalizations by adhering to guidelines Alexander has posited. First, investigators can operate under the working assumption that the beliefs, commitments, and practices of those we are researching are influenced by extra-personal systems of belief, commitment, and action with which they are acquainted. Second, mixed methods of inquiry can allow researchers to become familiar with the potentially influential wider systems of beliefs, commitment, and normative practices with which our participants may be familiar. Third, fine-grained qualitative field work can be used to uncover the beliefs, norms, and commitments and understand the rationale of practices amongst the participants. Fourth, researchers can consider relations between potentially influential wider systems of beliefs and commitment and normative practices and any system found in the beliefs, commitments and rationales of practice amongst those they are researching.

Learning More from the Current Cross-National Data

One of the misuses of cross-national comparisons that has emerged since large-scale cross-national comparisons were first conducted in the early 1960s has been the rank ordering of countries. The value of cross-national comparisons lies not in the ranking of nations to see which educational systems are superior to others, but rather to investigate why some countries differ in their achievement levels. The IEA, established in 1959, strongly emphasized that "horse race" analyses that rank ordered countries were just first *and* necessary steps toward understanding cross-national differences (Keeves, 1995).

The move from *educational tourism* (pre-1960), where visitors from one country formally observed the educational systems of foreign countries and offered rich descriptions of teaching practices, students' behavior and learning opportunities, and school structures, to large-scale international comparisons (post-1960) was only feasible because sophisticated methods of inquiry were developed. Prior to the 1960s, educational researchers did not have the tools to make such cross-national comparisons, but improved methods in survey design and statistical analyses such as inference statistics and sampling, coupled with technological advances in the use of computers for data analyses, opened the door for cross-national comparative research. Interestingly enough, cross-national data, in one form or another, moved from detailed ethnographic accounts across countries and the use of qualitative inquiry to a somewhat sole reliance on quantitative methods, given the introduction of internationally valid standards of such inquiry by the IEA. Although quantitative methods allowed cross-national data to be compared on equivalent measures, such large-scale inquiry must be coupled with qualitative methods, as Husen (1967) has argued, in order to give us a rich portrait of the factors associated with educational achievements. Cross-national comparisons offer an awareness to nations that they "cannot borrow wholesale from each other [but rather] by looking at the other systems one can get a perspective that provides insights into how one could go about improving one's own system" (Keeves, 1995, p. 169).

The purpose of cross-national data should not solely be to list factors that are related to educational achievement. Such research also should be focused on the *processes*, in addition to the products, involved in educational systems in order to develop a greater understanding of how educational systems work. For example, how do teachers, students, parents, administrators, and others in the educational system make meaning of their experiences, and how does this influence issues of learning and teaching? The goal of cross-national research should not only be to construct models of teaching and learning processes in school, but it should also include the testing of these models against observed data in order to confirm or reject model structures.

Furthermore, we, like others (Husen, 1967; Keeves, 1995), firmly believe that the time is long overdue for an integration of more sophisticated statistical methods, such as multilevel analyses along with qualitative methods for in-depth inquiry and analyses of how individuals make meaning of their experiences within educational systems. In all likelihood, there is probably more variation within nations than between nations. When we focus exclusively on between-nation differences, we fail to detect the rich variation that exists within a nation of learners. Although it is interesting to look cross-nationally at achievement, it is difficult to simply look at the average achievement of a nation. Comparing averages can begin to give us a sense of the variation in achievement between nations, but it will not reveal whether there is substantial variation within a nation. This question can be easily addressed using current data collected by such cross-national examinations as TIMSS. The data gathered by TIMSS can be conceptualized as hierarchical in nature—students were sampled within countries. The question then becomes, given that there is variation in test scores overall, how much of this variation is attributable to differences between countries (Level 2) and how much is attributable to differences in students (Level 1). Intraclass correlations (calculated by fitting a multilevel model with no predictors) would help address this question. Although it is interesting to know that Country X has higher test scores, and that students in Country X spend more time in class, it also would be interesting to show that there is a correlation between these variables across countries. Although neither correlation nor regression can establish causal relationships (e.g., more time in class causes higher test scores), they would at least allow us to begin to determine if and where these variables covary. IEA has begun to conduct such multilevel analyses of cross-national data (Keeves, 1995) due to the expansion of statistical methods that allow for hierarchical linear modeling, for example, and there is a call for more of the same in future cross-national comparisons.

The Future of Cross-National Research

I have no objection in principle to creating better measuring instruments in order to find out how well our students are doing in science, in mathematics, in literature, in reading. . . . Of course we need standards and resources to make our schools work well in solving the myriad tasks they face. But resources and standards alone will not work. We need a surer sense of what to teach to whom and how to go about teaching it in such a way that it will make those taught more effective, less alienated,

and better human beings. . . . What we need is a school reform movement with a better sense of where we are going, with deeper convictions
about what kind of people we want to be. (Bruner, 1996, pp. 117-118)

As Bruner points out, we need to go beyond cataloging the different
ways in which education is delivered and move toward a deeper sense of
the purposes of education. We believe that the current data on cross-
national achievement and school systems are insufficient for us to make
informed recommendations about how to improve our own educational
system. We, and others, have argued that we cannot simply adopt the
educational methods of those nations whose students are performing well.
We need to understand how education is viewed, valued, and understood by the citizens of the culture whose outcomes we admire. If we are
to adopt some of their methods, we must do so in a culturally sensitive
way. Without information about the meaning of education, we cannot
begin to translate any of the methods used by other nations in a culturally
sensitive way—the exercise would be akin to translating a text without
knowing the language in which it has been written.

Integrating Survey and Qualitative Methods of Inquiry

Cross-national survey research can lead us to pertinent qualitative
research questions. Qualitative inquiries, in turn, can shape the questions
we attend to in future large-scale quantitative surveys. We believe that it
is time for qualitative methods of inquiry to once again be present in
cross-national data, as they were in the pre-1960s era. When integrated
with surveys, the more sophisticated methods of qualitative inquiry that
are now at our disposal can better serve our purposes of taking an in-
depth look at other countries' educational systems so that we may gain
insights about improving our own system.

A promising approach is found in Li's (2000) comparison of Chinese
and U.S. conceptions of learning using prototype research methods. In
general, prototype research methods require that the researcher interview
individuals to elicit words and phrases that are used to describe the domain in question. This elegant method uses emic concepts, yet employs
sophisticated quantitative analyses to understand the data. In this case, Li
obtained a cultural prototype of "intelligence through a five-step process
in which she asked increasingly larger groups of American and Chinese
students to relate any words or phrases related to learning. This culmi-
nated in a hierarchical cluster analysis of groups of ideas that represented
the students' conceptions of learning.

Li found little conceptual overlap between Chinese and American
conceptions of learning. American conceptions of learning did not include any words or phrases related to actual achievement. For the U.S.

students, the major focus is on thinking, which can be considered a hyper-cognized domain, one that is well developed in U.S. society (Levy, 1973). In contrast, Chinese students used words and phrases that related achievement as representing breadth and depth of knowledge, extraordinary ability, and the unity of moral development and knowledge. In short, American students appear to be hypercognized for the process of learning while the Chinese students appear to be hypercognized about attitudes for learning.

Li's contribution to our sociocultural understanding of achievement and motivation is significant, because she rises to the call for combined methods (e.g., Shweder, 1997). Yet Li goes one step further, in the sense that her sophisticated analyses of data were derived entirely from emic or qualitative understandings of learning in each culture.

A second positive approach is found in Stigler and Hiebert's (1999) use of qualitative methods to analyze the TIMSS video study, which included data on classroom learning and teaching. One of the most interesting findings that emerged from this analysis is that teaching, and not teachers, is a critical factor in the teaching and learning of mathematics when comparing Japan and the United States. American mathematics teaching tends to focus on procedural skills rather than conceptual understandings.

A second finding is that among U.S. and Japanese schooling processes, there are large differences in teaching *between* cultures, but not within cultures. That is, in comparison to the within-culture variation in teaching, there are much larger gaps between different countries in terms of teaching processes. Along this vein, Stigler and Hiebert took advantage of qualitative data to observe and document that teaching is very much a cultural activity that has embedded in it notions of learning that stem from cultural beliefs and practices. In their analyses, they state that teaching is very difficult to change given the cultural underpinnings. Such insights would have been very difficult, nearly impossible, to arrive at if qualitative methods were not used for such inquiry.

Conclusion

We believe that researchers conducting cross-national investigations need to be aware of their own culture and context and the extent to which it influences both their investigations and their interpretations of their findings. As Sir Michael Sadler stated in a now famous lecture delivered in Guildford:

> In studying foreign systems of education, we should not forget that the things outside the schools matter even more than the things inside the

schools, and govern and interpret the things inside. We cannot wander at pleasure among the educational systems of the world, like a child strolling through a garden, and pick off a flower from one bush and some leaves from another, and then expect that if we stick what we have gathered into the soil at home, we shall have a living plant. (Sadler, 1979, p. 49)

REFERENCES

Alexander, R. (2000). *Culture and pedagogy*. London: Blackwell.

Ames, C., Ames, R., & Felker, D. W. (1977) Effects of competitive reward structure and valence of outcome on children's achievement attributions. *Journal of Educational Psychology 69*(1), 1-8.

Ames, C., & Archer, J. (1987). Mothers' beliefs about the role of ability and effort in school learning. *Journal of Educational Psychology, 71*, 409-414.

Beaton, A., Mullis, I., Martin, M., Gonzalez, E., Kelly, D., & Smith, T. (1996). *Mathematics achievement in the middle school years: IEA's Third International Mathematics and Science Study*. Chestnut Hill, MA: Boston College, Center for the Study of Testing, Evaluation, and Educational Policy.

Bempechat, J. (1998). *Against the odds: How 'at risk' students exceed expectations*. San Francisco: Jossey-Bass.

Bempechat, J. (2000). *Getting our kids back on track: Educating children for the future*. San Francisco: Jossey-Bass.

Bempechat, J., & Abrahams, S. (1999). "You can't oppress yourself": Conceptions of achievement and opportunity in post-apartheid South Africa. *Teachers College Record, 100*, 841-859.

Bempechat, J., & Drago-Severson, E. (1999). Cross-national differences in academic achievement: Beyond etic conceptions of children's understandings. *Review of Educational Research, 69*, 287-314.

Bempechat, J., Graham, S., & Jimenez, N. (1999). The socialization of achievement in poor and minority students: A comparative study. *Journal of Cross-Cultural Psychology, 30*, 139-158.

Bempechat, J., London, P., & Dweck, C. S. (1991). Children's conceptions of ability in major domains: An interview and experimental study. *Child Study Journal, 21*(1), 11-35.

Bruner, J. (1990). *Acts of meaning*. Cambridge, MA: Harvard University Press.

Bruner, J. (1996). *The culture of education*. Cambridge, MA: Harvard University Press.

Cobb, P., Wood, T., Yackel, E., Nicholls, J., Wheatley, G., Trigatti, B., & Perlwitz, M. (1991). Assessment of a problem-centered second-grade mathematics project. *Journal for Research in Mathematics Education, 22*, 3-29.

Cole, M. (1988). Cross-cultural research in the socio-historical tradition. *Human Development, 31*, 137-151.

Cole, M. (1996). *Cultural psychology: A once and future discipline*. Cambridge, MA: Harvard University Press.

Cole, M., & Scribner, S. (1973). *Culture and thought*. New York: John Wiley & Sons.

Cole, M., & Wertsch, J. V. (1996). Beyond the individual-social antimony in discussions of Piaget and Vygotsky. *Human Development, 39*, 250-256.

Covington, M. V., & Omelich, C. L. (1979). Effort: The double-edged sword in school achievement. *Journal of Educational Psychology, 71*(2), 169-182.

Dweck, C. (1999). *Self-theories: Their role in motivation, personality and development*. New York: Psychology Press.

Dweck, C. S., & Bempechat, J. (1983). Children's theories of intelligence: Consequences for learning. In S. G. Paris, G. M. Olson, & H. W. Stevenson (Eds.), *Learning and motivation in the classroom*. Hillsdale, NJ: Lawrence Erlbaum Associates.

Eccles, J. (1993). School and family effects on the ontogeny of children's interests, self-perceptions, and activity choices. In J. Jacobs (Ed.), *Nebraska Symposium on Motivation: Vol. 40. Developmental perspectives on motivation* (pp. 145-208). Lincoln: University of Nebraska Press.

Elkind, D. (1988). *The hurried child: Growing up too fast too soon*. New York: Addison-Wesley.

Elkind, D. (1994). *Ties that stress: The new family imbalance*. Cambridge, MA: Harvard University Press.

Elliott, J.G., Hufton, N.R., Hildreth, A., & Illushin, L. (1999). Factors influencing educational motivation: A study of attitudes, expectations and behaviour of children in Sunderland, Kentucky and St. Petersburg. *British Educational Research Journal, 25*, 75-94.

Elliott, J.G., Hufton, N., Illushin, L., & Willis W. (2001). The kids are doing all right: Differences in parental satisfaction, expectation and attribution in St. Petersburg and Sunderland, Kentucky. *Cambridge Journal of Education, 31*, 179-204.

Greenfield, P. (1994). Independence and interdependence as developmental scripts: Implications for theory, research, and practice. In R. Cocking and P. Greenfield (Eds.), *The cross-cultural roots of minority child development* (pp. 1-37). Hillsdale, NJ: Lawrence Erlbaum Associates.

Harkness, S., & Super, C. (1992). Parental ethnotheories in action. In I. E. Sigel, A. V. McGillicuddy-DeLisi, & J. J. Goodnow (Eds.), *Parental belief systems: The psychological consequences for children* (2nd ed., pp. 373-391). Hillsdale, NJ: Lawrence Erlbaum Associates.

Haste, H. (1994). *The sexual metaphor*. Cambridge, MA: Harvard University Press.

Hess, R., & Azuma, H. (1991). Cultural support for learning. *Educational Researcher, 20*(6), 2-8.

Hess, R. D., Chih-Miei, C., & McDevitt, T. M. (1987). Cultural variations in family beliefs about children's performance in mathematics: Comparisons among People's Republic of China, Chinese-American, and Caucasian-American families. *Journal of Educational Psychology, 79*, 179-188.

Holloway, S. (1988). Concepts of ability and effort in Japan and the United States. *Review of Educational Research, 58*, 327-345.

Holloway, S. D. (2000). *Contested childhoods: Diversity and change in Japanese preschools*. London: Routledge.

Holloway, S. D., Kashiwagi, K., Hess, R. D., & Azuma, H. (1986). Causal attributions by Japanese and American mothers about performance in mathematics. *International Journal of Psychology, 21*, 269-286.

Holloway, S., & Minami, M. (1996). Production and reproduction of culture: The dynamic role of mothers and children in early socialization. In D. Shwalb & B. Shwalb (Eds.), *Japanese childrearing: Two generations of scholarship* (pp. 164-75). New York: Guilford Press.

Hufton, N. R., & Elliott, J. G. (2000). Motivation to learn: The pedagogical nexus in the Russian school: Some implications for transnational research policy borrowing. *Educational Studies, 26*(1), 115-136.

Hufton, N. R., Elliott, J. G., & Illushin, L. (in press). Motivation to learn: The elusive role of culture: Qualitative accounts from three countries. *British Educational Research Journal, 27*(5).

Husen, T. (1967). *International study of achievement in mathematics*. New York: John Wiley & Sons.

Kagan, J. (1989). *Unstable ideas: Temperament, cognition, and self.* Cambridge, MA: Harvard University Press.

Keeves, J. P. (1995). The case for international comparisons. In J. J. Lane (Ed.), *Ferment in education: A look abroad* (pp. 169-189). Chicago: University of Chicago Press.

Kitayama, S. (2000). Collective construction of the self and social relationships: A rejoinder and some extensions. *Child Development, 71,* 1143-1146.

Kitayama, S., Markus, R., Matsumoto, H., & Noraskkunkit, V. (1997). Individual and collective processes in the construction of the self: Self-enhancement in the United States and self-criticism in Japan. *Journal of Personality and Social Psychology, 72,* 1245-1267.

Lampert, M. (1990). When the problem is not the question and the solution is not the answer: Mathematical knowing and teaching. *American Educational Research Journal, 27,* 29-63.

Lave, J. (1977). Tailor-made experiments and evaluating the intellectual consequences of apprenticeship training. *The Quarterly Newsletter of the Institute for Comparative Human Development, 1,* 1-5.

Lave, J. (1988). *Cognition in practice.* Cambridge, England: Cambridge University Press.

Lawrence-Lightfoot, S., & Davis, J. H. (1997). *The art and science of portraiture.* San Francisco: Jossey-Bass.

Lee, C. (1987). China's integrated approach to child care and socialization. Paper presented at the Society for Research in Child Development, Baltimore.

LeVine, R. (1977). Child rearing as cultural adaptation. In P. Leiderman, S. Tulkin, & A. Rosenfeld (Eds.), *Culture and infancy: Variations in the human experience* (pp. 15-27). New York: Academic Press.

Levy, R. I. (1973). *Tahitians: Mind and experience in the Society Islands.* Chicago: University of Chicago Press.

Li, J. (2000). What do U.S. and Chinese college students think learning is? Exploring learning models of American and Chinese. Paper presented at the 16th biennial meeting of the International Society for the Study of Behavioral Development, Beijing, China.

Li, J. (in press). Chinese conceptualization of learning. *Ethos.*

Markus, H., & Kitayama, S. (1991). Culture and the self: Implications for cognition, emotion, and motivation. *Psychological Review, 98,* 224-253.

Markus, H. R., Mullally, P. R., & Kitayama, S. (1997). Selfways: Diversity in modes of cultural participation. In U. Neisser & D. A. Jopling (Eds.), *The conceptual self in context: Culture, experience, self-understanding* (pp. 13-61). Cambridge, England: Cambridge University Press.

Marsh, H. W., & Shavelson, R. J. (1985). Self-concept: Its multifaceted, hierarchical structure. *Educational Psychologist, 20,* 107-125.

McKnight, C., Crosswhite, F., Dossey, J., Kifer, E., Swafford, J., Travers, K., & Cooney, T. (1987). *The underachieving curriculum: Assessing U.S. school mathematics from an international perspective.* Champaign, IL: Stipes.

Meyer, J., Ramirez, F., & Soysal, Y. (1992). World expansion of mass education, 1870-1980. *Sociology of Education, 65,* 128-149.

Miller, P. (1996). Instantiating culture through discourse practices: Some personal reflections on socialization and how to study it. In R. Jessor, A. Colby, & R. Schweder (Eds.), *Ethnography and human development: Context and meaning in social inquiry* (pp. 183-204). Chicago: University of Chicago Press.

Mouer, R., & Sugimoto, Y. (1986). *Images of Japanese society: A study in the social construction of reality.* London: Routledge and Kegan Paul.

Mouer, R. E., & Sugimoto, Y. (1990). *Images of Japanese society: a study in the social construction of reality.* London; New York: Kegan Paul International.

Munroe, R., & Munroe, R. (1997). A comparative anthropological perspective. In J. Berry, Y. Poortinga, & J. Pandey (Eds.), *Handbook of cross-cultural psychology: Vol. 1. Theory and method.* Boston: Allyn & Bacon.

Nicholls, J., & Hazzard, S. (1993). *Education as adventure: Lessons from second grade.* New York: Teachers College Press.

Nicholls, J. G. (1978). The development of the concepts of effort and ability, perception of own attainment, and the understanding that difficult tasks require more ability. *Child Development, 49,* 800-814.

Nicholls, J. G. (1989). *The competitive ethos and democratic education.* Cambridge, MA: Harvard University Press.

Nicholls, J. G., Cheung, P. C., Lauer, J., & Patachnick, M. (1989). Individual differences in academic motivation: Perceived ability, goals, beliefs, and values. *Learning and Individual Differences, 1,* 63-84.

Nicholls, J. G., Cobb, P., Wood, T., Yackel, E., & Patachnick, M. (1990). Assessing students' theories of success in mathematics: Individual and classroom differences. *Journal for Research in Mathematics Education, 21*(2), 109-122.

Ogbu, J. (1986). The consequences of the American caste system. In U. Neisser (Ed.), *The school achievement of minority children: New perspectives.* Hillsdale, NJ: Lawrence Erlbaum Associates.

Peak, L. (1991). *Learning to go to school in Japan.* Berkeley: University of California Press.

Pirie, S., & Kieren, T. (1992). Creating constructivist environments and constructing creative mathematics. *Educational Studies in Mathematics, 23,* 505-528.

Quihuis, G., Bempechat, J., Jimenez, N. V., & Boulay, B. A. (in press). Identifying students' implicit theories of intelligence: A study of meaning making in context. In J. Bempechat & J. Elliott (Eds.), *Achievement motivation in culture and context: Understanding children's learning experiences* (Vol. 96 [Summer]). San Francisco: Jossey-Bass.

Reese, L., Balzano, S., Gallimore, R., & Goldenberg, C. (1995). The concept of "educación": Latino family values and American schooling. *International Journal of Educational Research, 23,* 57-81.

Rogoff, B. (1990). *Apprenticeship in thinking: Cognitive development in a social context.* New York: Oxford University Press.

Roopnarine, J., & Carter, D. B. (1992). The cultural context of socialization: A much ignored issue! In J. Roopnarine & D. B. Carter (Eds.), *Annual advances in applied developmental psychology: Vol. 5. Parent-child socialization in diverse cultures* (pp. 245-251). Norwood, NJ: Ablex.

Sadler, M. (1979). *Selections from Michael Sadler: Studies in world citizenship.* Liverpool, England: Dejall & Meyorre.

Schurmans, M., & Dasen, P. (1992). Social representations of intelligence: Cote d'Ivoire and Switzerland. In M. V. Cranach, W. Doise, & G. Mugny (Eds.), *Social representations and the social bases of knowledge* (pp. 144-152). Lewiston, NY: Hogrefe & Huber.

Scribner, S. (1983/1992). Mind in action: A functional approach to thinking. *The Quarterly Newsletter of the Laboratory of Comparative Human Cognition, 14,* 103-110.

Serpell, R., & Hatano, G. (1997). Education, schooling, and literacy. In J. Berry, P. Dasen, & T. S. Saraswathi (Eds.), *Handbook of cross-cultural psychology: Vol. 2. Basic processes and human development* (pp. 339-375). Norwood, NJ: Ablex.

Shore, B. (1996). *Culture in mind: Cognition, culture, and the problem of meaning.* New York: Oxford University Press.

Shweder, R. (1990). Cultural psychology—What is it? In J. Stigler, R. Shweder, & G. Herdt (Eds.), *Cultural psychology: Essays on comparative human development* (pp. 1-43). New York: Cambridge University Press.

Shweder, R. (1997). The surprise of ethnography. *Ethos, 25,* 152-163.

Spiro, M. (1993). Is the Western conception of the self "peculiar" within the contexts of world cultures? *Ethos, 21,* 107-153.

Sternberg, R. J. (1990). Prototypes of competence and incompetence. In R. J. Sternberg & J. Kolligian, Jr. (Eds.), *Competence considered* (pp. 117-145). New Haven, CT: Yale University Press.

Stevenson, H., Chen, C., & Lee, S. (1993). Mathematics achievement of Chinese, Japanese, and American children: Ten years later. *Science, 259,* 53-58.

Stevenson, H., & Lee, S. (1990). Contexts of achievement: A study of American, Chinese, and Japanese children. *Monographs of the Society for Research in Child Development, 55* (1-2, Serial No. 221).

Stevenson, H., & Stigler, J. (1992). *The learning gap.* New York: Simon and Schuster.

Stevenson, H. W., Lee, S., & Stigler, J. W. (1986). Mathematics achievement of Chinese, Japanese and American children. *Science, 231,* 693-699.

Stigler, J., & Hiebert, J. (1999). *The teaching gap.* New York: Free Press.

Stigler, J. W., & Perry, M. (1988). Mathematics learning in Japanese, Chinese, and American classrooms. In G. B. Saxe & M. Gearhart (Eds.), *Children's mathematics* (Vol. 41). San Francisco: Jossey-Bass.

Stigler, J. W., & Perry, M. (1990). Mathematics learning in Japanese, Chinese, and American classrooms. In J. W. Stigler, R. A. Shweder, & G. Herdt (Eds.), *Cultural psychology: Essays on comparative human development* (pp. 328-353). Cambridge, England: Cambridge University Press.

Tobin, J., Wu, Y., & Davidson, D. (1989). *Preschool in three cultures.* New Haven, CT: Yale University Press.

Tudge, J., Hogan, D., Snezhkova, I., Kulakova, N., and Etz, K. (2000). Parents' child-rearing values and beliefs in the United States and Russia: The impact of culture and social class. *Infant and Child Development, 9,* 105-121.

Vygotsky, L. (Ed.). (1978). *Mind in society.* Cambridge, MA: Harvard University Press.

Weiner, B. (Ed.). (1972). *Theories of motivation: From mechanism to cognition.* Chicago: Markham.

Weiner, B. (1984). Principles for a theory of student motivation and their application within an attributional framework. In R. E. Ames & C. Ames (Eds.), *Research on motivation in education: Student motivation.* New York: Harcourt Brace Jovanovich.

Weiner, B. (1985). An attributional theory of achievement motivation and emotion. *Psychological Review, 92,* 548-573.

Weiner, B., Russell, D., & Lerman, D. (1979). The cognition-emotion process in achievement-related contexts. *Journal of Personality and Social Psychology, 37,* 1211-1220.

White, M. (1987). *The Japanese educational challenge.* New York: Free Press.

White, M., & LeVine, R. (1987). What is an "ii ko" (good child)? In H. Stevenson, H. Azuma, & K. Hakuta (Eds.), *Child development and education in Japan* (pp. 55-62). New York: Freeman.

6

Measuring Family Background in International Studies of Education: Conceptual Issues and Methodological Challenges

*Claudia Buchmann**

In all societies, the family plays a crucial role in shaping the educational experiences and achievement of children and the transmission of status from one generation to the next. Throughout the world, children of high-status parents are more likely to get ahead in school. Three interrelated processes—the transmission of financial capital, the transmission of cultural resources, and the transmission of social capital from parents to children—are most often called on to explain this phenomenon. But only fairly recently have studies begun to incorporate all three processes into empirical investigations of family background in determining children's educational status. In this chapter, I review the measurement of family background, tracing its increasingly complex conceptualization and examining the methods used to assess the impact of family background on educational outcomes in international and comparative research. Then I assess the quality and content of family background items of past large-scale international surveys in detail. Specifically, I focus on several surveys conducted by the International Association for the Evaluation of Educational Achievement (IEA): the Six Subject Study, the First and Second International Mathematics Studies, the Second International Science Study, and the Third International Mathematics and Science Study. I also discuss the Program for International Student Assessment, a current in-

*Claudia Buchmann is an assistant professor of sociology at Duke University.

ternational survey of student skill and knowledge being organized by the Organization for Economic Cooperation and Development (OECD).

Examining how large-scale international surveys have dealt with the challenge of measuring family background in a wide range of societies is a valuable exercise; they constitute an impressive foundation of knowledge on what works and what does not. Based on an assessment of these surveys, I offer recommendations for future international studies of educational achievement to consider in the conceptualization and measurement of family background. These include ways to replicate the successes and avoid the pitfalls of prior conceptualizations of family background, as well as ways to expand the measurement of family background to better account for the multidimensional influences and processes of families that have been found to be related directly to children's academic success.

WHY MEASURE FAMILY BACKGROUND?

Why is it important to measure family background well in international comparative studies of education? There are many good answers to this question, but the most pressing for policy makers relate to the following factors:

(1) The importance of controlling for family influences in investigations of the impact of schools on children's learning and achievement, so that we can examine school effects net of family background effects. As Coleman (1975, p. 359) stated more than twenty years ago: "In the attempt to discover effects of school factors on achievement, perhaps the principal villain is the fact that student populations in different schools differ at the outset, and because of this difference, it is not possible merely to judge the quality of a school by the achievements of the students leaving it. It is necessary to control in some way for the variations in student input with which the teachers and staff of the school are confronted." It is crucial to know how students in a population are distributed on a wide range of family factors that are themselves important predictors of achievement; only then can we assess the role of the school in achieving its social and economic objectives, most notably its efficacy in providing greater equality of educational opportunity.

(2) The necessity to improve our knowledge of the ways that the family, as an institution, affects children's ability and motivation to learn as well as academic achievement. A better understanding of how family background and home environment relate to student learning can help societies formulate policies that may serve to intervene in detrimental family processes or enhance beneficial ones. We are constantly looking

for ways to alter educational institutions to improve children's lives. The same thinking should be applied to the family institution, especially in this era of rapidly changing family life.

(3) The importance of controlling for family influences in comparative research on educational achievement. If, in addition to mean levels of achievement, we want to compare the *distribution* of educational achievement across societies, we need to measure the social conditions across which achievement (or any other educational outcome) is distributed. Family background is one of the most important social conditions to consider when trying to compare populations cross-nationally. This point can be demonstrated with a simple hypothetical two-country comparison. If Country A greatly outperforms Country B on some measure of achievement, it may be tempting to attribute this difference to the quality of education in the two countries. But if upon further investigation we discover that background characteristics of the two comparison populations are very different—Country A has an ethnically and culturally homogeneous population and relatively low income inequality; Country B is culturally and ethnically diverse, is marked by great income inequality, and has experienced a rapid influx of first-generation immigrants from poor countries—then it becomes clear that the differences in achievement scores may say more about the differences of the student populations than about the quality of education in the two countries. The broad distribution of background influences may well be related to a wider distribution of achievement scores in that context. Moreover, the goals and challenges facing the educational system in Country B are likely quite different from those in Country A. Some would use such examples to argue that comparing societies with their attendant cultural, social, and educational differences is a futile exercise. I believe such comparisons can cumulate in new knowledge on learning processes and school effectiveness if we strive to measure and account for these variations in social conditions in comparative research on educational achievement.

One or more of these goals have guided much of the international research on the relationship between family influences and educational outcomes. The following section reviews this literature and its contributions to these longstanding issues.

FAMILY BACKGROUND AND EDUCATIONAL OUTCOMES: WHAT DO WE KNOW?

Although socioeconomic status has always been at the core of the concept of family background, over time, the concept has expanded to include other aspects of families—such as family structure, parental involvement with children's schooling, and cultural and educational resources—in order to reflect the complex, multidimensional ways in which family background and home environment influence individual educational outcomes. Here I focus on how the concept of family background has grown from the initial specification of socioeconomic standing of the family of origin, to include family structure and other demographic characteristics, as well as family social and cultural capital.

Socioeconomic Status

Three components—parent's education, parent's occupation, and family income—typically comprise the measure of family socioeconomic status (SES). Status attainment research begun by sociologists in the United States more than three decades ago laid the foundation for this conceptualization of socioeconomic status and a methodology—usually path analysis and multiple regression techniques with large survey data sets—to investigate the intergenerational transmission of status. In the classic study, *The American Occupational Structure,* Blau and Duncan (1967) present a basic model of the stratification process in which father's education and occupational status explain son's educational attainment, and all three variables, in turn, explain son's occupational attainment. Around the same time, Sewell and colleagues at the University of Wisconsin began publishing papers that addressed questions regarding the relative impacts of family background and schooling on subsequent educational and occupational attainments (Sewell, Haller, & Portes, 1969; Sewell & Hauser, 1975). A notable aspect of the "Wisconsin model" of status attainment was its focus on social-psychological factors, such as aspirations and motivation, in conjunction with family socioeconomic status in determining student achievement. In this regard, the Wisconsin model attempted to specify the mediating mechanisms by which family origins influenced individual educational and occupational outcomes. While Blau and Duncan specified father's occupation and education as separate influences, the Wisconsin researchers usually combined these measures, along with mother's education and family income, into a single measure of socioeconomic status (Haller & Portes, 1973, p. 63). Despite these measurement differences, both models concluded that socioeconomic status strongly determined educational attainment.

These classic works established a framework for the study of family background on educational attainment in a wide range of contexts. By the early 1980s, more than 500 papers had attempted to replicate or extend their basic findings (Campbell, 1983). Some researchers applied these constructs to nationally representative samples in the United States (Jencks, 1972); others examined their generalizability to very different countries and contexts (Gerber & Hout, 1995; Hansen & Haller, 1973; Smith & Cheung, 1986). Human capital models in economics, in which family background and schooling decisions determined education and earnings outcomes (Becker & Tomes, 1979), also contributed to this growing field.

A thorough review of the burgeoning research on the relationship between family SES and educational outcomes could easily fill a book; instead Table 6-1 provides a reasonably representative sample of the international research on the relationship between socioeconomic status and educational attainment and achievement published since 1970. For each study, the table includes the country of focus, the definition and measurement of SES, the educational outcome studied, and key findings regarding the impact of SES on attainment or achievement. By focusing solely on family background and its relationship to educational outcomes, this summary necessarily neglects other information,[1] but permits an assessment of the conceptualization and measurement of socioeconomic status in international studies of educational outcomes.

The table reflects several interesting aspects of the field in general. First, most studies utilized survey data and statistical methods to examine the relationship between family SES and educational outcomes. Some early studies only reported correlations or used analysis of covariance to investigate these relationships, but the bulk of research in this field has relied on multivariate modeling strategies such as regression analysis.

Second, the research on educational attainment and the research on achievement have developed along somewhat distinct lines, with the former often the purview of sociologists, economists, and demographers, and the latter more often studied by educational researchers and policy analysts. Table 6-1 reflects this development by listing studies of attainment (or in some cases, enrollment) in Panel A, and studies of achievement in Panel B. This distinction should not be overstated; certainly sociologists such as Coleman and others made significant contributions to the early study of educational achievement. Nonetheless, it draws attention to some differences in the scope and interests of these two domains of research. For example, although the impact of family background factors is often a central concern in the research on educational attainment, much of the research on educational achievement is concerned with the effects of school factors, curriculum, or pedagogy; family background receives secondary consideration or is treated merely as a control variable. This is partly due to a longstanding preoccupation with finding "school effects" in response to early studies, such as the Coleman Report (Coleman et al., 1966), which seemed to suggest that school-level differences had little impact on variation among individual children in terms of their academic success.

Third, there is more international and comparative research on the determinants of attainment than on the determinants of achievement, largely because achievement data are more difficult to acquire. National population censuses and surveys on diverse topics frequently contain data on the educational histories of all household members that can be used to construct measures of educational attainment. But achievement data must be gathered through the administration of cognitive tests or, in the case of grade-point average or national exam scores, the acquisition of students' school records, both of which are time-consuming research strategies. The fact that so many of the studies of achievement in Table 6-1 utilize IEA data underscores the importance of these large-scale international surveys as major data sources for research on educational achievement. Here I briefly discuss the major methods and findings of these two interrelated lines of work: research on educational attainment and research on educational achievement.

Research on Educational Attainment

Building on the foundation laid by status attainment research in the United States, much research has examined the role of social origins in determining educational and occupational status and mobility in a range of countries. Some researchers have examined how this relationship changes over time with large societal changes, such as the expansion of formal schooling, the industrialization of society, or the transition from socialism to capitalism. Regardless of their larger agendas, studies in this realm have contributed greatly to our understanding of how family socioeconomic status shapes educational attainment in a wide range of contexts.

Family background has been treated more systematically in research on educational attainment than in research on achievement. The influence of the Blau-Duncan and Wisconsin models is clearly evident; most studies in Panel A conceptualize socioeconomic status as either father's education and occupation or a composite measure of these and other family background factors. Some researchers have had to alter this approach due to data limitations or considerations of the local context, but still, the systematic approach to the measurement of family background is striking.

Occupational status typically is measured via scales that have been developed to generalize the prestige associated with occupations across a wide range of societies. The earliest of these was the Socioeconomic Index (SEI) scale formulated by Duncan (1961) for the United States and subsequently modified by other researchers for other countries. Many of the studies in Panel A use a modified Duncan SEI scale for father's occupational status. Also building on Duncan's scale, comparative stratification

TABLE 6-1   International Studies of the Relationship Between Family
Socioeconomic Status and Educational Outcomes

Panel A: Attainment

Study	Country	Measures of Family Socioeconomic Status
Hansen & Haller, 1973	Costa Rica	Occupational status, consumption status (index of parental education, house construction, and household possessions)
Kerckhoff, 1974	Great Britain	Father's education, father's occupational status
Currie, 1977	Uganda	Father's education, father's occupational status
Cochrane & Jamison, 1982	Thailand	Father's education, mother's education, land ownership
Simkus & Andorka, 1982	Hungary	Father's occupation
Behrman & Wolfe, 1984	Nicaragua	Father's education, mother's education, number of siblings, mother present
Mukweso, Papagiannis, & Milton, 1984	Zaire	Father's education, father's occupational status, index of consumption goods
Whyte & Parrish, 1984	China	Father's education, father's occupational status
Robinson & Garnier, 1985	France	Father's education, father's class
Smith & Cheung, 1986	Philippines	Father's education, father's occupational status
Jamison & Lockheed, 1987	Nepal	Father's education, father's literacy, father's modernity, caste, household landholdings
King & Lillard, 1987	Malaysia	Father's education, mother's education
Pong & Post, 1991	Hong Kong	Father's occupational status, mother's education
Lin & Bian, 1991	China	Father's education, father's occupational status
Paterson, 1991	Scotland	Father's occupation, mother's education., household composition
Shavit & Pierce, 1991	Israel	Mother's education, father's education, father's occupational status
Stevenson & Baker, 1992	Japan	Father's education, mother's education, family income

Outcome	Results
Attainment	Indirect (through aspirations) on attainment
Attainment	Positive effects on attainment
Attainment	Positive effects on attainment
Enrollment	Education vars positive on enrollment
Attainment	Indirect (through aspirations) on attainment
Attainment[a]	Positive effect on attainment
Attainment	Positive effects on attainment; stronger effect of mother's ed. than father's ed. on all children
Attainment	Positive effects on attainment
Attainment	Positive effects on attainment
Attainment	Positive effects on attainment
Attainment	Positive effects on attainment
Enrollment	Positive effects on attainment
Attainment	Positive effects on attainment; larger effects of mother's ed. on daughters' attainment
Attainment	Positive effects on attainment
Attainment	Positive effects on attainment
Attainment	Positive effects on attainment
Attainment	Positive effects on attainment
University enrollment	Positive effects on university enrollment

continues

TABLE 6-1   Continued

Study	Country	Measures of Family Socioeconomic Status
Hout, Raftery, & Bell, 1993	United States	Father's education, father's occupational status, mother's education
Blossfeld, 1993	Germany	Father's education, father's occupational status
De Graaf & Ganzeboom, 1993	Netherlands	Father's education, father's occupational status
Jonsson, 1993	Sweden	Father's education, father's occupational status
Kerckhoff & Trott, 1993	England Wales	Father's education, father's occupational status
Cobalti & Schizzerotto, 1993	Italy	Father's education, father's occupational status
Buchmann, Charles, & Sacchi, 1993	Switzerland	Father's education, father's occupational status
Tsai & Chiu, 1993	Taiwan	Father's education, father's occupational status, mother's education
Treiman & Yamaguchi, 1993	Japan	Father's education, father's occupational status
Mateju, 1993	Czechoslovakia	Father's education, father's occupational status
Szelenyi & Aschaffenburg, 1993	Hungary	Father's education, father's occupational status
Heyns & Bialecki, 1993	Poland	Father's education, father's occupational status
Shavit, 1993	Israel	Father's education, father's occupational status
Lillard & Willis, 1994	Malaysia	Father's education, father's earnings, mother's education
Fuller, Singer, & Keiley, 1995	Botswana	Mother's education, mother's employment status, senior male's employment status, household quality and possessions
Gerber & Hout, 1995	Soviet Russia	Parents' education, occupational status of main income earner in household

Outcome	Results
Attainment[a]	Positive effects on attainment
Attainment[a]	Positive effects on attainment
Attainment[a]	Positive effects on attainment
Attainment[a]	Positive effects on attainment
Attainment[a]	Positive effects on attainment
Attainment[a]	Positive effects on attainment
Attainment[a]	Positive effects on attainment
Attainment[a]	Positive effects on attainment
Attainment[a]	Positive effects on attainment
Attainment[a]	Positive effects on attainment
Attainment[a]	Positive effects on attainment
Attainment[a]	Positive effects on attainment
Attainment[a]	Positive effects on attainment
Attainment	Positive effects on attainment; mother's ed. stronger for daughters
Enrollment (drop out)	Mother's education significantly related to dropout; no effects of other variables
Attainment[a]	Positive effects on attainment

continues

TABLE 6-1   Continued

Study	Country	Measures of Family Socioeconomic Status
Pong, 1996	Malaysia	Household head's earned income, mother's education
Tansel, 1997	Cote D'Ivoire Ghana	Father's education, mother's education Total household expenditure
Zhou, Moen, & Tuma, 1998	China	Father's education, father's occupational status
Wong, 1998	Czechoslovakia	Father's education, household possessions
Buchmann, 2000	Kenya	Parent's education, household financial status

Panel B: Achievement

Study	IEA Data	Country	Measures of Family Socioeconomic Status
Comber & Keeves, 1973	FISS	19 countries	Home background (index)
Rosier, 1974	FISS	Australia	Home circumstances (index)
Shukla, 1974	FISS	India	Father's occupation, father's education, mother's education, use of dictionary, number of books in the home, family size
Pollock, 1974	FISS	Scotland	Father's occupation, number of books in the home, family size
Heyneman, 1976		Uganda	Parents' occupation, parents' education, household possessions
Lanzas & Kingston, 1981		Zaire	Education of relative with greatest influence on student's life (e.g., mother, father, uncle, grandparent)
Cooksey, 1981		Cameroon	Mother's and father's education, mother's and father's occupation, home amenities (running water, electricity, toilet, refrigerator, cooker)
Niles, 1981		Sri Lanka	Family SES (index of father's occupation, father's education, mother's education, family income)
Heyneman & Loxley, 1983	SISS	29 countries	Father's occupation, father's education, mother's education, books in home, dictionary or other measure of consumption in home

Outcome	Results
Enrollment	Positive effects on enrollment
Enrollment, Attainment	Positive effects of father's and mother's education; mother's education stronger for daughters in Ghana
Entry to 3 levels of schooling	Positive effects on entry at all levels
Attainment	Positive effects on attainment
Enrollment	Positive effects on enrollment

Outcome	Results
Science achievement	Positive effect
Science achievement	Positive effect
Hindi and science achievement in the home	Positive effect of father's occ. and books
Science achievement	Positive effect of father's occ.
National exam performance	Positive effect
English achievement	Modest positive effect for students living with parents; no effect for those living with relatives
National exam performance	Positive effect on on performance
Achievement	Positive effect
Science achievement	Positive effect, but smaller than school effects, especially in poorer countries

continues

TABLE 6-1 Continued

Study	IEA Data	Country	Measures of Family Socioeconomic Status
Heyneman, Jamison, & Montenegro, 1984		Philippines	Parent's education
Lockheed, Vail, & Fuller, 1986	SIMS	Thailand	Father's occupation, mother's education, home language
Lockheed, Fuller, & Nyirongo, 1989	SIMS	Thailand	Mother's education, father's occupation
		Malawi	Mother's education, father's occupation, electricity in home, radio in home
Riddell, 1989		Zimbabwe	Father's occupation, father's education, electricity in the home
Jimenez & Lockheed, 1989	SIMS	Thailand	Father's occupation, mother's education, home language
Holloway, Fuller, Hess et al., 1990		Japan United States	Father's occupation, father's education, mother's education
Lee & Lockheed, 1990	SIMS	Nigeria	Father's occupation (professional versus non-professional)
Katsillis & Rubinson, 1990		Greece	Family SES (index of father's education, father's occupation, mother's education, family income), father's class status
Lockheed & Longford, 1991	SIMS	Thailand	Father's occupation, mother's education, home use of four-function calculator, home language
Zuzovsky & Aitkin, 1991	SISS	Israel	Family SES (index of father's occupation, mother's education, household composition)
Gamoran, 1991	SIMS	United States	Parent's education
Baker, Riordan, & Schaub, 1995	SIMS	Belgium New Zealand Thailand Japan	Father's occupation, mother's education, home language

[a]Attainment measured in terms of transitions following Mare (1981).

Outcome	Results
Science, math Filipino achievement	Positive effect net of textbooks
Math achievement	Positive effect on math pretest; negligible effect on math posttest, net of pretest
Math achievement	Positive effect
Math and language (math and language)	No effect of ed. or occ.; positive effect of housing measures
English and math achievement	Positive effect
Math achievement	Father's occupation positive on achievement gains for males in single-sex schools, mother's ed. for females
Educational achievement	Positive effects
Math achievement	Positive effects, net of school type
Achievement (GPA)	Positive effects of family SES on achievement; no effect of father's class status
Math achievement	Positive effects
Science achievement	Positive effect but varies by school
Math achievement	Positive effect
Math achievement	Used as a control to model effect of mixed versus single-sex schools

researchers have devoted considerable effort to developing internationally comparative scales of occupational prestige and testing their reliability cross-culturally. Two of these scales, the Standard International Occupational Prestige (SIOP) scale (Treiman, 1977) and the International Socioeconomic Index (ISEI) of occupational status (Ganzeboom, DeGraaf, & Treiman, 1992), have been used extensively in international research. More recently, Ganzeboom and Treiman (1996) have developed a prestige and status scale for the 1988 International Standard Classification of Occupations (ISCO) of the International Labor Office that will likely be used extensively in future research. Although most prior research has relied on paternal occupational status in constructing this measure, recent empirical evidence indicates that mother's occupational status has a strong impact on educational achievement (Dronkers, 1989) and attainment (Kalmijn, 1994), independent of father's education and occupational status. Such findings, combined with the increasing prevalence of women's full-time labor force participation throughout the world, suggest that mother's occupational status should be included as a measure of family background in future research.

The inclusion of mother's education has been more common, perhaps because early status attainment research indicated that mother's education had positive effects on children's schooling, net of father's education and occupational status (Mare, 1981; Sewell & Hauser, 1975). In many cases, maternal and paternal education are highly correlated and researchers use one or the other as a measure of parental education. In contexts where mothers spend more time with their children or where males typically are absent from the household, it is reasonable to expect that mother's education should have a stronger impact than father's education, and researchers have used mother's education as the measure for parental education (see Fuller, Singer, & Keiley, 1995, for the case of Botswana). Another strategy has been to use the sum of both parents' schooling.

As in the case of occupational status, scales have been developed for measuring educational attainment with the goal of ensuring comparability cross-nationally. CASMIN and ISCED are two such scales. The International Standard Classification of Education (ISCED) was originally developed by UNESCO and is regularly used by UNESCO and other international organizations for reporting national education statistics. The CASMIN categories were developed as part of a project known as "Comparative Analysis of Social Mobility in Industrial Nations." Mueller and colleagues at the University of Mannheim, Germany developed CASMIN with the express purpose of facilitating comparative research on social stratification and mobility. Table 6-2 presents the details of both of these classification schemes.

TABLE 6-2   ISCED and CASMIN Educational Classification Schemes

ISCED (International Standard Classification of Education-1997)

0.   Preprimary level of education
1.   Primary level of education (first stage of basic education)
2.   Lower secondary level of education (second stage of basic education)
3.   Upper secondary level of education
4.   Postsecondary, nontertiary education
5.   First stage of tertiary education (not leading directly to an advanced research qualification)
6.   Second stage of tertiary education (leading to an advanced research qualification)

CASMIN (Comparative Analysis of Social Mobility in Industrial Nations)

1a.   Less than compulsory level; no formal certificate
1b.   Minimum, compulsory general elementary certificate
1c.   Minimum, compulsory general education plus basic vocational qualification
2a.   Advanced vocational qualification or intermediate general education plus vocational qualification
2b.   Intermediate academic or general qualification
2c.   Full maturity secondary certificate (Abitur, A-level)
3a.   Lower tertiary certificate (usually vocational)
3b.   Higher tertiary certificate (university degree or above)

SOURCES: UNESCO (1997); Mueller & Karle (1993).

ISCED and CASMIN are similar in that they focus on the levels of education completed—elementary, secondary, and tertiary education—and specify some subdivisions at each level. The CASMIN scale goes a step further to distinguish general or academic credentials from vocational credentials. Though they are not without problems (see Kerckhoff, Ezell, & Brown, 2002), these scales have facilitated international comparisons of educational systems and educational stratification.

Developing reliable measures of family wealth or income in studies of educational attainment has been more complicated than developing measures of parental education or occupational status because it is very difficult to get high response rates on income questions, and the accuracy of responses is often suspect. Capturing good comparative measures of wealth in international research is even more problematic, because income and wealth categories seldom are comparable across societies with different income distributions and levels of economic development. These and other challenges with collecting income data have led many researchers to use other measures as proxies for family wealth, such as indices of home possessions and/or home structural characteristics. Some researchers argue that such indices are even better approximations of long-term wealth, because they reflect earnings over a lifetime or the purchasing power of families, while income measures only reflect a particular time point (Filmer & Pritchett, 1999; Liebowitz, 1974; Wong, 1998).

Although generalizations about the large body of research on family background and educational outcomes gloss over the rich details from specific studies, they are nonetheless useful for tracing the progress of this research. First, as the last column of Table 6-1 shows, virtually all studies find that socioeconomic status has a substantial impact on educational attainment across a wide range of contexts. Second, father's education usually is found to be a stronger determinant than occupational status or mother's education, although the latter measures are also usually important. Finally, family socioeconomic status tends to have a larger impact on educational attainment and achievement in the earlier stages of the student's life course than in later ones. But even in later stages—especially in societies where higher education involves substantial cost—family effects are still evident (Steelman & Powell, 1989).

Research on Educational Achievement

In the past three decades, a great deal of research has focused on the role of family background and school effects on educational achievement. The stimuli for much of this research were two major projects, the Coleman Report (Coleman et al., 1966) in the United States and the Plowden Report in Great Britain (Peaker, 1971), which generally concluded that family background was more important than school factors in determining children's educational achievement. These studies sparked a great deal of interest in assessing the determinants of educational attainment and achievement and set off a lively debate regarding the roles of family and school factors in this process.

This debate was limited largely to industrialized countries, primarily the United States and Great Britain, until Heyneman (1976) published the results of his "Coleman Report for a developing country". In his study of seventh-grade students from 67 primary schools in Uganda, Heyneman replicated the design of the Coleman Report and found significant effects of school facilities and weak effects of family background on academic achievement. He believed these results to be due to the greater variance in physical facilities of schools and the smaller variance of social class in Uganda.

In subsequent research with IEA data, Heyneman and Loxley (1983) generalized these findings to other developing countries and found that the portion of the variance in achievement attributable to family background was generally much smaller, and that attributable to school quality generally much larger, in developing versus industrialized countries. They concluded that "the poorer the country, the greater the impact of school and teacher quality on achievement" (p. 1180). By the mid-1990s, more than 100 studies of school effects had been conducted in a wide range of developing countries, the majority of which found significant effects of school factors, net of family background, on achievement (see Fuller, 1987, and Fuller & Clarke, 1994, for reviews). Most of these studies utilized the production function approach[2] and regression analysis to identify the specific determinants of achievement and make inferences about the relative importance of the various inputs to student performance.

From these studies, some general cross-national patterns regarding school effects on student achievement have emerged. Although U.S.-based research suggests that student-teacher ratios and teacher salaries are most important school inputs for student achievement (Card and Krueger, 1992; Hedges, Laine, & Greenwald, 1994), studies in developing countries have found that more basic material inputs such as textbooks, libraries, and teacher training strongly determine achievement (Behrman & Birdsall, 1983; Heyneman & Jamison, 1980; Heyneman & Loxley, 1983; Lockheed, Vail, & Fuller, 1986). Expensive inputs, such as science laboratories, increased teachers' salaries, and reduced class size, appear to have little effect (Cohn & Rossmiller, 1987). The general conclusion is that basic material inputs are most important in contexts that have inadequate or highly variable educational resources (developing countries), but are less important in contexts where a minimum level of basic resources has been achieved (industrialized countries).

The school effects literature, however, has been critiqued extensively on various fronts and some have questioned the validity of claims regarding cross-national variations in the patterns of school effects. Some critics have questioned the adequacy of the measurement of family background in studies of achievement, which generally has been less systematic than that in research on educational attainment. Specifically, numerous school effects studies have used inadequate or inappropriate controls for family background. Fuller and Clarke comment astutely on this problem:

> The aggregate influence of schooling in developing countries has probably been overstated due to the underspecification of student background factors. . . . The greatest weakness here is the lack of social class measures that are culturally relevant to the particular society or community being studied. If imprecise SES indicators from the West are simply imported and error terms contain unmeasured elements of family background that are highly correlated with school quality, achievement effects will be mistakenly attributed to school factors. Evidence from Indonesia, Malawi, Thailand, and Zimbabwe shows that, when multi-

ple, situationally relevant indicators of class and ethnicity are utilized, the remaining proportion of achievement variance that can possibly be related to school factors diminishes (Lockheed, Fuller, & Nyirongo, 1989; Ross & Postlethwaite, 1989, 1992). In Indonesia, Ross and Postlethwaite included 11 modern possessions and 10 types of livestock to validly discriminate families' levels of wealth and social class; together, over half of the total variance explained was attributable to these factors, for achievement in Bahasa, math, and science. (Fuller & Clarke, 1994, p. 136)

Of course, as with all international comparative research, the challenge is to walk the fine line between sensitivity to local context and the concern for comparability across multiple contexts. Although researchers should gauge the appropriateness of "Western-based" measures in non-Western contexts and alter them accordingly, they must also remember that the use of widely divergent measures or concepts leads to results that are less comparable than when similar measures and models are used.

Others have criticized school effects studies on methodological grounds, specifically their reliance on OLS regression analysis and the use of the R-squared measure to determine the impact of family and school effects on student achievement. As Riddell (1989, p. 487) notes, "[C]riticism of such arbitrary use of the proportion of variance as a measure of importance is at least as old as the criticism of the Plowden report. Yet such criticism does not seem to have prevented its continued misuse." Another methodological caveat of the school effects research involves the "misapplication of a single-level model to a reality that is clearly hierarchical" (Riddell, 1989, p. 484). This problem was likely exacerbated by the use of aggregate data, which inflate estimated effects of family background relative to classroom and school effects (Bidwell & Kasarda, 1980).

In the late 1980s, a new generation of "effective school" research in the United States revisited longstanding questions regarding school and family effects on achievement with multilevel modeling techniques (Aitkin & Longford, 1986; Raudenbush & Bryk, 1986). These analytical strategies allow researchers to take account of the hierarchical nature of most educational data, thereby addressing some of the methodological shortcomings of prior work. Only a few studies have utilized multilevel models to examine school effects in international research, and their results are quite interesting. In contrast to previous research utilizing the production function approach, these studies find greater effects of family background than school factors on educational achievement in Zimbabwe (Riddell, 1989) and Thailand (Lockheed & Longford, 1991). For example, in their analysis of Thai data, Lockheed and Longford find that school-level differences contributed 32 percent of the explained variance in student mathematics achievement, while family and individual factors contributed 68 percent of the explained variance. These studies raise questions about past generalizations regarding the differential effects of family background and school factors in developing versus developed countries. Moreover, they have reinvigorated discussions over the proper way to measure and study school effects (for a recent exchange, see Hanushek, 1995; Kremer, 1995). Clearly, the long debate regarding school effects is far from resolved, and more research is needed before definitive conclusions can be established.

Beyond Socioeconomic Status: Other Measures of Family Background

As important as it is, family socioeconomic status captures only one aspect of family background in determining individuals' educational outcomes. Over time the definition of family background has grown increasingly complex, as substantial research has found that family structure, parental involvement, educational resources in the home, and family social and cultural capital often have independent influences, net of socioeconomic status, on children's educational outcomes.

Family Structure

Substantial research demonstrates that features of family structure, such as the number of children or the presence of one versus two parents in the household, have ramifications for educational outcomes. Studies of industrialized countries consistently document an inverse relationship between family size and educational performance that persists net of parental education and family income (Blake, 1989; Downey, 1995; Steelman & Powell, 1989). A prominent explanation for this relationship is the "resource dilution hypothesis," which stresses that material resources and parental attention are diluted with additional children in the household. Negative associations between sibship size and educational outcomes have been replicated in some developing countries, including Thailand (Knodel, Havanon, & Sittitrai, 1990), Malaysia (Parish & Willis, 1993; Pong, 1997), the Dominican Republic, and the Philippines (Montgomery & Lloyd, 1997). Similarly, there are well-documented negative effects of single parenthood on children's educational outcomes in the United States and other industrialized countries. These range from a greater probability of school dropout to lower achievement, and have been attributed in part to economic stress associated with female headship and in part to the lack of human or social capital in the household (McLanahan & Sandefur, 1994; see Seltzer, 1994, for a review).

Importantly, recent research in developing countries suggests that cross-cultural differences may mitigate the disadvantages of large family size or single parenthood on children's schooling. In some societies, extended family systems and a more collectivist cultural orientation may offset the otherwise detrimental impacts of these family features. For example, Lloyd and Blanc (1996) found that extended family networks in sub-Saharan Africa enable children with academic promise to move to households of "patron" family members, who help them gain access to higher quality schools. In Malaysia, Pong (1996) found that children of divorced mothers, but not of widowed mothers, have lower school participation rates than children of two-parent families. These results are likely due to the buffering role of large kinship systems in Malaysia, whereby widows receive more material support from family members than do divorced mothers (p. 248).

These studies remind researchers to be cognizant of important sociocultural variations as they design questions on family background, and specifically family structure, in cross-national surveys. If such questions are designed carefully, they could be immensely useful to researchers trying to map cross-cultural variations in the relationship between family structure and educational outcomes. Although single-country studies such as those already mentioned point to possible sociocultural patterns in this relationship, the lack of comparable international data on family structure and schooling to date has hindered comparative cross-national research on this topic.

Family Social and Cultural Capital

In addition to human capital (parental education, occupational status) and financial capital (wealth), families may possess social capital, which exists in the relations among persons (Coleman, 1988), and cultural capital, or knowledge of socially valued cultural cues (Bourdieu & Passeron, 1977; DiMaggio, 1982; Lareau, 1989). Both of these concepts have become very popular among social scientists and policy makers as empirical evidence of the importance of social and cultural capital as predictors of children's school success expands rapidly.

Coleman, one of the early and most influential proponents of social capital, defined the term as a social structural asset for the individual that facilitates certain beneficial actions and outcomes for those who occupy a given social structure. "Trust, obligations and expectations, norms, relations of authority, and shared information are all examples of social capital because they are resources that arise from the social relationships of individuals who share membership in a common social structure" (Carbonaro, 1998, p. 296). Social capital exists both within the family and between the family and external others (Coleman, 1988, pp. S109-116). Within the family, social capital relates to parent-child ties such as the attention parents devote to their children and their children's education. Outside the family it pertains to social relationships among parents and parents' relationships with the institutions (e.g., schools) in the community.

Families also vary in the degree to which they possess cultural capital, or "widely shared, high-status cultural signals (attitudes, preferences, formal knowledge, behaviors) used for social and cultural exclusion" (Lamont & Lareau, 1988, p. 156). The concept is typically operationalized as participation in high-brow cultural activities, such as reading literature, attending concerts, and visiting art museums as well as the presence of cultural objects (books, music) in the home (Teachman, 1987). Several studies have found that cultural capital, measured as student or parental participation in and preferences for such activities, has significant positive effects on educational attainment (De Graaf, 1986; DiMaggio 1982).

Of course, the cultural codes that are considered valuable should vary from society to society (De Graaf, De Graaf, & Kraaykamp, 2000, p. 93). Because societies differ in the institutionalization of high culture, it is important to consider how cultural capital is determined by national differences in educational structures and other societal characteristics. For example, it appears that Bourdieu's original conception of cultural capital is more appropriate for the case of his home country, France, than for the United States or Great Britain. In fact, some researchers have argued that an emphasis on high-brow cultural activities misses other aspects of cultural capital that should be more relevant to educational success for some groups and in some societies (Buchmann, 2002; De Graaf et al., 2000; Farkas, 1996). Among low-status or poor populations, a conceptualization of cultural capital that focuses on the reading habits and linguistics skills of parents may be more relevant. Parents can transmit linguistic and cognitive skills to children through their own reading behaviors and by helping children become familiar with reading. Research has found parental reading habits to be beneficial to children's educational performance (Farkas, 1996). In the Netherlands, parental reading habits were more important for children from low social origins than for children from high socioeconomic backgrounds (De Graaf et al., 2000). Finally, research on immigrant populations finds that the ability to speak the language of school instruction is a valuable form of cultural capital that promotes students' aspirations and achievement (Stanton-Salazar & Dornbush, 1995).

Compared to the research on other aspects of family background, the study of social and cultural capital as it relates to children's schooling is still in its early stages, and the concepts of social and cultural capital continue to be refined. As in the case of research on family structure, there has been relatively little comparative research on this topic, thus we do not yet understand how these forms of capital and their impact on educational outcomes vary across societies.

In sum, our knowledge of the relationship between family background and educational outcomes has expanded greatly in recent decades. Indeed, substantial evidence from virtually every society in the world demonstrates that individuals' social origins impact their educational experiences. In addition to identifying this fundamental relationship, research has detailed some of the nuances and variations in this relationship across societies. Moreover, significant progress has been made in understanding how family background matters, how family structure intervenes in the relationship between SES and educational outcomes, and the mechanisms by which parents are able to transmit social status to their children via social and cultural capital. Much work remains to be done in terms of further specifying the multidimensional impacts of family environment on children's schooling, finding ways to improve schools in order to raise the achievements of children from all social backgrounds, and minimizing the impact of such inequalities to the greatest extent possible.

Large-scale international surveys have played a central role in producing the knowledge just discussed and will likely play a greater role in the future. Because they are a major source of standardized and comparative data on the issues of concern to educational researchers and policy makers, they can be especially valuable for comparative cross-national research. But for these surveys to be most useful for addressing central empirical and policy-oriented questions, they must be responsive to the knowledge amassed from the large field of research discussed. The design of these surveys, and their instrumentation regarding family background in particular, will determine the kinds of research questions that can be handled with such survey data, whether specific knowledge gaps can be rectified, and the kinds of answers that might be possible.

FAMILY BACKGROUND MEASURES IN LARGE-SCALE INTERNATIONAL SURVEYS OF EDUCATION

To some degree, large-scale international assessments of educational achievement have followed a similar trajectory to that of the empirical literature discussed, in that the conceptualization and measurement of family background in such surveys has grown more complex and, with some exceptions, extensive over time. But these surveys also have been criticized for their approaches to measuring family background. In an early critique, Inkeles (1979) faults IEA for, among other things, under-analyzing "the relation between school achievement and separate social groups (social class, race, religious or ethnic groups)" (cited in Noah, 1987, p. 144; see also Theisen, Achola, & Boakari, 1983). More recently, Goldstein (1995, p. 12) summarized these studies' measurement of family background in this way: "With some exceptions, such as the IEA second mathematics study, there is little reliable background extra-institutional information about the characteristics of students' parents, home amenities, etc. This limits the kinds of causal explanations which can be offered."

Are such criticisms valid? How well have large-scale international surveys of educational achievement measured the central components of family background? How could these measures be improved in future studies? To address these questions, I review and assess the family background measures from five major surveys conducted by IEA in the past 30 years. I also discuss a major study of the OECD currently in progress, the Program for International Student Assessment (PISA), that undoubtedly will be a major source of international data for researchers in the near future.[3]

IEA and PISA Surveys

According to Postlethwaite, executive director of IEA from 1962 to 1972, the main purpose of the IEA survey research has been "to study the relationship between relevant input factors in the social, economic, and pedagogic realms and outputs as measured by performance on international tests . . . the main multivariate analyses of the data [have] attempted to discover the major input and process variables accounting for variation in a given population between students within countries and schools within countries" (Postlethwaite, 1974, p. 158).

The First International Mathematics Study (FIMS) was conducted between 1962 and 1965 in twelve countries, with the goal of examining differences among various educational systems and the relationship between these differences and variations in academic achievement. Major results of the study were published by Husen (1967). The Six Subject Survey, which included what has since become known as the First International Science Study (FISS), began in 1966 with the goal of assessing student achievement in the areas of science, reading comprehension, literature, French as a foreign language, English as a foreign language, and civic education. Major results of the study were published by Comber and Keeves (1973). The Second International Mathematics Study (SIMS) was administered in 20 educational systems between 1980 and 1982, and IEA published a report on the results in 1987. The Second International Science Study (SISS) began in 1981 with the goal of providing an overview of science education in 26 educational systems for three target populations: students at the 10-year-old level, at the 14-year-old level, and in the final year of secondary school. SISS results were published in 1987.

The Third International Mathematics and Science Study (TIMSS) is the most recent and perhaps the most ambitious of the IEA surveys. The study was conducted in 1995 for three populations of students (primary school, middle school, and late secondary school) in 42 countries. Of these, 26 countries (along with 12 additional countries that were not involved in the 1995 survey) participated in TIMSS-R, a followup survey of eighth-grade students in 1999. A third assessment is scheduled for 2003. In addition to the major reports and publications of results by IEA, the survey data have been and will continue to be used extensively by researchers interested in a variety of topics related to education.

Finally, the Programme for International Student Assessment (PISA) has been organized by OECD as a major assessment of skills and knowledge in the domains of "reading literacy, mathematical literacy, and scientific literacy" as well as the general problem-solving skills of 15-year olds in 32 countries (OECD, 2000). A summary of results from the 2000 survey focusing primarily on reading literacy was published (OECD, 2001); second and third assessments are to be administered in 2003 and 2005, focusing on mathematics and scientific literacy, respectively.[4]

To investigate the conceptualization and measurement of family background in each of these international studies, I consulted the student background section of each questionnaire, as well as additional documentation for each survey. Table 6-3 provides an overview of the five IEA studies and PISA and their coverage of family background in three broad domains: family socioeconomic status, family structure, and family social and cultural capital. The social and cultural capital domain is further subdivided into educational resources, parental involvement, cultural capital, and minority and residential status.

From the table it is clear that the number of questions has expanded and the conceptualization of features of family life has grown increasingly complex over time. FIMS contained only the most basic questions regarding family socioeconomic status. FISS, SIMS, and SISS included questions in four of the six domains of family background covered in Table 6-3. TIMSS covered five domains and PISA will cover all six domains to some degree.

Measuring Socioeconomic Status

Although all studies include items for parents' education and all but TIMSS include measures of occupational status, the actual measurement of these factors has varied from survey to survey. Over time, measurement flaws made in earlier surveys were corrected with an eye toward improving the validity and comparability of measures. For example, in FIMS parental education was measured as years of schooling. But the measurement of years of schooling is not comparable across different educational systems; twelve years of education in the United States is generally equivalent to the completion of secondary school, but in other educational systems secondary school may consist of fewer or more years. Perhaps in response to this problem, FISS and SISS used the level of education completed, but assigned arbitrary years of education to each level, such that response options consisted of grade 10 or less, grade 11, and grade 12 and 0, 1-2, 3-4, or 4+ years of postsecondary education. This scheme created a new problem in that it could not account for variations in educational level for parents with fewer years of school. In countries where the majority of adults did not complete at least ten years of school, substantial differences in educational attainment were entirely masked. It is surprising that the problem was not found in the analysis of FISS data and that SISS replicated this coding scheme.

Measurement of parental education was improved in SIMS and TIMSS; in each case, general levels of schooling were used. It is unclear why ISCED educational categories were not used, because ISCED is the most common internationally standardized classification scheme for educational attainment. Nor can ISCED categories be derived from the classification schemes used in these surveys because they are not as specific as those in ISCED (see Table 6-2). ISCED distinguishes between the completion of lower and upper secondary school, and the completion of a first university degree and additional degrees at the tertiary level (e.g., M.A. and Ph.D.). Although the consequences of this coding decision likely are not severe, it means that researchers cannot easily link the data from these surveys to the other abundant sources of information that use ISCED categories. Fortunately, TIMSS allowed countries to alter the response categories to fit their educational systems. This option seems to provide comparability between countries while capturing country-specific features of educational systems. It also is possible that ISCED categories can be derived from the country-specific educational classifications for some countries. PISA does use ISCED categories for the coding of parents' educational attainment, thus ensuring that researchers will be able to use PISA data in conjunction with other UNESCO and OECD data.

In terms of occupational status, early studies focused on father's occupation in a format that asked for job title and activities. In the First International Mathematics Study, these responses were coded according to a common occupational classification scale for all countries (Husen, 1967, Vol. 1, pp. 138-144). The First International Science Study asked each country to use the occupational classification that was generally employed in social science research in that country; in the Second International Science Study, this format was followed again, but classifications were then collapsed into a four-category scale consisting of: (1) professional and managerial workers, (2) clerical workers, (3) skilled workers,

TABLE 6-3 Family Background Measures in Large-Scale International Assessments of Educational Achievement

Study	Socioeconomic Status	Family Structure	Educational Resources
First International Mathematics Study (IEA 1967)	Father's education[a] Mother's education[a] Father's occupation[f] Mother's employment status[h]		
First International Science Study (IEA 1973)	Father's education[b] Mother's education[b] Father's occupation[b]	Number of siblings Student's birth order	Dictionary Books Daily newspaper
Second International Mathematics Study (IEA 1985)	Father's education[c] Mother's education[c] Father's occupation[g] Mother's occupation[i]		Abacus Slide rule Four-function calculator Scientific calculator Programmable calculator Computer
Second International Science Study (IEA 1987)	Father's education[b] Mother's education[b] Father's occupation[g] Mother's occupation[j]	Number of siblings Student's birth order	Dictionary Books
Third International Mathematics and Science Study (IEA 1995)	Father's education[d] Mother's education[d] Home possessions	Who lives at home with you? Total people in home	Dictionary Books Calculator Computer Desk

Social and Cultural Capital		
Parental Involvement	Cultural Capital	Minority and Residential Status
Help with homework Check spelling Encourage reading Ask about school		
Help with homework Parental perceptions of math		Home language
		Country of birth (student, mother, father) Home language Number of years in country
	How often: read a book, visit museum, attend concert, go to theatre, go to movies, watch educational TV.	Born in country? (student, mother, father) If no, student's age at migration to country Home language

continues

TABLE 6-3 Continued

Study	Socioeconomic Status	Family Structure	Educational Resources
Programme for International Student Assessment (OECD 2000)	Father's education[e] Mother's education[e] Father's occupation[k] Mother's occupation[k] Home possessions	Number of siblings Student's birth order Who lives at home with you?	Dictionary Books Calculator Textbooks Desk Quiet place to study Internet Educational software Computer Musical instrument

Coding Schemes
Education:
[a]Grade completed 1-17+.
[b]Grade completed 10 or less, 11, 12, 0, 1-2, 3-4, 4+ years of postsecondary education.
[c]Less than primary, finished primary, less than secondary, finished secondary, trade certificate, attended college, finished college.
[d]Finished primary, some secondary, finished secondary, some vocational/technical, some university, finished university. Countries were allowed to alter this coding scheme.
[e]ISCED categories.

and (4) semiskilled/unskilled workers (Keeves & Saha, 1992). Using SISS data, Keeves and Saha analyzed several alternative occupation scales, including the four-category scale, a two-category (white-collar/blue-collar) scale, and the Treiman SIOP scale. They found that both the four-category scale and the Treiman scale were most appropriate across a range of countries, and that the Treiman scale was better able to discriminate among higher occupational status categories.

The surveys also varied in their consideration of mother's occupational status. FIMS asked a question on mother's employment status (no job, part-time, full-time), but did not provide an option for recording her occupational status, if employed. SIMS was the first study to record both mother's and father's occupational status, and used wording that allowed the student to answer the question for either mother/father or female/male guardian.

TIMSS differed markedly from prior studies in that it did not include questions on parental occupation. TIMSS organizers believed the prob-

Social and Cultural Capital

Parental Involvement	Cultural Capital	Minority and Residential Status
Help with homework Parental involvement Time talking; eating main meal together; discussing social, political, and cultural issues	How often in past year: visit museum, attend concert, go to theatre, go to movies, go to sporting events.	Born in country? (student, mother, father) Home language

Occupation:
f Title and job activities of father.
g Title and job activitities of father/guardian.
h No job, part-time, full-time employment status of mother.
i No job, part-time, full-time, if employed, title and job activities of mother/female guardian.
j Title and job activities of mother.
k Title, job activities, and occupational status (measured through ISEI) of father/ mother.

lems in gathering parental occupational status noted in prior IEA surveys raised questions about the feasibility of gathering reliable and usable data on parental occupation in TIMSS (Larry Suter, personal communication, September 11, 2000). Indeed the challenges of collecting wealth and occupational status are well known. As Keeves and Saha (1992, p. 166) explain:

> [A]ny direct measure of the financial resources of the economic characteristics of the home cannot be collected in studies of educational achievement where the data are obtained from students in schools and classrooms. Even to ask questions about father's occupation is problematic in some countries. IEA has always encountered sensitivities in obtaining data for this indicator of social status, which have intensified with the increasing awareness of issues associated with confidentiality of information that is gathered from surveys and stored within computer systems. The usefulness of such information in establishing relationships between home background and achievement outcomes has been widely recognized and appropriate questions have generally been in-

cluded in questionnaires. Nevertheless, in some countries, the amount
of missing data as a consequence of non-response has commonly been
substantial.

Such concerns, along with knowledge that several participating countries
would not allow questions on parental occupation and wealth, likely led
to the decision to exclude questions regarding parental occupational status from TIMSS. Thus the measurement of socioeconomic status was limited to two components: parental education and home possessions. To
measure home possessions, countries were invited to add up to twelve
items on home possessions beyond the educational resources listed in
Table 6-3 that were standard for all countries. The final list of home possessions varied substantially across countries.

In the ongoing search to solve the problem of developing standard,
internationally comparable measures of wealth in the absence of income
data, household possessions have been the focus of much recent attention, especially in the fields of development economics and health. The
measurement of household possessions usually is applied to examining
wealth differences as they relate to health outcomes, such as immuniza-
tion coverage, child mortality (Hammer, 1999), or nutrition (Rutstein,
1999), but is readily applicable to the study of educational outcomes. As
noted, some researchers believe household assets capture wealth better
than income, because income can fluctuate greatly over time and assets
may reflect a more stable and continuous source of wealth.

Current research should be of considerable value to the designers of
future large-scale surveys in this regard. Using Demographic and Health
Surveys (DHS) in 35 developing countries, economists Filmer and
Pritchett (1999) created an "asset index" from survey questions on household possessions (e.g., radio, television, bicycle) and housing characteristics (presence of electricity, the type of construction materials used). There
was substantial overlap in the questions asked in different countries, but
the precise list of variables derived from the questions varied from 9 in
some countries to 21 in others. The variables were aggregated into an
index using principal components analysis[5] (p. 88). The asset index was
calculated separately for each country. Within each country, individuals
or households were sorted and assigned to wealth groups (poor, middle,
rich) on the bases of their values for the asset index (p. 89). Filmer and
Pritchett are careful to point out that the levels of the asset index are not
directly comparable across countries (e.g., poor households in Brazil do
not have the same standard of living as the poor in Turkey) and the gap
between rich and poor likely varies between countries (e.g., the gap between poor and rich households in Brazil could be larger than the gap
between poor and rich households in Turkey). But the asset index performs as well as more traditional measures of wealth, and has the addi-

tional advantage of being comparable across countries. Thus, the real value of such an asset index is that it can be used to evaluate the distribution of educational outcomes across different socioeconomic status groups within countries. By applying such strategies to the study of educational achievement, we can begin to ask questions like, "How do the poorest 30 percent of students in Country A compare to the poorest 30 percent of students in Country B in terms of math achievement, both absolutely and relative to the rich in each country?" This is not a trivial question, because it helps to focus attention on the subpopulations for which high rates of achievement are most often elusive.

The inclusion of household possession questions also may help address problems of missing and inaccurate data on family background. All surveys that collect data on family background from students themselves have problems with nonresponse or inaccuracies. For example, an analysis of data from the U.S. High School and Beyond Survey, which asked questions of students and parents, found low correlations between student and parent responses for some family background factors: .21 for the presence of a specific place to study, .35 for the presence of an encyclopedia, .44 for mother's occupation, and .87 for father's education (Koretz, 1992). Such discrepancies between student and parent responses raise serious questions about the accuracy of these data. It also appears that nonresponse regarding parents' education questions for TIMSS and TIMSS-R is quite high. In the U.S. sample for TIMSS-R, roughly 25 percent of students did not complete the question on father's education and 19 percent did not complete it for mother's education; nonresponse for the item on number of books in the home was much lower, around 2 percent (Larry Suter, personal communication, October 18, 2000). A recent study that used TIMSS data to examine the influences of educational achievement in ten European countries reports that missing data on parents' education was too high in all countries (more than 20 percent) to allow some kind of imputation to replace missing values (Bos & Kuiper, 1999). Instead, the researchers used the "number of books in the home" measure as a proxy variable; as in the United States, this variable apparently had a much lower rate of nonresponse in European countries.

Researchers Boe and May at the University of Pennsylvania are working to develop an index for socioeconomic status using TIMSS data on household possessions. One challenge, however, is the current lack of standardization across countries on a core group of household possessions. Thus, although the addition of household assets measures in TIMSS was clearly an improvement over prior surveys, future surveys should try to ensure some level of comparability across countries on a core set of possession measures. A careful assessment of the reliability and validity of home possessions as a measure of SES within countries and as a construct that holds cross-nationally may determine that home possessions data can provide better and more comparable measures of socioeconomic status than parental education and occupation.

Measuring Family Structure

FISS was ahead of its time in measuring both birth order and number of siblings, and SISS used the same format. Some studies did not include any measures of family structure, and worse yet, TIMSS included questions on household configuration in such a way that the elements of family structure likely most important for educational outcomes cannot be definitively determined. Students were asked to indicate (yes/no) whether the following people lived at home with them most or all of the time: mother, father, one or more brothers, one or more sisters, stepmother, stepfather, one or more grandparents, other relatives, other nonrelatives. Finally, they were asked to supply the total number of people living in their home. The best that researchers can do with these data is to distinguish children living with both biological parents from children living with single parents. But the potential wealth of information on other aspects of family structure is compromised by the question format. There is no way to deduce the total number of siblings, the child's birth order, or the actual structure of the family (i.e., total number of adults in the household). Also, in its focus on living arrangements rather than family configuration, the survey provides no data on family structure for children who do not live at home (a common situation in some countries). In the measurement of family structure, then, TIMSS did a poorer job than surveys that preceded it. PISA follows a similar format but has the advantage of asking an additional question about the total number of older and younger brothers and sisters so that the sibship size and birth order of each student can be determined. This is a notable improvement over the TIMSS format.

Measuring Social and Cultural Capital

Designers of the early IEA studies appear to have recognized the importance of educational resources in the home as a measure of cultural capital that can facilitate educational success. With the exception of FIMS, all studies include some measures of educational resources that are expected to be related to student achievement. Over time the types of resources included reflect technological changes in educational resources themselves. FISS and SISS asked only about reading materials (dictionary, books, daily newspaper). SIMS included a question on the presence of a computer in the home, even at a time before home computers were common in many countries. PISA is most specific in this regard and asks about computer-related resources, such as educational software and access to the Internet, to appropriately reflect the rapid changes in computer usage for educational activities in recent years.

Other measures of cultural capital are relatively recent additions to large-scale international surveys. Only TIMSS and PISA include questions regarding parent's/children's participation in cultural activities. Given recent research findings on the importance of other forms of cultural capital, especially parent's reading habits, future surveys should consider adding one or two questions to address this aspect as well. Finally, the more recent surveys ask questions regarding immigrant status and the language spoken in the home. Thus, they provide researchers with a valuable source of data to examine the role of immigrant status and home language in children's educational achievement cross-nationally.

Parental involvement, a primary indicator of social capital within the family, is measured less systematically. Early studies included questions about parent's help with homework and involvement in children's schooling more generally, but neither SIMS nor TIMSS included questions on this topic. PISA asks several interesting questions on parental involvement, including whether parents and children eat a main meal together and how much time they spend talking to each other, in addition to whether parents assist children with homework.

Assessment

In sum, in order to assess the progress in the measurement of family background in these surveys over the past decades, it may be useful to revisit the main reasons for measuring family background stated at the outset of this paper, because the adequacy of family background measures may vary according to the goals toward which they are applied. In terms of the first goal of controlling for family influences in order to examine school effects net of family effects, substantial progress has been made in the more than thirty years since the first IEA survey was conducted. Many of the flaws, such as those in the measurement of parental education and occupation, were addressed and improved in subsequent surveys. Recent surveys have been more cognizant of the multidimensional influences of family life and, in contrast to prior surveys, have incorporated questions regarding family cultural capital, home language, and immigrant status.

In terms of the second goal of studying family background as a determinant of educational achievement in its own right, the measurement of family background also has improved. Growing awareness of the central importance of family background in determining educational achievement is reflected in reports based on data from international achievement surveys. Early reports, such as those based on FISS data, paid little attention to socioeconomic status or other aspects of family background. Home background influences were aggregated into a single construct and used primarily as a control variable in analyses of the impact of school factors on educational achievement (Comber & Keeves, 1973). Analyses of SISS data treated family background in somewhat greater detail and not just as a control variable. For example, Postlethwaite and Wiley (1992, pp. 125-128) presented a complex path analysis in which family SES was hypothesized to influence students' views regarding science, their liking of school, and their science achievement (see also Keeves, 1992). Published reports based on TIMSS data provide the most detailed summaries of family background influences on academic achievement. Each of the five reports published thus far (Beaton et al., 1996a, 1996b; Mullis et al., 1997a, 1997b, 1998) devotes a chapter to family factors and provides summary statistics for various measures of family background as they relate to achievement in each country. For example, Beaton et al. (1996a, 1996b) report mean achievement scores for each response category for questions relating to the number of books in the home, highest level of education for either parent, and the presence of study desk, dictionary, and computer in the home. Even this relatively simple presentation of bivariate relationships improves on past reports and underscores the strong correlations between aspects of family background and educational achievement. Thus, although the primary focus of international assessments of educational achievement remains on school factors and processes, the attention devoted to family background factors in both the design of the surveys and the reports of the data is greater today than ever.

Although the general picture is one of progress, in hindsight it is also apparent that some inconsistencies in data collection might have been avoided. Most notably, these are the lack of parents' occupational status and the weaknesses of the family structure data in the TIMSS survey. The implications of these weaknesses are becoming apparent as researchers begin to utilize the TIMSS data. The American Institutes for Research recently "polled" researchers conducting secondary analyses using TIMSS data on the perceived advantages and disadvantages of TIMSS. In the report of their findings to the TIMSS-R Technical Review Panel, they summarized researcher's opinions in the following way: "[T]he overwhelming consensus was that TIMSS was the richest, most comprehensive set of truly comparable cross-national data ever collected." On the downside, among other things, researchers "wished there was more background information on family socioeconomic status" (American Institutes for Research, Memorandum to Members of the TIMSS-R Technical Review Panel, 2000, p. 4). The limitations of the family background data in TIMSS are further reflected in current research projects attempting to study the impact of family background on educational outcomes or control for family background in assessments of school factors. Most of these studies use only one measure of family background, either parental education (e.g., Schiller, Khmelkov, & Wang, 2000) or number of books in the home (e.g., Boe, Turner, Leow, & Barkanic, 1999; Bos & Kuiper, 1999); they acknowledge that these are incomplete measures of family background, but that TIMSS offers few alternatives. Thus, for the explicit purpose of examining the relationship between family background and educational outcomes across nations, further improvements are necessary in the measurement of family background in cross-national surveys of educational achievement.

Finally, it appears that the data from IEA studies have been underutilized in terms of the third goal of comparing the *distribution* of educational achievement within and across societies. Much more energy has been devoted to comparing nations in terms of average achievement than to comparing nations in terms of the dispersion of math and science achievement scores or other educational outcomes. This is unfortunate for two reasons. First, as mentioned previously, awareness of variations in terms of family background and other factors of student populations provides crucial context for comparing average performance across nations; without such contextual qualifications, differences in achievement scores may reveal very little about the effectiveness of educational systems being compared. Second, investigations of the achievement gaps between students from poor versus rich (single-parent versus two-parent, educated versus uneducated) families could yield valuable information regarding how the distribution of achievement scores relate to other inequalities within societies. Cross-national comparisons of such achievement gaps would go far beyond the usual comparison of average achievement scores across countries. For example, if such analyses revealed that some countries have comparatively small achievement gaps between rich and poor students, these cases could be informative for countries struggling with large performance gaps by socioeconomic status. Focused investigation on the achievement of poorest students and those attending resource-impoverished schools across societies also might be illuminating. Some countries with relatively high average achievement scores might look quite different when examined from this perspective.

Recently, Berliner similarly emphasized the necessity to look at the extremes in addition to the averages in the case of the results of TIMSS-R for the United States:

> The U.S. average masks the scores of students from terrific public schools and hides the scores of students attending shamefully inadequate schools. . . . Average scores mislead completely in a country as heteroge-

neous as ours. We have many excellent public schools, and many that are not nearly as good. Those who want to undermine our public schools often condemn the whole system rather than face the inequities within it. They should focus their attention instead on rescuing the under-funded and ill-equipped schools that are failing children in our poorest neighborhoods. (*The Washington Post*, January 28, 2001, p. B3)

Indeed, focused analyses of factors related to low achievement of students from low-SES or otherwise impoverished backgrounds in the United States and other countries could shed considerable light on the reasons for their underperformance and suggest remedies targeted to student populations in great need of assistance.

As first step in this direction, a recent report by the U.S. Department of Education (2000) makes a concerted effort to examine the distribution of student achievement across subpopulations of U.S. students (by economic circumstances, family configuration, parental education, etc.) and to compare the averages of these subpopulations to the average achievement scores of other nations (see Figure 6-1). These comparisons are revealing and generally demonstrate that students from low socioeconomic circumstances (as indicated by the home possessions measure) perform substantially worse than the international average, while average achievement scores for students of middle and upper socioeconomic status is equal to or above the international average. As this example demonstrates, investigations of the distribution of achievement scores within and between societies can provide valuable information. The accurate examination of the distribution of educational outcomes requires that we measure the social conditions, especially family background, across which such outcomes are distributed.

Undoubtedly, large-scale international surveys have contributed much to understanding the effects of family background on educational outcomes, the impact of school effects net of family effects on educational achievement, and the determinants of unequal educational opportunities and outcomes within and across societies. The fact that so many of the studies in Panel B of Table 6-1 utilize IEA data is further testimony to the great value of these surveys. To ensure that future surveys continue to make such contributions and improve on knowledge gleaned from prior research, they should take advantage of the solid foundation that prior surveys contribute to the conceptualization and measurement of family background. Toward that goal, I offer several recommendations for consideration. The first relates to the treatment of prior survey data; the remaining recommendations relate to the development of future surveys.

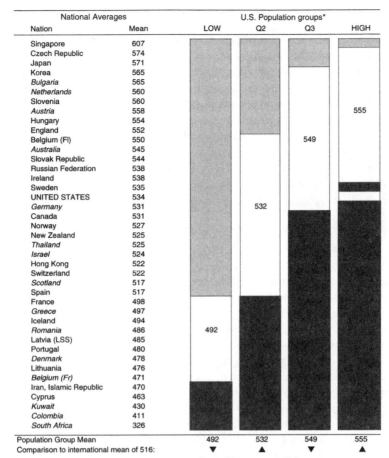

National Averages		U.S. Population groups*			
Nation	Mean	LOW	Q2	Q3	HIGH
Singapore	607				
Czech Republic	574				
Japan	571				
Korea	565				
Bulgaria	565				
Netherlands	560				
Slovenia	560				
Austria	558				555
Hungary	554				
England	552				
Belgium (Fl)	550			549	
Australia	545				
Slovak Republic	544				
Russian Federation	538				
Ireland	538				
Sweden	535				
UNITED STATES	534				
Germany	531		532		
Canada	531				
Norway	527				
New Zealand	525				
Thailand	525				
Israel	524				
Hong Kong	522				
Switzerland	522				
Scotland	517				
Spain	517				
France	498				
Greece	497				
Iceland	494				
Romania	486	492			
Latvia (LSS)	485				
Portugal	480				
Denmark	478				
Lithuania	476				
Belgium (Fr)	471				
Iran, Islamic Republic	470				
Cyprus	463				
Kuwait	430				
Colombia	411				
South Africa	326				
Population Group Mean		492	532	549	555
Comparison to international mean of 516:		▼	▲	▼	▲

*Population Group Identification: LOW=1st quartile; Q2= 2nd quartile; Q3= 3rd quartile; HIGH= 4th quartile

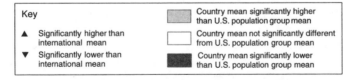

Key		Country mean significantly higher than U.S. population group mean
▲	Significantly higher than international mean	Country mean not significantly different from U.S. population group mean
▼	Significantly lower than international mean	Country mean significantly lower than U.S. population group mean

FIGURE 6-1 Family wealth and science achievement: Science total scores; upper grade, Population 2; 1995.

NOTES: Nations not meeting international sampling guidelines shown in italics.
Unshaded areas indicate 95 percent confidence interval of population group mean.
Population group mean scores are shown in unshaded area in approximate position.
The French-speaking (Belgium-Fr) and the Flemish-speaking (Belgium-Fl) populations of Belgium were sampled separately. The placement of Sweden may appear out of place; however, statistically the placement is correct. Latvia (LSS) indicates only Latvian-speaking schools were sampled.
SOURCE: U.S. Department of Education (2000, p. 77).

RECOMMENDATIONS

1. One of the great benefits of TIMSS has been the ease of use of the data files for secondary analysis, especially the ability for researchers to download them from the TIMSS Web site. If prior surveys, especially SIMS and SISS, could be made similarly accessible via the Internet, it is likely that more researchers would utilize these valuable sources of international data to address questions related to family background and educational outcomes. Moreover, researchers might be encouraged to consider comparing the results of these surveys over time if they had easy access to all three data sources. This is one relatively straightforward way to further the productive synergies between the researchers conducting secondary analyses of the survey data and the survey organizers.

2. Measures of parental education and occupational status are core components of family background that should be incorporated, when possible, into future surveys. Although the problems of missing data and concerns regarding reliability are likely to continue, the value of data gathered on these core concepts often will outweigh these caveats. In some cases, such as with young student populations who might not provide accurate answers or in countries where collecting such information is forbidden by law, incorporating these measures is not feasible. In other cases, as with older student populations, such data can provide valuable information on family background. Survey designers should weigh the advantages and disadvantages of obtaining information on parents' education and occupation and collect it where possible.

3. Future studies should follow the examples set by TIMSS and PISA and include questions on home possessions as a proxy for wealth. Following the methods of Filmer and Pritchett and other researchers, effort should be devoted to devising a common core of possessions that would allow for cross-national comparisons, but also allow for additional components of this construct to capture variations in home possessions that are of particular interest within nations. Recent and ongoing research on the construction of indices using home possession measures should provide a valuable source of information as survey designers consider how to best measure socioeconomic status with measures of home possessions. Until a definitive conclusion is drawn, however, surveys should strive to include multiple measures of socioeconomic status, namely parents' education, parents' occupation, and home possessions.

4. Relatedly, a careful assessment of prior IEA survey data should be conducted to determine the extent of problems related to nonresponse, validity, and reliability of various measures of family SES. Such an assessment could reveal how these problems vary by country or question format and could offer clear recommendations on which types of questions

are likely to yield the most robust and valid information on family socio-economic status.

5. Large-scale international surveys are the best source of comparative data available to study the relationship between family background and educational outcomes across a wide range of societies. Although the investigation of this relationship has not always been the primary concern of survey designers, these surveys do have the (perhaps unenviable) burden to provide researchers with the best family background data possible. Thus in the areas where knowledge is weakest, namely the mapping of cross-cultural variations in the impact of family structure and social/cultural capital on educational outcomes, these surveys have an especially large contribution to make. Therefore, family structure and social/cultural capital should be incorporated consistently as aspects of family background. The questions on family structure must be formulated carefully, so that the most important elements of family structure, namely number of brothers and sisters and headship of the household (e.g., single parent versus two biological parents versus stepparent) can be determined. Surveys should include the multiple dimensions of family social and cultural capital, including parental involvement, and parent's/children's participation in cultural activities. Surveys organizers should attend to the ongoing research in these areas; as the concepts of social and cultural capital continue to be refined, survey questions may need revision.

6. More generally, a strategy of standardization on core components of a concept, combined with options for nations to include variations, could be an efficient and fruitful way to measure the multiple dimensions of family background and simultaneously fill the need for comparative, yet context-sensitive measures. Researchers interested primarily in international comparisons could utilize the core standardized components, and researchers interested in examining questions of particular concern within a country could take advantage of the context-sensitive measures.

7. The conceptualization of "the family" varies from society to society. Problems regarding different definitions of "family" and "household" could be minimized by explicitly supplying respondents the definition they should use when answering survey questions. For example, before asking about parents' educational and occupational status, the PISA questionnaire clarifies its definition of "parent" for the respondent in the following way:

> Some of the following questions are about your mother and father (or those person[s] who are like a mother or father to you—for example, guardians, step-parents, foster parents, etc.). If you share your time with more than one set of parents or guardians, please answer the following

questions for those parents/step-parents/guardians you spend the most time with. (OECD, 2000, p. 6).

Such clarifications help assure that respondents use the same definition of family or family members as that intended by the survey.

It is important to remember that family background is only one of the many topics covered in international studies of educational achievement. Considering their scope, both in terms of content and geographic coverage, the accomplishments of these studies are extremely impressive. Large-scale international surveys have been a valuable source of data for researchers and policy makers concerned with understanding the determinants of educational outcomes. As Husen (1987, p. 33) notes,

> Cross-national comparisons of student achievements and attitudes provide a unique opportunity for disentangling the relative effect of the factors that the child brings to school. These are the social influences at large and home background in particular, on the one hand, and the key factors operating in the school situation on the other hand.

Careful consideration and measurement of family background factors can help to ensure that future surveys continue to provide detailed and comprehensive data with which to address longstanding questions regarding children's learning processes and educational achievement throughout the world.

NOTES

1. For example, most of the studies listed in the table consider other independent or dependent variables (especially occupational status). Some studies employ cross-sectional data; others use longitudinal data. This information, as well as the broader goals of each research project, cannot be gleaned from Table 6-1; the studies should be consulted directly (see References).
2. This approach focuses on the relationship between measurable educational inputs and school outcomes and is derived from the notion that the output of the educational process, namely individual student achievement, is related directly to a series of inputs (Hanushek, 1995, pp. 228-229). Family inputs commonly are measured by parental education, income, wealth, and family size. School inputs typically are conceptualized as teachers' characteristics, school organization, and community factors.
3. I do not discuss other major surveys such as the International Assessment of Educational Progress (IAEP) or International Adult Literacy Survey because their questionnaires did not include major sections on the family background of respondents.
4. An additional survey project worthy of note is the Southern Africa Consortium for Monitoring Educational Quality (SACMEQ). In the past decade, this project conducted two assessments (SACMEQ I and II) of conditions of schooling and the quality of primary education in 15 countries in Eastern and Southern Africa. Like the IEA surveys, SACMEQ surveys gathered data on students, teachers, and school administrators, but they also contain family background questions appropriate for developing country contexts. For example, family wealth is assessed with questions on livestock holdings,

household possessions, and structural conditions of the home. Interestingly, the questions on home possessions in TIMSS and PISA were modeled after the SACMEQ survey (I am grateful to an anonymous reviewer for this information). Further information about SACMEQ can be obtained from Kenneth N. Ross, International Institute for Educational Planning (IIEP), UNESCO, Paris, France.

5. As Filmer and Pritchett (1999, p. 88) explain, principal components analysis is a technique closely related to factor analysis that is used for "summarizing the information contained in a large number of variables to a smaller number by creating a set of mutually uncorrelated components of the data." For a detailed discussion of this procedure, see Filmer and Pritchett (1998).

REFERENCES

Aitkin, M., & Longford, N. (1986). Statistical modeling issues in school effectiveness studies (with discussion). *Journal of the Royal Statistical Society, Series B, 149*, 1-43.

Baker, D. P., Riordan, C., & Schaub, M. (1995). The effects of sex-grouped schooling on achievement: The role of national context. *Comparative Education Review, 9*, 468-481.

Beaton, A., Mullis, I., Martin, M., Gonzalez, E., Smith, T., & Kelly, D. (1996a). *Science achievement in the middle school years: IEA's Third International Mathematics and Science Study*. Chestnut Hill, MA: Boston College.

Beaton, A., Mullis, I., Martin, M., Gonzalez, E., Smith, T., & Kelly, D. (1996b). *Mathematics achievement in the middle school years: IEA's Third International Mathematics and Science Study*. Chestnut Hill, MA: Boston College.

Becker, G. S., & Tomes, N. (1979). An equilibrium theory of the distribution of household income and intergenerational mobility. *Journal of Political Economy, 84*, S279-S288.

Behrman, J. R., & Birdsall, N. (1983). The quality of schooling: Quantity alone is misleading. *American Economic Review, 73*, 928-946.

Behrman, J. R., & Wolfe, B. (1984). The socioeconomic impact of schooling in a developing country: Is family background critical? Are there biases due to omitted family background controls? *Review of Economics and Statistics, 66*, 296-303.

Bidwell, C. E., & Kasarda, J. D. (1980). Conceptualizing and measuring the effects of school and schooling. *American Journal of Education, 88*, 401-430.

Blake, J. (1989). *Family size and achievement*. Berkeley: University of California Press.

Blau, P. M., & Duncan, O. D. (1967). *The American occupational structure*. New York: John Wiley & Sons.

Blossfeld, H. P. (1993). Changes in educational opportunities in the Federal Republic of Germany: A longitudinal study of cohorts born between 1916 and 1965. In Y. Shavit & H. P. Blossfeld (Eds.), *Persistent inequality: Changing educational attainment in thirteen countries* (pp. 51-74). Boulder, CO: Westview.

Boe, E., Turner, H. M., May, H., Leow, C. S., & Barkanic, G. (1999). The role of student attitudes and beliefs about mathematics and science learning in academic achievement: Evidence from TIMSS for six nations (Center for Research and Evaluation in Social Policy Data Analysis Report No. 1999-DAR3). Unpublished manuscript, University of Pennsylvania.

Bos, K., & Kuiper, W. (1999). Modelling TIMSS data in a European comparative perspective: Exploring influencing factors on achievement in mathematics in grade 8. *Educational Research and Evaluation, 5*, 157-179.

Bourdieu, P., & Passeron, J. C. (1977). *Reproduction in education, society and culture*. Beverly Hills, CA: Sage.

Buchmann, C. (2000). Family structure, parental perceptions and child labor in Kenya: What factors determine who is enrolled in school? *Social Forces, 78*, 1349-1379.

Buchmann, C. (2002). Getting ahead in Kenya: Social capital, shadow education and achievement. *Research in Sociology of Education, 13,* 135-161, forthcoming.

Buchmann, M., Charles, M., & Sacchi S. (1993). The lifelong shadow: social origins and educational opportunity in Switzerland. In Y. Shavit & H. P. Blossfeld (Eds.), *Persistent inequality: Changing educational attainment in thirteen countries* (pp. 177-192). Boulder, CO: Westview.

Campbell, R. T. (1983). Status attainment research: End of the beginning or beginning of the end? *Sociology of Education, 56,* 47-62.

Carbonaro, W. J. (1998). A little help from my friend's parents: Intergenerational closure and educational outcomes. *Sociology of Education, 71,* 295-313.

Card, D., & Krueger, A. B. (1992). Does school quality matter? Returns to education and the characteristics of public schools in the United States. *Journal of Political Economy, 100,* 1-40.

Cobalti, A., & Schizzerotto, A. (1993). Inequality of educational opportunity in Italy. In Y. Shavit & H. P. Blossfeld (Eds.), *Persistent inequality: Changing educational attainment in thirteen countries* (pp. 155-176). Boulder, CO: Westview.

Cochrane, S. H., & Jamison, D. T. (1982). Educational attainment and achievement in rural Thailand. In A. Summers (Ed.), *Productivity assessment in education* (pp. 41-60). San Francisco: Jossey-Bass.

Cohn, E., & Rossmiller, R. A. (1987). Research on effective schools: Implications for less developed countries. *Comparative Education Review, 31,* 377-399.

Coleman, J. S. (1975). Methods and results in the IEA studies of effects of school on learning. *Review of Educational Research, 45,* 335-386.

Coleman, J. S. (1988). Social capital in the creation of human capital. *American Journal of Sociology, 94*(Suppl.), S95-S120.

Coleman, J. S., Campbell, E. Q., Hobson, C. J., McPartland, J., Mood, A. M., Weinfield, F. D., & York, R. L. (1966). *Equality of educational opportunity.* Washington, DC: U.S. Department of Health, Education, and Welfare.

Comber, L. C., & Keeves, J. (1973). *Science education in nineteen countries.* Stockholm: International Association for the Evaluation of Educational Achievement.

Cooksey, B. (1981). Social class and academic performance: A Cameroon case study. *Comparative Education Review, 25,* 403-418.

Currie, J. (1977). Family background, academic achievement and occupational status in Uganda. *Comparative Education Review, 21,* 14-28.

De Graaf, N. D., De Graaf, P. M., & Kraaykamp, G. (2000). Parental cultural capital and educational attainment in the Netherlands: A refinement of the cultural perspective. *Sociology of Education, 73,* 92-111.

De Graaf, P. M. (1986). The impact of financial and cultural resources on educational attainment in the Netherlands. *Sociology of Education, 59,* 237-246.

De Graaf, P. M., & Ganzeboom, H. B. G. (1993). Family background and educational attainment in the Netherlands for the 1891-1960 birth cohorts. In Y. Shavit & H. P. Blossfeld (Eds.), *Persistent inequality: Changing educational attainment in thirteen countries* (pp. 75-100). Boulder, CO: Westview.

DiMaggio, P. (1982). Cultural capital and school success: The impact of status cultural participation on the grades of U.S. high school students. *American Sociological Review, 47,* 189-201.

Downey, D. (1995). When bigger is not better: Family size, parental resources and children's educational performance. *American Sociological Review, 60,* 746-761.

Dronkers, J. (1989). Working mothers and the educational achievements of their children. In K. Hurrelmann & U. Engel (Eds.), *The social world of adolescents* (pp. 185-198). Berlin, Germany: Walter de Gruyter.

Duncan, O. D. (1961). A socioeconomic index for all occupations. In A. J. Reiss (Ed.), *Occupation and social status* (pp. 109-161). New York: Free Press.

Farkas, G. (1996). *Human capital or cultural capital? Ethnicity and poverty groups in an urban school district.* New York: Aldine de Gruyter.

Filmer, D., & Pritchett, L. (1998). *Estimating wealth effects without income or expenditure data— or tears: Educational enrollment in India* (World Bank Policy Research Working Paper No. 1994). Washington, DC: Development Economics Research Group (DECRG), The World Bank.

Filmer, D., & Pritchett, L. (1999). The effect of household wealth on educational attainment: Evidence from 35 countries. *Population and Development Review, 25,* 85-120.

Fuller, B. (1987). What school factors raise achievement in the developing world? *Review of Educational Research, 57,* 255-292.

Fuller, B., & Clarke, P. (1994). Raising school effects while ignoring culture? Local conditions and the influence of classroom tools, rules, and pedagogy. *Review of Educational Research, 64,* 119-157.

Fuller, B., Singer, J., & Keiley, M. (1995). Why do daughters leave school in southern Africa? Family economy and mothers' commitments. *Social Forces, 74,* 657-680.

Gamoran, A. (1991). Schooling and achievement: Additive versus interactive models. In S. W. Raudenbush & J. D. Willms (Eds.), *Schools, classrooms and pupils: International studies of schooling from a multi-level perspective* (pp. 37-51). San Diego, CA: Academic.

Ganzeboom, H. B. G., DeGraaf, P. M., & Treiman, D. J. (1992). A standard international socio-economic index of occupational status. *Social Science Research, 21,* 1-56.

Ganzeboom, H. B. G., & Treiman, D. J. (1996). Internationally comparable measures of occupational status for the 1988 international standard classification of occupations. *Social Science Research, 25,* 201-239.

Gerber, T. P., & Hout, M. (1995). Educational stratification in Russia during the Soviet period. *American Journal of Sociology, 101,* 611-660.

Goldstein, H. A. (1995). Interpreting international comparisons of student achievement. *Educational Studies and Documents* (No. 63). Paris: UNESCO.

Haller, A. O., & Portes, A. (1973). Status attainment process. *Sociology of Education, 46,* 51-91.

Hammer, J. (1999). *Child mortality and household wealth in a collection of DHS data.* Washington, DC: Development Economics Research Group (DECRG), The World Bank.

Hansen, D. O., & Haller, A. O. (1973). Status attainment of Costa Rican males: A cross-cultural test of a model. *Rural Sociology, 38,* 269-282.

Hanushek, E. A. (1995). Interpreting recent research on schooling in developing countries. *World Bank Research Observer, 10,* 227-246.

Hedges, L. V., Laine, R. D., & Greenwald, R. (1994). Does money matter: A meta-analysis of studies of the effects of differential school inputs on student outcomes. *Educational Researcher, 23,* 5-14.

Heyneman, S. P. (1976). Influences on academic achievement: A comparison of results from Uganda and more industrialized societies. *Sociology of Education, 49,* 200-211.

Heyneman, S. P., & Jamison, D. T. (1980). Student learning in Uganda: Textbook availability and other factors. *Comparative Education Review, 24,* 206-220.

Heyneman, S. P., Jamison, D. T., & Montenegro, X. (1984). Textbooks in the Philippines: Evaluation of the pedagogical impact of a nationwide investment. *Educational Evaluation and Policy Analysis, 6,* 139-150.

Heyneman, S. P., & Loxley, W. A. (1983). The effect of primary school quality on academic achievement across twenty-nine high- and low-income countries. *American Journal of Sociology, 88,* 1162-1194.

Heyns, B., & Bialecki, I. (1993). Educational inequalities in postwar Poland. In Y. Shavit & H. P. Blossfeld (Eds.), *Persistent inequality: Changing educational attainment in thirteen countries* (pp. 303-336). Boulder, CO: Westview.

Holloway, S. D., Fuller, B., Hess, R. D. et al. (1990). The family's influence on achievement in Japan and the United States. *Comparative Education Review, 34,* 196-207.

Hout, M., Raftery, A. E., & Bell, E. O. (1993). Making the grade: Educational stratification in the United States, 1925-1989. In Y. Shavit & H. P. Blossfeld (Eds.), *Persistent inequality: Changing educational attainment in thirteen countries* (pp. 25-50). Boulder, CO: Westview.

Husen, T. (1967). *International study of achievement in mathematics: A comparison of twelve countries.* Stockholm: Almqvist and Wiksell International.

Husen, T. (1987). Policy impact of IEA research. *Comparative Education Review, 31,* 29-46.

Inkeles, A. (1979). National differences in scholastic performance. *Comparative Education Review, 23,* 391.

Jamison, D. T., & Lockheed, M. E. (1987). Participation in schooling: Determinants and learning outcomes in Nepal. *History of Political Economy, 35,* 279-306.

Jencks, C. S. (1972). *Inequality: A reassessment of the effects of family and schooling in America.* New York: Basic.

Jimenez, E., & Lockheed, M. E. (1989). Enhancing girls' learning through single-sex education: Evidence and a policy conundrum. *Educational Evaluation and Policy Analysis, 11,* 117-142.

Jonsson, J. O. (1993). Persisting inequalities in Sweden. In Y. Shavit & H. P. Blossfeld (Eds.), *Persistent inequality: Changing educational attainment in thirteen countries* (pp. 101-132). Boulder, CO: Westview.

Kalmijn, M. (1994). Mother's occupational status and children's schooling. *American Sociological Review, 59,* 257-275.

Katsillis, J., & Rubinson, R. (1990). Cultural capital, student achievement, and educational reproduction: The case of Greece. *American Sociological Review, 55,* 270-279.

Keeves, J. P. (1992). *The IEA Study of Science III: Changes in science education and achievement: 1970-1984.* Oxford, England: Pergamon Press.

Keeves, J. P., & Saha, L. J. (1992). Home background factors and educational outcomes. In J. P. Keeves (Ed.), *The IEA Study of Science III: Changes in science education and achievement: 1970-1984* (pp. 165-186). Oxford, England: Pergamon Press.

Kerckhoff, A. C. (1974). Stratification processes and outcomes in England and the U.S. *American Sociological Review, 39,* 789-801.

Kerckhoff, A.C., Ezell, E.D., & Brown, J.S. (2002). Toward an improved measure of educational attainment in social stratification research. *Social Science Research, 31,* 1-25.

Kerckhoff, A. C., & Trott, J. M. (1993). Educational attainment in a changing educational system: The case of England and Wales. In Y. Shavit & H. P. Blossfeld (Eds.), *Persistent inequality: Changing educational attainment in thirteen countries* (pp. 133-154). Boulder, CO: Westview.

King, E. M., & Lillard, L. A. (1987). Education policy and school attainment in Malaysia and the Philippines. *Economics of Education Review, 6,* 167-181.

Knodel, J., Havanon, N., Sittitrai, W. (1990). Family size and the education of children in the context of rapid fertility decline. *Population and Development Review, 16,* 31-62.

Koretz, D. (1992). *Evaluating and validating indicators of mathematics and science education* (RAND Note N-2900-NSF). Santa Monica, CA: RAND.

Kremer, M. (1995). Research on schooling: What we know and what we don't (a comment on Hanushek). *World Bank Research Observer, 10,* 247-254.

Lamont, M., & Lareau, A. (1988). Cultural capital: Allusions, gaps and glissandos in recent theoretical developments. *Sociological Theory, 6,* 153-168.

Lanzas, A., & Kingston, W. (1981). English achievement in Zaire: The effects of family status and residential disruption. *Comparative Education Review, 25,* 431-441.

Lareau, A. (1989). *Home advantage: Social class and parental intervention in elementary education.* Philadelphia: Falmer.

Lee, V. E., & Lockheed, M. E. (1990). The effects of single-sex schooling on achievement and attitudes in Nigeria. *Comparative Education Review, 34,* 209-231.

Liebowitz, A. (1974). Home investments in children. *Journal of Political Economy, 82,* S111-S131.

Lillard, L. A., & Willis, R. J. (1994). Intergenerational educational mobility: Effects of family and state in Malaysia. *Journal of Human Resources, 29,* 1126-1166.

Lin, N., & Bian, Y. (1991). Getting ahead in urban China. *American Journal of Sociology, 97,* 657-688.

Lloyd, C. B., & Blanc, A. K. (1996). Children's schooling in sub-Saharan Africa: The role of fathers, mothers and others. *Population and Development Review, 22,* 265-298.

Lockheed, M. E., Fuller, B., & Nyirongo, R. (1989). Family effects on students' achievement in Thailand and Malawi. *Sociology of Education, 62,* 239-255.

Lockheed, M. E., & Longford, N. T. (1991). School effects on mathematics achievement gain in Thailand. In S. W. Raudenbush & J. D. Willms (Eds.), *Schools, classrooms and pupils: International studies of schooling from a multi-level perspective* (pp. 131-148). San Diego, CA: Academic.

Lockheed, M. E., Vail, S., & Fuller, B. (1986). How textbooks affect achievement in developing countries: Evidence from Thailand. *Educational Evaluation and Policy Analysis, 8,* 379-392.

Mare, R. D. (1981). Change and stability in educational stratification. *American Sociological Review, 46,* 72-87.

Mateju, P. (1993). Who won and who lost in a Socialist redistribution in Czechoslovakia? In Y. Shavit & H. P. Blossfeld (Eds.), *Persistent inequality: Changing educational attainment in thirteen countries* (pp. 251-272). Boulder, CO: Westview.

McLanahan, S. S., & Sandefur, G. D. (1994). *Growing up with a single parent: What hurts, what helps.* Cambridge, MA: Harvard University Press.

Montgomery, M. R., & Lloyd, C. B. (1997). *Excess fertility, unintended births and children's schooling* (Policy Research Division Working Paper No. 100). New York: Population Council.

Mueller, W., & Karle, W. (1993). Social selection in educational systems in Europe. *European Sociological Review, 9,* 1-23.

Mukweso, M., Papagiannis, G. J., & Milton, S. (1984). Education and occupational attainment from generation to generation: The case of Zaire. *Comparative Education Review, 28,* 52-68.

Mullis, I., Martin, M., Beaton, A., Gonzalez, E., Kelly, D., & Smith, T. (1997a). *Science achievement in the primary school years: IEA's Third International Mathematics and Science Study.* Chestnut Hill, MA: Boston College.

Mullis, I., Martin, M., Beaton, A., Gonzalez, E., Kelly, D., & Smith, T. (1997b). *Mathematics achievement in the primary school years: IEA's Third International Mathematics and Science Study.* Chestnut Hill, MA: Boston College.

Mullis, I., Martin, M., Beaton, A., Gonzalez, E., Kelly, D., & Smith, T. (1998). *Mathematics and science achievement in the final years of secondary school: IEA's Third International Mathematics and Science Study.* Chestnut Hill, MA: Boston College.

Niles, F. S. (1981). Social class and academic achievement: A third world reinterpretation. *Comparative Education Review, 25,* 419-430.

Noah, H. (1987). Reflections. *Comparative Education Review, 31,* 137-149.

Organization for Economic Cooperation and Development. (2000). *Program for international student assessment.* Paris: Author.

Organization for Economic Cooperation and Development. (2001). *Knowledge and skills for life: First results from PISA 2000.* Paris: Author.

Parish, W. L., & Willis, R. J. (1993). Daughters, education, and family budgets: Taiwan experiences. *Journal of Human Resources, 28,* 863-898.

Paterson, L. (1991). Trends in attainment in Scottish secondary schools. In S. W. Raudenbush & J. D. Willms (Eds.), *Schools, classrooms and pupils: International studies of schooling from a multi-level perspective* (pp. 37-51). San Diego, CA: Academic.

Peaker, G. (1971). *The Plowden children four years later.* London: National Foundation for Educational Research in England and Wales.

Pollock, J. G. (1974). Some reflections on the Scottish national data. *Comparative Education Review, 18,* 279-291.

Pong, S. L. (1996). School participation of children from single-mother families in Malaysia. *Comparative Education Review, 40,* 231-249.

Pong, S. L. (1997). Sibship size and educational attainment in Peninsular Malaysia: Do policies matter? *Sociological Perspectives, 40,* 227-242.

Pong, S. L., & Post, D. (1991). Trends in gender and family background effects on school attainment: The case of Hong Kong. *British Journal of Sociology, 42,* 249-271.

Postlethwaite, T. N. (1974). Introduction. *Comparative Education Review, 18,* 157-163.

Postlethwaite, T. N., & Wiley, D. E. (1992). *The IEA Study of Science II: Science achievement in twenty-three countries.* Oxford, England: Pergamon Press.

Raudenbush, S. W., & Bryk, A. S. (1986). A hierarchical model for studying school effects. *Sociology of Education, 59,* 1-7.

Riddell, A. R. (1989). An alternative approach to the study of school effectiveness in third world countries. *Comparative Education Review, 33,* 481-497.

Robinson, R. V., & Garnier, M. A. (1985). Class reproduction among men and women in France: Reproduction theory on its home ground. *American Journal of Sociology, 91,* 250-280.

Rosier, M. J. (1974). Factors associated with the learning of science by students in Australian secondary schools. *Comparative Education Review, 18,* 180-187.

Ross, K., & Postlethwaite, T. N. (1989). *Indonesia quality of basic education.* Djakarta, Indonesia: Ministry of Education and Culture.

Ross, K., & Postlethwaite, T. N. (1992). *Indicators of the quality of education: A summary of a national study of primary schools in Zimbabwe* (International Institute for Educational Planning Research Report No. 96). Paris: UNESCO.

Rutstein, S. (1999). *Health, nutrition and population country fact sheets.* Calverton, MD: Macro International.

Schiller, K. S., Khmelkov, V. T., & Wang, X. Q. (2000). *International differences in the effects of family structure on mathematics achievement.* State University of New York, Albany.

Seltzer, J. (1994). Consequences of marital dissolution for children. *Annual Review of Sociology, 20,* 235-266.

Sewell, W. H., Haller, A. O., & Portes, A. (1969). The educational and early occupational attainment process. *American Sociological Review, 34,* 82-92.

Sewell, W. H., & Hauser, R. M. (1975). *Education, occupation and earnings: Achievement in the early career.* New York: Academic.

Shavit, Y. (1993). From peasantry to proletariat: Changes in educational stratification of Arabs in Israel. In Y. Shavit & H. P. Blossfeld (Eds.), *Persistent inequality: Changing educational attainment in thirteen countries* (pp. 337-350). Boulder, CO: Westview.

Shavit, Y., & Pierce, J. L. (1991). Sibship size and educational attainment in nuclear and extended families: Arabs and Jews in Israel. *American Sociological Review, 56,* 321-330.

Shukla, S. (1974). Achievements of Indian children in mother tongue (Hindi) and science. *Comparative Education Review, 18,* 237-247.

Simkus, A., & Andorka, R. (1982). Educational attainment in Hungary. *American Sociological Review, 47,* 740-751.

Smith, H. L., & Cheung, P. L. (1986). Trends in the effects of family background on educational attainment in the Philippines. *American Journal of Sociology, 9,* 1387-1408.

Stanton-Salazar, R. D., & Dornbush, S. M. (1995). Social capital and the reproduction of inequality: Information networks among Mexican-origin high school students. *Sociology of Education, 68,* 116-135.

Steelman, L. C., & Powell, B. (1989). Acquiring capital for college: The constraints of family configuration. *American Sociological Review, 54,* 844-855.

Stevenson, D. L., & Baker, D. P. (1992). Shadow education and allocation in formal schooling: Transition to university in Japan. *American Journal of Sociology, 97,* 1639-1657.

Szelenyi, S., & Aschaffenburg, K. (1993). Inequalities in educational opportunity in Hungary. In Y. Shavit & H. P. Blossfeld (Eds.), *Persistent inequality: Changing educational attainment in thirteen countries* (pp. 273-302). Boulder, CO: Westview.

Tansel, A. (1997). Schooling attainment, parental education, and gender in Cote d'Ivoire and Ghana. *Economic Development and Cultural Change, 45,* 825-856.

Teachman, J. (1987). Family background, educational resources and educational attainment. *American Sociological Review, 52,* 548-557.

Theisen, G. L., Achola, P. P. W., & Boakari, F. M. (1983). The underachievement of cross-national studies of achievement. *Comparative Education Review, 27,* 46-68.

Treiman, D. J. (1977). *Occupational prestige in comparative perspective.* New York: Academic.

Treiman, D. J., & Yamaguchi, K. (1993). Trends in educational attainment in Japan. In Y. Shavit & H. P. Blossfeld (Eds.), *Persistent inequality: Changing educational attainment in thirteen countries* (pp. 229-250). Boulder, CO: Westview.

Tsai, S. L., & Chiu, H. Y. (1993). Changes in educational stratification in Taiwan. In Y. Shavit & H. P. Blossfeld (Eds.), *Persistent inequality: Changing educational attainment in thirteen countries* (pp. 193-228). Boulder, CO: Westview.

UNESCO. (1997). *International Standard Classification of Education (ISCED-1997).* Paris: UNESCO.

U.S. Department of Education. (2000). *Mathematics and science in the eighth grade: Findings from the Third International Mathematics and Science Study.* Washington, DC: National Center for Education Statistics.

Whyte, M. K., & Parish, W. L. (1984). *Urban life in contemporary China.* Chicago: University of Chicago Press.

Wong, R. S. (1998). Multidimensional influences of family environment in education: The case of socialist Czechoslovakia. *Sociology of Education, 71,* 1-22.

Zhou, X., Moen, P., & Tuma, N. B. (1998). Educational stratification in urban China, 1949-94. *Sociology of Education, 71,* 199-222.

Zuzovsky, R., & Aitkin, M. (1991). Curricular change and science achievement in Israeli elementary schools. In S. W. Raudenbush & J. D. Willms (Eds.), *Schools, classrooms and pupils: International studies of schooling from a multi-level perspective* (pp. 25-36). San Diego, CA: Academic.

7

Advancements in Conceptualizing and Analyzing Cultural Effects in Cross-National Studies of Educational Achievement[1]

*Gerald K. LeTendre**

[T]hose who have conducted the [International Association for the Evaluation of Educational Achievement] IEA studies have been well aware that educational systems, like other aspects of a culture, have characteristics that are unique to a given culture. In order to understand why students in a particular system of education perform as they do, one must often reach deep into the cultural and educational history of that system of education (Purves, 1987, p. 104).

The problem of "culture" has engaged researchers of cross-national trends in education and schooling for decades and continues to invigorate a lively theoretical and methodological debate today. Scholars interested in comparative studies of education can still find themselves in a quandary as there is, to date, no single definition of culture or method of cultural analysis that is agreed on by all researchers. Researchers in the field still debate questions such as "How can an understanding of differences in cultures help us to better understand international differences in student achievement?" "How can an analysis of culture help us to understand what are and are not possible lessons to be learned for the U.S. in terms of improving student achievement?" or "When is culture an important factor and when is it not?"

Nonetheless, there have been significant advances in how culture has been conceptualized in cross-national studies of educational achievement.

*Gerald LeTendre is Chair of the Comparative and International Education Committee and the Harry and Marion Eberly Faculty Fellow at the Pennsylvania State University.

Both theoretically and methodologically, the study of educational achievement has been advanced by borrowing from cross-national work in the subfields of sociology of education, anthropology of education, cultural psychology, and qualitative studies in education. The traditional "national case study" model—in which idealized models of the nation's education system were developed and analyzed—commonly used in the earliest days of the IEA has given way to studies which take into account national and regional diversity as well as studies that try to account for cross-national factors that can affect a range of nations. At both the micro- and macrosocial levels, an analysis of cultural effects has been advanced by better theory, research designs, and data sets and powerful software capable of analyzing huge data sets. The development of iterative, multi-method research designs has allowed researchers to overcome major epistemological problems that previously separated qualitative and quantitative researchers, allowing cultural analyses to inform cross-national studies at all stages of the research.

In this chapter, I will review the advances that have been made in conceptualizing and studying culture in cross-national or comparative studies of schools and educational systems. I will show how models of cultural dynamics can be integrated with quantitative data in studies of educational achievement and cultural effects. Already, many researchers in the subfields of anthropology of education, sociology of education, and comparative education now routinely use mixed method designs to account for cultural effects (see Caracelli & Green, 1993; Tashakkori & Teddlie, 1998). I will summarize the most important methodological advances in modeling cultural effects on student achievement in two large recent IEA studies, and propose new models of multimethod research design that can integrate cultural analyses and quantitative analyses in the same study. Finally, I will discuss the problems inherent in trying to create large, qualitative, public databases: the kind of databases that further the integration of cultural analysis in studying many aspects of educational achievement.

HOW TO DEFINE "CULTURE"?

Virtually every aspect of education can be described as "culture," depending on how the writer uses the term. In the quote cited at the beginning of this chapter, Purves states that the entire educational system is part of the national culture. Defining just what culture is has been an elusive task (see Hoffman, 1999, for an essay on the various definitions of culture used in comparative education studies). Using the broadest definition, even the most basic patterns of instructional practice are seen as the result of culture. Taking this stance, basic concepts such as "academic achievement" are regarded as socially constructed or "cultural" phenomena by the researcher (see Goldman & McDermott, 1987; Grant & Sleeter, 1996). From this perspective, it is useless to argue what may or may not be a cultural effect because culture permeates and affects all social interactions.

The idea that culture or cultural effects can be reduced to a set of variables has, as Hoffman (1999, pp. 472-474) notes, led to a dead end in comparative education. This kind of epistemological impasse has long kept qualitative and quantitative researchers from uniting in a common study of the cross-national causes and correlates of educational achievement. Invested in one mode of investigation, both quantitative and qualitative researchers find themselves bogged down in fruitless epistemological debates, missing a way to bridge qualitative and quantitative approaches to research: incorporating both methods in a larger research project designed to identify and test patterns of causality. While quantitative analysts tend to assume that a universal causal model with discrete variables can be readily identified and implemented in cross-national research, qualitative analysts tend to assume that the first problem to overcome in a cross-national study is how to model causation.

Early comparativists frequently used textual descriptions or statistical summaries of nations or national systems of education as the basis for a comparative methodology (Bereday, 1964). This approach was limited because it assumes a pervasive, ill-defined cultural effect. In searching for what Jones termed "a scientific methodology" (Jones, 1971, p. 83) comparativists employed models in which nations as a whole were identified as culturally homogeneous units, that is, the "national case study" (see Passow, 1984).[2] This led the field of comparative and international education to be dominated largely by "area experts" who studied the educational system of specific nations or regions. Content analyses of "comparative" studies of education printed in major academic journals reveal a predominant focus on only one country (Ramirez & Meyer, 1981) and a lack of comparative research design (see also Baker, 1994).

Rust, Soumare, Pescador, and Shibuya (1999, p. 107) aptly demonstrate that over the past 20 years, few studies appearing in the major comparative journals cite the major theorists of the field of comparative education, and that "Very little attention has been given to data collection and data analysis strategies." However, outside of the comparative education journals, there has been significant debate about how to improve data collection and data analysis strategies. The basic strategy of combining cross-national achievement and survey data, widely employed in IEA studies, provoked lively debates, particularly around the Second International Mathematics Study (Baker, 1993; Bradburn, Haertel, Schwille, & Torney-Purta, 1991; Rotberg, 1990; Westbury, 1992, 1993). However, these debates did not address the basic concept of culture.[3] The authors generally accepted an implicit model of culture as a historically static set of values (or language) specific to, and homogeneous among, a particular nation that could be readily modeled using discrete variables and linear equations.

The problem with attempting to measure culture as a set of discrete variables that function in the same way across nations can be demonstrated by reference to attempts to understand what constitutes effective teaching within any given nation. The creation of ever more detailed national-level data sets has reached a dead end in IEA studies. For example, in 1984, Passow (p. 477) identified "quality of teachers" as *one* possible "teacher variable" to consider. In the IEA classroom study (Anderson, Ryan, & Shapiro, 1989), "quality of teachers" was measured in many different ways with sets of variables addressing specific areas— including knowledge of the field, instructional practice, and belief systems—any number of which could be construed as "cultural." In the Third International Mathematics and Science Study (TIMSS), a host of variables measured a wide range of teacher behaviors, beliefs, and backgrounds. Table 7-1 provides a partial list of variables related to teacher quality in the TIMSS Population 2 teacher questionnaire that many qualitative analysts would consider to measure cultural effects.[4]

Faced with such an alarming number of variables, researchers have turned to qualitative studies to help orient research and guide analysis and interpretation. The work of cross-cultural psychologists, such as Stevenson and Stigler, attempted to understand how teacher quality affects student achievement by incorporating theories that specific beliefs about teaching and learning were "cultural" and drove more effective instructional practice (see Stevenson & Stigler, 1992; Stigler & Hiebert, 1998). Both Stevenson and Stigler argue that Japanese teachers' emphasis on persistence rather than innate ability led them to believe they could increase the achievement of all students, thus providing motivation to work harder to ensure that all students make academic progress.

The idea that what makes a "good" teacher (or a good classroom) depends on the culturally influenced expectations of students, parents, and the teachers themselves has been expanded by the work of anthropologists and educational researchers (see, e.g., Anderson-Levitt, 1987, 2001; Crossley & Vulliamy, 1997; Daniels & Garner, 1999; Flinn, 1992; LeTendre, 2000; Shimahara, 1998). Scholars in subfields such as anthropology of education or sociology of education who engage in cross-national work now tend to employ a model of culture as a dynamic system. Rather than attempt to create more and more numerous sets of variables, these researchers emphasize the respondent's perceptions of the social world, individual-level interactions, variation in cultural norms within

TABLE 7-1   Teacher Variables in TIMSS, Population 2

Time on Task in Classroom	Time Outside of Classroom	Implementation
Time teaching textbook	Preparing/grading exams	Ability tracked or detracked
Time spent on topics (20 main topics)	Planning lessons	Use of calculators
Time on introduction of topic	Updating student records	Use of review
Time on review	Reading/grading student work	Use of quizzes
Frequency of computer use	Professional study	Small-group activities
Frequency of use of graphs or charts	Meetings with other teachers/students/ parents	Paper-pencil exercises
Time on small-group activities		Hands-on lab
Time on topic development		Assign homework
Frequency of teacher/ student interaction		Oral recitation/drill
		Ask students to explain reasoning
		Type of homework assigned

SOURCE: TIMSS Population 2 Mathematics/Science Questionnaire.

nations and sources of conflict (e.g., historical, regional, linguistic, racial, etc.) around key concepts, roles, and institutions.

As early as 1976, IEA scholars called for increased attention to alternative ways to model cultural effects:

> The most interesting, and perhaps the most useful, approach to cross-national research proceeds not in terms of existing country-wide units, but on the basis of sub-national units. This means that it may be more interesting (for comparative work) to inquire about the correlates of achievement with, say, metropolitan areas across several countries, or among the children of the poor, or among girls, each group taken together across nations, than it is to regard individual countries as the logical, or only, units of analysis. (Passow, Noah, Eckstein, & Mallea, 1976, p. 293)

Many scholars now recognize that the static, national case study approach ultimately masks more important findings regarding the range of cultural variation within national subunits; conflicting educational expectations held by religious, linguistic or ethnic groups; and the degree to which cultural change affects the nation in question. For example, Shimahara (1998, pp. 3-4) squarely places his recent volume as a contribution to cross-national studies of education in that it brings to bear a contextual (i.e., cultural dynamic) perspective on classroom management:

> Yet the majority of international comparisons tend to be sketchy and cursory, paying scant attention to the national and cultural context of schooling. Such a problem is glaring in a broad array of writings. . . . Even *The Handbook of Research on Teaching*, presumably the most authoritative project on teaching of the American Educational Research Association, suffers from the same shortcomings. Authors refer to teaching practices in other countries without offering contextual interpretations.

Shimahara, in this and previous works, has attempted to bring anthropological theory and qualitative methods to cross-national studies of education and achievement in the last ten years. The importance of "culture" in explaining the schooling process, or more basically, in identifying the boundaries of school as an institution, has played an increasing role in the IEA's studies.

ADVANCES IN MODELING CULTURE

Researchers engaged in cross-national studies of educational systems have begun to use models of culture where culture is seen as a pervasive set of values, habits, and ideals that permeate every social institution and, in fact, construct the boundaries of acceptable or even imaginable behavior (see Douglas, 1986 for a theoretical synthesis), but do not assume that culture is historically static or homogeneous within national boundaries. Researchers conducting comparative studies that use a cultural dynamic approach to study educational achievement, for example, first document the range and variation in respondent's definitions and knowledge of key concepts (e.g. achievement), social roles (e.g. teacher), and institutions (e.g. school). They then proceed to analyze patterns of consensus or conflict around such concepts, at the same time comparing recorded belief statements with observed behaviors. The same process is carried out in a second country and the patterns of consensus or conflict within each nation are then compared (see Anderson-Levitt, 2001; LeTendre, 2000; Shimahara and Sakai, 1995; Spindler, 1987).

Two recent major IEA studies—Civic Education and TIMSS—both attempted to incorporate more dynamic models of culture and made significant methodological and theoretical advances over previous studies as they incorporated extensive qualitative components. The decision to combine qualitative and quantitative data collection in different research components of the same study indicates an understanding that a combined qualitative/quantitative approach will maximize understanding of educational processes cross-nationally. In the TIMSS-Repeat (TIMSS-R), an expanded video component has been retained with the explicit intent of providing the opportunity for holistic analysis that incorporates a more dynamic model of culture. The intended coding procedures of the TIMSS-R video data will include both inductive and deductive components. The researchers stated they will:

> Develop a holistic interpretive framework for each country to which specific teaching codes can be linked. We refer to this as "conserving" for each country the context or meaning of a given analytic code, for example the meaning of the use of chalkboards and overhead projectors. (TIMSS-R Video Study Web site at www.lessonlab.com/timss-r/video coding.htm)

These advances in integrating qualitative and quantitative methods in cross-national studies of academic achievement parallel the areas of experimentation by scholars in many fields. In demography, family studies, and other fields, whole journal issues recently have been devoted to investigation of qualitative methods. For example, Asay and Hennon (1999) suggest innovations in interviewing for international family research derived from qualitative educational studies. An entire issue of *The Professional Geographer* is dedicated to qualitative methods, including "Use of Storytelling" and "The Utility of In-Depth Interviews" (*The Professional Geographer*, Vol. 51, No. 2). Essentially, several fields are converging on a combined analytic strategy that mixes quantitative and qualitative data in order to answer distinct but related questions about a given phenomenon.

HOW CULTURAL ANALYSES IMPROVE OUR UNDERSTANDING OF ACHIEVEMENT

How can an understanding of differences in national cultural dynamics help us to better understand international differences in student achievement? How can an analysis of culture help us to understand what are and are not possible lessons to be learned for the United States in terms of improving student achievement? The answer lies in the richness of details—the "thick description"—that high quality qualitative studies provide. This kind of data allows researchers to address three major problems in current social science research: how to capture daily life, how to improve interpretation, and how to model dynamic systems. More accurate data on daily life form the basis for more accurate comparisons of national cultural dynamics and improve our knowledge of the implications and problems that need to be faced if programs or reforms are to be transferred from one nation to another.

Capturing Daily Life

Researchers in a variety of fields are drawn to qualitative methods as a way of more accurately documenting and portraying the social experiences of groups of interest. As Asay and Hennon (1999, p. 409) write: "Qualitative methodologies are often chosen for family research because of their ability in gaining 'real life' and more contextualized understanding of the phenomenon of interest." Researchers from several fields appear to see qualitative methods as a way to capture more accurate portrayals of the social world. Epistemologically, these researchers believe that an analysis of system dynamics will produce results distinct from an analysis of the causal relationships between parts of the system. Stigler and Hiebert (1999) noted that in studying the videotapes of teachers in three nations, it was more important to see how the lessons formed a whole than to count frequencies of coded categories. Simply put, qualitative analyses provide insight into how the cultural dynamic is working at the time of the study.

On another level, although surveys, structured interviews, or observation instruments can capture a myriad of codeable behaviors or characteristics (such as the desire to go to college), they largely fail to capture the assumed meanings that people make in every social interaction. For example, in my own work, I found that all adolescents said they wanted to go on to college (LeTendre, 2000). Yet what was meant by college differed dramatically. One young U.S. adolescent boy said to me: "I'd like to go to college, like an electrician's program like my uncle went to, but if not that I'd like to be a lawyer." Survey questions about future academic aspirations generally fail to capture the complexity, and confusion, that characterizes adolescent educational decision making (see LeTendre, 1996; Okano, 1995). This student (and many others I interviewed) saw all forms of post-high school training as "college."

The fact that an adolescent thinks there is essentially no difference between the kind of training needed to be a journeyman electrician and a lawyer suggests that his or her educational trajectory will be affected adversely by a lack of knowledge of the basic educational opportunity structure (see also Gambetta, 1987; Gamoran & Mare, 1989; Hallinan, 1992; Kilgore, 1991; Lareau, 1989). Similarly, Stigler and Hiebert (1999) note that in studying teacher practice in classrooms, coding and analyzing discrete variables fails to accurately model the effect of specific actions in context. Such contextualized knowledge opens new lines of inquiry for the researcher, and presents the possibility of identifying what features of the system are likely to be linked with areas of interest and what are not. That is, holistic analysis of the dynamic system can highlight pertinent cultural features or subsystems that can be targeted for more intense study. Qualitative data allow researchers to document the extent to which behaviors vary and to which disagreement is raised, and the kinds of behaviors about which people argue. This kind of highly detailed, descriptive data allows for a more accurate interpretation of the entire body of data we have about a given country.

Improving Interpretation

By analyzing culture as a dynamic system, researchers increase the accuracy of interpretation of the results of qualitative or combined qualitative/quantitative studies in terms of bringing them closer to how the respondents themselves see things. This was made dramatically clear to me in my own work. I found that certain academically competent Japanese students were highly worried and concerned about the upcoming high school examination—a fact that would not be predicted from either a conflict or sponsorship model of educational selection (LeTendre, 1996). A reanalysis of field notes and interview transcriptions, however, revealed the role that strong emotions played in the decision-making process and suggested a new theoretical interpretation: Students who have high test scores are perceived by their teachers to need less counseling about high school placement, but this lack of counseling makes the students feel that their choices are less "safe" or "good" than lower achieving students who receive more counseling. High-achieving Japanese students were not able to reassure themselves emotionally, via contact with teachers, that their choices were sound choices, creating anxiety.

Too often, highly statistical analyses of educational achievement fail to record accurately how teachers, students, parents, and administrators interpret the world around them, thus preventing accurate causal modeling of the social system in question. For example, one could theorize that a culture of competition in Japan (Dore, 1976) drives high-stakes testing and the large cram-school system (see also Rohlen, 1980; Zeng, 1996). Yet ethnographic studies of U.S. schooling (Eckert, 1989; Goldman & McDermott, 1987; Grant & Sleeter, 1996) also document a culture of competition, yet there has been little high-stakes testing or cram-school development in the United States. The expression of academic competition is affected by patterns of relationships between key concepts, roles, and institutions, and these patterns differ between the United States and Japan.

In the United States, competition pervades all aspects of student life in schools, particularly social life, and adolescents spend considerable energy in vying for social popularity or athletic supremacy. In U.S. schools, there are distinct and separate social status hierarchies that split arenas of competition, "jocks" opposed to "nerds" (see Eckert, 1989). In Japan, there is less differentiation of social status hierarchies, and all social status hierarchies are affected by academic performance (Fukuzawa & LeTendre, 2001). Even in working-class high schools, there is a comparative lack of a strong countercultural movement (compare Kinney, 1994; Okano, 1993; Trelfa, 1994, with Grant & Sleeter, 1996; Jenkins, 1983; or MacLeod, 1987). Without understanding the cultural context of competition—the ways in which adolescents (and teachers) make sense of academic competition and how it affects their lives—we could not model accurately the role of academic competition in either the United States or Japan, much less conduct a systematic comparison of the effect of competition on student achievement and socialization. Nonetheless, ethnographic studies by themselves provide limited data for national policy decisions. National survey and testing data are needed if researchers wish to formulate and test hypotheses at a national level.

A combination of qualitative and quantitative data has gained wide support as a way to increase accuracy of interpretation. In summarizing the future strategy of IEA basic school subjects, Plomp (1990, p. 9) writes, "[I]ncreased attention will be paid to ways of combining quantitative and 'narrative' methodologies in order to provide potential for rich interpretations for the statistical data, and in this way providing decision makers which [sic] more comprehensive information." Plomp (then IEA chairman), like researchers in other fields, believed that some form of qualitative data was needed to accurately interpret survey results.

Modeling Dynamic Systems

Attempts to model cultural effects by using an increasingly large array of variables in cross-national studies failed because the potential number of variables that can be considered cultural is so large. Identifying what a cultural variable is (as well as measuring its impact) tends to devolve into arguments about how to define culture. This strategy also has another limitation.

Defining cultural variables assumes that any given variable will have the same effect across time and place: that the cultural dynamic will function in the same way over time and across regions. The prevailing understanding of cultures is that they are systems in flux that cannot be studied in some state of equilibrium or against some initial steady state. There are no steady states or states of equilibrium for nations. The cultural dynamic is essentially a "moving target" that constantly changes and does not have a readily identifiable trajectory. Grand cultural theories of early anthropology (regarding progressive evolution from sociocultural states of savagery through barbarism to civilization) have been abandoned and criticized for their inherent racial and/or cultural prejudice. Scholars of national educational systems and cross-national education studies must try to understand the workings of a system with limited knowledge of what states the system has passed through (i.e., historical context) and no knowledge of what states the system is likely to go through (developmental trajectory).

Modeling culture as a dynamic system offers a way to understand the overall patterns of interactions that occur in the culture at the time it is observed. Modeling culture as a dynamic system shifts the analytic focus from identifying discrete, quantifiable cultural variables (and their statistical relation to other variables) to a focus on recording and documenting participants' understandings and social interactions. Modeling culture as a dynamic system also implies that individuals are trying to make sense out of their world, and that there will be significant individual variation in terms of what kinds of classes of things or people affect individual perceptions and behavior.

Modeling culture as a dynamic system generates sets of questions about the overall functioning of the system. In discussing the limitations of observational instruments to capture classroom environments Anderson and colleagues (1989, p. 299) noted that "Differences among studies appear to exist in the categories of questions that are formed (whether *a priori* or *post hoc*). Furthermore, and both as expected and as appropriate, the categories formed seemed to depend on the purpose or purposes of the study." An analysis of cultural effects, in which culture is modeled as a dynamic system, is designed to ask different questions from studies that try to identify causal relationships (defined *a priori*) between specific variables in the system.

Integrating Qualitative Analyses

Some combination of qualitative and quantitative data is necessary if we are to understand, model, and compare national educational systems. The problem remains in determining what the best way is to integrate an analysis of cultural effects or qualitative studies with quantitative studies in order to improve cross-national studies of achievement. Because the basic research designs and rationales of qualitative and quantitative studies "ask very different questions of the data," an overarching strategy of combined analysis seems most appropriate (see Tashakkori & Teddlie, 1998). Qualitative studies, on their own, offer ways to capture daily life, improve interpretation, and model dynamic systems but suffer some significant limitations. See Goldthorpe (1997, pp. 3-17) for a critique of such methods in comparative social science research.

In the next section, I compare the relative strengths and weaknesses of two large cross-national studies of achievement, TIMSS and the IEA Civic Education Study. Both studies represented advances in modeling culture in terms of large, cross-national studies, yet they represented very different approaches to integrating qualitative and quantitative components. This point is crucial because, as I will show in the case of TIMSS, simply conducting simultaneous quantitative and qualitative studies does not address the problem of creating an overarching framework for analysis. It is this framework that allows the results of the different research components to be used in ways that increase the overall analytic strength of the study. Thus, although the Civic Education Study gathered far less culturally nuanced data (from the standpoint of a qualitative researcher), the data were better integrated into the overall study than in TIMSS.

An analysis of these two studies shows that (1) qualitative studies intended to improve conceptualizing and analyzing of cultural effects must be open ended or flexible enough to capture essential national variation and provide an understanding of how key concepts, roles, and institutions (e.g., civics or academic achievement) are perceived by different groups of actors within the nation; and (2) larger studies must have an iterative, componential design in order to successfully integrate the analysis of qualitative and quantitative data.

COMPARISON OF TIMSS AND
THE IEA CIVIC EDUCATION STUDY

All IEA studies follow a rigorous research design process that includes extensive planning and review phases. TIMSS and the IEA Civic Education Study are of particular interest in that the designers explicitly tried to incorporate qualitative components into the research design in order to investigate cultural effects. In many cross-national studies, national differences or "culture" were studied using an exploratory/confirmatory combination of quantitative components. Both the IEA Computer Study and the Organization for Economic Cooperation and Development (OECD) International Adult Literacy Survey employed this methodology. TIMSS, in particular, represented a major methodological advancement over previous IEA studies by generating two large qualitative databases—the results of the video and case study components.

Both TIMSS (see Schmidt, McKnight, & Raizen, 1997; Stevenson & Nerison-Low, 2000; Stigler & Hiebert, 1998) and the IEA Civic Education Study (Torney-Purta, Schwille, & Amadeo, 1999; Torney-Purta, Lehmann,

Oswald, & Schultz, 2001) generated large amounts of qualitative data in the form of national case studies as well as massive amounts of quantitative data from surveys and assessment instruments. Both studies provide insights into how we can integrate more effectively an analysis of culture into cross-national studies of achievement. Important differences between the two studies—in terms of the number of separate study components, the sequencing of the components, and the overall strategy for analyzing the components—make these two studies an ideal methodological case study. In this section, I will compare how cultural effects were modeled and studied, contrast the research designs in terms of component models, and identify the research design strengths that improve the integration of qualitative and quantitative data.

In discussing TIMSS and the Civic Education Study, I will limit my discussion to the qualitative components and their role in providing an analysis of cultural effects. Given my familiarity with the TIMSS case study component, I will devote more discussion to it than to the video study. Those interested in learning more about the case studies can consult the following: Office of Educational Research and Improvement (1998, 1999a, 1999b) and Stevenson and Nerison-Low (2000). Those interested in the video studies can consult Stigler & Hiebert (1998, 1999). In addition, links to major TIMSS documents can be found at the National Center for Education Statistics Web site.

The TIMSS Case Study: Collision of Two Methodologies

The TIMSS study components (achievement, curriculum, survey, case study, and video) all were carried out simultaneously, but the emphasis given to each component was different. The most emphasis (in terms of data collection and analysis) was placed on the achievement tests, the surveys, and the curriculum analysis (see Figure 7-1). Although this type of diagramming represents the complexity of the TIMSS research design in a simplistic manner, it highlights important features of the overall research design (compare with Figure 7-2). The sequential process of data collection and analysis in the IEA Civic Education Study allowed the qualitative data to have a far greater impact on the overall analysis than in TIMSS.

The overall analytic strategy for TIMSS was to identify models of causal relationships between discrete variables. Contrast this approach with the mixed methods design in Brewer and Hunter (1989), Morgan (1998), or Tashakkori and Teddlie (1998). TIMSS also differed from other IEA studies in that multiple topics were studied (e.g., student achievement, instructional practices, K-12 policy issues), whereas in many IEA studies there is typically one topic, such as computer use. Each compo-

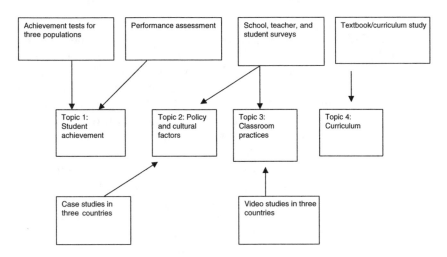

FIGURE 7-1   Schematic of TIMSS research design. See also NRC (1999, p. 3).

nent of TIMSS (e.g., the case study, the video study) was tailored to study a particular subject in a specialized way: questionnaires addressed instructional practice and opportunity to learn (OTL); interviews and observations addressed overall perceptions of the educational system. This specialization in each component led to problems in coordinated analysis that I will address in more detail.

In addition, the size of each component was much larger than in most studies that employ mixed methods. Within the TIMSS each component produced large amounts of data—larger than many single studies conducted by the average educational researcher. More than 40 countries participated in TIMSS, with at least three nations participating in each component. Several of the components, such as the achievement tests, surveys, curriculum study, and case studies, measured multiple age ranges, a fact that further complicated the analysis needed to adequately assess the results of any one component.

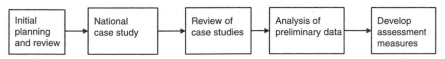

FIGURE 7-2   Schematic of IEA Civic Education Study research design (mixed iterative).

This simple fact of "data overload" meant that the potential insight to be gained by comparing the databases has not yet been achieved, as researchers have devoted their energies to concentrating on only one or two components. Data overload has been a problem in using TIMSS to inform educational policy. Some policy initiatives were trapped in debates informed by premature or incomplete analysis (LeTendre, Baker, Akiba, & Wiseman, 2001). "However, the very richness and complexity of the study has been a source of dissonance between the research and policy communities," notes BICSE (National Research Council, 1999, p. 2).

The case study component of TIMSS was an ambitious attempt to integrate then state-of-the-art qualitative methods in a cross-national study of educational achievement. Methodologically, the case study component was influenced by the Whitings' groundbreaking six-culture study (Whiting & Whiting, 1975)[5] and the rationale and methods for the case study component were developed in a context distinct from the typical IEA study. The "Study Plan for the Case Studies" (Stevenson & Lee, n.d.) makes passing reference to the "Second IEA International Studies," but does not cite or quote extensively from either IEA studies or from major figures publishing qualitative work in the field of comparative and international education (e.g. Altbach & Kelly, 1986). In a draft of the "Justification for the Case Studies (undated, p. 2)," the authors note: "To our knowledge, there have been no detailed qualitative studies that compare everyday practices at home and at school that might contribute to differences in students' level of academic achievement in science and mathematics. This is the major goal of the case studies."

The implementation of the case study component, in retrospect, was weakened by a lack of a preliminary synthesis of methodological issues relating to cross-national or cross-cultural studies of schooling. In both the anthropological literature and the comparative/international literature, there were numerous studies that dealt precisely with the issue of how "everyday practices at home and at school" influence student achievement, although these studies did not have the cross-national scope of TIMSS.[6] This lack of a multidisciplinary integration of qualitative methods meant that the case study team itself had to work through methodological issues during the study (e.g., how to deal with analysis of data in the field) rather than focus on integrating the case study data with other TIMSS components.

A second design problem was the placement of the case studies in the overall TIMSS research design and the overall timeline of TIMSS. Although attempts were made to coordinate the efforts of the TIMSS survey team and the case study team, by the time both teams met in late August 1994, the questions and procedures for the survey component of the main study and the case study already had been set. This meant that the quantitative (achievement tests, main study surveys, curriculum analysis) and qualitative (case studies, video studies) studies were carried out largely in isolation from each other.

The original intent of the overall TIMSS design was integrative. The initial focus on why there are differences in test scores, classroom practices, and teaching standards all suggested that the case studies were to follow a methodological approach similar to that used in qualitative studies of education; the case studies would be analyzed and contrasted with the data from the video and main survey and achievement study. This kind of integrated analysis never occurred because of time constraints, the amount of data collected, and the lack of a comprehensive analysis plan that could bridge epistemological differences between the study components.

The main problem was time. In traditional ethnographic fieldwork, data analysis begins as soon as the fieldworker enters the field. All "data" collected (e.g., interview transcripts, observations, records of informal conversations) are understood to be affected by the researcher's biases, status in the field, and the contextual situation in which data were generated. The analysis of data begins with outlining how researchers make meaning out of what they are told or saw, how valid these interpretations are compared to subsequent interpretations based on more experience, and how these interpretations lead to more finely developed questions about the field (see Goetz & LeCompte, 1984). Such analysis typically leads researchers to highlight conflicting points of view, to call attention to the hidden or implicit assumptions research participants are making, and to infer, for the naïve reader, the meanings participants intended when the researchers write up the study (see Wolcott, 1994). Inference and inductive thinking are incorporated as part of the analytic strategy in most branches of qualitative inquiry (see Glaser & Strauss, 1967; Hammersley & Atkinson, 1983; Lincoln & Guba, 1985).

To use such analysis to inform quantitative research designs requires early integration. The kind of analysis generated in the TIMSS case studies is most useful in the early stages of survey or instrument design, when important questions about meaning in specific linguistic or cultural contexts are being assessed. As Ercikan (1998, p. 545) noted, "In the case of international assessments, multidimensional abilities can differ from one country to another due to cultural, language, and curriculum differences. Cultural difference can influence intrinsic interest and familiarity of the content of items." Because of the TIMSS timeline, the case study data were unavailable to the designers of the survey and test instruments, leaving researchers and reviewers to try to integrate the results of the components as "finished products."

The IEA Civic Education Study: Mixed Methods

The IEA Civic Education Study, like TIMSS, used both quantitative and qualitative methods. However, the research design of the Civic Education Study incorporated quantitative and qualitative data in a mixed-methods approach wherein experts moved back and forth between two sets of data and where the findings of the qualitative data could be used to alter the collection of quantitative data. The organizing committee for the Civic Education Study began by calling on the expertise of national experts and the IEA general assembly to support a study of civic education. Although the study, like previous IEA studies, used an implicit model of nation as the "case" or unit of analysis, the committee members evinced a belief that "civics" as a topic was likely to be strongly linked with national cultures and values in a way that studies of previous IEA topics were not.

The committee proposed a series of national case studies, but ones that emphasized a cultural conflict model or social construction of reality perspective. The most common case study format in IEA studies is the summative case study (see also Stake, 1995; Yin, 1994). Summative case studies are designed to provide the qualitative equivalent of a descriptive statistics report in a statistical study. Apparently what some reviewers expected (or hoped) the TIMSS case studies would provide. Although the TIMSS case studies were clearly "ethnographic" (see Merriam, 1988) studies, the Civic Education case studies were mixtures of historical and ethnographic case studies. Both studies, then, have features that place them in the ethnographic tradition where the implicit model of culture used is a dynamic or conflict model. In both studies, the case study components provided a "thick description" of culture that would allow significant questioning of how phenomena (e.g., ideals of citizenship and beliefs about learning mathematics) were culturally formed and acted out in the schools of participating nations.

The research design of the Civic Education cases diverged significantly from TIMSS in that the people doing the case study were not required to have ethnographic or qualitative training. There was no attempt to follow a model like the Whitings' six-culture study, wherein the problem of cultural translation was made explicit. Rather, following a more traditional IEA model, country representatives were picked from a pool of qualified scholars in each nation to compile the case study. Furthermore, the fieldwork for the Civic Education case studies was much less in comparison to TIMSS and the historical or document analysis work was greater.

Nonetheless, the Civic Education Study encountered problems similar to those faced in TIMSS. In the early stages, an organizing committee created overarching questions much in the way that the four TIMSS case study topic areas were created. However, rather than let the country representatives then create their own set of core questions, the Civic Education committee created an initial set of 15 questions that all country representatives were required to answer. These 15 questions were revised and a set of 18 new questions, more focused on contested or conflicting views, was created.

The creation of the case study proceeded as an interchange among the national representatives, panels of experts in each nation, and the Civic Education organizing committee. In the Civic Education Study, panels of experts in each nation played a major role in crafting the case study itself, although most of the work in creating the final study was the work of the national representative. This created tensions among the representatives, some of whom wanted to significantly amend the original 18 questions, and the organizing committee members, who wanted to keep the questions standard for all participating countries.

This dissatisfaction led to sustained dialogue about the research process and the inclusion of ideas from national representatives in the ongoing conduct of the research to a far greater extent than was possible in TIMSS. Although the TIMSS components collected data simultaneously, the Civic Education team collected and reflected on data sequentially, allowing the research process to move along lines more in keeping with the ideals of mixed methods research. The exchanges between representatives and the committee allowed new questions and interpretations that "arose from the data" to guide how subsequent data would be collected and interpreted (see Glaser & Strauss, 1967).

The overall research design of the IEA Civic Education study is summarized in Figure 7-2. This design follows the integrated process suggested by Morgan (1998), but I emphasize the iterative nature of the analysis because simply linking qualitative and quantitative data collection sequentially does not provide the analytic power generated in the Civic Education Study. There the analytic power of each kind of data was maximized because as it was being analyzed, the second stage of research was being formed. Major findings (and limitations) at each stage were incorporated into the beginning of the next stage maximizing the analytic potential of the study.

IDENTIFYING RESEARCH DESIGN STRENGTHS

Over time the IEA and other cross-national studies have shifted from summative national to case studies that incorporate more historical and cultural material, identifying within-country variation, subpopulations, economic inequality, and other factors. The Civic Education case studies were more of a mixture of ethnographic and historical material than has been typical in the past, but it was the TIMSS Case Study that truly represents a methodological advancement in conceptualizing and analyzing cultural effects in cross-national studies.

This point is crucial. Although the TIMSS Case Study project generated truly ethnographic case studies, their potential went untapped. The IEA Civic Education case studies were far more limited in terms of the data generated, but their placement in the overall research design allowed the more limited data to be used in a far more efficient manner. The scholars responsible for compiling the Civic Education case studies were integrated into a meta-discussion of larger research design issues in a way that the TIMSS case study (and even video study) personnel were not. This integration allowed the "strength" of qualitative studies—to generate high-quality hypotheses grounded in empirical reality—to be incorporated into the overall research process.

The fact that the Civic Education case studies were more limited in focus (addressing only civic education and concentrating on the mid-teen years) allowed them to be used in a more effective way and points out a simple, yet daunting problem in effectively using studies of cultural dynamics: data overload. The TIMSS case study component generated a rich database of interviews with, and observations of, students, teachers, parents, and administrators that span the K-12 system in all three countries. But the amount of data makes the database hard to use. The initial cleaning and ordering of the files took well over a year for the University of Michigan team and another six months was required to import the data into NUD*IST and provide basic case-level codes.[7] Simply preparing the case study database for analysis presented a major time commitment.

The integration of qualitative studies, that model culture as a dynamic system, with other studies requires careful research design strategy. In dealing with national systems of education, issues of regional variation, the presence of subcultures, and variation in teacher practices over the course of schooling and a host of other issues mean that to achieve an integrated use of different forms of analysis, the study must have an extended time frame.

INTEGRATING A CULTURAL ANALYSIS: AN ITERATIVE, MULTIMETHOD APPROACH

The Civic Education Study demonstrates that an integration of cultural analysis and quantitative analysis can be achieved in cross-national studies through careful research design. If research is designed to maximize the interaction of the components over the course of the research project, then such study can document the reality of day-to-day living, identify pertinent cultural factors, improve accuracy of interpretation, and integrate macrosocial and microsocial perspectives. On the other hand, if the research design does not allow such integration, the overall analysis may suffer from data overload, temporal disjunctures, or other factors that decrease the overall effectiveness of the research. Future research designs must systematically integrate the knowledge derived from one database with the knowledge from other databases in an iterative analytic process.

The results of TIMSS and the IEA Civic Education Study provide insights into how to organize such research. The use of an iterative multimethod model appears most likely to maximize the analytic capacity of individual components in multilevel, multisite approaches and is especially crucial in integrating qualitative components aimed at providing a holistic analysis of phenomena of interest. The IEA Civic Education Study employed an iterative model in which qualitative studies were used to generate ideas for further quantification, but several variations of such a model are feasible. The analytic power of the research design to identify and explain the impact of cultural effects can be maximized by paying attention to the analytic strengths of different kinds of data collected in the component studies, by controlling the temporal relationship of components to each other, by controlling the relative emphasis given to each component, and by using an overall integrated data analysis and instrument generation strategy.

Choosing Components to Maximize Analytic Strength

Research designs that incorporate mixed methods maximize the researcher's ability to compare the knowledge derived from one component with that derived from another. For example, the fact that Japanese teachers assign less homework in seventh and eighth grades than U.S. teachers (variables in the student and teacher surveys) can be combined with interview and observation data from the case studies that reveal "no homework" policies in some Japanese elementary schools and the role of cram schools in remediation. Such comparison of the databases generally has been assigned to one of two categories by methodologists: triangulation or complementarity (Greene, Caracelli, & Graham, 1989, p. 259; Tashakkori & Teddlie, 1998, p. 43).

Triangulation

The term triangulation is used in several ways in qualitative studies in education, but here I mean using multiple measures to assess a specific phenomenon. For example, teacher surveys, teacher logs, structured observations, and videos of classroom practice all can be used to measure instructional practice such as the assignment of homework. Each method will record the instructional practice in slightly different ways, but these measures can be related to one another to provide a more accurate assessment of homework assignment. Triangulation also provides researchers with the opportunity to revise their instruments and fine tune their overall research design (see U.S. Department of Education, 1999).

Such triangulation can occur between study components or within components if the component is large enough. For example, in the TIMSS-R video study (which sampled about 100 schools in eight nations), the videotape data were complemented by a student questionnaire, a teacher questionnaire, samples of student work, samples of materials used in the lesson, and samples of tests given (http://www.lessonlab.com/timss-r/instruments.htm). These multiple measures of classroom practices can be used to enhance the measurement of instructional practices deemed of interest.

Triangulation is costly both in terms of time and analytic effort. In very large projects like TIMSS, future research designs would do well to identify a specific phenomenon or areas of related phenomena (e.g., how teachers achieve equity of opportunity to learn within classrooms) and design components to allow triangulation of measures around these phenomena of interest. When the study includes a wide range of grade levels, like TIMSS, it is important to take into account the fact that there may be different organizational environments and/or cultural expectations for different levels of schooling in a given nation. For example, widespread "no homework" policies at the elementary level in Japan give way to significant homework assignment in the middle school years. Triangulation of measures would need to be performed on more than one age level in multilevel studies, increasing the risk of data overload.

The TIMSS data offer the possibility of triangulation among teacher surveys, student surveys, case study observations, and the video studies at the Population 2 level for three nations. However, to engage in extensive triangulation of measures even at this level has been daunting. To use triangulation at every level of a multigrade level study like TIMSS likely would be cost prohibitive in terms of collection and unlikely to result in data that could be used by researchers in a timely manner. Rather than triangulating methods at each level, maximizing complementarity of components in early stages of the research would be a more effective way to identify the cultural aspects of a phenomenon (such as opportunity to learn) in different nations and/or regions, providing a path for more specific and limited triangulation of measures in subsequent components.

Complementarity

Survey studies, case studies, and other field-based observational studies can be used either in a confirmatory or exploratory way (Tashakkori & Teddlie, 1998, p. 37). However, survey research typically is used in a confirmatory manner (i.e., to test formal hypotheses), while case studies and other field-based observational studies generally are used to explore given social situations in depth. In multiage level, multinational studies like TIMSS, survey questionnaires offer the potential to generate data that can be used to test hypotheses about the impacts of belief structures on a cross-national level. The TIMSS survey data at the student, teacher, and school levels can be combined with the achievement data to allow researchers to test what factors, cross-nationally, are associated with academic achievement, although they do not allow causal modeling.

Cross-sectional survey data of the kind presented in TIMSS are less useful to the overall analysis process than longitudinal survey data, especially surveys that have been developed with input from ongoing qualitative research. In TIMSS, the case study data complement the survey data (in three nations) by providing researchers with highly detailed descriptions ideal for exploratory (i.e., hypothesis generating) work. These case studies also provide a global description of the public educational systems in these three nations that allows researchers to see how different organizations (i.e., Japanese cram schools and public schools) or groups (e.g., teachers and parents) interact at different levels. However, if survey questions had been derived with input from analysis of the case study data, it is likely that such questions would have provided more insight into how intranational variation in belief structures compared with international variation (for a preliminary attempt to achieve this comparison, see LeTendre, Baker, Akiba, Goesling, and Wiseman, 2001).

To maximize the complementarity within the overall research design, however, more interaction between the exploratory components (case studies or other field studies) and the development of survey instruments is needed. One of the problems in trying to use both the TIMSS case study and survey databases is that sometimes there is good overlap (e.g., in the coverage of homework) and sometimes poor overlap (e.g., in the coverage of family background) between the two components. Initiating exploratory, qualitative components first, and overlapping the analysis of these components with the development of survey, test, or observation instruments, would maximize the overall complementarity of the components.

Finally, as Adam Gamoran pointed out in a review of this paper, a more sophisticated overarching analysis design might have improved the purely quantitative components of TIMSS. A pretest/posttest design combined with longitudinal or time-series surveys of practices and beliefs would have allowed analysts of TIMSS to test more complex causal models. In planning such large cross-national studies, the temporal relationship of key components is crucial to the overarching design.

Temporal Relationship of Components

The IEA Civic Education project provides a good model for the ideal temporal relationship of components: researchers involved in each stage of research should be integrated into the planning and initial analysis of subsequent stages (an analytic "pass the baton" metaphor, if you will). In this way, important knowledge about the problems and limitations of each component is conserved. Such temporal sequencing also increases the complementarity of the components, as key questions that arise in early stages of the research can then drive the development of research focus and instrument creation in subsequent stages.

In large projects such as TIMSS, temporal sequencing may create substantial costs if all components are given equal weight. In most multi-method research designs, not all components are given the same emphasis or have the same analytic weight as other components. In smaller studies with only two components (a survey and a case study), researchers may place more emphasis on data collection and analysis on one component versus another. In cross-national studies like TIMSS, the complexity of the research design suggests that temporal sequencing and relative emphasis on components must be manipulated as part of the overall research design.

Relative Emphasis of Components

Tashakkori and Teddlie (1998), for example, note that most multi-method research designs assign more or less emphasis to the component studies. The use of a small, "pilot" qualitative study with a subsequent "main" quantitative study is common in much social science research. A small pilot study, perhaps involving focus groups and some limited open-ended interviews, typically is used to generate a first draft of a survey. Future cross-national studies, which must address multiple levels of schooling, could benefit from a research design that systematically manipulates both the emphasis and temporal sequence of the components.

For example, a study using multiple components with three stages of data collection might be conducted on the quality of teacher classroom practice. Simultaneous observational or video studies of a limited number of classrooms could be conducted along with a study based on teacher records or journals. Analysis of these data might highlight one aspect of classroom practice (such as classroom management styles) as being a key factor affecting instructional quality. This material then could be used to generate a survey or an observation instrument that would be pilot tested. This pilot study would be likely to raise further questions or reveal other areas of interest that then would be incorporated into the final research design, where revised quantitative instruments and more focused qualitative study (perhaps a case study) would be used to gather the main body of data.

AN INTEGRATED ANALYSIS STRATEGY FOR COMPONENTS

Finally, in very large studies like TIMSS, more than one line of research could occur simultaneously, with links across lines increasing the analytic power of each component. Qualitative and quantitative components should be organized in iterative stages, culminating in a final database that could be collected on a larger scale.

For example, in a study of student academic achievement, components such as video studies of classrooms, like those conducted in TIMSS and TIMSS-R, could be integrated by having fewer classrooms, but recording each classroom for longer periods of time. Ideally, the beginning, middle, and end of similar units (such as electricity) should be taped at the same grade level to provide information about patterns of unit flow. In addition, keeping teacher and student logs in videotaped classrooms would provide more accurate assessment (U.S. Department of Education, 1999). The videotapes and logs would be collected in the first stage of research and used as stimuli for focus groups of teachers or parents in subsequent qualitative components designed to highlight cultural effects on teaching.[8] The results of these focus group interviews, along with the original videos and/or logs, would serve as the basis for creating instruments or video strategies for the final phase that would address identified patterns. That is, more attention might be directed at comparing veteran and novice teachers, area specialists and nonspecialists, classes of heterogeneous ability, and classes of homogeneous ability if these groups or interactions appear to be especially relevant in the nations in question.

DATA RELEASE AND ANALYSIS

The timely release of data and the incorporation of a large group of secondary analysts also should be considered as part of the overall research strategy. The release of TIMSS data via the World Wide Web by the Boston University team was a major breakthrough in the dissemination of cross-national data. The high quality of the technical reports and data packaging has allowed scholars around the world to use the TIMSS survey and achievement data to engage in significant debates about effects and methods and what areas need future studies. Largely because of confidentiality issues, neither the TIMSS case study nor the video study data have been released or analyzed in the way that the survey and achievement data have. Future studies should consider ways to disseminate qualitative data that would allow a larger pool of researchers to access the data and link the analysis of qualitative data with the analysis of quantitative data.

Several strategies for data release are possible. First, to address the issue of maintaining subject confidentiality, transcripts of the classroom dialogue in video studies could be edited to delete identifying information and be released along with the corresponding surveys and coded observations. Although this kind of qualitative data would not provide the rich analytic possibilities of the visual data, it would allow access to the data by a larger range of scholars, increasing the possibility of new insights. Researchers who use such textual data might then seek to work with the original video data, following protocols for maintaining confidentiality that the National Center for Education Statistics already has in place.

With case study data, the problem of maintaining confidentiality is slightly different. In the TIMSS case study, even after deleting distinguishing remarks and inserting pseudonyms, reviewers familiar with the school systems studied could readily identify field sites. The power of qualitative data to capture the gestalt or cultural dynamic of a given place means that it is impossible to protect subject anonymity without substantially lessening the analytic capacity of the data. However, releasing portions of the data collected might be feasible. Logs or diaries kept by teachers could be edited to delete identifying remarks, then released. Verbatim transcripts, with identifying text deleted, also might be released. Scholars who analyzed these initial data sets then might seek to work with the original data under specified guidelines.

CONCLUSION: PROBLEMS THAT REQUIRE
FURTHER ATTENTION AND EXPERIMENTATION

The major challenge in incorporating cultural analyses in studies of student achievement is that most research in either qualitative sociology or cultural anthropology is exploratory and is thus designed specifically to raise questions, not test hypotheses formally derived from an existing body of theory. For some researchers trained in quantitative methods, the basic techniques of qualitative research violate what they perceive as the basic requirements of "good science." For example, using snowball sampling, where informants lead the research on to other informants, is a classic technique in qualitative research, especially among "hidden" (e.g., drug users, runaways, gay teenagers in schools) populations. Yet many quantitative researchers regard a "random sample" as the sine qua non of good research. Framing qualitative research as a type of "pilot study" does not readily work to bridge this gap as it reduces the qualitative research to such an extent as to make it worthless to pursue and quantitative researchers are likely to voice the same objections to the quality of the pilot study.

Cultural analyses should be incorporated as methodologically distinct, but integrated, components in cross-national studies of schooling so that the effects of beliefs, values, ideological conflicts, or habitual practices can be incorporated into the analysis. Patterns, both within nations and across nations, can be compared and contrasted to improve our understanding of what values, beliefs, or practices are accentuated, legitimized, or even institutionalized. Such analyses, when joined with various types of national quantitative assessments, would more clearly identify the overall similarity or dissimilarity of basic cultural patterns around schooling and would increase understanding of what kinds of reforms or innovations would or would not transfer from one nation to another.

Documenting the range of cultural variation within nation states is perhaps the most important role for cultural analysis in cross-national studies of educational achievement. A wide range of scholars (both quantitative and qualitative) have argued that the unit of the nation state is an inadequate analytic unit because it misses crucial regional variation as well as variation in subpopulations (such as racial, ethnic, linguistic, religious, or other minority groups). Detailed description of cultural variation with regard to core beliefs would greatly inform both quantitative research and policy creation. Documenting cultural change is crucial to understanding how current beliefs or values may or may not hold for the future and thus may or may not be relevant in subsequent assessments or policy recommendations.

Large cross-national studies of educational achievement that attempt to incorporate significant qualitative components in order to analyze cultural effects on learning are a relatively new type of study. TIMSS, with its large number of components and enormous databases, was a groundbreaking study and offers future researchers important lessons. The study of mixed methods is itself relatively new in social sciences, and promises to yield substantial breakthroughs in the future. Advances in computer or software technology (such as programs that allow visual and textual data to be analyzed simultaneously) have radically changed the nature of qualitative research and likely will continue to affect possibilities for research. Within qualitative research, specific forms of research (e.g., case studies or focus group research) have seen substantial methodological debate and evolution in the past 15 years.

In summary, my assessment of the current state of research is that we, as a community of scholars, have only begun to investigate ways to collect, analyze, and apply (to policy formation) these rich data sets. Further methodological improvements are certain to occur.

We are currently in a period where many possibilities exist for combining data and creating new methods for analyzing data. Some problems, like data overload, remain but such problems are not new—historians have dealt with them for centuries. New analytic tools promise the ability to analyze larger data sets with more consistency.

Effectively utilizing large qualitative data sets will require continued support for innovation and experimentation in analysis. Funding specifically for research on how to analyze these large data sets would increase the ability of the academic community in general to access the potential of the data. Just as hierarchical linear model (HLM) analysis has transformed research on school effects, so too, do new programs or strategies for integrating large qualitative and quantitative databases offer the potential to transform cross-national research. Such innovation will require time, money, and patience as dead ends and temporary failures are inevitable in any scientific undertaking, but the potential advances make this area one that deserves continued support and emphasis within the broader scientific community.

NOTES

1. I would like to thank Lynn Paine, Andy Porter, and Adam Gamoran for their insightful feedback and comments on previous drafts of this chapter.
2. Within the past 15 years, the major journals in the field of comparative education have seen more and more articles that draw on critical or postmodern theories to analyze the "culture" of schooling (Taylor, 1996). The 1998 theme of the Comparative and International Education Society (CIES) was "Bringing Culture Back In." Clearly, many scholars who would identify themselves as comparativists are interested in issues of culture, yet the fact that the CIES organizers agreed that culture was something that needed to be "brought back in" suggests that significant problems remain in integrating studies that focus on a cultural analysis with more traditional "national case studies" of education and educational achievement.
3. Even studies of the global spread of institutional forms of schooling—which tend to be highly influenced by a social construction of meaning perspective—often focus on society-level variables and ignore the cultural implications of institutional theory (e.g., Boli & Ramirez, 1992; Meyer, Ramirez, & Soysal, 1992).
4. Some readers initially may review this list and question why "time on small group activities" might be related to culture. In the case of Japan, previous research has shown that small groups are associated with cultural ideals and play a special role in Japanese education (Hendry, 1986; Lewis, 1995; Peak, 1991; Tobin, Wu, & Davidson, 1989). Small groups play a key role in Japanese society, and teacher beliefs and attitudes about group functioning have been linked to a shared set of beliefs (culture) that drive student-teacher interactions (Fujita, 1989).

5. The director, Dr. Harold Stevenson, was a leading expert in cross-cultural studies in psychology and had conducted numerous cross-national psychological studies of the effects of schooling (Stevenson, Azuma, & Hakuta, 1986; Stevenson, Lummis, Lee, & Stigler, 1990; Stevenson, Parker, Wilkinson, Bonnevaux, & Gonzalez, 1978). Also, one of the more influential advisors on the case study component, Dr. Robert Levine, had worked on the original six-culture study.

6. The edited series of ethnographic case studies produced by Waveland Press has many volumes dealing explicitly with cultural impacts on education (e.g., Rosenfeld, 1971; Wolcott, 1967).

7. NUD*IST is one of several qualitative data analysis packages used by qualitative researchers. These packages allow the researcher to create coding schema and index large textual databases. See Miles and Huberman (1994).

8. This method has been used by Tobin, Wu, and Davidson (1989) as well as Fujita and Sano (1988) to generate powerful insights into how implicit (i.e., cultural) expectations for classroom practices affect teacher work roles and child development.

REFERENCES

Altbach, P., & Kelly, G. (Eds.). (1986). *New approaches to comparative education.* Chicago: University of Chicago Press.

Anderson, L., Ryan, D., & Shapiro, B. (1989). *The IEA Classroom Environment Study.* New York: Pergamon Press.

Anderson-Levitt, K. (1987). National culture and teaching culture. *Anthropology and Education Quarterly, 18*, 33-38.

Anderson-Levitt, K. (2001). *Teaching culture.* Cresskill, NJ: Hampton Press.

Asay, S., & Hennon, C. (1999). The challenge of conducting qualitative family research in international settings. *Family and Consumer Sciences Research Journal, 27*(4), 409-427.

Baker, D. (1993). Compared to Japan, the U.S. is a low achiever . . . really: New evidence and comment on Westbury. *Educational Researcher, 22*(3), 18-20.

Baker, D. (1994). In comparative isolation: Why comparative research has so little influence on American sociology of education. *Research in Sociology of Education and Socialization, 10*, 53-70.

Bereday, G. (1964). *Comparative method in education.* New York: Holt, Rinehart & Winston.

Boli, J., & Ramirez, F. (1992). Compulsory schooling in the Western cultural context: Essence and variation. In R. Arnove, P. Altbach, & G. Kelly (Eds.), *Emergent issues in education: Comparative perspectives* (pp. 15-38). Albany, NY: State University of New York Press.

Bradburn, N., Haertel, E., Schwille, J., & Torney-Purta, J. (1991). A rejoinder to "I never promised you first place." *Phi Delta Kappan, June,* 774-777.

Brewer, J., & Hunter, A. (1989). *Multimethod research: A synthesis of styles.* Newbury Park, CA: Sage.

Caracelli, V., & Greene, J. (1993). Data analysis strategies for mixed-method evaluation designs. *Educational Evaluation and Policy Analysis, 15*(2), 195-207.

Crossley, M., & Vulliamy, G. (Eds.). (1997). *Qualitative educational research in developing countries.* New York: Garland.

Daniels, H., & Garner, P. (Eds.). (1999). *World yearbook of education 1999: Inclusive education.* London: Kogan Page.

Dore, R. P. (1976). *The diploma disease.* Berkeley: University of California Press.

Douglas, M. (1986). *How institutions think.* Syracuse, NY: Syracuse University Press.

Eckert, P. (1989). *Jocks and burnouts: Social categories and identity in the high school.* New York: Teachers College Press.

Ercikan, K. (1998). Translation effects in international assessments. *International Journal of Educational Research, 29*, 543-553.

Flinn, J. (1992). Transmitting traditional values in new schools: Elementary education of Pulap Atoll. *Anthropology and Education Quarterly, 23*, 44-58.

Fujita, M. (1989). It's all Mother's fault: Childcare and the socialization of working mothers in Japan. *Journal of Japanese Studies, 15*(1), 67-92.

Fujita, M., & Sano, T. (1988). Children in American and Japanese day-care centers: Ethnography and reflective cross-cultural interviewing. In H. Trueba and C. Delgado-Gaitan (Eds.), *School and society: Learning through culture* (pp. 73-97). New York: Praeger.

Fukuzawa, R., & LeTendre, G. (2001). *Intense years: How Japanese adolescents balance school, family and friends.* New York: RoutledgeFalmer.

Gambetta, D. (1987). *Were they pushed or did they jump? Individual decision mechanisms in education.* New York: Cambridge University Press.

Gamoran, A., & Mare, R. D. (1989). Secondary school tracking and educational equality: Compensation, reinforcement, or neutrality. *American Journal of Sociology, 94*, 1146-1183.

Glaser, B., & Strauss, A. (1967). *The discovery of grounded theory.* Chicago: Aldine.

Goetz, J., & LeCompte, M. (1984). *Ethnography and qualitative design in educational research.* Orlando, FL: Academic Press.

Goldman, S., & McDermott, R. (1987). The culture of competition in American schools. In G. Spindler (Ed.), *Education and cultural process* (pp. 282-300). Prospect Heights, IL: Waveland Press.

Goldthorpe, J. (1997). Current issues in comparative macrosociology: A debate on methodological issues. *Comparative Social Research 16*, 1-26.

Grant, C., & Sleeter, C. (1996). *After the school bell rings.* London: Falmer Press.

Greene, J., Caracelli, V., & Graham, W. (1989). Toward a conceptual framework for mixed-method evaluation designs. *Educational Evaluation and Policy Analysis, 11*(3), 255-274.

Hallinan, M. (1992). The organization of students for instruction in the middle school. *Sociology of Education, 65*(April), 114-127.

Hammersley, M., & Atkinson, P. (1983). *Ethnography: Principles in practice.* New York: Routledge.

Hendry, J. (1986). *Becoming Japanese: The world of the pre-school child.* Manchester, England: Manchester University Press.

Hoffman, D. (1999). Culture and comparative education: Toward decentering and recentering the discourse. *Comparative Education Review, 43*(4), 464-488.

Jenkins, R. (1983). *Lads, citizens and ordinary kids: Working-class youth life-styles in Belfast.* London: Routledge & Kegan Paul.

Jones, P. E. (1971). *Comparative education: Purpose and method.* St. Lucia: University of Queensland Press.

Kilgore, S. (1991). The organizational context of tracking in schools. *American Sociological Review, 56*, 189-203.

Kinney, C. (1994). From a lower-track school to a low status job. Unpublished doctoral dissertation, University of Michigan, Ann Arbor.

Lareau, A. (1989). *Home advantage: Social class and parental intervention in elementary education.* London: Falmer Press.

LeTendre, G. (1996). Constructed aspirations: Decision-making processes in Japanese educational selection. *Sociology of Education, 69*(July), 193-216.

LeTendre, G. (2000, August). Downplaying choice: Institutionalized emotional norms in U.S. middle schools. Paper presented at the American Sociological Association, Washington, DC.

LeTendre, G., Baker, D., Akiba, M., & Wiseman, A. (2001). The policy trap: National educational policy and the Third International Mathematics and Science Study. *International Journal of Educational Policy Research and Practice, 2*(1), 45-64.

LeTendre, G., Baker, D., Akiba, M., Goesling, B., & Wiseman, A. (2001). Teachers' work: Institutional isomorphism and cultural variation in the U.S., Germany and Japan. *Educational Researcher, 30*(6), 3-16.

Lewis, C. (1995). *Educating hearts and minds.* New York: Cambridge University Press.

Lincoln, Y., & Guba, E. (1985). *Naturalistic inquiry.* Beverly Hills, CA: Sage.

MacLeod, J. (1987). *Ain't no makin' it.* Boulder, CO: Westview Press.

Merriam, S. (1988). *Case study research in education.* San Francisco: Jossey-Bass.

Meyer, J., Ramirez, F., & Soysal, Y. (1992). World expansion of mass education, 1870-1980. *Sociology of Education, 65*(2), 128-149.

Miles, M. B., & Huberman, A. M. (1994). *Qualitative data analysis: An expanded sourcebook.* Thousand Oaks, CA: Sage.

Morgan, D. (1998). Practical strategies for combining qualitative and quantitative methods: Applications to health research. *Qualitative Health Research, 8*(3), 362-376.

National Research Council. (1999). *Next steps for TIMSS: Directions for secondary analysis.* Board on International Comparative Studies in Education, A. Beatty, L. Paine, & F. Ramirez, Editors. Board on Testing and Assessment, Commission on Behavioral and Social Sciences and Education. Washington, DC: National Academy Press.

Office of Educational Research and Improvement. (1998). *The educational system in Japan: Case study findings.* Washington, DC: U.S. Department of Education.

Office of Educational Research and Improvement. (1999a). *The educational system in the U.S.: Case study findings.* Washington, DC: U.S. Department of Education.

Office of Educational Research and Improvement. (1999b). *The educational system in Germany: Case study findings.* Washington, DC: U.S. Department of Education.

Okano, K. (1993). *School to work transition in Japan.* Philadelphia: Multilingual Matters.

Okano, K. (1995). Rational decision making and school-based job referrals for high school students in Japan. *Sociology of Education, 68*(1), 31-47.

Passow, A. H. (1984). The I.E.A. National Case Study. *Educational Forum, 48*(4), 469-487.

Passow, A. H. P., Noah, H., Eckstein, M., & Mallea, J. (1976). *The National Case Study: An empirical comparative study of twenty-one educational systems.* New York: John Wiley & Sons.

Peak, L. (1991). *Learning to go to school in Japan.* Berkeley: University of California Press.

Plomp, T. (1990). IEA: Its role and plans for international comparative research in education. Paper presented at the American Educational Research Association, Boston.

Purves, A. (1987). IEA agenda for the future. *International Review of Education, 33*, 103-107.

Ramirez, F., & Meyer, J. (1981). Comparative education: Synthesis and agenda. In J. Short (Ed.), *The state of sociology: Problems and prospects* (pp. 215-238). Newbury Park, CA: Sage.

Rohlen, T. (1980). The *Juku* phenomenon: An exploratory essay. *Journal of Japanese Studies, 6*(2), 207-242.

Rosenfeld, G. (1971). *Shut those thick lips.* New York: Holt, Rinehart & Winston.

Rotberg, I. (1990). I never promised you first place. *Phi Delta Kappan, December,* 296-303.

Rust, V., Soumare, A., Pescador, O., & Shibuya, M. (1999). Research strategies in comparative education. *Comparative Education Review 43*(1), 86-109.

Schmidt, W., McKnight, C., & Raizen, S. (1997). *A splintered vision.* Dordrecht, Netherlands: Kluwer Academic.

Shimahara, N. (Ed.). (1998). *Politics of classroom life: Classroom management in international perspective.* New York: Garland.

Shimahara, N., & Sakai, A. (1995). *Learning to teach in two cultures.* New York: Garland.

Spindler, G. (1987). Cultural dialogue and schooling in Schoenhausen and Roseville: A comparative analysis. *Anthropology and Education Quarterly, 18*(1), 3-16.

Stake, R. (1995). *The art of case study research.* Thousand Oaks, CA: Sage.

Stevenson, H., Azuma, H., & Hakuta, K. (Eds.). (1986). *Child development and education in Japan.* New York: W. H. Freeman.

Stevenson, H., & Lee, S. (n.d.). *Study plan for the case studies.* Ann Arbor: University of Michigan.

Stevenson, H., Lummis, M., Lee, S., & Stigler, J. (Eds.). (1990). *Making the grade in mathematics: Elementary school mathematics in the United States, Taiwan and Japan.* Reston, VA: National Council of Teachers of Mathematics.

Stevenson, H., & Nerison-Low, R. (2000). *To sum it up: TIMSS case studies of education in Germany, Japan and the United States.* Philadelphia: Mid-Atlantic Eisenhower Consortium for Mathematics and Science Education.

Stevenson, H., Parker, T., Wilkinson, A., Bonnevaux, B., & Gonzalez, M. (1978). Schooling, environment, and cognitive development: A cross-cultural study. *Monographs of the Society for Research in Child Development, 43* (3, Serial No. 175).

Stevenson, H., & Stigler, J. (1992). *The learning gap.* New York: Summit Books.

Stigler, J., & Hiebert, J. (1998). Teaching is a cultural activity. *American Educator (Winter),* 4-11.

Stigler, J., & Hiebert, J. (1999). *The teaching gap: Best ideas from the world's teachers for improving education in the classroom.* New York: Free Press.

Tashakkori, A., & Teddlie, C. (1998). *Mixed methodology: Combining qualitative and quantitative approaches.* Thousand Oaks, CA: Sage.

Taylor, A. (1996). Education for democracy: Assimilation or emancipation for aboriginal Australians. *Comparative Education Review, 40*(4), 426-438.

Tobin, J., Wu, D. Y., & Davidson, D. H. (1989). *Preschools in three cultures: Japan, China and the United States.* New Haven, CT: Yale University Press.

Torney-Purta, J., Lehmann, R., Oswald, H., & Schultz, W. (2001). *Citizenship and education in twenty-eight countries: Civic knowledge and engagement at age fourteen.* Amsterdam: IEA Secretariat.

Torney-Purta, J., Schwille, J., & Amadeo, J.A. (1999). *Civic education across countries: Twenty-four national case studies from the IEA Civic Education Project.* Amsterdam: IEA Secretariat.

Trelfa, D. (1994). *Educating the working-class: Perceptions of relevance of schooling among Japanese vocational high school students.* Ann Arbor: University of Michigan.

U.S. Department of Education. (1999). *Measuring classroom instructional processes: Using survey and case study fieldtest results to improve item construction* (Working Paper No. 1999-08). Washington, DC: National Center for Education Statistics.

Westbury, I. (1992). Comparing American and Japanese achievement: Is the United States really a low achiever? *Educational Researcher, 21*(5), 18-24.

Westbury, I. (1993). American and Japanese achievement . . . again: A response to Baker. *Educational Researcher, 22*(3), 18-20.

Whiting, B., & Whiting, J. (Eds.). (1975). *Children of six cultures: A psycho-cultural analysis.* Cambridge, MA: Harvard University Press.

Wolcott, H. (1967). *A Kwakiutl village and school.* Prospect Heights, IL: Waveland Press.

Wolcott, H. F. (1994). *Conducting case studies: Collecting the evidence.* Thousand Oaks, CA: Sage.

Yin, R. (1994). *Case study research: Design and methods.* Thousand Oaks, CA: Sage.

Zeng, K. (1996). Prayer, luck, and spiritual strength: The desecularization of entrance examination systems in east Asia. *Comparative Education Review, 40*(3), 264-279.

Part III

Making Inferences

8

The Measurement of Opportunity to Learn[1]

*Robert E. Floden**

Sometimes it seems as though, in the United States at least, the attention to student opportunity to learn (OTL) is even greater than the attention to achievement results. For the Third International Mathematics and Science Study (TIMSS), the finding that the U.S. curriculum is "a mile wide and an inch deep" may be better remembered than whether U.S. students performed relatively better on fourth-grade mathematics or on eighth-grade science. To be sure, the interest in what students have a chance to learn is motivated by a presumed link to achievement, but it is nonetheless striking how prominent OTL has become. As McDonnell says, OTL is one of a small set of generative concepts that "has changed how researchers, educators, and policy makers think about the determinants of student learning" (McDonnell, 1995, p. 305).

Over more than three decades of international comparative studies, OTL has come to occupy a greater part of data collection, analysis, and reporting, at least in studies of mathematics and science learning. The weight of evidence in those studies has shown positive association between OTL and student achievement, adding to interest in ways to use OTL data to deepen understanding of the relationships between schooling and student learning. In the broader realm of education research, its use has been extended to frame questions about the learning opportunities for others in education systems, including teachers, administrators,

---

*Robert Floden is professor of teacher education, and of measurement and quantitative methods, in the College of Education at Michigan State University.

and policy makers. In education policy, the concept is used to frame questions about quality of schooling, equal treatment, and fairness of high-stakes accountability. It seems certain to play a continuing part in international studies, with a shift toward use as an analytic tool now that the general facts of connections to achievement and large between-country variations have been repeatedly documented.

Given its importance, it is worth considering what hopes have been attached to OTL, how it has been measured, how it has actually been used, and what might be done to improve its measurement and productive use. This chapter will address these several areas by looking at the role of OTL in international comparative studies and at its use in selected U.S. studies of teaching, learning, and education policy. Most attention will fall on studies of mathematics and science learning because those are the content areas where the use of OTL has been most prominent, in part because it has seemed easier to conceptualize and measure OTL in those subject areas.

WHAT IS OTL?

The most quoted definition of OTL comes from Husen's report of the First International Mathematics Study (FIMS): "whether or not . . . students have had the opportunity to study a particular topic or learn how to solve a particular type of problem presented by the test" (Husen, 1967a, pp. 162-163, cited in Burstein, 1993). (The formulation, with its mention of both "topic" and "problem presented by the test," hints at some of the ambiguity found both in definition and in measurement of OTL.) Husen notes that OTL is one of the factors that may influence test performance, asserting that "If they have not had such an opportunity, they might in some cases transfer learning from related topics to produce a solution, but certainly their chance of responding correctly to the test item would be reduced" (Husen, 1967a, pp. 162-163, cited in Burstein, 1993).

The conviction that opportunity to learn is an important determinant of learning was incorporated in Carroll's (1963) seminal model of school learning, which also extended the idea of opportunity from a simple "whether or not" dichotomy to a continuum, expressed as amount of time allowed for learning. By treating other key factors, including aptitude and ability as well as opportunity to learn, as variables expressed in the metric of time, Carroll's model created a new platform for the study of learning. One important consequence was that the question became no longer "*What* can this student learn?" but "*How long* will it take this student to learn?" Questions of instructional improvement have, as a result, been reshaped to give greater prominence to how much time each student is given to work on topics to be mastered. In the United States, this new view of aptitude contributed to the shift from identifying *which students* could learn advanced content to working from the premise that *all students* could, given sufficient time, learn such content. That shift supports the interest in opportunity to learn as a potentially modifiable characteristic of school that could significantly affect student learning.

Carroll posits that the degree of student learning is a function of five factors:

1. Aptitude—the amount of time an individual needs to learn a given task under optimal instructional conditions.
2. Ability—[a multiplicative factor representing the student's ability] to understand instruction.
3. Perseverance—the amount of time the individual is willing to engage actively in learning.
4. Opportunity to learn—the time allowed for learning.
5. Quality of instruction—the degree to which instruction is presented so as not to require additional time for mastery beyond that required by the aptitude of the learner.
(Model as presented in Borg, 1980, pp. 34-35)

Of these factors, the first three are characteristics of the student; the last two are external to the child, under direct control of the teacher, but potentially influenced by other aspects of the education system. The model specifies the functional form of the relationship, starting with the general formulation that the degree of learning is a function of the ratio between time spent learning and time needed to learn:

$$\text{Degree of learning} = f\,\frac{\text{Time spent learning}}{\text{Time needed to learn}}$$

The model elaborates on this function, expressing "time spent learning" as the product of "opportunity to learn" and "perseverance," and "time needed to learn" as a product of "aptitude," "quality of instruction," and "ability to understand instruction" (see Figure 8-1). (The last three variables are scaled counterintuitively, so that a low numerical value is associated with what one would typically think of as "high" aptitude or "high" quality of instruction.)

Carroll's model, with its general emphasis on the importance of instructional time, was elaborated by Bloom (1976) and Wiley and Harnischfeger (1974). The concept of OTL has been differentiated so that it involves more than a simple time metric. One set of distinctions has separated the intentions for what students will study from the degree to which students actually encounter the content to be mastered. Imagine a

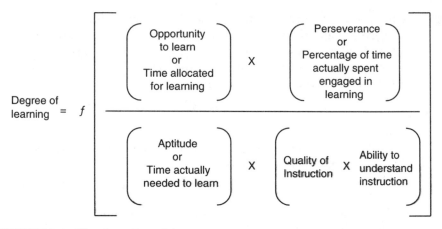

FIGURE 8-1   The Carroll model.
SOURCE: Berliner (1990). Reprinted with permission of Teachers College Press.

progression that starts at a distance from the student—say with a national policy maker—and goes through successive steps, nearer and nearer to the student, ending with content to which the student actually attends. At each step in this chain, a form of OTL exists if the content is present to some degree and does not exist if the content is absent.

Studies could attempt to measure the degree of any of these types of OTL: To what extent is the topic emphasized in the national curriculum? In the state curriculum? In the district curriculum? In the school curriculum? How much time does the teacher plan to spend teaching the content to this class? How much time does the teacher actually spend teaching the topic? How much of that time is the student present? To what degree does the student engage in the corresponding instructional activities? (In Carroll's model, the latter may be part of "perserverance.") For each level, common sense and, in some cases, empirical evidence suggest that OTL will be related to whether or how well students learn the content.

International comparative studies, and the International Association for the Evaluation of Educational Achievement (IEA) studies in particular, have divided this chain of opportunities into two segments, or "faces" of the curriculum: the intended curriculum and the implemented curriculum. (A third "face" of the curriculum, the "attained curriculum," is what students learned. That represents learning itself, rather than an opportunity to learn.) For each link in this chain, a study could measure opportunity to learn as a simple presence or absence or as having some degree of emphasis, usually measured by an amount of time intended to be, or actually, devoted to the topic. At the level of national goals, for example, one could record whether or not a topic was included, or could record some measure of the relative emphasis given to a topic by noting how many other topics are mentioned at the same level of generality, by examining how many items on a national assessment are devoted to the topic, or by constructing some other measure of relative importance. For the implemented curriculum, emphasis on a topic could be measured by the amount of time spent on the topic (probably the most common measure), by counting the number of textbook pages read on the topic, by asking the teacher about emphasis given to the topic, and so on.

Early studies that used time metrics for opportunity to learn[2] looked at several ways of deciding what time to count. These studies looked for formulations that would be highly predictive of student achievement and that could be used to make recommendations for changes in teaching policy and practice. Wiley and Harnischfeger (1974) began by looking at rough measures of the amount of time allocated in the school day, finding a strong relationship between the number of hours scheduled in a school year and student achievement. The Beginning Teacher Evaluation Study (BTES) (Berliner, Fisher, Filby, & Marliave, 1978) also found that allocated time, in this case the time allocated by individual teachers, was related to student achievement. To obtain an even stronger connection to student achievement, the investigators refined the conception of opportunity to learn, adding information about student engagement in instructional tasks and about the content and difficulty of the instructional tasks to their measurement instruments.

Following the work of Bloom (1976), Berliner and his colleagues argued that student achievement would be more accurately predicted by shifting from allocated time to "engaged" time. That is, students are more likely to learn if they not only have time that is supposed to be devoted to learning content, but also are paying attention during that time, if they are "engaged." Pushing the conception even further, they argued that the student should not only be engaged, but should be engaged in some task that is relevant to the content to be learned. That is, the opportunity that counts is one in which the student is paying attention, and paying attention to material related to the intended learning. Finally, the research group studied what level of difficulty was most related to student learning, asking whether it was more productive for students to work on tasks where the chance of successfully completing the task was high, moderate, or low. They found that student achievement was most highly associated with high success rate.[3] Therefore, the version of opportunity to learn that they found to be tied most closely to student learning is what they dubbed "Academic Learning Time" (ALT), defined as "the amount of time a student spends engaged in an academic task [related to the intended learning] that s/he can perform with high success" (Fisher et al., 1980, p. 8).

Measuring this succession of conceptions of OTL—allocated time, engaged time, time on task, Academic Learning Time—requires increasing amounts of data collection. Allocated time can be measured by asking teachers to report their intentions, through interview, questionnaire, or log. Measuring engaged time requires an estimate of the proportion of allocated time that students were actually paying attention.[4] Measuring time on task requires a judgment about the topical relevance of what is capturing the students' attention. Measuring Academic Learning Time requires an estimate of the degree to which students are completing the tasks successfully.

In their study of the influence of schooling on learning to read, Barr and Dreeben (1983) supplemented data on amount of time spent with data on the number of vocabulary words and phonics concepts students studied. Building on their own analysis of the literature growing out of Carroll's model, they investigated how the social organization of schools, especially the placement of students into reading groups, worked to influence learning, both directly and through the mediating factor of content coverage by instructional groups. They argue that Carroll's model is a model for *individual* learning, rather than *school* learning, in the sense that it describes learning as a function of factors as they influence the student, without reference to how those factors are produced within the social settings of the school or classroom.

For large-scale international comparative studies, these conceptions of OTL suggest a continuum of tradeoffs in study design. Each conception of OTL has shown some connection to student achievement. The progression of conceptions from system intension to individual time spent on a topic moves successively closer to the experiences that seem most likely to influence student learning. But the problems of cost and feasibility also increase with the progression. The model of learning suggests that the link will be stronger if OTL is measured closer to the student; policy makers, however, are more likely to have control of the opportunities more distant from students.

Questionnaires have been used in international studies to gather information on allocated time, tied to specific content. Such questionnaires give information on time allocation and the nature of the task, but shed little light on student engagement in the tasks, or on students' success rate. Ball and her colleagues' pilot study of teacher logs (Ball, Camburn, Correnti, Phelps, & Wallace, 1999) raises questions about teachers' ability to estimate the degree of student engagement. (Nearly a century ago, Dewey [1904/1965] claimed that it is difficult for anyone to determine when a student is paying attention. The difficulty probably increases with the age of students.) Teachers might be able to report on the students' success rate at a task, but that success rate probably varies across tasks, suggesting that measurement at a single time (e.g., with a questionnaire) would be unlikely to capture difficulty for the school year as a whole. Given the ambiguity about whether engagement is a part of OTL or of a student's perseverance, it is probably best for large-scale international studies to leave student engagement out of the measurement of OTL.

It should be clear the OTL is a concept that can have a variety of specific interpretations, each consistent with the general conception of students having had the opportunity to study or learn the topic or type of problem. Past international studies have chosen to include measurements of more than one of these conceptions, which may be associated with one another, yet remain conceptually distinct.

WHY IS OTL IMPORTANT?

For international comparative work, OTL is significant in two ways: as an explanation of differences in achievement and as a cross-national variable of interest in its own right. In the first case, scholars and policy makers wish to take OTL into account or "adjust" for it in interpreting differences in achievement, within or across countries. If a country's low performance on a subarea of geometry, for example, is associated with little opportunity for students to learn the content of that subarea, there is no need to hunt for an explanation of the low score in teaching technique or poorly designed curriculum materials: The students did not know the content because they had never been taught it. In the second case, scholars and policy makers take an interest in which topics are included in a country's curriculum (as implemented at a particular grade level, with a particular population) and which are excluded or given minimal attention. Policy makers in a country might, for example, be interested to see that some countries have included algebra content for all students in middle school, contrary to a belief in their own country that such content is appropriate for only a select group, or only for older students.

The language of the FIMS reports suggests that the reason for asking whether students had an opportunity to learn content was to determine whether the tests used would be "appropriate" for the students: "Teachers assisting in the IEA investigation were asked to indicate to what extent the test items were appropriate for their students. This information is based on the perception of the teacher as to the appropriateness of the items" (Husen, 1967b, p. 163). The implication suggested is that if a student had not had the opportunity to learn material, testing the student on the material would be inappropriate, in the sense that the student could not be expected to answer the questions. At the level of a country, taking results for content that students had not had the opportunity to learn at face value also would be inappropriate. Information about OTL has value because it gives a way of deciding whether it is appropriate to look at national achievement results for particular content.

In the same spirit, reports on the Second International Mathematics Study (SIMS) warn against comparing the performance of two countries unless both countries had given students the opportunity to learn the content.

> It is interesting to note that students in Belgium (Flemish), France, and Luxembourg were among those who had their poorest performance on the geometry subtest. In those three systems, the study of geometry constitutes a significant portion of the mathematics curriculum, and these results are an indication of the lack-of-fit between the geometry curriculum in those systems and geometry as defined by the set of items used in this study. These findings underscore the importance of interpreting these achievement results cautiously. They are a valid basis for drawing comparisons only insofar as the items which defined the subtests are equally appropriate to the curricula of the countries being compared. (Robitaille & Garden, 1989, p. 123)

Although some scholars deny that comparative studies should be taken as some sort of "cognitive Olympics," many news reports treat them as such.[5] Information on OTL provides a basis for deciding whether a country's poor performance should be attributed to a decision not to compete.

Adjustments for OTL are also of interest for those scholars who see comparative research as a search for insights into processes of teaching and learning, rather than a way to determine winners and losers. Because of the variation in national education systems, information on the achievement in other countries can be a source of ideas for how teaching processes, school organization, and other aspects of the education system affect student achievement. Comparative research can help countries learn from the experiences of others. To the extent that research is able to untangle the various influences on student achievement, it can help in developing models of teaching and learning that can be drawn on in various national contexts, avoiding some of the pitfalls that come from simply trying to copy the education practices of countries with high student achievement.

> The issue . . . is not borrowing versus understanding. Borrowing is likely to take place. The question is whether it will take place with or without understanding. . . . Understanding . . . is a prerequisite to borrowing with satisfactory results. (Schwille & Burstein, 1987, p. 607)

OTL can be an important determinant of student achievement. If OTL is not taken into account, its effects may be mistakenly attributed to some other attribute of the education system. A general rule in developing and testing models of schooling is that misspecification of the model, such as omitting an important variable like OTL, can lead to mistaken estimates of the effects of other factors.

In addition to its uses for understanding achievement results and their links to education systems, OTL is of interest in its own right. One of the insights from early comparative studies was a picture of the common-alities and differences in what students in varying countries had the opportunity to learn. As one of the SIMS reports puts it: "A major finding of this volume is that while there is a common body of mathematics that comprises a significant part of the school curriculum for the two SIMS target populations . . . , there is substantial variation from system to system in the mathematics content of the curriculum" (Travers & Westbury, 1989, p. 203). An understanding of similarities and differences across countries gives each nation a context for considering the learning opportunities it offers. A look at the within-country variation in OTL also provides a basis for considering current practice and possible alternatives. What variation in OTL occurs across geographic regions in a country? Across social classes? Between boys and girls? The variation found in other countries is a basis for reflecting on the variation in one's own country.

HOW HAS OTL BEEN MEASURED
IN INTERNATIONAL COMPARISONS?

I will focus on FIMS, SIMS, and TIMSS, the three international comparative studies in which OTL has played the most significant role. The First International Mathematics Study (Husen, 1967a, 1967b) included the definition of OTL quoted earlier, as "whether or not . . . students have had the opportunity to study a particular topic or learn how to solve a particular type of problem presented by the test." The FIMS report describes the questions asked about OTL as "based on the perception of the teacher as to the appropriateness of the items" (Husen, 1967a, p. 163). The choice of the word "appropriate" suggests that the intent in measuring OTL was to prevent interpreting low scores due to lack of OTL as indicative of some deficiency in teachers or students. If the item was not taught to students, then it would be "inappropriate" for those students.

The actual question put to teachers to measure OTL was as follows:

> To have information available concerning the appropriateness of each item for your students, you are now asked to rate the questions as to

whether or not the topic any particular question deals with has been covered by the students *to whom you teach mathematics and who are taking this set of tests*. Even if you are not sure, please make an estimate according to the scale given below.

Please examine each question in turn and indicate in the way described below, whether, in your opinion

A. All or most (at least 75 percent) of this group of students have had an opportunity to learn this type of problem.

B. Some (25–75 percent) of this group of students have had an opportunity to learn this type of problem.

C. Few or none (under 25 percent) of this group of students have had an opportunity to learn this type of problem.

The FIMS investigators used the responses to these questions to create an OTL scale score for each item, assigning the center of the percentage interval in the response as the numeric value for the scale:

> These ratings were scaled by assigning the value 87.5 (midway between 75 and 100) to rating A, 50 to rating B, and 12.5 to rating C. The ratings given by a teacher to each of the items in the tests taken by his students were averaged, unrated items being excluded from the calculations. For each teacher there was thus a mean rating and the mean score made by his pupils on the tests rated. (Husen, 1967a, pp. 167-168)

A criticism of this approach to measuring OTL is that it left unclear whether an opportunity to learn "this type of problem" referred to the topic that the item was intended to represent or something specific about the way the problem was formulated. Teachers might be interpreting the question as asking whether they expected students to be able *to get the problem right*, rather than whether they had *worked on* the corresponding topic.

For SIMS, the single question was replaced by a pair of questions, in an attempt to disentangle OTL from teacher judgments about students' likelihood for being able to solve a particular problem. Thus, teachers were asked both about whether the mathematics related to the test item has been taught or reviewed (the OTL question) and about the percentage of students in the class who would get the problem correct.

Specifically, teachers responded to the following pair of questions for each item on the SIMS test:

1. What percentage of the students from the target class do you estimate will get the item correct without guessing?
2. During this school year, did you teach or review the mathematics needed to answer the item correctly? (Flanders, 1994, p. 66)

Asking this pair of questions allows the teacher to indicate that students had studied the topic independently of whether they learned it well enough to answer the test item correctly. OTL might not lead to success because they had not studied the topic in the particular formulation used in the test item or they had not put enough effort into learning the topic. In at least some SIMS analyses, the two items were simply combined into a single scale, which seems difficult to interpret, at least in terms of appropriateness. Is it inappropriate to give a difficult test item on a topic that students did study? Does the teachers' prediction that students would have a difficult time answering the item correctly (given that they had the opportunity to learn it) mean that teaching had disappointing success, or that the item is somehow not really a test of the topic, perhaps because it seems "tricky" or tangential to the topic? This aspect of OTL measurement was changed again in TIMSS (to using multiple items to illustrate a topic), suggesting that researchers were not satisfied with combining opportunity to learn with predicted student success on the item.

The FIMS approach to the OTL question also leaves unspecified when students had the opportunity to learn the type of problem. That omission reduces information about the country's mathematics curriculum. It also might be important, for the appropriateness of the item for the test, to know whether the content was studied recently or some time further in the past.[6]

For SIMS, teachers also were asked OTL questions for each item. Unlike FIMS, the presumption was that OTL was the same for all students in the class: All either had or had not received the opportunity to learn how to answer the item. For content covered, teachers were asked whether the content was covered during the year of the study or earlier. For content not covered, teachers were asked whether students would learn the content later, or not at all. (In either case, the item would be "inappropriate" for these students.) Teachers also predicted what proportion of their students would get the item right.

This SIMS approach still confounds opportunity to learn the mathematical topic with information about students' familiarity with specific features of the test item that are either irrelevant or tangential to the mathematics topic. The measurement of OTL in TIMSS gets more separation between topic and item by naming a topic, giving more than one item to illustrate the topic, then asking the teacher about opportunity to learn how to "complete similar exercises that address this topic." Thus teachers are encouraged to think about OTL at a topic, rather than specific item, level. Having multiple illustrations of a topic should clarify what is the core of a topic and what is peripheral. (Information on each illustrative item is collected by asking the teachers to indicate, for each item, whether it is "appropriate" for a test on this topic.)

The SIMS questions about *when* a topic is taught are expanded from the FIMS questions. For topics taught during the year of the study, the teacher is asked to specify whether the topics already have been taught, are currently being taught, or will be taught later in the year. For topics not taught during the year of the study, TIMSS added two new options to those included in SIMS. The new possibilities are: "Although the topic is in the curriculum for THIS grade, I will not cover it," and "I DO NOT KNOW whether this topic is covered in any other grade."

TIMSS also asked teachers whether they think "students are likely to encounter this topic *outside* of school this year." This question could shed some light on items where students performed well despite lack of opportunity to learn in school. If students were likely to encounter the topic outside school, the item might be considered inappropriate as an indicator of the success of the education system because mastery of topic should be credited to either institutions or experiences outside the system. No question is asked about whether students might study the topic elsewhere in school (e.g., in science), which would give further understanding of student success despite lack of opportunity to learn in the target class. In this case, the item still might be appropriate if the intent was to understand the performance of the education system as a whole.

OTHER APPROACHES TO MEASURING OTL

Measurement of OTL has not been restricted to international comparisons. As noted, the conceptualization of OTL used in international studies drew on studies of U.S. education, and vice versa. Just as methods of measuring OTL have been changing in international studies, U.S. domestic research has included changing approaches to measurement, which can be drawn on in planning for future measurement of OTL in international comparisons.

Using Teacher Logs to Gather Information on Instruction

One line of OTL work in the United States was initiated by Porter and his colleagues at Michigan State University in the Content Determinants Project (Porter, Floden, Freeman, Schmidt, & Schwille, 1988). As part of the instrumentation for a study of teachers' decisions about what to teach, the project developed a system for classifying elementary school mathematics content. Classification began with analysis of tests and textbooks. The classification served as the basis for a system in which teachers reported on the content of their mathematics instruction, either through a questionnaire or through logs completed over the course of the school year. Like the TIMSS OTL questions, teachers were asked to list the topics they covered, rather than to say something about how well their students would do in responding to particular test items. This teacher log approach has been adapted by other researchers, including Knapp (Knapp & Associates, 1995; Knapp & Marder, 1992) and Ball (Ball et al., 1999), as well as being used in Porter's subsequent research.[7]

In a recent study of mathematics courses taken in the first year of high school, Gamoran, Porter, Smithson, and White (1997) compared several approaches to the measurement of OTL, looking for the representation that would have the highest association with differences in student achievement. They found the largest correlation with an index that represented content at a fine level of detail and included information both about the amount of time (actually, proportion of class time) spent on tested material and the distribution of that time across the topics tested. The highest correlations came when emphasis was distributed in a pattern similar to the distribution of content coverage on the achievement test.

This research team used teacher questionnaires to gather information on the content coverage in high school mathematics courses intended to provide a bridge between elementary and college preparatory mathematics. The questionnaires focused specifically on the content on which students would be tested in this study. They asked both about which mathematics topics were covered (from among 93 topics that might be covered in such mathematics courses) and what sort of "cognitive demand" the instruction made on students. Cognitive demand

> was defined according to six levels: (1) memorize facts, (2) understand concepts, (3) perform procedures/solve equations, (4) collect/interpret data, (5) solve word problems, and (6) solve novel problems. (Gamoran et al., 1997, p. 329)

Content was classified according to both topic and cognitive demand, yielding 558 different topic/demand possibilities. Teachers used this scheme to record the content they taught; test items were classified using the same scheme. Gamoran and his colleagues (1997) found that correlations with achievement were highest when the analysis used the combination of topics and cognitive demand, rather than looking only at topic or demand. Using the intersection, the correlations were 0.451 with class gains and 0.259 with student gains. "Using topics only, the correlations with student achievement gains were –0.205 at the class level and 0.103 at the student level. For cognitive demand only, the correlations were 0.112 at the class level and 0.069 at the student level" (p. 331).

Gamoran also tried different approaches to using the information on coverage. He looked at both the proportion of instructional time spent on the tested topics and at how the pattern of time spent on tested topics matched the distribution of topic coverage on the test. He labeled the first "level of coverage," and computed it by dividing the total amount of time teachers reported spending on the 19 topics covered on the test by the total amount of time spent in these mathematics classes. Because the test covered only 19 of the 558 possible mathematics topics, values of this index are small, with averages across different types of mathematics classes ranging from 0.046 to 0.086.

Gamoran labels the match of distribution to the pattern of topics on the test "configuration of coverage." The configuration is a measure of the match between the relative time spent on each tested topic and the number of test items on that topic. The index of configuration would be reduced, for example, if a large proportion of time were spent on one tested topic, at the expense of time on other tested topics. The index used is created so that 1.0 represents a perfect match in configuration, with lower values occurring as the pattern of time departs from that perfect match.

Gamoran and colleagues tried several different ways and found that the effect on achievement of these two indicators—level and configuration of coverage—was most stable when they were combined as a product, rather than added together or used as two separate variables. Based on these results, they use a model that assumes that

> level and configuration are ineffective alone and matter only in combination. This assumption seems reasonable: Great range with shallow depth and great depth in a narrow range of coverage both seem unlikely to result in substantial achievement. (Gamoran et al., 1997, p. 331)[8]

Elsewhere, Porter characterizes the correlations obtained by this combination of level and configuration, using content recorded as the intersection of topic and cognitive demand, as indicating that the connection between content of instruction and student achievement is high: "From these results, it is possible to conclude that the content of instruction may be the single most powerful predictor of gains in student achievement under the direct control of schools" (Porter, 1998, p. 129).

The high correlations with student achievement gains make it appealing to use a similar approach to measurement of OTL in future international comparisons. The fact that the measure has a strong empirical relationship to achievement gains is strong evidence that the measure has adequate reliability and predictive validity. Two factors raise questions about the adoption of this approach, however.

The first is a practical concern. The level of detail found to be most highly correlated with student outcomes goes beyond information collected in international studies. TIMSS asked OTL questions at a detailed level of content, but when the study asked teachers to report on the amount of time spent on different topics, the content categories were collapsed into a smaller set. Would the burden on teachers of having to report such specific content, with the amount of time (e.g., number of class periods) spent on the content, be tolerable for a large-scale study? (Gamoran's study collected information on 56 classrooms in 7 schools.) To date, the burden of international assessments has not led to problems with data collection, but the question deserves attention.

A second concern is a question about the interpretation of an approach to measuring content coverage that gives credit for a pattern of content emphasis, among tested topics, that most closely matched the distribution of emphasis on the achievement test used. Gamoran found that using this information gives a higher correlation with student achievement gains. But what does that match with the pattern of topics included on the test mean for students' opportunity to learn? Somehow it seems strange to have OTL depend on the relative emphasis of topics on the test; on the other hand, if the purpose of measuring OTL is to take account of the effects of OTL when trying to understand educational processes, perhaps it is best to use the representation that yields the strongest link to learning.

Perhaps the key to thinking about whether to adjust OTL information according to emphasis on the test is to ask whether the distribution of items on the test represents an ideal or standard. As the standards movement in the United States has evolved, assessments sometimes match adopted curriculum standards, but at other times the different schedules for development of standards and assessments results in a misalignment. If the pattern of topic coverage on the test represents agreement about relative value, then it seems sensible to adjust aggregate indices of OTL according to the distribution of test items. If the pattern of coverage does not represent such agreement, that creates a problem for interpreting any aggregate score.[9]

Web-Based Approaches to Teacher Logs

Ball and her colleagues have been pilot testing the use of Web-based technology to gather detailed information from teachers about their classroom instruction. They have been exploring this approach because they also have concerns about the feasibility of trying to collect detailed information on instructional content and processes. They focused on elementary school mathematics and reading. The scope of desired information includes length of lesson, grouping of students, nature of student activity, topics and materials used, and level of student engagement. In their pilot test (Ball et al., 1999), they were able to get teachers to use the logs regularly, but they report that further work is needed to gather trustworthy data about the topics and other characteristics of instruction. Still, their work is suggestive of an approach that might, in the future, increase the feasibility of collecting more detailed information about students' opportunity to learn.

As part of the pilot test for this data collection, researchers observed 24 lessons for which the teacher also entered a report on the instruction. A comparison of teacher and researcher reports on these lessons gave information on the validity of the teacher reports. For reports of length of lesson, the reports differed by an average of more than eight minutes per lesson, where lessons averaged around a total of 50 minutes. For questions about student activity, teachers chose from about six options (in both reading and mathematics), with the possibility of multiple options chosen in one lesson. The options included "students read trade books," "worked in textbooks," "worksheets," and "teacher-led activity." Agreement between researchers and teacher reports was about 75 percent for both reading and mathematics.

Ball indicated that the pilot test results were encouraging for the ability of the Web-based instrument to capture number and duration of lessons, but that more work was needed to get valid information about topic, instructional task, student and teacher activity, and student engagement. She saw validity problems arising from ambiguity of the meanings of the topic and activity descriptions. She also suggested that teachers may have difficulty remembering details of the lesson between the time the lesson is finished and the time, later in the same day, when teachers would record it. Note that she is concerned by a gap of a few hours, raising even more serious questions about surveys that ask teachers to report on instruction for an entire year.

> We need to have confidence about what the items mean to teachers. Central here is understanding how teachers interpret items and how they represent their teaching through their responses in the log. Thus, there are threats to validity that deal with teachers' understanding of the log's questions, language, and conceptualization of instruction. Other researchers have found that the validity of items related to instruction is weaker with respect to instructional practices most associated with current reforms (e.g., everyone is likely to report that they hold discussions in class, engage children in literature, or teach problem solving). Another potential problem entails teachers' ability to recall details of a lesson many hours after that lesson occurred. (Ball et al., 1999, p. 31)

Ball and her colleagues have decided not to use the Web-based approach because of the concerns about teachers' access to the necessary computer equipment (Ball, personal communication, February 2001). Such concerns seem likely to be even more salient in any international studies conducted in the near future.

Measuring Content Coverage in Reading Instruction

Barr and Dreeben (1983) conceptualized the content of early reading instruction as the vocabulary words and phonics elements that students encountered. Because the teachers in their study taught reading by having students work sequentially through basal reading materials, the investigators were able to use progress through the materials to determine the amount of content covered. The first-grade teachers in the study were asked during the year and at the end of the year to indicate how far each of the reading groups had made it through the materials. An analysis of those materials was used to determine how many basal vocabulary words and how many phonics concepts would be covered at each location in the basal. This use of progress through the curriculum as a way to measure content coverage places low demands on the teacher's memory of what has or has not been taught, but it will only be appropriate when teachers stick closely to the curriculum materials, without omitting or reordering sections.

Concerns About the Reliability and Validity of Teacher Logs and Surveys

Mayer (1999) recently has argued that little is known about the reliability and validity of teacher surveys used to collect information about instructional practice. His particular focus is on the use of "reform" practices, such as those recommended in the National Council of Teachers of Mathematics (NCTM) teaching standards. He identifies two pieces of prior research: Smithson and Porter's (1994) look at the instruments used in Reform Up Close (1994) and Burstein and colleagues' investigation (Burstein et al., 1995) of instruments used to study secondary school mathematics.

Smithson and Porter asked teachers to keep logs over the course of a school year, recording information both on content and on instructional practices. They also asked the teachers to complete a survey, asking for similar information about either the prior half-year or the half-year to come. A comparison between the survey and the logs was used to understand how much information would be lost by using only a survey, which is a less expensive data collection strategy, but one that might suffer from difficulty in recalling what happened many weeks ago, or in predicting how the year is going to run. According to Mayer's summary, the correlations between teacher practices reported on the survey and those reported on the logs ranged from 0.21 (for "write report/paper") to 0.65 (for "lab or field report"). Smithson and Porter found these correlations encouraging, but Mayer takes them as evidence of the unreliability of survey reports of such practices.

Burstein also compared teacher logs and surveys, but his research added a second administration of the survey, allowing for a look at the consistency in survey responses over time, as well as comparison of survey results to reports on logs. The comparison of surveys to logs found agreement of 60 percent or less for all types of instructional activities, a result that both Burstein and Mayer view as discouraging. The readministration of the survey yielded perfect agreement for 60 percent of all responses. Again, Mayer views this degree of agreement as low, concluding that "surveys and logs do not appear to overlap enough to prove with any degree of confidence that the surveys are reliable" (Mayer, 1999, p. 33).

Mayer makes an additional contribution by conducting a study of Algebra I teachers that compares teacher survey reports to classroom observations. The categories of practice for the study were chosen to permit a contrast between "traditional" teaching practices (e.g., lecturing) and the types of practices advocated in the NCTM teaching standards (National Council of Teachers of Mathematics, 1991). The traditional approaches were ones in which students

- listen to lectures,
- work from a textbook,
- take computational tests, or
- practice computational skills.

The NCTM approaches were ones in which students

- use calculators,
- work in small groups,
- use manipulatives,
- make conjectures,
- engage in teacher-led discussion,
- engage in student-led discussion,
- work on group investigations,
- write about problems,
- solve problems with more than one correct answer,
- work on individual projects,
- orally explain problems,
- use computers, or
- discuss different ways to solve problems.

Results are based on 19 teachers in one school district who vary considerably in instructional practice. Each teacher was asked to complete a survey at the beginning and end of a four-month period, and was observed three times during this period. The survey asked teachers to say how often they used each practice ("never," "a few times a year," "once or twice a month," "once or twice a week," "nearly every day," or "daily") and how much time was spent in the practice on days they did use it ("none," "a few minutes in the period," "less than half," "about half," "more than half," or "almost all of the period"). These two pieces of information were converted to numbers of days per year and minutes per day respectively.[10] The product of the two numbers was then an estimate of the number of minutes spent using the practice during the year.

Mayer found that the correlation of the time estimates between the responses on the two survey administrations (four months apart) ranged from 0.66 to a negative 0.09. Although Mayer found these results consistent with his earlier conclusion that surveys give unreliable reports of instructional practice, he also reported that aggregating the reports to form a composite index of NCTM practice produced a measure with "encouraging" reliability (0.69). Comparison of this composite index with the classroom observations showed that teachers had some tendency to report more use of NCTM practices than were observed. But he also found that correlation between the composite index from the survey and the observations was strong (0.85). His overall conclusion is that existing survey instruments give unreliable information on individual instructional practices (e.g., amount of time spent listening to lectures), but that acceptable reliability can be obtained by forming composites, or perhaps by refining the questions teachers are asked.

Mayer's results suggest that logs could be used to measure instructional practices at a fairly high level of generality (e.g., NCTM-like practice versus traditional practice). That is a caution worth attending to, but it does not have direct consequences for the measurement of OTL. The measures Mayer studied asked teachers to describe their practices, rather than asking them to report on the topics they covered. Mayer's study does, however, stand as a reminder that the reliability of teacher reports, whether in logs or in surveys, is an issue that deserves attention when developing OTL measures. Achievement tests are developed over several iterations, taking care that the measures used for research have high reliability. Measures of OTL require a similar process of development to attain levels of reliability that will allow for fruitful uses of the measure. As noted already, when measures have shown high associations with student achievement and achievement gains, those associations are themselves strong evidence of the reliability of the measures, because unreliability attenuates the observed relationship with other variables.

Timing of the Measurement of OTL

Over the sequence of international science and mathematics studies, the amount of information collected about *when* students had opportunity to learn content has increased. As noted previously, FIMS did not ask for any information about when students had the opportunity; SIMS asked, for topics taught during the year of the study, whether the topic already has been taught, is currently being taught, or will be taught later in the year; TIMSS added the possibilities that the topic is a part of the curriculum that the teacher will omit and that the teacher does not know whether the topic is taught at another grade.

What are the possible advantages of gathering information about OTL at various points in time? How feasible is measurement at different points in time? For the purpose of describing OTL (the second of the two major purposes discussed early in this paper), the most accurate description would come from asking teachers what students have an opportunity to learn at the grade they teach. Information gathered cross-sectionally (e.g., by asking sixth-grade teachers what they cover, as information for what opportunities eighth graders have had) would be useful if the curriculum has been stable for several years; that information would be less useful in times of curriculum change. Asking teachers to report about opportunities to learn at other grades would reduce the number of teachers who would have to give information, but the information would likely be less accurate.

What about the timing of OTL measures when the purpose is to adjust for differences in OTL in interpreting achievement results or in understanding relationships within the education system? Accurate information about opportunities prior to the test could be used much as information about opportunities during the tested year: Low achievement on topics students had never been taught should not be taken as an indication of poor instruction or poor student motivation; low achievement on topics that were taught in prior years suggests either that students do not review material often enough to retain it or that the material was not mastered initially.

Information about opportunities to learn at a later time do not call for a shift in thinking about what the achievement results indicate about the school system's effectiveness in teaching the topic. Data on later teaching of the topic would, however, affect the overall picture of a country's mathematics instruction. It would help to distinguish, for example, between countries that teach a topic later in the curriculum (perhaps because of judgments about difficulty for younger students) and countries that have decided not to include the topic in their curriculum.

The difficulties of determining what content students have studied in prior years would be avoided if studies included information about achievement in the previous year, that is, if data were available on achievement *gains*, rather than merely on achievement attained. It would be unnecessary to adjust for opportunities to learn in prior years if gains, rather than attainment, were the learning outcome under consideration, because the effects of the prior opportunities to learn would be represented in the initial achievement measure.

HOW HAS OTL BEEN USED?

In the series of international comparative studies of mathematics and science, the OTL data have been used in both the intended ways described at the beginning of this chapter: as a basis for "appropriately" interpreting the achievement results and as a description of the curricula actually implemented within and across the participating countries. Data on OTL have been presented alongside achievement data, as well as being presented on their own. For the most part, the use of the data in the comparative reports has been as commentary on patterns of performance on particular topic areas, rather than attempting any overall adjustment of achievement in light of OTL. That is probably wise, given imprecision of the OTL measures and the inevitable debates that would ensue about the technical details of any adjustment procedure.

Burstein's analysis of the SIMS longitudinal study (Burstein, 1993) is an exception that could serve as a starting point for developing this approach to adjustment. For the eight education systems that participated in the longitudinal study, Burstein looked at the effect of adjusting the results by creating subtests of items based on OTL data. Data from the question about teaching or reviewing the topic were combined with data from the question asking whether the topic had been taught previously to create an index of whether a teacher reported "teaching, reviewing, or assuming [because it had been taught earlier] the content necessary to answer the test item had been taught" (p. xxxvi). Burstein created subtests by selecting those items that 80 percent of the teachers reported "teaching, reviewing, or assuming." For each of the resulting eight subtests (one for each education system), he then computed the achievement results for all eight systems. The result was a series of tables, each representing the items that students had the opportunity to learn in a particular system. Each table presented, for that subtest, the pretest, posttest, and gain results for each country, plus the corresponding OTL data—the number of items on the subtest that at least 80 percent of the country's teachers reported teaching, reviewing, or assuming.

These tables showed both the broad range of OTL across systems and the effects on absolute and comparative performance of varying the test to match the OTL for system. Of the 157 test items common to all these eight systems, the number of items reaching the 80 percent OTL threshold ranged from 48 to 103. In this analysis, the general result was that systems tended to have higher pretest, posttest, and gain scores on their own system-specific test. The between-system rankings remained about the same, though there were some differences in the magnitude of differences. This analysis demonstrates the possibility for using OTL data to make overall adjustments, which go some way toward making comparisons more plausible. The study also demonstrates the possibility and value of looking at gain scores, rather than simply examining attained achievement. Burstein notes, however, that overall rankings are still problematic in SIMS because the overall item pool did not capture the curricula of all countries, and because the mix of items in the overall pool unevenly represented the various system curricula.

The OTL data also have been used as a basis for noting that a conclusion of comparative research is that OTL is related to achievement, a finding that should no longer be news, but somehow continues to be striking. In the following paragraphs, I will look more closely at the OTL-based conclusions drawn in the series of mathematics and science assessments, with particular attention to Westbury and Baker's exchange about how looking at OTL shapes interpretation of differences in TIMSS between Japanese and U.S. achievement.

Husen's report on FIMS (1967b) noted that OTL was correlated with achievement, with modest results within countries (because of little within-country OTL variation) but substantial correlations between countries.

> Within countries the correlations between achievement scores and teachers' perceptions of students' opportunities to learn the mathematics involved in the test items were always positive and usually substantial. Between countries they were large (0.62 and 0.90 for 1 a and 3 a). The conclusion is that a considerable amount of the variation between countries in mathematics scores can be attributed to the difference between students' opportunities to learn the material tested. (p. 195)

Husen's report (1967b) treats this attribution of difference as a rationale for looking at countries' achievement in light of how "appropriate" the tests were for what was taught in the country. The report seems to consider the differences in OTL as a given context, rather than a basis for possible shifts in national curriculum policy. In the report, these large correlations were not listed among the findings about relations between mathematics achievement and curriculum variables. OTL is apparently seen as a control variable, not a curriculum variable. The report states:

> One of the most striking features of the results is the paucity of general . . . relationships between mathematics achievement and curriculum variables investigated. The correlations between achievement scores and these curriculum variables, when based on the pooled data from all countries, were usually quite low. The weakness of many of the relation-

ships that were found limits their usefulness in curriculum planning. (p. 197)

It seems from this statement that, for FIMS, OTL was not seen as a curriculum variable and did not seem to be considered useful in curriculum planning.

In interpretation of the SIMS results, however, OTL began to be seen as a policy relevant curriculum variable. The OTL data continued to be used as a basis for interpreting achievement data, giving a basis for deciding whether test items were appropriate for particular countries, but commentators also began to argue that a country's pattern of OTL was an appropriate topic for policy discussion, rather than a given part of the context. That is, the discussions began to suggest that the conclusion that might be drawn from seeing low achievement on an item with low OTL was that the country should consider giving students more opportunities to learn how to solve the item, rather than that the low achievement was simply the result of use of an item inappropriate for that country.

To be sure, the OTL results in SIMS continued to be used as a basis for pointing out that some tests results reflected the fact that a set of items was inappropriate for a country. In the main report of SIMS (Robitaille, 1989), achievement results were presented in great detail, with graphic displays that combined each country's achievement results with its OTL results, and with commentary on specific items that pointed out that some low results reflected a mismatch between what was taught in a country and the items used on the SIMS test.

But SIMS reporting also began to shift discussion to questions about whether a country's combined pattern of achievement and OTL might suggest that policies should seek to change OTL, rather than treating it as a given. In an exchange published in *Educational Researcher*, Westbury and Baker (Baker, 1993a, 1993b; Westbury, 1992, 1993) debated how to interpret the U.S.-Japanese difference on SIMS mathematics achievement. They agreed that OTL needs to be taken into account in interpreting the achievement differences. In the analysis that opens the exchange, Westbury uses different course types as a way to describe curricular differences. For example, Westbury notes that the U.S. eighth graders may be in any of four course types: remedial, typical, enriched, or algebra, while Japanese students at that age are all in the single course type. Westbury uses OTL data to describe differences among the U.S. course types, noting that "it is only the U.S. *algebra* course type that has a profile similar to Japan's course" (Westbury, 1992, p. 20). He then compares achievement for that course type to the Japanese achievement, trying to equate for OTL. He finds that the achievement difference disappears, even in a further analysis that tries to account for any selectivity of the U.S. algebra courses.

Baker responds with an analysis that uses OTL data to restrict analysis, class by class, to the material teachers report they taught during the year, finding that Japanese students learned 60 percent of the content taught, as contrasted with only 40 percent for the U.S. students. In his rejoinder, Westbury contends that he was trying to ground the comparison in "a notion of *intentional* curricula," which includes a wider range of factors, for which looking at courses as a whole was more appropriate.

The debate illustrates some of the detailed analytic choices that can be made about how the OTL data are used in interpreting achievement data. Perhaps more important is that the debate illustrates the shift in the discussion from seeing OTL as a background variable to seeing the connections between OTL and achievement as the grounds for national reconsideration of curricular coverage. Westbury's argument is that the ways in which OTL information shifts interpretation are grounds for changing the opportunities. Rather than seeing the SIMS results as a reason for emulating Japanese schooling practices, the results are a reason for making different decisions about what students should have a chance to learn. Westbury's initial argument (modified somewhat in light of Baker's response) is that the differences in achievement are explained entirely by differences in curriculum coverage. Thus OTL data are used as a basis for shifting discussions about how to make U.S. education more effective from organizational and teaching variables to curricular choices.

In the TIMSS reporting, particularly reporting about curriculum and OTL in the United States, the emphasis has shifted even further toward the problems with existing patterns of OTL. The implemented curriculum in the United States is no longer a given part of the context; it has become the problem to be faced. The stress to be put on differences in learning opportunities was foreshadowed in the extensive cross-national curriculum analysis done as an early part of TIMSS (Schmidt, McKnight, & Raizen, 1997; Schmidt, McKnight, Valverde, Houang, & Wiley, 1997). The description of the U.S. curriculum as "a mile wide and an inch deep" may be the TIMSS result that has been most widely repeated.

The importance assigned to OTL in interpretation of the achievement data can be readily seen in the chapter titles of *Facing the Consequences* (Schmidt, McKnight, Cogan, Jakwerth, & Houang, 1999): "Curriculum does matter" and "Access to curriculum matters." The argument in these chapters follows those made in earlier studies by identifying topic areas within a subject area and comparing relative performance in those areas to corresponding data on OTL.

One of the assumptions in this argument is that transfer of learning across topics is limited, so that additional time spent on measurement, for example, will not be of much help in learning how to work problems on relations of fractions. That is, opportunity to learn is important for each topic area, not just for mathematics or science as a whole. If mathematics or science learning were simply increasing mastery of a single skill, then it would not matter what topics were studied. Students who learned more mathematics would do better on all topics. A look at the relative performance of different countries on different topics reveals that students differ in their knowledge of mathematics across topics. U.S. eighth graders, for example, do relatively well at rounding, but are at the bottom of the pack in measurement units. So test performance is, to some extent, topic specific.

The next step in the OTL analysis would be comparing the results by topic area to the differences in OTL for those topic areas. In *Facing the Consequences*, however, OTL information was only included as part of general claims about the diffuse nature of the U.S. curriculum, in comparison to the curricula from other countries.[11] That diffuseness is given as an explanation of the moderate gains in U.S. student learning between adjoining years. The degree to which OTL differences explain the varying topic-level performance in the United States (or any other country) will need to be determined from OTL analyses like those of Westbury and Baker. That earlier exchange illustrates both that the effects found could be substantial (as when Westbury's analysis erased the differences in achievement) and that more than one strategy for analysis may be used, and may yield substantially different interpretations. Analyses like these should be pursued in future studies, as OTL data are used as part of the process of modeling the determinants of student achievement.

SOCIAL SUPPORTS AS OTL

Adding to the possibilities for analysis and interpretation, opportunity to learn could be construed more broadly to include factors beyond classroom instructional time, however defined. Students, for example, might have a better opportunity to learn instructional content because they receive help outside of school. Such help might be participation in formal educational programs, such as the often-mentioned Japanese tutoring programs, or they might be experiences that look less like school-away-from-school, perhaps help with homework from a parent, or even practice with a skill in a work or recreational activity. Students who are encouraged to read at home, for example, have more opportunity to learn the skills of reading than students who read only during class time.

Differences in this more broadly defined OTL are substantial, both within countries and across countries. In acquisition of written literacy, for example, children with literate parents have out-of-school opportunities to learn that are not available to illiterate parents. Thus what appears as an effect of schooling may sometimes come from out-of-school learning, but the importance of out-of-school learning will vary by content area and by country.

> In most industrialized countries the path to early literacy begins in the home and continues through formal instruction in school. There is an interdependence between the two sources, since formal instruction gains its full effectiveness on the foundation established and maintained by parents and family members. In many developing countries, however, high rates of parental illiteracy make it impossible for parents to enter directly into the process of helping their children learn how to read. In these societies, instruction in reading depends primarily on what the child encounters in school. (Stevenson, Lee, & Schweingruber, 1999, p. 251)

Such differences in family-based opportunities to learn may account for some of the well-documented associations between family background (including social class, income, levels of mother's and father's education) and achievement. Such associations have been found within countries, in the United States most famously in the Coleman report (Coleman et al., 1966). Effects of family background on achievement also have been found in cross-national studies such as SIMS. "Just like its IEA predecessors, the SIMS results of the analyses of the effects of background characteristics on achievement (status) at either pretest or posttest occasions showed the strong relationships of such variables as the pupil's mother's education, father's education, mother's occupation, and father's occupation with cognitive outcomes," note Kifer and Burstein (1992, p. 329). "The immediate evidence and external evidence agree in attributing more variation in student achievement to the family background than to school factors. The reason is not far to seek. It is that parents vary much more than schools," adds Peaker (1975, p. 22).[12]

Such family background variables are like OTL in that they may provide an explanation for achievement differences that otherwise might be attributed to differences in the education system. To understand the connections between schooling and achievement, some of the effects of family background can be statistically "controlled," either by including measures of the background variables in statistical models used to estimate links between schooling and achievement or by including measures of prior achievement, which would themselves be highly associated with family background.

SIMS investigators concluded that including prior achievement was a necessary approach for controlling both the effects of experiences prior to the school year and the effects of differences in curriculum based on those prior experiences (Schmidt & Burstein, 1992). They also found that including prior achievement in the analysis—looking at learning across the year rather than merely at achievement—greatly reduced the influence of such background variables. "The background characteristics of students are not strongly related to *growth* because the pretest removes an unknown but large portion of the relationship between those characteristics and the posttest," note Kifer and Burstein (1992, p. 340, emphasis added).

The strategy of focusing on achievement *gains* as a way of controlling for differences in background factors seems implicit in the arguments for importance of curriculum in the TIMSS publication, *Facing the Consequences* (Schmidt et al., 1999). Using items that appear on tests at more than one level, and taking advantage of the fact that tested populations include students at more than one grade level, Schmidt and his colleagues are able to estimate gains in achievement across grades. While acknowledging that gains across grades could be due in part to "life experience" (i.e., opportunities to learn outside school), they argue that the associations of the gains with curriculum content at the corresponding grade levels indicate that curriculum, that is, OTL within schools, is an important factor in learning the content of these items.

> The general purport of all specific items discussed above is that, while developmental and life experience factors may be involved in accounting for achievement changes, curricular factors undoubtedly are. . . . The main evidentiary value of examining these link items is that their differences rule out explanations based on factors such as maturation, life experience, or some general measure of mathematics or science achievement. (Schmidt et al., 1999, pp. 158-159)

In summary, connections between OTL and student achievement typically are conceived as within-school phenomena. Students do, however, sometimes have other opportunities to learn outside the classroom, opportunities that are often linked to differences in family background. The significance of these outside opportunities will vary by content area: Families differ substantially in the opportunities young children have to acquire basic literacy; families likely will vary much less in the opportunities they provide for learning how to compute the perimeter of a rectangle (because such knowledge is less likely to be part of the ordinary lives of any families). Thus, evidence about the connection between OTL and student achievement may be easier to interpret for topics that are more "academic," that is, more distinctively school knowledge. Although differences in how "academic" that content is will vary by school subject (e.g., chemistry is more academic than reading), looking at individual items can make it easier to identify content that is unlikely to be learned outside school. Looking at measures of gain, rather than status, is another way to simplify interpretation of the effects of school OTL.

WHAT HAS RESEARCH SHOWN ABOUT
THE STRENGTH OF OTL EFFECTS?

Empirical support for the influence of time spent engaged in learning on student achievement was provided by the Beginning Teacher Evaluation Study (BTES), which used a combination of teacher logs and classroom observations to record how much time a sample of elementary school teachers "allocated to reading and mathematics curriculum content categories (e.g., decoding consonant blends, inferential comprehension, addition and subtraction with no regrouping, mathematics speed tests, etc.)" (Fisher et al., 1980). (Classroom observations also were used to estimate the fraction of allocated time that students actually engaged in the learning opportunities.) BTES found substantial differences in the time teachers allocated (i.e., in OTL) and found statistically significant associations between time allocated and student achievement. These are samples of the early empirical evidence that if students spend more time working on a topic, they will learn more about the topic. Or, conversely, and perhaps more important in the context of international comparative studies, if students spend little or no time working on a topic, they will learn little about it. As the quote from Husen (p. 232) suggests, the exceptions come either when the student is able to transfer learning from another topic or when the student spends time outside of school on the topic (e.g., learning from parents or independent reading, even though the topic is not studied as part of formal education).

The BTES research found positive associations between student achievement and each of these measures of OTL. For the full set of Academic Learning Time variables, the effects on student achievement were statistically significant for some, but not all, of the specific content areas tested in grades two and five reading and mathematics. Overall, about a third of the statistical tests were significant at the 0.10 level. The magnitudes of the effects are indicated by the residual variance explained by the ALT variables, after the effect of prior achievement has been taken into account. Those residual effects ranged in magnitude from 0.01 to 0.30, with an average on the order of 0.10 (Borg, 1980, p. 67).

Barr and Dreeben (1983) found a high correlation (0.93) between the number of basal vocabulary words covered and a test of vocabulary knowledge, accounting for 86 percent of the variance on that test. The correlation was also high with a broader test of reading at the end of first grade (0.75) and even with a reading test given a year later (0.71). For phonics, the correlations with content coverage were somewhat lower, 0.62 with a test of phonics knowledge, 0.57 with first-grade achievement, and 0.51 with second-grade achievement.

Barr and Dreeben's attention to the social organization of schooling led them to examine whether the correlation between coverage and achievement comes because students with higher aptitude cover more content. They found that groups with higher mean aptitude do cover more content, but that the correlation between individual student aptitude and achievement was close to zero. Thus the investigators conclude that student aptitude affects how much content they cover through affecting assignment to group, but, given assignment to group, it is content coverage, not aptitude, that is the major determinant of learning, especially for vocabulary.

In FIMS, the within-country relationship between OTL and achievement was positive, but varied. As Husen (1967a, pp. 167-168) wrote, "There was a small but statistically significant positive correlation between the scores and the teachers' ratings of opportunity to learn the topics. There was, however, much variation between countries and between population within countries in the size of these coefficients." The small magnitude of the relationship in some countries may have been due to limited variation in OTL within those countries, that is, in the uniformity of curriculum in those countries. The between-country association between OTL and student achievement, however, was substantial, with correlations of 0.4 to 0.8 for the different populations. "In other words, students have scored higher marks in countries where the tests have been considered by the teachers to be more appropriate to the experience of their students" (p. 168).

For SIMS, the Westbury-Baker exchange mentioned earlier shows that the relationship between OTL and achievement was, at least in Westbury's initial analysis, strong enough to explain all of the Japan-U.S. differences in achievement. Thus OTL can be a powerful explanatory variable when looking at particular, fairly narrow comparisons.

The more general analysis of OTL data for SIMS, however, did not yield results that were striking enough to be given attention in general conclusions of the study. An overall OTL variable was included in a broader search for patterns in the data (Schmidt & Kifer, 1989). The within-country analysis used a hierarchical model with predictive variables that included student gender, language of the home, family help, hours of mathematics homework, proportion of class in top one-third nationally, class size, school size, and teacher's age. The model was estimated for each country by achievement topic area (i.e., arithmetic, algebra, geometry, measurement, statistics, total). The frequency of the importance of each variable was reported in a table of the number of statistically significant betas for each topic area over the 20 countries. What is striking about the table (Schmidt & Kifer, 1989, p. 217) is that none of the between-class or between-school variables has more than 4 (out of a possible 20) significant betas for any topic area. The OTL variable has one significant beta over countries for each of the five subtests and one for the total test.

Among the between-class or between-school variables, that puts it below class size, proportion of class in top third nationally, class hours of mathematics per week, and about the same as teacher age. This is, at best, a modest effect within countries. That is consistent with the FIMS results, where within-country associations between OTL and achievement were positive, but weak to modest. Perhaps these modest associations were due, as in the case of FIMS, to relatively small within-country variation in OTL in most countries. (The United States is unusual in the extent of within-country OTL variation.) For FIMS, between-country associations were substantial. Beyond the Westbury-Baker exchange, I did not locate any reports of the between-country OTL-achievement associations from SIMS.

As noted, the TIMSS reports document the cross-country variation in the content of curricular materials, but I did not locate reports on the variation in teachers' reported OTL.[13] Given the important role the differences in national curriculum differences have played in policy discussions, the TIMSS curriculum analysis deserves further attention by scholars within and outside the community that has carried out the TIMSS studies.

CONCLUSION

The sequence of international comparative studies of mathematics and science has given increasing attention to variation in OTL, both in data collection and in reporting. OTL information has obvious importance for the interpretation of achievement differences within and across countries. OTL's link to curricular intentions has become a major spur for discussions about an individual country's curriculum, at least in the United States. The positive association between OTL and student learning has been documented in a number of studies, although the measured association between OTL and achievement or achievement gains has been quite varied. Some analyses show a weak connection; Westbury's analysis produced a dramatic effect of taking OTL into account. Some of the variation in strength of association can be attributed to the amount of variation in OTL; some can be attributed to reliance on teachers' memories of content coverage; some may be due to learning outside school or to transfer of learning from one topic to another.

The number of reports making extensive use of the currently collected OTL data seems small. The complexities of analysis are likely daunting. The dramatic results in Westbury and Baker should make further analyses attractive. Their focus on a single pair of countries undoubtedly contributed to their ability to find clear (though somewhat contradictory) results.

What does this review suggest for future comparative studies? The importance of continuing to collect some OTL information is evident. Now, as before, interpretation of achievement or learning comparisons requires some understanding of what learning was intended and how much these intentions were realized, by nations and by teachers. Looking at specific topics, rather than general content areas, is more likely to yield measurable differences in OTL and stronger relationships to achievement. But finer grained work also places greater burdens on respondents and analysts.

Choices about what sort of OTL data to collect, and how, must be considered in light of the questions to be answered. Surely no further evidence is needed to support the conclusion that OTL has some positive effect on achievement. Attention now should turn to understanding the processes of teaching and learning, using information on OTL to help construct analytic models that can do a better job of identifying the separate, though perhaps interacting, effects of student aptitude, perseverance, quality of instruction, and opportunity to learn.

The work done to date with OTL suggests several principles that should be used in continuing to refine measures:

• The questions asked should allow for analyses that separate OTL from related variables, such as teachers' judgments about whether students have learned (as opposed to having the opportunity to learn) and student perseverance in working on a topic.

• Questions should also allow for separation of information about classroom processes from information about content coverage. The Carroll model separates OTL from quality of instruction. Keeping these distinct is important for building more accurate models of the influences on student learning. Moreover, methodological studies suggest that teachers are less reliable in giving retrospective information about time spent using different methods of instruction than they are in giving information about time spent on specific topics.

• Information about opportunities to learn in grades other than those tested is important for understanding a system's curriculum and for understanding connections between school practices and student learning. Information can be collected from teachers in the tested grades, but their reports may contain inaccuracies because of lack of communication within the system or because of changes in the curriculum over time. Information about student achievement in the prior year can give a better indication of prior learning. In past studies, some countries have seen such longitudinal designs as difficult to implement, but the added information they provide strongly suggests that they should be considered.

- Information also should be gathered about opportunities to learn topics outside the classrooms in the tested subject. The interpretation of achievement results will be influenced by whether students had opportunities to learn content outside school or in other subject areas (e.g., learning how to write reports in social studies classes or learning about measurement in science classes).
- Development of measures of OTL deserves the same care given to development of cognitive achievement measures. The reliability of OTL measures can be used as the basis for successive refinements, just as it is in selection and revision of test items. Ambiguous wordings of content descriptions should be detected and eliminated. In mathematics, the wording and organization of topic categories have benefited from decades of research; topic categories in other subject areas would benefit from similar cycles of testing and revision. Studies of the associations between student learning and various OTL variables can be used to determine what combinations and functional forms have the greatest predictive validity. Further work could be done to investigate the construct validity of OTL measures.

In short, researchers and policy makers have come to agree that OTL should be an important part of international comparative studies of achievement, in large part because OTL has been shown to have a link to student learning. In future studies, attention should shift from producing further evidence to support the existence of that link, toward using measures of OTL to build better models of the sources of student learning. Such models should give insight into the reasons students receive differing opportunities to learn and the reasons that student learning varies, given the same opportunities to learn. To make that shift, investments should be made, as they have begun to be in mathematics, into improving OTL measures so that they can better support fruitful research. Carroll's model of school learning remains a helpful general framework for such research, but should be supplemented to include the factors—system policies, classroom organization, teacher knowledge—that influence the opportunity to learn and the quality of instruction students experience.

NOTES

1. This paper has benefited substantially from comments on an earlier draft by Andy Porter, by other members of BICSE, and by Jack Schwille.
2. The word "early" is not quite accurate. Studies of time allocations in schools go back at least to the early 1900s. Although these studies did not use the language of "opportunity to learn," they were motivated by the thought that allocations of time were a determinant of student achievement. For a sketch of this distant history, see Borg (1980) or Berliner (1990).

3. The idea that student achievement will be highest when academic tasks are relatively easy for students (i.e., that students have a high success rate with them) seems sensible in some respects, but may depend on the subject matter involved and the focus of the achievement test. Berliner and his colleagues were looking at effects on the learning of basic skills. For higher level content, easy academic tasks might be less productive. Recent discussions of standards often use the phrase "challenging content," which seems inconsistent with the assignment of easy tasks. A basic principle in the Japanese mathematics lessons, captured in the TIMSS videotapes, seems to be that lessons should be structured around difficult problems.

4. "Engaged time" also may be seen as a part of Carroll's "perseverance," rather than OTL. How this should be treated in a research study depends on the purpose of the analysis. Engagement might be thought of as a function of individual student character-istics, or as another aspect of instruction that the educational system, through the teacher, might affect.

5. Schwille and Burstein (1987, p. 606) describe tensions within the research community itself between seeing international studies as between-country comparisons and seeing them as a set of within-country studies. They note, however, that IEA researchers often have denied interest in the "cognitive Olympics," given the difficulties of analysis that must take into account so many differences among countries, differences that are argu-ably important as control or explanatory variables.

6. In the first science study, the OTL questions were asked collectively of all teachers at the tested grade level in a school. That obscured any differences in OTL among teachers within a school. That problem was corrected in the mathematics studies.

7. Porter and his colleagues have combined an instrument for measuring instructional practices with one measuring instructional content in mathematics and science into a package they call the Surveys of Enacted Curriculum (SEC) (Porter & Smithson, 2001). This package is being used in several large-scale studies (Blank, Kim, & Smithson, 2000; Council of Chief State School Officers, 2000; Ware, Richardson, & Kim, 2000). The per-formance of this package in these studies should be useful in deciding how this pack-age might be adapted and refined for future research.

8. This empirical result appears to be at odds with interpretations of TIMSS results that suggest that Japanese teachers' treatment of a small number of mathematics and science topics in great depth leads to high overall levels of achievement.

9. Porter and Smithson (2001) offer a useful discussion of the role of studies of alignment between standards and assessments in studying the effects of policies on student learn-ing.

10. For the "how often" question, the conversion was: never = 0 days; a few times a year = 5 days; once or twice a month = 14 days; once or twice a week = 55 days; nearly every day = 129 days; daily = 184 days. For the "for how many minutes" question, the conver-sion was: none = 0; a few minutes in the period = 5 minutes; less than half = 15 minutes; about half = 25 minutes; more than half = 37.5 minutes; almost all of the period = 50 minutes.

11. TIMSS staff told me that the OTL information will be an important part of more de-tailed analyses presented in reports in preparation at the time this chapter was going to press.

12. Jack Schwille has pointed out to me that Peaker's attribution of more variance to family background than to schools is based on analyses that enter all family background vari-ables first. When, as is often the case, family background variables are correlated with school variables, it is difficult to determine how the shared variance should be appor-tioned. In any case, the effects of differences in family background on achievement consistently have been shown to be substantial.

13. These may appear in TIMSS reports that were in preparation at the time this paper went to press.

REFERENCES

Baker, D. P. (1993a). Compared to Japan, the U.S. is a low achiever . . . really: New evidence and comment on Westbury. *Educational Researcher, 22*(3), 18-20.

Baker, D. P. (1993b). A rejoinder. *Educational Researcher, 22*(3), 25-26.

Ball, D. L., Camburn, E., Correnti, R., Phelps, G., & Wallace, R. (1999). *New tools for research on instruction and instructional policy: A Web-based teacher log* (Document W-99-2). Seattle: University of Washington, Center for the Study of Teaching and Policy.

Barr, R., & Dreeben, R. (1983). *How schools work.* Chicago: University of Chicago Press.

Berliner, D. C. (1990). What's all the fuss about instructional time? In M. Ben-Peretz & R. Bromme (Eds.), *The nature of time in school* (pp. 3-35). New York: Teachers College Press.

Berliner, D. C., Fisher, C. W., Filby, N., & Marliave, R. (1978). *Executive summary of Beginning Teacher Evaluation Study.* San Francisco: Far West Regional Laboratory for Educational Research and Development.

Blank, R. K., Kim, J. J., & Smithson, J. L. (2000). *Survey results of urban school classroom practices in mathematics and science: 1999 report.* Norwood, MA: Systemic Research.

Bloom, B. S. (1976). *Human characteristics and school learning.* New York: McGraw-Hill.

Borg, W. R. (1980). Time and school learning. In C. Denham & A. Lieberman (Eds.), *Time to learn* (pp. 33-72). Washington, DC: U.S. Department of Health, Education, and Welfare, National Institute of Education.

Burstein, L. (1993). Prologue: Studying learning, growth, and instruction cross-nationally: Lessons learned about why and why not engage in cross-national studies. In L. Burstein (Ed.), *The IEA Study of Mathematics III: Student growth and classroom processes.* New York: Pergamon Press.

Burstein, L., McDonnell, L. M., Van Winkle, J., Ormseth, T., Mirocha, J., & Guitton, G. (1995). *Validating national curriculum indicators.* Santa Monica, CA: RAND.

Carroll, J. (1963). A model for school learning. *Teachers College Record, 64,* 723-733.

Coleman, J. S., Campbell, E. Q., Hobson, C. J., McPartland, J., Mood, A. M., Weinfeld, F. D., & York, R. L. (1966). *Equality of educational opportunity.* Washington, DC: U.S. Department of Health, Education, and Welfare.

Council of Chief State School Officers. (2000). *Using data on enacted curriculum in mathematics and science: Sample results from a study of classroom practices and subject content.* Washington, DC: Author.

Dewey, J. (1904/1965). The relation of theory to practice in education. In M. L. Borrowman (Ed.), *Teacher education in America: A documentary history* (pp. 140-171). New York: Teachers College Press.

Fisher, C. W., Berliner, D. C., Filby, N. N., Marliave, R., Cahn, L. S., & Dishaw, M. M. (1980). Teaching behaviors, academic learning time, and student achievement: An overview. In C. Denham & A. Lieberman (Eds.), *Time to learn* (pp. 7-32). Washington, DC: U.S. Department of Health, Education, and Welfare, National Institute of Education.

Flanders, J. (1994). Student opportunities in grade 8 mathematics: Textbook coverage of the SIMS test. In I. Westbury, C. A. Ethington, L. A. Sosniak, & D. P. Baker (Eds.), *In search of more effective mathematics education* (pp. 61-93). Norwood, NJ: Ablex.

Gamoran, A., Porter, A. C., Smithson, J., & White, P. A. (1997). Upgrading high school mathematics instruction: Improving learning opportunities for low-achieving, low income youth. *Educational Evaluation and Policy Analysis, 19*(4), 325-338.

Husen, T. (Ed.). (1967a). *International Study of Achievement in Mathematics: A comparison of twelve countries* (Vol. I). New York: John Wiley & Sons.

Husen, T. (Ed.). (1967b). *International Study of Achievement in Mathematics: A comparison of twelve countries* (Vol. II). New York: John Wiley & Sons.

Kifer, E., & Burstein, L. (1992). Concluding thoughts: What we know, what it means. In L. Burstein (Ed.), *The IEA Study of Mathematics III: Student growth and classroom processes* (pp. 329-341). New York: Pergamon Press.

Knapp, M., with others. (1995). *Teaching for meaning in high-poverty classrooms.* New York: Teachers College Press.

Knapp, M. S., & Marder, C. (1992). *Academic challenge for the children of poverty, Vol. 2: Study design and technical notes.* Washington, DC: U.S. Department of Education, Planning and Evaluation Service.

Mayer, D. P. (1999). Measuring instructional practice: Can policymakers trust survey data? *Educational Evaluation and Policy Analysis, 21*(1), 29-45.

McDonnell, L. M. (1995). Opportunity to learn as a research concept and a policy instrument. *Educational Evaluation and Policy Analysis, 17*(3), 305-322.

National Council of Teachers of Mathematics. (1991). *Professional standards for teaching mathematics.* Reston, VA: Author.

Peaker, G. F. (1975). *An empirical study of education in twenty-one systems: A technical report* (Vol. 8). Stockholm: Almqvist and Wiksell International.

Porter, A., Floden, R., Freeman, D., Schmidt, W., & Schwille, J. (1988). Content determinants in elementary school mathematics. In D. A. Grouws, T. J. Cooney, & D. Jones (Eds.), *Effective mathematics teaching* (pp. 96-113). Reston, VA: National Council of Teachers of Mathematics.

Porter, A. C. (1998). The effects of upgrading policies on high school mathematics and science. In D. Ravitch (Ed.), *Brookings papers on education policy* (pp. 123-164). Washington, DC: Brookings Institution Press.

Porter, A. C., & Smithson, J. L. (2001). Are content standards being implemented in the classroom? A methodology and some tentative answers. In S. H. Fuhrman (Ed.), *From the capitol to the classroom: Standards-based reform in the states. One hundredth Yearbook of the National Society for the Study of Education. Part II* (pp. 60-80). Chicago: University of Chicago Press.

Robitaille, D. F. (1989). Students' achievements: Population A. In D. F. Robitaille & R. A. Garden (Eds.), *The IEA Study of Mathematics II: Context and outcomes of school mathematics* (pp. 102-125). New York: Pergamon Press.

Robitaille, D. F., & Garden, R. A. (1989). *The IEA study of Mathematics II: Contexts and outcomes of school mathematics.* Oxford, England: Pergamon Press.

Schmidt, W. H., & Burstein, L. (1992). Concomitants of growth in mathematics achievement during the population a school year. In L. Burstein (Ed.), *The IEA Study of Mathematics III: Student growth and classroom processes* (pp. 309-327). New York: Pergamon Press.

Schmidt, W. H., & Kifer, E. (1989). Exploring relationships across Population A systems: A search for patterns. In F. D. Robitaille & R. A. Garden (Eds.), *The IEA Study of Mathematics II: Contexts and outcomes of school mathematics* (pp. 209-231). New York: Pergamon Press.

Schmidt, W. H., McKnight, C. C., Cogan, L. S., Jakwerth, P. M., & Houang, R. T. (1999). *Facing the consequences: Using TIMSS for a closer look at U.S. mathematics and science education.* Boston: Kluwer Academic Press.

Schmidt, W. H., McKnight, C. C., & Raizen, S. A. (1997). *A splintered vision: An investigation of U.S. science and mathematics education.* Boston: Kluwer Academic Press.

Schmidt, W. H., McKnight, C. C., Valverde, G. A., Houang, R. T., & Wiley, D. E. (1997). *Many visions, many aims, Vol. 1.: A cross-national investigation of curricular intentions in school mathematics.* Boston: Kluwer Academic Press.

Schwille, J., & Burstein, L. (1987). The necessity of trade-offs and coalition building in cross-national research: A critique of Theisen, Achola, and Boakari. *Comparative Education Review, 31*, 602-611.

Smithson, J. L., & Porter, A. C. (1994). *Measuring classroom practice: Lessons learned from the efforts to describe the enacted curriculum — The Reform Up Close Study*. Madison: University of Wisconsin-Madison, Consortium for Policy Research in Education.

Stevenson, H. W., Lee, S., & Schweingruber, H. (1999). Home influences on early literacy. In D. A. Wagner, R. L. Venezky, & B. V. Street (Eds.), *Literacy: An international handbook* (pp. 251-257). Boulder, CO: Westview Press.

Travers, K. J., & Westbury, I. (1989). *The IEA Study of Mathematics I: Analysis of mathematics curriculum*. Oxford, England: Pergamon Press.

Ware, M., Richardson, L., & Kim, J. (2000). *What matters in urban school reform*. Norwood, MA: Systemic Research.

Westbury, I. (1992). Comparing American and Japanese achievement: Is the United States really a low achiever? *Educational Researcher, 21*(5), 18-24.

Westbury, I. (1993). American and Japanese achievement . . . again: A response to Baker. *Educational Researcher, 22*(3), 21-25.

Wiley, D. E., & Harnischfeger, A. (1974). Explosion of a myth: Quantity of schooling and exposure to instruction, major educational vehicles. *Educational Researcher, 3*(4), 7-12.

9

Statistical Issues in Analysis of International Comparisons of Educational Achievement

Stephen W. Raudenbush and Ji-Soo Kim*

International comparisons of educational achievement have become influential in debates over school reform in the United States and other countries. Such studies provide evidence on how countries compare at a given time with respect to various cognitive skills; on how the average achievement in a society is changing over time; on the magnitude of inequalities in skill levels between subgroups within a society; and on differences in such inequalities between societies. Policy makers in countries that rank low in achievement can cite these data in urgent calls for reform. Researchers use such findings to develop explanations for why certain countries outperform other countries, why certain countries seem to be improving over time faster than others, and why inequality in outcomes appears more egregious in some societies than others. By motivating reform and generating new reform strategies, international comparative studies provoke public concern, heated controversy, and new lines of research.

This chapter considers statistical issues that arise in drawing conclusions from international studies of achievement. It is organized around two distinct but related uses of the data these studies yield.

The first use involves *description* and *comparison*: description of the average level of achievement within a society and comparison of such

*The first author is Professor, School of Education, Professor, Department of Statistics, and Senior Research Scientist, Survey Research Center, University of Michigan. The second author is an advanced doctoral student at the School of Education, University of Michigan.

achievement averages across societies; description of changes in achievement over time for each society and the comparison of such change trends across societies; description of inequality within a society and comparison of inequality between societies. Such description and comparison require statistical inferences and lead inevitably to substantive interpretations. This chapter will consider the statistical issues underlying the validity of such inferences and interpretations.

The second use of international comparative data involves *causal explanation*. Although such nonexperimental data cannot justify causal inference (Mislevy, 1995), the data are highly relevant to the development of causal explanations. When combined with collateral information on cross-national differences in curriculum and instruction and when viewed in light of the expert judgment of researchers and educators, comparative achievement data can help generate promising new explanations for why children are learning more in one nation than another (Schmidt, McKnight, & Raizen, 1997). Such explanations are central to policy formation and to the design of new research. Promising new explanations tend to be based on statistical inferences about associations among several variables. This chapter will consider the statistical issues underlying the validity of inferences about such multivariate associations.

The Third International Mathematics and Science Study (TIMSS) provides a prominent and useful example. That study aimed to *describe* the intended curriculum, the implemented curriculum, and the attained curriculum (that is, student achievement) in each of about 50 countries. Each of these three tasks involves description, but the aim is obviously to generate *explanations* for how curriculum, instructional practice, and student achievement are connected. Indeed, some coherent explanations for the connections between these three domains have emerged and now serve as a focus for new research and debate.

TIMSS is not alone in this regard. The International Adult Literacy Study (IALS) describes the social origins (e.g., parental education) of adults in each of many societies as well as those adults' educational attainment, level of literacy in each of several domains, current occupational status, and income. One purpose of that study is to *describe* levels of adult literacy in each country and to compare countries on their levels of adult literacy. But the design of the study points toward *explanation* of how social origins, education, and, especially, adult literacy are linked to economic outcomes. The rationale for such a design relies on a strong hypothesis that cognitive skill is ever more important to economic success in a global economy and that cross-national differences in literacy are highly salient to cross-national differences in economic success. The goal of *causal explanation* at least implicitly underlies the design of IALS even though IALS, as a cross-sectional survey, can never strongly test the many empirical connections implied by any theory for how social origins, education, and literacy are connected to individual and national economic outcomes. Hence this chapter will consider statistical issues underlying valid descriptions while also considering how statistical analysis can best contribute to the larger goal of causal explanation.

The problem of making valid comparisons across societies is multi-faceted. Any comparison is founded on the assumption that the outcome variables have the same meaning in every society and that the items designed to measure these variables relate similarly in each society (Mislevy, 1995). The task of translation of the tests into many languages—and of back translation to ensure that the translations are functionally equivalent—is daunting. The task of statistically equating the tests to ensure that they have equal difficulty across countries is also enormous. Yet these challenges are well beyond the scope of this chapter. We shall assume that the outcome variables are measured equivalently in every society in order to focus on the statistical issues of central interest. Of course, any shortcomings in outcome measurement and scaling will amplify the statistical problems discussed here.

We shall also assume that the sampling designs in each study are adequate to ensure that a sample that fits the specifications of the design will represent the intended population. This requires, for example, that sample design weights are available that adjust adequately for unequal probabilities of selection of persons in the target population.

This chapter also assumes that demographic variables and other explanatory variables (such as gender, ethnicity, parental education, books in the home) are sensibly measured within each society. But we cannot avoid a problem that inevitably arises in cross-national research: that some of these explanatory variables will have different meanings in different countries. For example, ethnic and language minority groups that appear in some societies are not present in others, and parental educational attainment is conceived and assessed differently in different countries.

With these constraints in mind, this chapter begins with the problem of description and comparison of national differences. It then turns to the role that statistical analyses of comparative data might play in causal explanations.

DESCRIPTION AND COMPARISON OF NATIONAL OUTCOMES

Accurate description of a nation's outcomes is a necessary but not sufficient condition for meaningful comparison. We consider three kinds of description as well as the comparison each informs: cross-sectional description for one cohort, between-cohort descriptions, and descriptions of change over time. Throughout this chapter we define a cohort as a birth cohort, that is, persons born during a given interval of time.

Cross-Sectional Description and Comparison

A valid description should be no more complex than is necessary to capture the key features of the data. It should apply to a well-defined population, and it should be estimated from a sample that represents that population well. We now consider the complexity of a description, the target population being described, and the realized sample as a basis for cross-sectional description.

Complexity of Description

A description is a summary of evidence. Such a summary must be complex enough to capture the essential features of the evidence, but it should be as simple as is justifiable to avoid fastening attention on irrelevancies. A one-number summary, typically the mean, is likely to provide an inadequate basis for comparison. If the nations being compared vary in *dispersion*, presenting means alone will omit important information about how the countries compare. Two nations with the same mean and varying dispersion would vary in the number of students who are especially low or high. If the outcome displays a skewed distribution, presenting the mean alone will mislead: Presenting the median may add useful information.

Interpreting national means is difficult without knowing how much of the variation in the outcome lies *within countries*. Outcomes such as achievement and literacy typically are measured on an arbitrary scale. Mean differences between nations might look big, but there is no way of assessing their magnitude without knowing how much variation lies within societies. Thus, for example, figures 1 through 3 of *Pursuing Excellence* (Takahira, Gonzales, Frase, & Salganik, 1998) give national means on mathematic achievement for "Population 1" (roughly, fourth graders according to the U.S. definition). These numbers seem to vary a lot: Singapore's mean is about 100 points higher than the international average. But without knowing something about the scale of this variable, we cannot discern whether this difference represents a big or small difference in mathematics proficiency. Figure 4 displays, for each country, the percentage of students who are above the 10th percentile internationally. This conveys some sense of how big the national differences are (e.g., 39 percent of Singapore's students score above the international 90th percentile). However, it conveys the size of national differences only for the upper end of the distribution.

One-number summaries fail to convey information about *uncertainty*. Figure 2 of *Pursuing Excellence* shows a U.S. mean of 565 on science achievement, while the mean for Japan is 574. This information alone does not help us decide whether the nations really differ. However, the figure also puts the nations in "blocks" according to whether they are "significantly different" from the United States. Japan is in the same block as the United States, so these two nations are not significantly different. In contrast, England, which scored 551, is significantly lower than the United States. This dichotomous approach encourages us to conclude that the United States and Japan, which differ by nine points, are similar, but the United States and England, which differ by 14 points, are different. Displaying confidence intervals is more informative because it allows the reader to gauge how much weight to put on an observed mean difference.

Mean differences will be misleading when *statistical interactions* are present. In the comparative context, an interaction occurs when the magnitude of the difference between countries depends on some background characteristic of the population (rural versus urban or male versus female). Two nations that look similar on average, for example, could differ dramatically if subgroups were compared. For example, to say that a given nation is at the international mean would convey no useful information by itself if boys in that nation were doing very well and girls were doing very poorly.

Mean differences also will be misleading in the presence of *confounding*. A confounding variable is a background characteristic that is related to achievement but is more prevalent in one country than another. To ignore such variables can lead to an error known as "Simpson's paradox." It is possible, in principle, that Nation A can have a *higher* mean than Nation B even though every subgroup in Nation A does *worse* than the corresponding subgroup in Nation B! This can occur when the more advantaged subgroups have larger relative frequency in the lower performing nation.

A salient confounding variable in the TIMSS design is student age. Much of the controversy around Population 3 (defined as students in their final year of secondary school or, for short, "school leavers," including U.S. seniors) focuses on national differences in age. However, even in the less controversial studies of Populations 1 and 2, age as a confounding variable becomes a potential concern. Population 1 includes, in each nation, the pair of adjacent school grades that contain the most nine-year-olds. This rule defines Population 1 as third and fourth graders in the United States, but this definition yields different grade sets in different countries. Yet TIMSS publications refer to Population 1 as "fourth graders." Now age is likely to be quite strongly related to achievement. If nations also differ with respect to the mean age of their samples, then age is a confounding variable. Although these national differences in age are likely to be small, one must keep in mind that most national differences in achievement also may be small (relative to differences within nations). Small differences in age might then contribute to nontrivial distortion in between-country comparisons. Moreover, as we shall see in the following example, grade-level comparisons between countries may be subject to misinterpretation as a result of selection bias.

By using TIMSS as an example, we do not mean to imply that TIMSS analyses are incorrect, that TIMSS reports are flawed, or that one should never report mean differences. Rather, our intent is to emphasize that analysts working on international comparative studies have several substantial responsibilities: (a) to explore aspects of the distribution of achievement other than the mean; (b) to report mean differences (or median differences) in the context of within-country variation; (c) to associate mean differences with confidence intervals; (d) to study interactions and report those that are especially salient; and (e) to study confounding variables and take necessary precautions that readers not misinterpret mean differences.

Just how much complexity must be reported must be decided on a case-by-case basis. A useful preliminary step is a graphical display that compares the cumulative distributions of an outcome between two countries. This leads to a pair of "S" curves. If the distance between these curves is essentially invariant and approximately equal to the mean difference, then the data lend some support to the reporting of mean differences as a partial summary of evidence. But if these S curves are nonparallel, the mean difference by itself is misleading. Such a display will not, of course, detect interactions or confounding. We will illustrate this idea in an example.

Defining the Target Population

Statistical inference requires a precise definition of the target population. Subtle differences between studies in this definition can lead to spurious differences in findings. International comparative research poses special challenges in this regard.

We have already referred to the cross-national differences in schooling systems that may lead to differences in mean age between societies, thus distorting comparisons between countries. TIMSS Population 3 entails a much more serious conceptual problem. Population 3 is defined as the population of those about to leave secondary school. Such a definition leaves great doubt about the meaning of the population in a given country and, hence, about the meaning of any comparisons between countries. First, many students will leave school before the time designated as the "school-leaving" time. In the United States, about 3–5 percent of all students drop out of school before 10th grade (Rumberger, 1995), and a larger number leave prior to high school graduation. Those students are not part of the TIMSS definition of Population 3. This is problematic. If such dropout rates vary by country, comparisons between countries will be biased, such that countries with the highest dropout rates will experience positive biases in their means. Even more problematic, distinctions between secondary and postsecondary school historically have become blurred. In the United States, persons failing to obtain a high school diploma may show up later in community colleges, where many will obtain GEDs (high school equivalency diplomas); some of these will go on to obtain bachelor's degrees. In reality, the designation of 12th grade as the "school-leaving age" has become quite arbitrary. Similar ambiguities will arise in other societies. For example, in some societies, students leave formal school earlier and obtain significant education in on-the-job-training programs.

In the ideal world, our international studies would define a population as all members of a fairly wide age interval (e.g., all persons between the ages of 5 and 25). We might then obtain a household sample of this age group, assess each participant, and estimate, for each society (and each subgroup), an age-outcome curve. Such a design would create an equated age metric and would include in the sampling frame persons who are dropouts and dropins and who receive various kinds of formal and informal schooling. Although such an ideal may be impossible to obtain, it would be worthwhile to explore better approximations to it. The designation of a population of "school leavers" or students in the final year of secondary school appears to produce serious and insoluble analytic problems.

Similar concerns arise in other studies. In IALS, adult earnings becomes an important outcome variable. It can be quite misleading to include young adults, say from 18 to 25, in such analyses because many of these young adults are in postsecondary school. Indeed, university students, who have high potential earnings, will have low earnings at these ages. Similarly, one does not wish to include retirees in the population definition when adult earnings is the outcome. One strategy is to include in the analysis only those adults between ages 25 and 59. However, the age at which postsecondary schooling terminates—and the age of retirement—may vary significantly from country to country. In a society with an early age of completion of a bachelor's-level education, 25 year olds will have more work experience than will those in a society where schooling takes longer. These differences may produce between-country differences in the outcomes that are misinterpreted.

The Realized Sample

No matter how well a survey is designed and administered, response rates will be less than 100 percent and they will vary from country to country. Nonresponse can therefore bias description for a given country and bias comparisons between countries. Three conditions are possible: nonresponse leading to data missing completely at random (MCAR), missing at random (MAR), or nonignorable missingness. Little and Rubin (1987) and Schafer (1997) describe strategies for minimizing bias that arises from nonresponse.

Example:
U.S. and Japanese Science and Mathematics Achievement in
Population 2

We use data from TIMSS to illustrate some key points raised in the previous discussion.

Comparing Distributions

Consider first the problem of using a single number to summarize national differences. Some have objected to this practice, arguing, for example, that students at the top of the U.S. distribution achieve similarly to students at the top of the Japanese distribution, while students at the bottom of the two distributions achieve very differently (c.f., Westbury, 1993). If so, the differences between the two distributions would not be captured by a single number such as an overall mean difference. As a first check on such an assertion, we compare the cumulative distributions of the two countries. Figure 9-1a does so for science achievement. The vertical axis is the percentile, and the horizontal axis is the overall science achievement score. In general, the Japanese distribution (curve furthest to the right) is higher on the achievement scale than is the U.S. distribution. However, the mean difference between the two societies is much larger at low percentiles than at higher percentiles. Indeed, the two countries appear to differ very little at the highest percentiles. Clearly, to summarize the differences between the two countries with a single number such as a mean difference would be misleading in this case. Of course, these national differences may not achieve statistical significance at any percentile, so more investigation is required.

When we turn to mathematics achievement (Figure 9-1b), the story

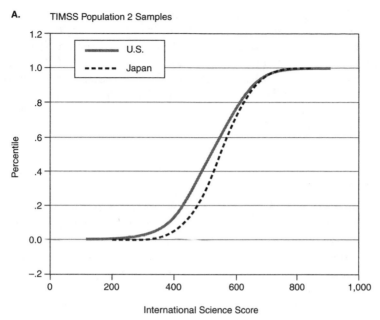

FIGURE 9-1a   Comparison of distributions (science outcome). TIMSS Population 2 samples.

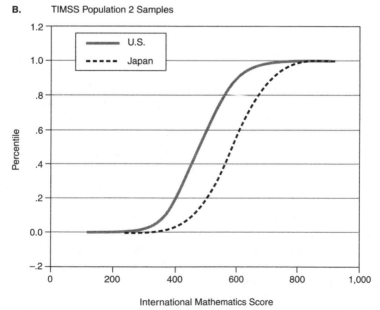

FIGURE 9-1b   Comparison of distributions (mathematics outcome). TIMSS Population 2 samples.

changes. The large mean difference between the two distributions appears roughly invariant across the percentiles (if anything, the differences are smallest at the lowest percentiles). Here a single mean difference does appear to capture the key feature of the difference in distributions. (Of course, we would go further to characterize the uncertainty about this mean difference by a confidence interval.) Note that Figure 9-1 does not provide a confidence interval for differences between the countries at any given percentile and is therefore appropriate only as a first check on how the distributions differ.

Age and Grade Effects

As mentioned earlier, country comparisons may be confounded by age even after controlling for grade. Even more perplexing, grade may be viewed as an outcome variable as well as a predictor of achievement because substantial numbers of students who fare poorly are likely to be retained in grade in some societies. This policy of grade retention may distort cross-national comparisons.

Figures 9-2a and 9-2b illustrate these difficulties. The figures provide scatterplots that display overall mathematics achievement (vertical axis) as a function of age (horizontal axis) for Population 2 (seventh and eighth graders). Figure 9-2a displays this association for Japan and Figure 9-2b does so for the United States. The figures reveal considerably more variability in age for the United States than for Japan. Moreover, the association between age and achievement differs in the two countries. Age and achievement are positively associated, as one might expect, in Japan. In contrast, the association between age and achievement in the United States, although curvilinear, is on average negative. Technically, there is an interaction effect between country and age. Thus, country comparisons will differ at different ages. What accounts for this interaction?[1]

This U.S. scatterplot seems to suggest that grade retention in the United States is affecting both the distribution of age and the age-outcome association. U.S. students who are older than expected, given their grade, plausibly have been retained in grade, and achieve at lower levels than their grade-level peers.[2]

The issue of confounding variables often arises in discussion of causal inference, and the reader may wonder whether we are criticizing TIMSS here for not supporting a causal inference. Indeed, the presence of confounding variables would certainly challenge the validity of causal inferences regarding national education systems as causes of national achievement differences. But our concern here simply involves accurate interpretation of descriptive statistics, not causal inference. The implied purpose of cross-national comparisons controlling for grade, as all TIMSS

in the Japanese Sample (Population 2)

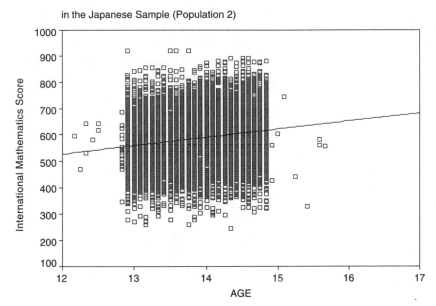

FIGURE 9-2a   Relationship between age and mathematics score in the Japanese sample (Population 2).

in the U.S. Sample (Population 2)

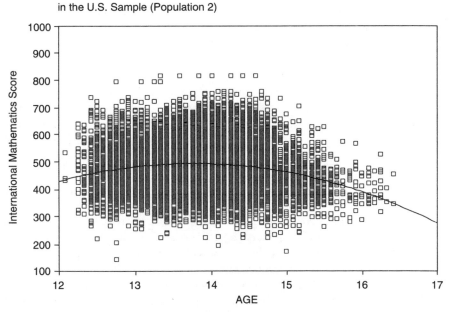

FIGURE 9-2b   Relationship between age and mathematics score in the U.S. sample (Population 2).

comparisons do, is to examine how students who are similar in exposure to schooling compare on outcomes. However, U.S. students who have been retained in grade have had more exposure to schooling than their younger, same-grade peers. This creates ambiguity about the meaning of cross-national comparisons and suggests that the mean differences between Japan and the United States, holding constant exposure to schooling, is larger than suggested by grade-specific comparisons.

The statistical problems of confounding (different age distribution in the two societies) and interaction (positive age effects in Japan, negative age effects in the United States) combine to raise questions about the conception of the target population. Students in the same grade in the two countries appear to vary in exposure to schooling as a function of grade retention, casting doubt on the meaning of country comparisons for Population 2, even after adjusting for age.[3] One might argue that the mean differences between the United States and Japan in mathematics are large in any case for Population 2, but comparisons between the United States and other countries may be quite sensitive to the differential selection of students into seventh and eighth grades.

Describing Differences Between Cohorts and Comparing Those Differences

Analysts will often wish to describe cohort differences within societies and compare societies with respect to those differences. For example, in TIMSS, the mean difference between Populations 1 and 2 is of interest. Some analysts have interpreted this mean difference as the average *gain* students make between the ages of nine and 13 (Schmidt & McKnight, 1998). The aim is then to compare countries with respect to their gain scores and to view national differences in gains as evidence of national differences in the effectiveness of the educational system operating for those between ages nine and 13. In interpreting such cohort differences as gains, the concerns mentioned are relevant and new concerns arise.

Applying our Framework for Sound Description

Using the framework developed earlier, it is clear that a comparison between cohorts within a society depends on principles of sound description. Thus, a description of cohort differences must be appropriately *complex*: Reporting a mean difference alone may omit important cohort differences in *dispersion*; reporting *uncertainty* (confidence intervals) associated with cohort differences is essential; statistical *interactions* between cohort and student background may be relevant; and certain *confounding* variables may give rise to misleading comparisons. A potentially confounding variable in TIMSS is, once again, student age. If, for any cohort, nations vary in the mean age of their populations, differences in mean age between cohorts will vary as well, and these differences are likely related to mean differences in achievement. Thus, age differences can masquerade as differences in "gains." In particular, if nations vary in the fraction of students retained in grade between grades four and eight, such differences will bias estimates of the "gains" of interest.[4]

Again using the framework already described, a description of cohort differences requires a viable definition of the target population for each cohort. Earlier, in the case of TIMSS, we concluded that the definition of Population 3 as "school leavers" is problematic, rendering problematic any cross-national comparison of cohort differences between, say, Population 2 and Population 3.

Finally, we have discussed the problem of response bias. The population for each cohort in each society may be well defined and the sample well designed, but the realized sample will be imperfect. Some degree of nonignorable missingness seems likely. Using statistical methods that are maximally robust to nonrandom sources of nonresponse is essential in any sound comparison of cohorts within a society and in any comparison between societies of these differences

In sum, any error in the description of the outcome for a single cohort in a single country is propagated in the comparison of two cohorts within a country and further propagated in the comparison between countries of such cohort differences.

Additional Challenges

Although all of the principles of sound statistical description apply in constructing cohort comparisons, three new concerns arise: the *metric* of the outcome, cohort differences in *demographic composition*, and *historical changes* in the causes of achievement.

The computation of cohort differences assumes, first, that the outcome is measured on a *common metric* across ages. A true equating requires that the same underlying construct be measured on each cohort and that the items in the tests for the separate cohorts be calibrated to lie on a common scale. This kind of equating seems unlikely when the cohorts are substantially different in age and the outcome involves math or science. When it is impossible to construct such a common metric, cohort comparisons must rely on some "relative standing" metric. For example, one might assign each person in each country a standard normal equivalent score defined as a distance of that person's achievement from the international mean for that person's cohort. This might be called "within-cohort" standardization. Cohort differences are then interpreted as differences in relative standing from one age to another. Some cohorts will display negative changes even though all children in that cohort are likely growing in math achievement. Moreover, the change in constructs assessed between cohorts can give rise to misleading results.

Suppose, for example, that Construct A is measured for grade four while Construct B is measured for grade eight. Assume for a moment that the target populations for the two grades are well-defined cohorts (persons born during a specified interval of time) and that no historical changes have occurred in the education system. Even then a cohort difference in relative standing confounds change over time with a difference between constructs. Consider the example depicted in Figure 9-3. A hypothetical nation is very proficient at teaching Construct A but very poor at teaching Construct B prior to grade four. Suppose that between grade four and grade eight, that nation promotes very substantial growth in both Constructs A and B. However, that nation's eighth graders are still comparatively low on Construct B given their low starting point. A distance between cohorts that describes change in relative standing will be, in fact, the distance between Construct A for grade four and Construct B for grade eight. This will be a small change for our hypothetical nation even though, in reality, that nation made substantial positive gains on both constructs.

Let us consider further the mean difference between two cohorts, say Cohort 4 (fourth graders) and Cohort 8 (eighth graders). Suppose the outcome is measured equivalently for both cohorts. Can we interpret a

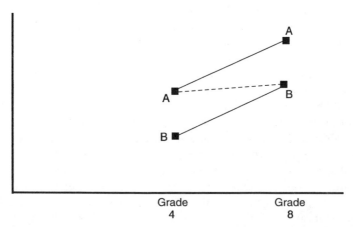

FIGURE 9-3   Construct A is assessed at Grade 4 while Construct B is assessed at Grade 8. The slope of the dotted line represents the estimated gain.

mean difference between these two cohorts as a measure of how much Cohort 8 learned between fourth and eighth grades? There is a substantial literature on inferences of this type (Nesselroade & Baltes, 1979). It is well known that a cross-sectional study of an age-outcome relationship confounds cohort and age. Only if cohort differences other than age are controlled can we interpret this mean difference as an age effect.

More specifically, the interpretation of a cohort mean difference as a mean gain assumes that Cohort 4's mean is equal to the mean of Cohort 8 when Cohort 8's members were in grade four. Of course, Cohort 8's status at grade four is missing. In essence, the logic is to use Cohort 4's mean as an imputation for this missing value of Cohort 8's mean at grade four. This imputation will be biased if Cohort 4 and Cohort 8 differ on variables other than age that are related to the outcome. For example, Cohort 4 may differ demographically from Cohort 8. This would occur, for example, if immigrants to a society tend to have younger children than natives of the society. As another example, suppose that the curriculum prior to grade four has changed since Cohort 8 was in the fourth grade. Then Cohort 4's observed status would not simulate Cohort 8's missing status at grade four. The first example (demographic differences between cohorts) can be addressed through statistical adjustment if the relevant demographic data are collected as part of the survey. But it is unlikely that data will be available on curricular change in the society because the data on the curriculum experienced by Cohort 8 during and after grade four but before grade eight will be missing. Thus, some uncertainty will remain about the veracity of interpreting cohort differences as age effects.

Now suppose that outcomes measured at the two grades are equated and that we know that cohort differences truly reflect age differences. Thus, according to the logic described, we can interpret cohort differences as *age-related gains in achievement*. Can we conclude further that international differences in such gains reflect differences in the effectiveness of the schooling systems in the countries compared? We shall consider this issue later under "The Role of International Comparative Data in Causal Explanation." That section will reveal substantial threats to the inference that age-related differences reflect the differential effectiveness of educational systems.

Describing National Changes Over Time
Based on Repeated Cross-Sections

An important goal of international studies of educational achievement is to describe the improvements in a nation's achievement over time and to compare nations with respect to their rates of improvement. A natural design for this goal is the repeated cross-section. Two alternative versions of the repeated cross-section come to mind:

1. **Hold age constant, let cohort vary.** TIMSS-R ("TIMSS Repeat") assessed eighth graders in 1995 and again in 1999. The idea is to treat differences in achievement between these two cohorts as reflecting changes in the operation of the educational system between 1995 and 1999.

2. **Hold cohort constant, let age vary.** TIMSS-R also assessed fourth graders in 1995 and eighth graders in 1999. This may be viewed as repeated observation of the same birth cohort (but see following discussion). Age-related differences between 1994 and 1999 are viewed as average learning gains for this cohort.

Advantages of the Repeated Cross-Section That Holds Age Constant

Recall that when nations were compared by comparing cohort differences (e.g., cross-sectional differences between Population 1 and Population 2 in TIMSS), age emerged as a potentially important confounding variable. In a repeated cross-sectional design, age reasonably might be viewed as fully controlled, provided the education system has not changed in its basic structure. If, for example, eighth graders in the United States in 1999 had the same age composition as eighth graders did in 1995, then the mean difference between time 1995 and 1999 in the United States will be unconfounded with age. If the population definition remains invariant in other nations as well, comparisons between nations in rates of change also will be unconfounded with age.[5]

Furthermore, recall that comparisons between cohorts in a cross-sectional study were likely confounded with differences in what outcomes were of interest. We noted, in particular, that it would be unlikely that outcome measures would be equated between cohorts within a cross-sectional study. In contrast, it should to be possible to equate assessments in a repeated cross-sectional study. The outcomes relevant to eighth graders in 1995 are likely to be quite similar to the constructs of interest for eighth graders in 1999. Thus, it should to be possible to "unconfound" outcome constructs with cohorts in this repeated cross-sectional study.

Threats to the Validity of the Repeated Cross-Sectional Design That Holds Age Constant

Nonresponse rates may differ over time. If they do, and if nonresponse is nonignorable, the effects of varying nonresponse can masquerade as historical change. However, the biggest threat to the repeated cross-sectional comparison is demographic change. A nation's population at a given age will change over time as a function of immigration, outmigration, and differential fertility of subgroups. If the demographic characteristics that are changing are also associated with achievement, trends in achievement will reflect, in part, this changing demography. Then it will be essential to measure and statistically control such demographic change if one hopes to interpret achievement trends as representing historical effects rather than demographic differences between cohorts. See Willms and Raudenbush (1989) for how such an analysis might proceed using a hierarchical model.

Advantages and Disadvantages of the Repeated Cross-Section That Holds Cohort Constant While Allowing Age to Vary

Suppose we sample fourth graders in 1995 and then sample eighth graders in 1999. We compute the mean difference and interpret it as an age-related gain. We then compare countries by their gains. This is a strong design to the extent that the 1995 and 1999 samples really represent the same birth cohort. Two threats to validity come to mind. First, immigration and outmigration may change the demographic composition of those sampled between the two years. Second, grade retention may censor the sample by excluding those who are retained between fourth and eighth grades, while adding fifth graders retained prior to ninth grade. Cross-national differences in immigration and grade retention would then bias inferences about natural differences in age-related gain.

THE ROLE OF INTERNATIONAL COMPARATIVE DATA IN CAUSAL EXPLANATION

The foregoing discussion reveals that sound explanations of national achievement differences require sound descriptions and sound comparisons: descriptions of achievement within a nation at a given time and comparisons between nations at a given time; description of cohort differences at a given time and comparison between nations on cohort differences; description of achievement trends over historical time and comparison between countries in terms of their achievement trends. We have considered the conditions required for such accurate description and comparison. However, even the soundest descriptions of nations and comparisons between nations do not justify causal inferences. Sound causal inferences require designs and analyses that can cope with the *counterfactual character* of causal questions.

When we claim that "Educational System 1 is more effective than

Educational System 2" for a given child, we imagine the following scenario: A child has two potential outcomes. The first potential outcome, Outcome 1, is the outcome that child would display if exposed to System 1. The second potential outcome, Outcome 2, is the outcome that child would display if exposed to System 2. To say that System 1 is more effective for the given child is to say that Outcome 1 is greater than Outcome 2 for that child. The counterfactual character of causal inference arises because it will not be possible to observe both Outcome 1 and Outcome 2 for a given child because that child will experience only one of the two systems. Thus the causal effect Outcome 1-Outcome 2 cannot be computed because either Outcome 1 or Outcome 2 will be missing. However, it is possible to estimate the *average* causal effect, for example, by randomly assigning children to System 1 or System 2. In this case, the population mean of the effect Outcome 1-Outcome 2 is equal to the population mean of System 1 minus the population mean of those in System 2. In the case of a randomized experiment, we can say that the mean of System 2 is a fair estimate of how those in System 1 *would have fared*, on average, had they received System 2 instead of System 1. (See Holland, 1986, for a clear exposition of the logic of causal inference.)

When random assignment is impossible, various quasi-experimental approximations to a randomized experiment are possible. How might cross-national researchers approach this problem? Four strategies appear prominent: comparing cohort differences, comparing historical trends, isolating plausible causal mechanisms, and comparing students within the same society who experience different systems of schooling. We consider each in turn.

1. Comparing cohort differences. The first approach to causal inference is to compute cross-sectional cohort differences for each society (e.g., differences between those in grade eight and those in grade four) and to compare those differences. Earlier, we considered difficulties in describing cohort differences as "gains." Cohort and age are confounded, so cohort differences might reflect differences other than age. Moreover, we saw that the U.S. eighth-grade sample was really a mixture of cohorts because of grade retention. Let us presume, however, that grades really do constitute cohorts and that cohort differences also in fact reflect age-related gains. Can we conclude that differences between nations in their gains reflect differences in the effectiveness of the educational systems?

To answer this question, we must reflect on a large literature that considers the adequacy of nonexperimental designs for drawing causal inferences. Our international survey can be likened to a pre-post quasi-experiment. In such a study, nonrandomly formed comparison groups (countries) are assessed prior to the introduction of a treatment. Next, different educational treatments are administered to each comparison group. Finally, a posttreatment assessment is administered. Differences between the gains of comparison groups are then taken to reflect differences in the effectiveness of the treatments being compared. This scenario is depicted in Figure 9-4. Here the treatments are the education systems of Country 1 and Country 2, as enacted between grades four and eight. The aim is to discern which country has the best educational system between those two grades. Country 1 makes a gain from A to B, while Country 2 makes a gain from C to D between grades four and eight. The magnitude of the quantity in curly braces (B-A)-(D-C) is the difference between mean gains of the two groups and is commonly regarded as a measure of difference in the effectiveness of the education systems as they operate between grades.

A substantial literature emerged during the late 1960s and 1970s on difficulties with this design and the interpretations it produces (Blumberg & Porter, 1983; Bryk & Weisberg, 1977; Campbell & Erlebacher, 1970). The problem with this design is that it requires that Point E be the expected status of children in Country 1 if the children in Country 1 instead had been educated in Country 2. That scenario is somewhat plausible if the scenario described in Figure 9-5 represented reality. Figure 9-5 shows achievement trends for the two groups of children based on two pretests, and then on posttest. In effect, Figure 9-5 tells us where the two countries' children were on a "pre-pretest." We see that, between this pre-pretest and the pretest, children of Countries 1 and 2 were growing at the same rate, on average. Then the children of Country 1 received a positive "de-

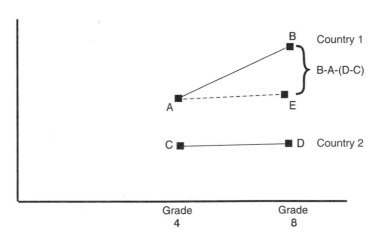

FIGURE 9-4   Causal inference based on two age groups.

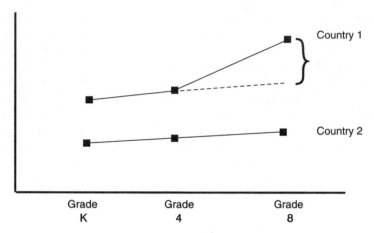

FIGURE 9-5   Scenario 1: Parallel growth prior to grade 4.

flection" by virtue of the educational system they experienced between grades four and eight in Country 1, creating a more rapid rate of growth than that experienced by children in Country 2. This deflection is taken as evidence of the causal effect of Country 1's educational system relative to that of Country 2 between grades four and eight.

Suppose, however, that the true scenario were that depicted in Figure 9-6. Under that scenario, children in Countries 1 and 2 were *growing at different rates prior to fourth grade*. Between fourth and eighth grades, their

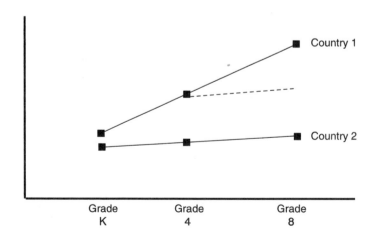

FIGURE 9-6   Scenario 2: Unequal growth prior to grade 4.

rates of growth remained unchanged. Thus, no deflection is discernible between grades four and eight. The data thus give no evidence that the two systems operated differently between grades four and eight. In both cases, the children grew along trajectories that were already in place prior to grade eight. (Moreover, the differences in trajectories prior to grade four may not reflect the contribution of formal schooling prior to grade four.)

The key problem with the two-point, pre-post quasi-experimental design is that the data provide no information about which scenario—Scenario 1 (Figure 9-5) or Scenario 2 (Figure 9-6)—is more plausible. Unless other data can be brought to bear or strong prior theory is available to rule out some of the possible scenarios, a pre-post design provides essentially no information about the relative effectiveness of the two systems between grades four and eight. The design forces the researcher to make an untestable assumption about where students in Country 1 would have been by grade 8 if those students had experienced the education system of Country 2.

2. Comparing historical trends. Earlier, we noted that historical trend data can eliminate confounding with age, but create a confounding between cohort and historical time (or "period"). Suppose we could adjust completely for cohort differences. Would differences in trends between societies then reveal differences in educational system effectiveness?

The problem in this case is that the changing effectiveness of the schooling system constitutes but one possible historical change that might account for the historical change in achievement. For example, as societies achieve higher and higher levels of educational attainment, parents are increasingly literate. Highly literate parents are better equipped than less literate parents to provide early experiences in the home that support literacy. Other secular trends—such as the increasing number of children in daycare, increasing nutrition, increasing survival rates of premature babies, changes in poverty rates, and changes in access to television and the Internet—can contribute to achievement trends even if the schooling system remained invariant in its effectiveness.

In sum, repeated cross-sections control age in allowing description of historical changes in achievement and comparison of countries in their achievement trends. And they facilitate comparisons over time with respect to a common outcome. However, historical time and cohort are confounded: Demographic differences between cohorts resulting from population change may masquerade as historical change. Moreover, changes in the operation of the schooling system will tend to be confounded with other secular trends that also may affect trends in achievement.

The repeated cross-section that controls cohort while allowing age to vary confronts a different problem: the confounding of age and historical time. Large age-related gains in achievement in a given country might be correlated with historical changes in that society other than changes in the operation of the education system.

3. Isolating plausible causal mechanisms. Researchers using TIMSS data have sought not only to make causal inferences about the impact of educational systems on student learning; they have also sought to identify specific causal mechanisms that would explain these national effects. Not only are such explanations potentially important for policy and theory, they also may compensate for lack of methodological controls. In particular, if one can identify specific educational processes that are strongly theoretically linked with higher achievement, and if those processes are also strongly associated empirically with country differences in achievement, the case for causation would be strengthened. Using this kind of logic, Westbury (1993, p. 24) wrote:

> It is, for instance, a curriculum-driven pattern of content coverage that determines algebra achievement and the distribution of opportunity to learn algebra at the eighth-grade level, and it is the way algebra is distributed in the United States that, in turn, plays a major role in determining America's aggregate standing on grade 8 math achievement in studies like [the Second International Mathematics Study] SIMS.

A common practice in research on TIMSS is to assess associations between a country's implemented curriculum or "opportunity to learn" (OTL) and student achievement and to view those associations as causal. A large and growing literature in statistics on time-varying treatments, however, reveals the serious perils in such inferences (Robins, Greenland, & Hu, 1999). The OTL that a teacher affords students must be viewed, at least in part, as a response to students' prior success in learning. OTL is then an outcome of prior learning as well as a predictor of later learning. A nation's curriculum represents not only an externally imposed "treatment," but also a historically conditioned set of expectations about how much students will know at any age. The curriculum is thus an endogenous variable. Standard methods of statistical analysis generally cannot reveal the causal impact of such endogenous treatment effects. Indeed, serious biases commonly accompany any attempt to do so. Control for prior achievement in a longitudinal study should reduce the bias, but one cannot rule out unmeasured causes of why OTL is greater for some students than for others.

4. Comparing students within societies who experience different

kinds of schooling. The strategies described for causal inference use data from other nations to estimate counterfactuals for U.S. children. More specifically, the strategy of comparing "gains" between Population 1 and Population 2 claims, in effect, that U.S. children would make gains similar to children in, say, Japan, if Japanese instructional approaches had been adopted in the United States. This chapter has criticized this kind of inference on somewhat technical grounds. Essentially, such inferences require extrapolations across societies: (a) that it is feasible to implement Japanese instructional methods in U.S. schools and (b) that if these methods were implemented, U.S. students would respond similarly to Japanese students. Causal inferences based on comparing trend data between nations require similar cross-national extrapolations. Such extrapolations, although intriguing, should not be confused with reasonable causal inferences.

Instead of basing causal inference on between-nation extrapolations, it makes more sense to develop hypotheses based on between-nation comparisons, but to test such hypotheses by conducting experiments *within* nations. In essence, we cannot really know how feasible it is to implement a new policy or how children in the United States will respond without actually trying to implement the policy in the United States.

While awaiting truly definitive experiments, it makes sense to contemplate *within-nation* analyses that *approximate* the experiment of interest. Consider the hypothesis that the U.S. math curriculum, in comparison to the curricula of other nations, lacks coherence, focus, and rigor, and that this curricular difference explains the observed national difference in math achievement (Schmidt et al., 1997). One might test this hypothesis *within* nations by identifying variation on coherence, focus, and rigor between schools within nations. One then would formulate a multilevel model of the association between curricular quality and outcomes.[6] The model would be constructed such that the difference between a child's outcome and the expected outcome for that child under the "typical" U.S. curriculum is a function of how far that child's experienced curriculum deviates from the U.S. average. The beauty of this model is that the causal inference is no longer just a large extrapolation. Rather than imagining how a student would do under a different nation's curriculum, we are imagining how the student would do under a curriculum actually observed in a U.S. school. The key challenge, however, is to estimate the "expected" outcome for each child under a typical U.S. curriculum. Surely it is true that a child's exposure to curricular quality depends on a variety of child and family characteristics, including but not limited to social background, ethnicity, and mathematics aptitude. To the extent that these characteristics also are related to achievement, they must be included in the model for "expected achievement" under the typical U.S. curriculum. Past research strongly suggests that prior aptitude, as measured by a pretest, is the most powerful confounding influence, as it tends to be most strongly related to curricular exposure and to mathematics achievement. Failure to include aptitude in the model will cast doubt on the validity of any causal inferences based on the within-country model. Unfortunately, TIMSS, unlike SIMS, for example, does not include a measure of prior aptitude. This fact seriously limits the utility of TIMSS for approximating the experiment that we wish we could conduct: one in which curricular practices suggested as potentially important in between-nation comparisons are selectively implemented within nations to study their causal effects.

Even if prior achievement were controlled and even if the analysis compared curriculum differences within societies as well as between societies, the potential endogeneity of these curricular variables would remain a concern. Certainly a good pretest would help control selectivity bias. However, teachers generally know much more than researchers do, even in the presence of a pretest, about the children they are assigned to educate. To the extent teachers use this knowledge to shape their instructional strategies, the concern will remain that OTL effects on achievement will be estimated with bias. Only a true experiment can fully resolve this issue, while within-country surveys can attempt to approximate the true experiment.

CONCLUSIONS

The ultimate utility of cross-national surveys is to support the improvement of public policy. Public policy inevitably is based on causal inferences because policy makers must make assumptions about what will happen if regulations or incentives or curricula change. Thus it is tempting to use available data to make strong causal claims. However, cross-sectional survey data generally provide a poor basis for causal inference.

If international surveys of achievement cannot support sound causal inference, of what value are they in thinking about how to improve schooling? We take the view that such data play a significant role in causal thinking by suggesting promising new causal explanations. For example, connections between the intended curriculum, the implemented curriculum, and the achieved curriculum in various countries participating in TIMSS have suggested a provocative explanation for shortcomings in U.S. math and science achievement (Schmidt et al., 1997). That explanation begins with a description of the intended curriculum in the United States as lacking in focus, rigor, and coherence within grades and across grades. These weaknesses are consistent with observable shortcomings in how teachers teach and with cross-national comparisons of achievement between the United States and other nations, nations whose intended and implemented curricula, by comparison, display high levels of focus, rigor, and coherence. This explanation thus suggests hypotheses about how very detailed changes in the curriculum would translate into changes in teaching and learning.

The explanation that Schmidt and colleagues have suggested appears consistent with the data from the curriculum study and achievement study of TIMSS and also may be well grounded in sound thinking about how mathematics education can best be organized to produce mathematical understanding and proficiency. However, other explanations can be constructed that will be equally consistent with the data from studies like TIMSS. Unfortunately, studies like TIMSS can supply no decisive evidence to arbitrate between such explanations. To test these explanations requires, instead, experimental trials of instructional approaches that embody the explanations of interest. We take the position that one cannot know how well an alternative intended and implemented curriculum would work in a given society without actually putting such a curriculum in place in that society and seeing what happens.

The essential utility of international studies of achievement, we believe, is to suggest causal explanations that can be translated into interventions that can be tested in experimental trials. We recommend analyses pointed toward such explanations and such interventions.

1. One might find data sets collected strictly within the United States or other countries, data sets that are longitudinal at the student level. Possible examples include the National Educational Longitudinal Study of 1988 (NELS) or The Early Childhood Longitudinal Study (ECLS). Such data sets would have to be scrutinized to determine if the key explanatory variables of interest (e.g., variables that capture curriculum and instruction) are available. The key explanatory variables are those suggested by cross-national work such as TIMSS.

2. One might design a new longitudinal study within a nation for the express purpose of testing hypotheses arising from TIMSS or other international comparative studies.

3. One might design a sequel to TIMSS that would collect longitudinal data at the student level in many countries. Multilevel analyses of such data could test hypotheses suggested by between-country comparisons within a number of societies, a powerful design indeed.

Difficulties with the third option include the high cost and managerial complexity of carrying on multiple longitudinal studies in varied nations. Moreover, the decision to "become longitudinal" must be integrated with other design options raised in this chapter. These include broadening the age range within countries and using a household survey rather than a school survey for older students.

Hybrid proposals might be considered. For example, one might encourage the United States to collaborate with a small number of carefully selected countries to design parallel longitudinal studies having the ambitious aim of linking curricular experiences with trajectories of student growth.

None of these suggestions is intended to undermine the utility of surveys of curriculum and achievement in many societies. Such surveys have proven their worth in generating important hypotheses for educational improvement within societies. Rather, the question is how to test those hypotheses. A combined program of longitudinal studies and experiments seems in order for this purpose.

Over the past several decades, statistical methods have greatly enhanced the capacity of researchers to summarize evidence from large-scale, multilevel surveys such as TIMSS and IALS. Our comparatively new understanding of missing data has allowed these studies to compare countries on many cognitive skills even though each examinee is tested on a comparatively small subset of items. Item response models create metrics for achievement and methods for discerning cross-national item bias. Improved graphical procedures enable us to visualize distributions of outcomes in complex and interesting ways. Hierarchical models enable us to study variation within and between countries and to compute sound standard errors for effects at each level.

More could be done to capitalize on these advances. For example, the magnitude of country-level differences could be assessed more sensibly in relation to differences between schools within countries and differences between children within schools using Bayesian inference for hierarchical models (Raudenbush, Cheong, & Fotiu, 1994).

However, upon reflection, our judgment is that the most important shortcoming in the analysis of cross-national international data is the lack of attention to recent advances in our understanding of sources of bias in analyses that suggest, implicitly or explicitly, causal interpretation. We have emphasized a need for greater sensitivity to biases that arise in how populations are defined (e.g., by the meaning of "grade" in the presence of retention or selective dropout), in how cross-national differences are interpreted, and in how we think about curriculum and opportunity to learn as causal mechanisms. These deep issues of design and interpretation cannot be resolved by sophisticated statistical analytic methods. Rather, attention to foundational logical issues is a basis of sound analyses and warranted substantive interpretations.

NOTES

1. This negative association between age and outcome in the United States is even more evident when we control for grade, though we do not show that effect here. The U.S. scatterplot excludes a small number of cases with extreme ages.
2. We evaluated an alternative hypothesis that nonnative speakers of English may be overrepresented among the older Population 2 students in the United States. About 12.4 percent of the U.S. sample did speak a language other than English at home, while no comparable variable exists in the Japanese data set. Yet language at home was not related to age in the U.S. data. Thus, although language at home is likely a confounding variable (it is plausible that the U.S. sample has more nonnative English speakers than the Japanese sample has nonnative speakers of Japanese), this does not explain the negative association between age and achievement in the United States. We are left with grade retention as the more plausible explanation. Other explanations involving differential selection of students into the U.S. and Japanese samples cannot, however, be ruled out.
3. By defining the population in terms of grade, the design effectively conditions inferences about countries on an endogenous variable rather than the desired exogenous variable.
4. The presence of students who have been retained in seventh and eighth grades contradicts the notion that Population 2 is a "cohort" (where cohort is defined as a subpopulation born during a given interval of time). Similarly, the absence of sixth graders who were retained also selects cases from a well-defined cohort. Thus a comparison between Populations 2 and 1 is not really a comparison of cohorts, and the meaning of the comparison is ambiguous.
5. This benefit is not likely, however, to extend to comparisons of Population 3. Dropout rates will likely vary over time and the notion of "school leaving" appears to be changing as well; for example, consider the changing role of community colleges in the United States.
6. An analysis using this type of model appears in Gamoran (1991), who used data from the Second International Mathematics and Science Study (SIMS) to assess curriculum effects. A major advantage of this analysis is that SIMS provided longitudinal data at the student level, thus allowing control of prior achievement. TIMSS does not.

REFERENCES

Blumberg, C., & Porter, A. (1983). Analyzing quasi-experiments: Some implications of assuming continuous growth models. *Journal of Experimental Education, 51*, 150-159.

Bryk, A., & Weisberg, H. (1977). Use of the non-equivalent control group design when subjects are growing. *Psychological Bulletin, 84*, 950-962.

Campbell, D., & Erlebacher, A. (1970). How regression artifacts in quasi-experimental evaluations can mistakenly make compensatory education look harmful. In J. Hellmuth (Ed.), *Compensatory education: A national debate, volume 3: The disadvantaged child* (pp. 185-210). New York: Brunner/Mazel.

Gamoran, A. (1991). Schooling and achievement: Additive versus interactive models. In S. W. Raudenbush & J. D. Willms (Eds.), *Schools, pupils, and classrooms: International studies of schooling from a multilevel perspective* (pp. 37-52). San Diego, CA: Academic Press.

Holland, P. (1986). Statistics and causal inference. *Journal of the American Statistical Association, 81*(396), 945-960.

Little, R., & Rubin, D. (1987). *Statistical analysis with missing data.* New York: John Wiley & Sons.

Mislevy, R. J. (1995). What can we learn from international assessments? *Educational Evaluation and Policy Analysis, 17*(4), 419-437.

Nesselroade, J., & Baltes, P. (1979). *Longitudinal research in the study of behavior and development.* New York: Academic Press.

Raudenbush, S. W., Cheong, Y. F., & Fotiu, R. (1994). Synthesizing cross-national classroom effect data: Alternative models and methods. In K. R. M. Binkley & M. Winglee (Eds.), *Methodological issues in comparative international studies: The case of reading literacy* (pp. 243-286). Washington, DC: National Center for Education Statistics.

Robins, J. M., Greenland, S., & Hu, F.-C. (1999). Estimation of the causal effect of a time-varying exposure on the marginal mean of repeated binary outcome. *Journal of the American Statistical Association, 94*(447), 687-700.

Rumberger, R. W. (1995). Dropping out of middle schools: A multilevel analysis of students and schools. *American Educational Research Journal, 32*(3), 583-625.

Schafer, J. (1997). *Analysis of incomplete multivariate data.* London: Chapman & Hall.

Schmidt, W. H., & McKnight, C. C. (1998). What can we really learn from TIMSS? *Science, 282*(5395), 1830-1831.

Schmidt, W. H., McKnight, C. C., & Raizen, S. A. (1997). *A splintered vision: An investigation of U.S. science and mathematics education.* Boston: Kluwer Academic.

Takahira, S., Gonzales, P., Frase, M., & Salganik, L. H. (1998). *Pursuing excellence: A study of U.S. twelfth-grade mathematics and science achievement in international context.* Washington, DC: National Center for Education Statistics.

Westbury, I. (1993). American and Japanese achievement . . . Again: A response to Baker. *Educational Researcher, 22*(3), 21-25.

Willms, J., & Raudenbush, S. (1989). A longitudinal hierarchical linear model for estimating school effects and their stability. *Journal of Educational Measurement, 26*(3), 209-232.

10

Drawing Inferences for National Policy from Large-Scale Cross-National Education Surveys[1]

Marshall S. Smith*

This chapter focuses on three questions:

1. What kinds of inferences may be validly drawn from large-scale, cross-national surveys about the effects on student achievement of differences among nations in the structure, content, and practice of education?

2. What inferences from past surveys have been used to inform national policy and were they methodologically and substantively reasonable?

3. Are there lessons from the past that might be used to improve the quality of policy considerations stimulated by results of TIMSS-R, the 1999 repeat survey of the 1995 Third International Mathematics and Science Study (TIMSS)?

Before addressing these questions, two clarifications are in order. First is the observation that "national policy" in the United States consists of two distinct parts: a formal part that is usually called "federal" policy and an "informal" part that is made up of consensus or near-consensus views of national organizations involved in education, informed media, policy analysts, state policy makers, and so forth. We are interested in both

---

*Marshall S. Smith is a professor of education in the School of Education at Stanford University and program director of education at the William and Flora Hewlett Foundation.

parts. Second, to simplify the discussion, I consider only implications for U.S. national policy and concentrate primarily on TIMSS, the most recent, ambitious, and methodologically sophisticated of the large-scale, cross-national surveys.[2] At various times in the discussion, I use examples from other cross-national surveys.

The extant literature on the cross-national educational surveys is daunting. The National Academies Web site alone has more than 100 papers on TIMSS. I recommend two papers previously prepared for the Academies on topics directly related to this chapter. Haertel's (1997) paper on what might be learned from the TIMSS data and Elmore's (1997) on the political and policy implications of TIMSS are thoughtful and powerful. I refer to both at various points in this discussion.

CONTEXT FOR THINKING ABOUT INFERENCES FROM TIMSS FOR NATIONAL POLICY

Some Recent History on the Use of Data from Cross-National Studies for Developing Policy

Educators and policy makers in the United States have long made comparisons between U.S. schools and students and those in other nations. At times, depending on the larger social and economic context, the comparisons have had considerable influence on education in America. In the late 1800s, for example, as schools and cities grew larger, the nation adopted the Prussian approach of sorting students into grades by age. After the Russians launched Sputnik in the 1950s, the federal government hurried to design and fund the development and implementation of the "new" mathematics and hands-on science curricula.

More formalized cross-national surveys in education began with the first International Association for the Evaluation of Educational Achievement (IEA) mathematics survey in 1964. That survey, and later ones in the 1960s and early 1970s in other subject areas, carried two general messages. First, although young U.S. students appeared to score well above the international average, U.S. students in grades beyond elementary school scored less well on the tests than did students in many other countries.

Second, the surveys underscored the importance of the content of the curriculum. Carroll (1963), for example, the author of a report on the IEA Foreign Language study, used the results to argue for his "model of school learning," which allocated a central role to curricular content. That curriculum is important—or as Carroll argued in conversation, that it was difficult to learn French in U.S. schools unless you were taught it—seems like an obvious idea in 2002. Carroll's work legitimately might be viewed as the precursor of the concept of opportunity to learn, a concept that has been embedded in three generations of IEA surveys and, in the late 1980s and into the 1990s, played an important role in discussions of U.S. national policy.

However, in the late 1960s and early 1970s, the effects of social and political processes on schools were taking clear precedence over curriculum content in education policy and reform discussions. With the notable exceptions of early childhood studies and scattered local efforts, the nation's diminished thirst for changes in curriculum might be attributed both to the influence of broad social movements taking place at this time and to the political and educational backlash against the post-Sputnik reforms of the late 1950s and early 1960s.

Similarly, the findings of the early cross-national studies that U.S. students in the later grades did not score as well as students in many other nations appear to have had little independent effect on policy deliberations during the late 1960s and into the early 1970s. Again, matters that addressed equality of opportunity—including community control, the growth and quality of Title I and Head Start, bilingual education, and desegregation—were primary concerns of education policy makers during this period. In addition, however, the public and policy makers often discounted results of early cross-national studies as unconvincing. After all, "everyone knew" that other nations had a much smaller percentage of eligible students in their secondary schools and that this explained the relatively low scores of the older U.S. students. Moreover, it was not until 1974 that the public discovered that Scholastic Aptitude Test (SAT) scores had peaked almost a decade earlier, a fact that might have provided support for the cross-national findings.

During the late 1970s, cross-national surveys continued to be unnoticed in policy debates at the national level.[3] National policy focused on how to improve the effectiveness of schools for poor and minority students even as SAT scores continued to drop and the progressive policies initiated in the 1960s were challenged by opposition to northern school desegregation and negative evaluations of Head Start and Title I.

The early years of the Reagan administration changed the nation's agenda. As SAT scores continued their fall and the nation struggled through severe inflation and fears of a decline in economic prosperity, national policy concerns turned away from a focus on lower achieving students toward the conclusion that our nation's human capital reservoir was being drained. Drawing on cross-national surveys carried out in the 1960s and early 1970s, a 1983 report released by the president found that "what was unimaginable a generation ago has begun to occur—others are matching and surpassing our educational attainments" (National Commission on Excellence in Education, 1983, p. 5). The policy recommendations of *A Nation at Risk*—more rigorous academic courses, longer school days and years, more homework, and overall a tougher program of study for U.S. students—were amplified by a variety of other reports put out by prestigious national organizations at roughly the same time.[4] A consensus of elite analysts and business and political groups emerged, a consensus that spawned a new "national policy." By and large the implementation of this new policy direction was initiated and carried out at the state level as governors and chief state school officers became more active in education reform. Federal-level policies changed little, and for a variety of reasons the federal government exerted little leadership until the end of the 1980s.

There is little question about the important role that cross-national survey data played in the arguments that were so badly presented in *A Nation at Risk* and the other reports. The reports, of course, did not rely exclusively on the international studies. Other test score and course-taking data also indicated a need to increase the academic rigor of U.S. schooling. Nonetheless, the cross-national survey results were prominently cited as showing the comparative inadequacy of U.S. education, to which the reports in turn linked the relative weakness of the U.S. economy. The now familiar argument was simple: The economic future of the United States was jeopardized because the students in countries that were our economic competitors had higher scores than U.S. students.[5]

When the Second International Mathematics Study (SIMS) was released in 1984, the political and educational climate was ripe for it to receive substantial attention. The two principal messages of SIMS to the U.S. public and policy makers were similar to earlier studies. The first, which reinforced the urgency of the emerging reforms, was that U.S. students achieved less well than did students of many other developed nations. The second message underscored the importance of curriculum and, in middle and secondary schools, tougher courses. Both messages found fertile soil in which to flourish.

The U.S. Educational Environment

"National education policy" in the United States—whether the emphasis was on equal opportunity in the 1960s and 1970s or the push for academic rigor in the 1980s—has generally a weaker influence on school practice than does national educational policy in many other countries. One reason for this is that the United States has a uniquely organized, managed, and governed education system. Most of the other nations that participated in TIMSS, for example, have a centralized system for control over curriculum specifications, the nature of instruction, and the treatment of low-achieving students.

In the United States, political control over most formal educational policy decisions resides in 50 states and a small number of very big cities, and reforms are implemented in 14,000 districts and 95,000 schools. Elmore (1997, p. 3) labeled the "two imperatives of educational governance in the United States as 'dispersed control' and 'political pluralism'" in the paper he did for a TIMSS seminar at the National Academies in 1997.

Understanding the nature and complexity of the U.S. educational system is important as we think about where and to whom policy implications from TIMSS might usefully be addressed. One simple conclusion might be that political and policy leadership can emanate from Washington D.C., but policy making that influences schooling is typically the province of the states and some large cities. Perhaps then comparisons more profitably might be made between other nations and individual states in the United States.

Though this might be a general rule, however, things are a little more complex. For example, during the 1960s and 1970s, the federal government became increasingly aggressive at protecting rights and providing services for students who lived in high-poverty areas, were disabled, or otherwise needed special help. On these issues the federal government both led and contributed to making policy.

Other conditions further demonstrate nationalizing influences in U.S. education while complicating the picture more. The past half-century has seen organized *national* interest groups in education expand dramatically in size and authority, and the forces of communication, transportation, and mobility have helped create schools that look, and are, extraordinarily alike from state to state across the nation. This is true even though states differ in the balance of state and local control, in their methods of financing schools, and in many of their specific policies. However, great differences remain in quality and performance among schools. Interacting with "dispersed control," the powerful national homogenizing forces have produced a system where there is far more variation in the quality and nature of schooling among schools within districts, and among districts within states, than there is among states.

As we enter the 21st century, the homogeneity among states has extended to the intentions and strategies of their reforms. Stimulated in the early 1990s by the National Governors Association, a wide variety of national education groups, and vigorous federal leadership and money, a standards-based reform movement has swept the country. Each of the 50 states, in policy talk and action, is attempting to implement its own brand of standards-based reform.

Viewed from one perspective, the national nature of the reforms and of the problems facing the reformers provides a simpler context for drawing policy implications from cross-national surveys than has existed in the past. In effect, federal and state policies are aligned with one another and with a national consensus about a desirable policy direction. At the same time, the variation among states in the nature of their politics and their finance and governance systems and the dispersed nature of control within states mean that no one can expect a uniform national response across or even within states to any particular policy.

What Levels of Government in the United States Should Be Interested in Policy Inferences from TIMSS?

The previous discussion suggests four points about what levels of government should be interested in policy inferences based on findings from TIMSS. First, regardless of whether a policy is initiated at the federal, state, or local level, it will be interpreted and potentially implemented within the context of state standards-based reforms in each of the 50 different states.

Second, even though new policies are interpreted within a common framework for reform, their implementation may vary from state to state and community to community and school to school. This suggests that the potential robustness of policies across state and local contexts should be examined.

Third, some policies, such as those affecting the content and structure of the curriculum and the nature of pedagogy, are more appropriately targeted for state and local governments and schools, even though the research, dissemination, and funding for these policies may come from the federal government, foundations or national interest groups. Regardless of who initiates a policy or new program, it ultimately will be implemented in states, districts, and schools.

Finally, the United States is considerably larger and politically more complex than any other nation studied in TIMSS. This makes direct application of lessons or policies from those other nations to the United States a questionable proposition. Consider, for example, a parallel situation within a single state in the Unites States. In this scenario, the superintendent of schools in Palo Alto, California, based on his experience in that affluent suburb, proposes a school reform to his fellow superintendent from Los Angeles. Likely the conversation would be polite, but the Los Angeles superintendent probably would not race home and initiate the reform. The differences between Palo Alto and Los Angeles are huge on a very large number of the important dimensions. The differences are equally large between small nations, such as Singapore or Iceland and larger, more complex nations, such as Germany or the United States. The closer the form of educational governance and the size and structure of the political entities, the more likely there will be easy transfer of ideas. All of the points lead us again to the proposition that policy inferences from most cross-national studies are generally more appropriate for states than for other entities in the United States. On the basis of size, complexity, and governance and fiscal responsibility, states are closer in character to many TIMSS nations than is the United States itself.

DIFFERENT KINDS OF INFERENCES

To "infer" means to reach a conclusion based on evidence. Most interesting inferences would require going beyond a simple descriptive conclusion such as "students in small classes achieve to a higher level than students in large classes." A next step would be to use such descriptive data and perhaps other data to argue that class size has some causal relationship to student achievement. To be convincing, this later step generally requires well-developed theory and/or a rigorous experimental design.

Assumptions Underlying Inferences

In most discussions of TIMSS, we assume a variety of things before we begin to make substantive inferences. We assume that the samples of students in the various countries are representative of the populations of students in those countries. We also assume that the TIMSS assessments are valid measures of mathematics and science content, as set out in the specifications for the assessments. Using these assumptions, we infer that the TIMSS assessments give us valid measurements of how much students in the various countries know of the specified mathematics and science. This allows us to say, for example, that compared to students in the other TIMSS nations, U.S. students achieve in math and science, as defined by the TIMSS assessments, relatively well in the fourth grade and relatively badly in the eighth grade.

However, unless we are convinced that the TIMSS mathematics and science assessments substantially measure what is taught in U.S. schools, we cannot say very much about what factors, other than curricular content, affect U.S. student achievement as measured by the TIMSS tests. For example, if teachers in U.S. schools do not teach science, or teach substantially different science than that measured by the TIMSS assessments, we do not have, from the TIMSS test data, sufficient evidence to say very much about the effects and quality of their teaching. A great deal rests on the alignment of the assessment with the curriculum.

Ironically, if the assessment is not fully aligned with the curriculum in a certain country and students in that country do badly in content areas of the assessment that are "underrepresented" in their curriculum, there is a plausible case to be made for the validity of the assessment, at least for making inferences about the effects of the curriculum on performance on the assessment. Indeed, the country might be motivated to alter its curriculum to place more emphasis on the "left-out" content area, if the country valued it.

I am not suggesting that the TIMSS assessment data are badly aligned with the curricula in U.S. schools—I know a great deal of effort was expended to ensure that the alignment was as close as possible. I also know that a variety of studies have been carried out on subdomains of science and mathematics that are represented in the TIMSS assessments and that have varying levels of alignment with typical U.S. curricula. I am simply pointing out that understanding how well the assessment is aligned with the curricula in various countries is a very important building block for making valid inferences from TIMSS data.

In addition to assumptions about the student assessment, we often have to make assumptions about the quality of other data gathered in TIMSS. I don't know enough about these data to suggest specific concerns, but I wonder, for example, whether there are independent measures of reliability or, even better, validity of the responses to the items for any of the questionnaires. I could imagine, for example, a number of legitimate ways to answer questions about teaching and the curriculum and school resources in the United States.

We already know that the assumption of a representative sample is violated for substantial numbers of countries, particularly at the Population 3 level (the school-leaving grade, grade 12 in the United States). For example, 16 of the 21 countries that participated in the Population 3 Upper Grade Mathematics Literacy assessment were in violation of the international sampling guidelines; one of the 16 was the United States. Even though there were substantial numbers of countries in violation in the other Populations (nine of 26 in Population 1 Upper Grade Science and 17 of 41 in Population 2 Upper Grade Science), the proportion of violators in Population 3 stands out. This fact, along with my own intuition about the lack of motivation of 12th-grade students on this assessment, makes me skeptical of the results of the Population 3 assessments. In the following discussion, I will focus only on Populations 1 and 2 (fourth and eighth grades).

Types of Inferences

Before we look at some examples of inferences from TIMSS, let's distinguish among three types of inferences: causal, "weak," and "synthetic."

Causal Inferences

For all sorts of reasons, the data from TIMSS and other cross-national surveys, combined with our lack of strong theoretical models, will not support causal inferences. For example, using only the TIMSS data, when analyzed with the most powerful statistical techniques, we cannot validly assert that differences in the pedagogy used by teachers in different nations result in differences in student achievement. We do not have adequate measures of differences in pedagogy nor a theory that is robust enough to account for the variation in the contexts of different nations. In economists' terms, we do not know enough about the production function. A very strong correlation does not overcome this weakness. Haertel said it well in 1997, shortly after TIMSS was released:

> These (TIMSS) descriptive data may suggest causal connections, but it is important to remember that TIMSS data alone cannot support any claims about causal relationships among variables. The rhetoric of "natural experiments" is seductive. It conjures up an image of the world as a great laboratory, with different countries trying alternative educational approaches and TIMSS as the common examination to see which approach worked best. But TIMSS is a comparative observational study, not an experiment. It involved the collection of data from scientific samples chosen to represent pre-existing populations, but those populations, the students of different nations, are not interchangeable. No group can be randomly assigned to any other nation's methods of child rearing or education. Students' experiences both in school and out of school vary in countless ways that have not been captured by the TIMSS study, and no statistical method can be relied upon to disentangle those innumerable influences unambiguously, nor to accurately quantify the effect on achievement of any one variable in isolation from all the others. (p. 2)

"Weak" Inferences

We are on sturdier ground when talking about TIMSS findings if we a) use qualifying language such as "supports the hypothesis that"; b) are able to support our inferences with similar findings from other research; and c) ground the findings and hypotheses in well-tested theory. A "weak" inference suggests a direction, indicates a hypothesis, or supports the elimination of a hypothesis. Admittedly, there are different grades of "weakness" in inferences from cross-national survey data. We might argue, for example, that a strong case for a causal inference would be presented by a cross-national panel study where a priori hypotheses about the effects of certain interventions were tested rigorously with appropriate methodological models and found to have strong effects. Unfortunately, our data, theory, and analyses of cross-national surveys, to date, are far from this optimal situation. Nonetheless, the findings would still cry out for further investigation and replication. The differences among the educational systems and cultures of nations are far too great to control away statistically. Every "inference" that may be made legitimately from analyses of the TIMSS data is a "weak" inference.

"Synthetic" Inferences

This kind of inference is a special case of a weak inference. A synthetic inference is the most powerful for policy purposes and the most speculative. It involves piecing together a story line (a "script" in Elmore's language) that integrates a variety of findings into a compelling and coherent picture. It typically draws on a variety of sources of information within a large study. It also may include other supporting data. Unlike a formal model, it often exists without precise parameters. Moreover, there is often no easy way to test the validity of the "story."

The "story line" from the presidential campaign in 2000 involved a complex set of inferences from a wide body of research that had convinced the candidates of the importance of testing, and of student and institutional accountability for improving educational achievement. An alternative "story line" often told by Jonathan Kozol, among others, rests on studies that support the position that providing more resources to needy schools is a viable strategy for improving achievement.

A third story line grew out of the TIMSS data and will be considered in the next section.

FOUR EXAMPLES OF INFERENCES FROM THE TIMSS STUDY

Now, let's take a look at four sets of findings or nonfindings from TIMSS and consider for each whether inferences about national policy legitimately might be made and whether such inferences, in fact, were made. The possible inferences in the first three sets of findings all fit the "weak" inference label; the last example fits in the category of "synthetic" inference.

- **A nonfinding—no single-variable "magic bullets."**

In the original TIMSS reports, there are no outstanding examples of single variables found to have special power to explain differences among countries in level of student *achievement*.[6] Difference in class size, the kind of governance system, and per-pupil expenditure, for example, are all viewed as operating within specific national contexts. As far as I know, these (non) findings received little attention at the national level. As a result, we were able to avoid the loose and inaccurate inference that because such factors did not have explanatory power *among* nations, they were not important *within* countries.

Suppose, however, that the TIMSS reports or reanalyses reported single-variable relationships at the national level between school resources and student achievement. Imagine, then, that class size had statistically differentiated among high- and low-scoring nations in TIMSS. In Washington in 1997-98, Democrats in the Clinton administration and in Congress were attempting to pass a bill to reduce class size in the early grades. They were supporting their position on the generally positive findings of the Tennessee experiment on class size. In that environment, if class size had been a powerful predictor of student achievement across nations, it would have been very difficult for Democrats to resist making an inference about national policy from the TIMSS data.

I have two points to make here. First, it is to their credit that the original TIMSS analysts did not attempt to create single-variable relationships and make something of them. It would have been easy for them to search for and erroneously find "statistically significant" relationships—after all, they were dealing with only 40+ degrees of freedom when they were using country analyses, and they could have tried out literally hundreds of different variables. Second, single-variable and other seemingly simple relationships derived from survey data are relatively easy for policy makers to understand and discuss. Even if informed analysts had cautioned against interpreting any cross-national relationship involving class size because of the tremendous differences among nations in the reasons why classes are relatively large or small, the impulse to use the finding to support the class size legislation would have been very powerful.

- **Benchmarking and "existence proofs."**

The fact that students in the "First in the World Consortium"[7] achieve at a level that is competitive with the highest scoring nations supported many policy makers in making the inference that U.S. students, in general, could succeed at far more challenging levels. Just as Jaime Escalante and District 2 in New York City are "existence proofs," so is the Consortium. Even though Consortium students, on average, are more advantaged than most U.S. students, the Consortium results have been seen to demonstrate that U.S. schools can be as effective as schools in the highest scoring nations. Given the right opportunities, the argument goes, all of our students can attain far higher standards of academic achievement.

The belief supported by this inference became national policy in 1983 in *A Nation at Risk*, a policy that was reiterated again by the governors and the president in the 1989 summit and at the federal level in the Goals 2000 and Improving America's Schools Act (IASA) legislation in 1994. In each instance, cross-national studies that showed that other students in other nations achieved at a consistently higher level than students in the United States were cited as evidence supporting the policy. The achievement of the TIMSS Consortium students dramatically buttressed the argument. There is good evidence from cognitive science and other fields outside of international comparative studies that supports the view that almost all U.S. students could be achieving to high academic standards. However, in my view the international surveys have been critical in forming a national alliance within the United States around this policy—without cross-national student achievement "benchmarks," it would have been much more difficult to align forces within the United States in support of more challenging standards.

A thought experiment that suggests the power of this kind of international benchmark is to ask what would have happened if the early cross-national surveys had found that U.S. students do better than most other nations, not just at the fourth grade level, but at the later grades as well. Would there have been *A Nation at Risk*?

The videos of teaching practice from the United States, Germany, and Japan provide a second benchmark. This time the benchmark is one created by strikingly different approaches to teaching—the simple and virtually uncontestable inference when these tapes are viewed is that differences in teaching lead to differences in student learning.

Inferences drawn from "benchmarks" of exemplary practice or achievement have a special authority because it is very difficult to prove or disprove them, unless further studies are carried out. But they provide an incentive to examine why they "exist." One of the challenges for BICSE might be to try to better understand under what conditions "benchmarks" can provide useful insights for potential policy inferences and future within-country studies. In the world of cross-national studies, this is essentially the problem of developing a theory for understanding the importance of differences among the contexts of different countries.

• **Students in the United States start out reasonably well as measured by fourth-grade scores in science and mathematics, and especially in science, but then fall behind between fourth and eighth grades.**

A number of possible inferences might arise from these findings. Consider first just the finding that U.S. fourth graders do comparatively well. In fact, in science, U.S. fourth-grade students did very well in TIMSS, statistically scoring lower than only one very small, quite wealthy nation. Moreover, this finding was not a surprise to observers of international comparative studies. Earlier math and science studies as well as a study of reading achievement all showed that U.S. fourth graders achieve at a relatively high level.

What kinds of inferences can we make from this finding of strong early achievement? Do these studies suggest the inference that we do not need more or improved early childhood education (preschool to third grade)—or that early childhood education should not be a national priority? They might, but I suspect that this particular inference has not been seriously considered by anyone who has anything to do with establishing national or state policy. In fact, I don't know of any inference for U.S. national or state policy that has been generated by the general finding that the U.S. fourth-grade students compare favorably with students from other nations.

We could speculate about several possible reasons for this. One could be that there is reputedly counterevidence from the National Assessment of Educational Progress (NAEP)—after all, our NAEP scores show that 38 percent of the nation's fourth graders "cannot read." Although psycho-metricians know that an arbitrary cut score that has little to do with an actual capacity to read creates this number, most politicians and people in the press appear to believe it means that our schooling is failing nearly two-fifths of fourth graders. Another reason people may overlook the finding on fourth-grade achievement is that it is politically unwise to suggest that early intervention is not a priority.

A third possibility concerns the difficulty of developing a politically plausible policy inference from a positive finding. If a finding is negative, remedies suggest themselves; if a finding is positive, our imagination often seems to be constrained to little other than proposing to expand the opportunity for the policy. The natural conservative nature of political action also operates as a constraint—"don't change if it ain't broke." A fourth and, I think, more compelling reason is that analysts and reporters have combined this finding with the fact that the distribution of student achievement in the United States typically has a larger variance than that of other nations. This line of reasoning leads to the valid point that although fourth-grade *average* scores may be high, many students do not achieve at an acceptable level.

Now, let us go beyond the fourth grade. U.S. eighth-grade TIMSS scores in science are a little above the median nation, though in the average range, and, in mathematics, considerably below the median. The drop in relative standing for the United States from fourth grade to eighth grade in mathematics and science is substantial and disturbing.

This finding was not a surprise to aficionados of cross-national surveys of achievement. Earlier international comparative studies in mathematics, science, and reading showed similar patterns.

For example, the Second International Mathematics Study (SIMS) received national attention because of a similar conclusion. Analyses of
SIMS data indicated that the U.S. curriculum in the middle grades, and
especially in eighth grade, was not as challenging as the curricula in other
nations. Recall that, in SIMS, pre- and post-eighth-grade achievement
data were collected, so it was possible to explore differences in achievement gains among and within countries during the eighth grade. The
cross-national average comparison in SIMS was that, on average, U.S.
eighth graders gained less during the year than did eighth graders in
other countries.

The more interesting analyses, however, used only data from the U.S.
sample. SIMS collected sufficient curriculum information within the
United States to be able to categorize different eighth-grade mathematics
classes into four groups (remedial, general, advanced, and algebra). Moreover, there was considerable variation in the scores of entering algebra
students. This allowed a within-country comparison of the gains of students within the four different types of eighth grade classes. It turned out
that after controlling for prior (pretest) achievement, students gained very
little from the "remedial" experience, a little more from the general curriculum, and a substantial amount from the advanced and algebra courses.

This particular analysis of eighth-grade curricular differences was an
entirely within-country study—it need not have been carried out under
the IEA umbrella. However, in conjunction with the cross-national comparative finding that U.S. eighth-grade students were lagging behind students in other nations, the within-country finding gained credibility and
lent support to the policy argument that U.S. students should take more
challenging courses in general, and eighth-grade algebra in particular.

During the middle and late 1980s and into the 1990s, this policy argument gained backing from a wide variety of state and local educators and
policy makers as well as organizations such as the College Board. Governors and federal policy makers urged local districts to make algebra available to larger numbers of students in the eighth and ninth grades. Although this erstwhile national policy was commendable, it also had its
critics, some of whom were scholars of international studies. It turns out
that many of the countries whose students do well in mathematics in
general and algebra in particular in eighth-grade international assessments actually prepare students in algebra over an extended number of
years. Algebraic concepts are introduced as early as third or fourth grade
and extended upon over the next few years. Instead of the content of
algebra being introduced and taught largely within a specific grade, it is

carefully integrated with other mathematics, as the child grows more able to learn and understand it. In other words, the inference that students should take an algebra course in eighth grade did not take into account the more extensive differences in mathematics curricula between nations.

Part of the reason that the U.S. policy developed in the way that it did is that many of the earlier grade teachers are not prepared to teach algebra content. Thus, to policy makers, there really was no alternative but to introduce it as a single-grade subject. Besides, I can hear them arguing, there are no studies that indicate that integration works better and algebra has always been a single-grade offering in the United States—this new policy just extends the opportunity to more students. The upshot of this is that a policy at least partly based on international findings was altered to fit the U.S. circumstances.

- **U.S. students in eighth and 12th grades score well below our nation's competitors in mathematics and science achievement. A plausible reason for this is that compared to other nations, U.S. curricula in mathematics and science lack focus, rigor, and coherence, and U.S. teaching emphasizes fragmented and disconnected bits of knowledge, rather than deep mastery of ideas.[8]**

It is not hard to **leap** from this "plausible reason" to at least suggest the inference that the United States needs a policy that leads to improving the focus, rigor, and coherence of mathematics and science curricula and that supports teaching that emphasizes mastery of ideas, rather than fragmented facts. The data supporting this "synthetic" inference are drawn from a number of separate places throughout TIMSS. The achievement data are taken from the assessments, the curriculum data from the achievement survey questionnaire and a separate data bank and analyses of the curricula in many nations, and the teaching data from questionnaires and videotapes.

Over the past few years, the *inferential leap* that this is what TIMSS shows has been publicly made or implied hundreds of times by many dozens of thoughtful people. In my former role as Under-Secretary and Acting Deputy Secretary of the U.S. Department of Education for most of the Clinton administration, I am one of those people; it was easy to do because it made a good story. The temptation to simplify complex results and to frame their implications into a story or capture them with a single example is very powerful, especially when talking to a lay audience or the press, which, of course, is where we should be most careful. Even when told with responsible caveats about cross-national survey data not supporting causal inferences, a story of this sort often leaves the audience with a clear impression that such inferences are justified.

This story has had a very successful run on the policy stage. There are at least three key reasons for this success that have to do with the nature and content of the story. In addition, the TIMSS rollout and the sustained effort at disseminating information also appeared to have an effect. First, the three key reasons:

1. The political stars were aligned. The story was easily seen as strongly supporting the goals of state standards-based reform, a policy advocated by the Clinton administration and governors across the nation. During the first few years of the Clinton administration, policies in education were focused specifically on policies that called for higher academic standards, challenging curricula aligned with the standards, and better training for teachers that would enable them to effectively teach the curricula. The key words were coherence and rigor—words that directly resonated with the story of the TIMSS results. The administration saw this and deliberately set out to use these results to support its policies.

2. The story is simple and plausible. It was supported with pictures communicated through easy-to-understand anecdotes and powerful videotapes of teachers from the United States, Japan, and Germany. The tapes showed striking differences between U.S. and Japanese teachers, differences that could be seen as helping to explain why Japanese students scored much higher on TIMSS assessments than U.S. students. Moreover, a widely available book, *A Splintered Vision*, authored by Schmidt, the principal U.S. TIMSS researcher, along with two colleagues (Schmidt, McKnight, & Raizen, 1997), presents a heavily documented version of the story.

3. The TIMSS data collection and analyses were conducted in a highly professional manner, and data from sources outside of TIMSS tended to corroborate at least parts of the story.

These three reasons created a rich environment for promoting the story. The alignment with current policy induced President Clinton and Secretary of Education Riley to be involved in releasing the data. Both saw the basic TIMSS data releases as well as the release of the data for the First in the World Consortium as powerful opportunities to support administration policies. The exposure for the administration was enhanced by the fact that different parts of the study were released over a six-month period, offering a number of opportunities for administration officials to comment to the press on the studies and their relationship to current policy.

Political and national interest group leaders amplified comments by the president and the secretary. Many education and business groups disseminated summaries of TIMSS findings and "implications" to their members.

The telling and dissemination of the story were enhanced by the videos of teachers from three nations, toolkits for teacher professional development, Web sites dedicated to TIMSS, extensive efforts by professional education groups, a public relations firm, and a tireless campaign by Schmidt.

Finally, the implicit and explicit imprimaturs of the National Center for Education Statistics (NCES) and BICSE at the National Research Council attested to the quality of the TIMSS work and corroborating data from earlier cross-national studies, and other research provided support to help validate the story.

TENTATIVE CONCLUSIONS ABOUT THE IMPACTS OF EARLY CROSS-NATIONAL SURVEYS AND TIMSS ON POLICY

What can we conclude from all of this? I have addressed two of the questions posed at the beginning of this chapter. The first had to do with the kinds of inferences that may legitimately be drawn from cross-national survey data. I argued against the possibility of drawing causal inferences and for a careful examination of context and corroborating data from other sources in drawing "weak," noncausal policy inferences. I also argued that the politically most powerful "weak" inference is a "synthetic" inference made up of a number of parts that together tell a plausible story. The TIMSS data provide a powerful example of a "synthetic" inference.

The second question had to do with past cross-national surveys and whether the findings from these surveys have been used to inform national policy. I argued that the early survey findings initially had little effect beyond raising issues such as the fact that U.S. secondary school students had lower test scores than students in many other nations and the importance of content and students' opportunity to learn. However, I also argued that the early cross-national studies were quite influential 10 to 20 years after they were released in helping to actually establish the policy directions for the rash of reports that came out in the early 1980s, including *A Nation at Risk*. I believe it is safe to say that the earlier reports stimulated a great deal of "policy talk" at the national level, which in time supported policy changes at state and local levels.

In this section I continue to consider the impact of TIMSS. One thing we are certain of is that the findings of TIMSS were widely disseminated, discussed, and used in policy circles. The results of TIMSS were a topic of conversation and a source of information for officials at all levels of the Clinton administration, in Congress, in numerous state houses and state departments of education, and throughout the extended national policy community. Experience with other international assessments suggests that timing is critical—findings typically will be used when the political and policy climate is ready. In this case the climate was ready. A further question has to do with whether the effect of TIMSS on policy has been only to support existing policy—or has it had a substantial independent impact on policy? That is, would state and/or federal policy have been different if there had been no Third International Mathematics and Science Study?

We do know that 14 districts or clusters of districts, including the First in the World Consortium, the Miami-Dade County Public Schools, and the Smart Consortium of districts in Ohio, as well as 13 states, opted to be part of TIMSS-R and took various administrative and policy steps to help students prepare for it.[9] We might infer from this that TIMSS and the advent of TIMSS-R have influenced policy formulation and development in a substantial number of states and communities around the nation. In these places TIMSS seems to have had more than a supportive and marginal effect. I hope studies are conducted of whether, how, and why these districts and states have taken the step of using TIMSS-R as a lever for reform.

It may be too early tell whether TIMSS has had a true independent effect at the federal level. At this point I think the weight of the evidence is that there were not independent effects. As far as I can tell, both from my own experience and from the literature, federal policies were not directly affected by the TIMSS results. In other words, the relevant education policies of the federal government (including the legislative and administrative branches) were not changed because of the results of TIMSS.

However, without question the TIMSS results reinforced the existing policies.

There is an irony here, for often a study will be widely discussed and disseminated if it broadly supports current policy, in which case it is unlikely to have a powerful independent influence on policy. On the other hand, a study that does not support existing policy may not be as widely disseminated. In this instance, we may need to wait some time to see the effects of the study, as in the cases of the international comparative studies carried out in the 1960s and 1970s.

ISSUES AND QUESTIONS THAT BICSE MIGHT ADDRESS THAT DRAW FROM OUR EXPERIENCES WITH TIMSS AND/OR TIMSS-R

This section addresses the last question I posed at the beginning of this chapter. Are there lessons from the past that might be used to improve the quality of inferences that might be made in the future from TIMSS, TIMSS-R, and their successors? As I thought about this issue, I broadened the section to include issues and ideas that might be part of BICSE's agenda as it works to make cross-national studies more robust, valid, and useful. These thoughts are intended to be provocative.

1. There is no way to fully control either policy makers from making "magic bullet" or other erroneous causal inferences from international data or researchers from promoting them. But BICSE might do a few things to reduce the chance that mischief results from either a sloppy original report or a reanalysis of the cross-national data. One might be to put out some voluntary standards for the use and interpretation of cross-national survey data. The standards might cover topics such as the usefulness of a priori theory and approaches for adjusting degrees of freedom when many equations or comparisons are explored and not reported.

2. This chapter suggests that states have been an important consumer of information about TIMSS, perhaps the most important. A substantial number of states administered TIMSS-R and the results were reported in the spring of 2001. The fact that a state deliberately signed up for TIMSS-R indicates that it might pay more attention to the results than it would if the results were based on a national sample. Could BICSE suggest guidelines and develop useful benchmarks for state policy makers as they interpret the results of the national data and of the data on their own states? Are there ways to think about the appropriateness of various policy inferences suggested by TIMSS-R for different state environments?

3. What kinds of national inferences will be drawn when the nation shows only modest gains at best when the TIMSS-R (1999) and TIMSS (1995) scores are compared? Perhaps BICSE could help policy makers, the press, and the public better understand what magnitude of student achievement gains are possible or likely over certain time periods. How fast can a system (teachers, curriculum, etc.) change to the point where it is having a substantially increased effect? Can we benchmark against average gains of other countries? What are expected gains and extraordinary gains? These questions were crafted before TIMSS-R was released.

Now after the TIMSS-R release, we know a little more now about how large a gain countries might expect to achieve over four years. The average gain for a country participating in both the TIMSS and TIMSS-R eighth-grade assessments in mathematics was two points. The U.S. score for 1999 was nine points higher than the U.S. score for 1995. Unfortunately this difference was not statistically significant, so it shows up in the report as "no gain." Of interest is that another nation also had a nine-point gain that was found to be statistically significant. This suggests that the United States was close to showing a statistically significant result.

Also of interest is that a subgroup of U.S. students, African-Americans, did show a statistically significant gain in eighth-grade mathematics. U.S. students showed no statistical or even suggestive gain in science achievement.[10]

With respect to what effect TIMSS-R has had, I must admit I know little. However, my sense is that it had little impact in Washington, D.C. I wonder, for example, how many readers of this chapter knew that African-American students made a statistically significant gain on the TIMSS test of mathematics between 1995 and 1999. I suspect that state and local press were far more attuned to the TIMSS-R state results when they were released in late spring than the Washington, D.C. press was to the release of the national TIMSS-R results.

4. I understand that in TIMSS-R we will have videos of teaching from seven or so countries. Suppose that one of the countries has both very high eighth-grade mathematics scores and a substantially different way of teaching than the Japanese? What will be a reasonable inference about differences in the effectiveness of various pedagogies? Can BICSE help with this? My own suspicion is that we will find that coherent, challenging instruction carried out well by teachers who understand the content will explain differences in achievement far better than differences in styles of instruction.

5. State standards-based reform in the United States has reached early adolescence. We are facing difficult implementation issues—and possible mid-course corrections to the reforms in various states. Are there lessons that might be drawn from TIMSS that would inform state or national policy as we work through this period? Are there other TIMSS-R countries going through major reforms? How are they doing? Cross-national studies offer insights into major differences in the policies of different nations; can they offer insights into implementation problems? States might contrast themselves with smaller countries that participate in TIMSS-R. It also might be worth focusing on the experiences at the federal and state levels of other nations that have a federal form of government. Australia, Canada, and Germany, for example, have states or provinces that operate as semiautonomous entities in much the same way that our states operate.

6. Is it possible for BICSE to consider some side studies that might help to inform the interpretation of possible policy inferences? For example, what are the effects of jukus on the test taking of eighth graders in Japan and Korea? Does the curriculum of a juku in a particular country reinforce the curriculum in the country's schools? Or does the juku experience provide students with knowledge and skills that they do not receive in school? Perhaps when we compare the schooling experiences of U.S. students with students in countries where there is a high use of

jukus, we should include the juku experience in the analysis. Another issue for BICSE to examine is what we know about context. What makes a policy robust enough to travel, to be appropriate across a wide variety of contexts? What makes a context amenable to change? Can we imagine a theory that would inform us about what kinds of ideas travel to and from countries that are very different in culture and experience?

7. Finally, a big question. The U.S. eighth and 12th graders who did so badly in SIMS in the early 1980s are now fueling the dot.com revolution. The eighth and 12th graders who did badly in the international mathematics and science studies in the 1960s and 1970s led the United States out of the traditional ways of doing business in the late 1980s and early 1990s. I was recently in Japan and China. In both countries they are examining their educational system to try to understand how to stimulate creativity in their students. Is it possible that the cross-national studies are leading the United States astray by measuring the wrong things? Is measuring success in student learning of the academic content of schools the same thing as measuring potential human capital? The Secretary's Commission on Necessary Skills (SCANS) established in the early 1990s proposed five competencies, in addition to basic and advanced academic skills, as necessary for people to have when they enter the modern workplace.[11] The five competencies include interpersonal skills, knowledge of systems, and the use of technology and information. Considerable evidence exists that motivation and the skill of working in groups have powerful effects on the quality of a person's work. Perhaps the SCANS commission and the Japanese and Chinese are on the right track in worrying about creating learning environments that foster skills and characteristics such as creativity and interpersonal skills as well as academic learning. These are not new questions but they continue to deserve attention.

NOTES

1. I gratefully acknowledge the thoughtful comments of Jennifer A. O'Day on drafts of this chapter and of Catherine Sousa and Tricia Tupano for their help in pulling together information that helped me to formulate the issues contained in the chapter. I also appreciate the time and energy that the Board on International Comparative Studies in Education (BICSE) members and staff spent on reviewing drafts of this chapter.
2. For a review of some of the "effects" of TIMSS on policies in other countries, see Macnab (2000). See also Lew and Kim (2000). Lew's e-mail address is hclew@cc.knuje.ac.kr. For other studies, contact the American Institutes for Research, in Palo Alto, CA and Washington, D.C., for its extensive bibliography; visit the National Academies Web site (www.nationalacademies.org); and visit the Consortium for Policy Research in Education Web site (www.cpre.org) or write the Consortium at the University of Pennsylvania, School of Education, Philadelphia, PA. Also visit the TIMSS Web site at Michigan State University, E. Lansing, Michigan (http://ustimss.msu.edu).

3. I served in the Carter administration for four years in two formal education policy development roles as a political appointee. I can recall no instance where the cross-national studies were important sources of policy information.

4. *A Nation at Risk* op cit.; Education Commission of the States, Task Force on Education for Economic Growth, *Action for Excellence*, Denver: 1983; Committee for Economic Development: Research and Policy Committee, *Investing in Our Children: Business and the Public Schools*; Committee for Economic Development, 1985. National Science Board, Commission on Precollege Education in Mathematics, Science and Technology, *Educating Americans for the 21st Century*, Washington, D.C.: National Science Foundation, 1983.

5. It should come as little surprise that there were substantial weaknesses in the inferences and policy conclusions drawn from analyses of test scores (including scores from the cross-cultural assessments). The stories of two sets of inferences are instructive. Only the second study refers to international comparative data. I quote from a report of a talk about the national commission reports that I gave in 1984 in the U.S. Capitol Building in Washington to a seminar organized by the Federation of Behavioral, Social and Cognitive Scientists.

   a. "Test Scores of College-Bound Youth—Several reports mention the decline in the number of students who scored over a certain level on the Scholastic Aptitude Test (SAT). . . . There has been a fairly dramatic decline in the number and percentage of people that score above that level (650 and 700), particularly on the verbal test. This . . . may represent a decline in the capacity of our most able students." One response to this in the reports was to argue for increased rigor in high school courses, particularly in mathematics and science. "However, . . . since 1975 the College Board test scores for advanced mathematics, chemistry and physics have gone up slightly, while at the same time more students are taking the tests." These latter data were not mentioned in the reports.

   b. Comparisons with other countries—"The IEA mathematics test cited in *A Nation at Risk* was administered in 1964. The other IEA tests used as examples by the commissions were administered between 1967 and 1972. An interesting irony is associated in the commissions' use of data collected in 1964. There is a continual theme through the reports that suggests that the nation's schools ought to return to the way they were in the 1950s and early 1960s when there was more discipline and control, before students were coddled and before lots of electives were offered. Of course, the 1964 IEA tests of 13- and 17-year-olds were administered to students who went through a major part of their schooling in the 1950s."

6. However, there may be a tendency in some of the "production function"-like reanalyses of the TIMSS data to highlight single variables, a tendency that should be watched.

7. See Dunson (2000) for a description of the First in the World Consortium.

8. See Elmore (1997) and Dunson (2000).

9. See Dunson (2000).

10. See http://nces.ed.gov/timss/timss-r/highlights.asp.

11. See http://wdr.doleta.gov/SCANS/whatwork/whatwork.html.

REFERENCES

Carroll, J. (1963). A model for school learning. *Teachers College Record, 64,* 723-733.

Committee for Economic Development. (1985). *Investing in our children: Business and the public schools.* Research and Policy Committee. NY: Author.

Dunson, M. A. (2000). *From research to practice and back again: TIMSS as a tool for educational improvement.* Consortium for Policy Research in Education Policy Brief RB-30, Graduate School of Education, University of Pennsylvania.

Education Commission of the States. (1983). *Action for excellence.* Task Force on Education for Economic Growth. Denver: Author.

Elmore, R. F. (1997, February). Education policy and practice in the aftermath of TIMSS. Paper prepared for Learning from TIMSS: An NRC Symposium on the Results of the Third International Mathematics and Science Study, convened by the Board on International Comparative Studies in Education, National Research Council, National Academy of Sciences, Washington, D.C.

Haertel, E. H. (1997, February). Exploring and explaining U.S. TIMSS performance. Paper prepared for Learning from TIMSS: An NRC Symposium on the Results of the Third International Mathematics and Science Study, convened by the Board on International Comparative Studies in Education, National Research Council, National Academy of Sciences, Washington, D.C.

Lew, H.-C., & Kim, O.-K. (2000, April). What is happening in Korea after TIMSS? A rough road for remodeling math classes. Paper presented at the 78th Annual Meeting of the National Council of Teachers of Mathematics, Chicago.

Macnab, D. S. (2000). Forces for change in mathematics education: The case of TIMSS. *Educational Policy Analysis Archives, 8*(15).

National Commission on Excellence in Education. (1983). *A nation at risk: The imperative for educational reform.* Washington, D.C.: U.S. Government Printing Office.

National Science Board. (1983). *Educating Americans for the 21st century.* Commission on Precollege Education in Mathematics, Science and Technology. Washington, D.C.: National Science Foundation.

Schmidt, W., McKnight, C. C., & Raizen, S. (1997). *A splintered vision of U.S. science and mathematics education.* Dordrecht, Netherlands: Kluwer Academic.

Conclusion

11

Large-Scale, Cross-National Surveys of Educational Achievement: Promises, Pitfalls, and Possibilities

*Brian Rowan**

Large-scale, cross-national surveys of schooling and student achievement have been part of the education landscape in the United States for nearly 30 years. The origins of such work can be traced to the twelve-country First International Mathematics Study conducted by the International Association for the Evaluation of Educational Achievement (IEA) in 1964. Since then, at least one, and sometimes several such surveys of student achievement have been conducted each decade. The United States already has participated in six cross-national surveys of mathematics and science achievement, four surveys of reading/literacy/language achievement, two surveys of civics education, and several surveys of student achievement in other domains (for a list of studies, see Table 4-1 of Chromy [this volume]).

What is striking about this corpus of work, besides its growing size, is that cross-national surveys of achievement have been fielded at a more rapid pace each decade since the 1960s. Only one such survey was fielded in the 1960s, and it covered only mathematics achievement. In the 1970s, there was again just a single study, but this one covered six academic subjects. Beginning in the 1980s, however, the pace accelerated. There were two surveys of math and science achievement in the 1980s, and another two in the 1990s. Moreover, the 1990s saw a reading survey, an

*Brian Rowan is a professor of education and study director for the Study of Instructional Improvement in the School of Education at the University of Michigan.

adult literacy survey, an early childhood survey, a language education survey, and a civics education study.

In this chapter, I discuss these large-scale, cross-national surveys of student achievement. I confine my discussion of this work to a small set of questions about the methodology used in the studies, questions raised by the Board on International Comparative Studies in Education (BICSE) and addressed by the chapters in this volume. In particular, this chapter considers the following three questions:

• Looking at the history of large-scale, cross-national surveys of student achievement, what progress has been made in conducting studies that are increasingly valid and increasingly informative?

• What opportunities lie ahead for improving the quality of such studies, both methodologically and in terms of information yield?

• How important is it to have international surveys of student achievement on a regular basis and with participation of a constant set of countries?

In the following pages, I do *not* address these questions directly. Rather, my approach is to answer these questions in the context of a larger discussion about the purposes of cross-national studies of education, particularly studies focused on issues of student achievement. Clearly, one cannot think wisely about the validity of large-scale, cross-national education surveys, or about the methods they use, the information they yield, or how regularly they should be conducted, without also thinking about the goals such studies are intended to achieve. The problem, of course, is that the large-scale, cross-national surveys discussed in this volume have been complex studies, designed to achieve multiple purposes and to inform multiple audiences of researchers, policy makers, and citizens from participating countries around the world. In this light, an evaluation of such studies, and a discussion about how they might be improved, requires us to think carefully about the goals we want such studies to achieve.

An excellent discussion of these goals can be found in a 1993 monograph published by the National Research Council (1993). This brief monograph advances the view that the world's varied education systems provide a kind of "natural laboratory" that allows interested parties in the United States to look at variations in schooling cross-nationally, to connect variations in educational organization and practice to variations in student achievement, and to use these analyses to think about how to improve the U.S. education system. In this view, data from cross-national surveys of student achievement can be analyzed in two important ways to inform instructional improvement in the United States. First, data on student achievement in the United States can be compared to data on student achievement in other countries, and such comparisons can be used in a "benchmarking" process that sets standards for student achievement in the United States. Second, data from cross-national surveys can be used to investigate how cross-national variations in school and classroom characteristics affect variations in student achievement in the hopes that this sort of analysis will tell us something about how to alter patterns of schooling and improve student achievement in this country.

In this chapter, I treat these two fundamental goals as the context for a discussion of the promises, pitfalls, and possibilities of cross-national surveys of student achievement. I turn first to the problem of cross-national comparisons of student achievement and to the use of such comparisons as benchmarks for student achievement in the United States. In discussing these issues, I pay special attention to the chapters by: Linn, Chromy, Hambleton, Raudenbush and Kim, and Smith in this volume, each of which takes up methodological problems relevant to the benchmarking issue. I then turn to the use of data from cross-national surveys to estimate how changes in schooling practices can improve student achievement in the United States. Here I pay special attention to the chapters prepared for this volume by: Bempechat, Jimenez, and Boulay; Buchmann; Floden; LeTendre; Raudenbush and Kim; and Smith. Only after having looked at these issues do I directly address the questions posed for me by BICSE, and at that, only in the limited way permitted by page constraints.

INTERNATIONAL COMPARISONS AS BENCHMARKS

As Smith (this volume) shows, large-scale, cross-national surveys of student achievement have figured centrally in debates about educational standards in the United States since the 1980s, when findings about the performance of U.S. students on the first international surveys of student achievement were called to the attention of the American public in *A Nation at Risk* (National Commission on Excellence in Education, 1983). Since that time, the cross-national studies have evolved into a kind of decennial "cognitive Olympics" in the United States, as Husen (1987, p. 131), one of the most thoughtful advocates of cross-national research in education, feared they might. In this environment, each new release of international data is given widespread attention, not only by researchers and policy makers, but also—as a result of widespread press coverage—by the public at large. Indeed, the international comparisons have become one of the few grand spectacles in American education, surpassing even the release of data from National Assessment of Educational Progress in terms of pure drama in coverage.

All of this has been controversial, especially in the eyes of those who think reports based on international comparisons have unfairly portrayed the performance of U.S. schools (Berliner & Biddle, 1995; Bracey, 1997). As we shall see, there *is* room for improvement in the ways that international comparisons of student achievement are reported to audiences in the United States. But a case can be made that even the poorly crafted, early reports on international studies of educational achievement performed an important service in American education. Since *A Nation at Risk*, the cross-national surveys of student achievement have served to dramatize issues of educational performance in the United States, mobilizing friend and foe of the system alike to articulate their aspirations for our education system and helping to launch what has become an important, and continuing, public debate about education standards in this country.

A discussion of the consequences of this debate, and the ensuing focus on standards in American education, is beyond the scope of this chapter. Suffice it to say for now, however, that there are two views on this issue. On the positive side, many observers believe the international comparisons (and other attempts to dramatize student achievement in the United States) are leading to the development of much more ambitious and appropriate standards for student learning in American schools. But other observers see a dark side to this development, especially the increased use of standardized test results to dramatize problems of student achievement in the United States. Increasingly, critics are arguing that standardized tests have become the nearly exclusive "coin of the realm" in judging the adequacy of America's schools and that the heavy reliance on such tests as tools of education accountability is leading to an unnecessary and harmful *narrowing* of instructional goals and processes in American schools. It is for this reason, then, that the role of the international comparisons in setting "benchmarks" for student achievement requires special scrutiny, for good benchmarks must not only portray American students' achievement fairly in comparison to students in other nations, but also must assess academic goals that we truly want to hold for our students.

I will raise two interrelated sets of questions about these issues. One set of questions concerns whether the international studies of educational achievement have been designed and managed to produce fair comparisons of student achievement across nations. In examining this problem, I will discuss the extent to which the various tests used in cross-national comparisons are aligned with curricular content emphasized in the nations participating in the comparisons and the extent to which the samples used in making comparisons provide the kind of level playing field required for a fair benchmarking process. Here, I will argue that steady progress is being made despite difficult challenges.

A second set of questions concerns the validity of international comparisons as benchmarks of student achievement in the United States. Here I will inquire more deeply into the curricular content of the achievement tests used in the international studies, discuss the wisdom of comparing achievement at the various age levels sampled in international comparisons, and quibble with the ways the results of these comparisons have been reported and interpreted, not only in the popular press, but also among responsible researchers. My point in this section will be that a variety of issues need attention before international comparisons can be used as clear and unambiguous benchmarks for educational achievement in the United States.

Fielding the Cross-National Studies

Three chapters in this volume discuss the difficulties associated with fielding "fair" cross-national surveys of student achievement and the progress that has been made in this area since the earliest surveys were mounted. Linn's chapter discusses the problems associated with developing achievement tests for the surveys. Chromy discusses problems associated with selecting and realizing samples of students. Hambleton discusses the translation or adaptation of research instruments for use in multiple countries. Overall, each of these chapters notes particular methodological problems faced by the researchers conducting cross-national surveys, but each also communicates a sense that significant progress has been made in addressing these problems.

Consider Linn's chapter on the achievement tests used in cross-national surveys. It is apparent from his discussion that there are difficult problems related to constructing achievement tests for cross-national comparisons, in large part because of differences that exist in national curricula across participating nations. But Linn's chapter also shows the increasing care that researchers have given to the task of aligning tests to national curricula in successive cross-national studies. In the latest studies, for example, achievement tests were constructed only after extensive examination of national curricula and detailed consultation with curriculum experts from participating countries. From this perspective, it appears that sound efforts have been made to ensure "fairness" in testing by allowing analysts from particular nations not only to have detailed knowledge about the alignment of all test items to national curricular goals, but also by allowing analysts from different nations to analyze achievement results using only items that meet an alignment standard for their own country.

Linn also details important progress in constructing and scaling achievement tests over time. The latest studies use elaborate content matrices to choose test content, and they use complex matrix sampling designs and item response theory to allow researchers to place all respondents on the same achievement scale (and subscales) even though a given respondent has answered only a subset of test items. Developments in scaling, in particular, allow researchers to conduct much more sophisticated analyses of the achievement test data from cross-national surveys. In the latest studies, for example, researchers can examine variations in student achievement within nations more completely and in a much more fine-grained way than previously possible. All of this further enhances the fairness of cross-national comparisons by allowing researchers to examine differences in student achievement among groups of students and/ or across curricular domains that are more or less aligned to national standards.

In combination with Linn's chapter, Hambleton's chapter shows that progress also has been made in adapting achievement tests and other data collection protocols for use in the many different nations involved in the cross-national studies. Hambleton, for example, lists the various steps now being used by responsible testing agencies to develop tests for use in cross-national settings, where language and culture are important considerations in test construction. Linn describes the care taken in the most recent cross-national surveys to pretest items and examine item parameters in different national populations. All of this should lead the consumer and user of cross-national data to the conclusion that—despite enormous difficulties—careful instrument development procedures can be (and are being) used to improve the validity and appropriateness of cross-national survey data.

Finally, Chromy's chapter discusses issues of sampling in the cross-national surveys of student achievement, tracing the various sampling designs used in different studies and the strategies used to ensure that these sampling designs are realized in different nations. His chapter describes a process in which sampling procedures of increasing rigor were developed through time, not only through more careful delineation of sampling plans, but also through more careful development of procedural manuals, reporting forms, and other approaches that enhance the comparability of data across participating nations and that allow analysts to take into account deviations from the uniform sampling procedures when these occurred. In fact, the development of these procedures, and careful monitoring of sample realization, is what now allows analysts (like Smith, this volume) to be able to observe (and take into account) the ways in which deviations from the standard sampling plan affect inferences about national differences in student achievement.

The discussion to this point, then, suggests that much progress has been made in developing sound procedures for fielding cross-national surveys of student achievement. This is no mean feat, because the problems here are formidable. The most difficult part of any research effort is the sheer mounting of the data collection effort, and all the more so when that effort is large and complex. Such problems have been especially pressing in large-scale, cross-national surveys because many of the participating countries have lacked the required "technical" infrastructure to mount complex survey research efforts prior to their participation in the surveys. In fact, the maintenance of the research infrastructure required to mount complex surveys in nations that historically have lacked such capacity is one reason to consider mounting large-scale, cross-national surveys on a frequent basis, for delaying successive waves of research in some nations runs the risk of allowing investments in the research infrastructure to be eroded.[1]

Reporting and Interpreting the Results

The progress just reported addresses some of the criticisms made about early cross-national comparisons of student achievement, especially complaints that the U.S. didn't face a "level" playing field in such comparisons. But a number of problems remain to be addressed before we can conclude that international comparisons of student achievement provide us with truly useful benchmarks for student achievement in the United States. In this section, for example, I discuss how the results of cross-national studies can be analyzed to better inform the overall debate about educational standards in this country, and I point to possibilities for future studies that might provide even more useful information than we now gain from the cross-national surveys. Overall, my message is that deeper and more probing analyses of the cross-national data are needed if they are to be used in a truly informative debate about education standards in this country.

Issues Related to Achievement Tests

One problem I want to address is the extent to which the achievement tests used in cross-national surveys supply the kinds of "benchmarks" for student achievement that we want in the United States. It is well known that the average test scores for American students in cross-national surveys rarely lie at the top of the cross-national performance distribution and that our students frequently perform more in the middle of the pack (or below), depending on the test. What we do *not* know from most published reports of these comparisons, however, is the kinds of academic performances being measured on cross-national achievement tests or the extent to which these tests reflect our desired standards for student learning. In fact, Linn's chapter (this volume) presents some fascinating insights into test content and format that call into question the extent to which the tests used in cross-national surveys provide the most useful benchmarks for student learning in American schools.

Even the most casual observer probably knows that current discussions of academic standards in American education increasingly present an *ambitious* set of goals for what we want students to know and be able to do at different points in their education careers. The emergence of these ambitious standards, however, has been only partly driven by the results of international surveys of student achievement. Equally important to this development has been a sea change in how instructional psychologists and psychometricians in the United States think about school learning. Increasingly, American educators are becoming concerned not simply with the extent to which items on achievement tests adequately sample various content domains in the school curriculum, but also with the level of "cognitive demand" of test items and the types of performance these items are designed to elicit from students.

Linn's discussion (this volume) reflects this interest, and he therefore spends considerable time discussing not only how cross-national surveys arrive at their tables of curricular content, but also how items are constructed to reflect more ambitious levels of "cognitive demand" and more authentic forms of academic performance. In this regard, Linn warns us that despite much progress, the achievement tests used in the most recent cross-national studies continue to include a preponderance of multiple-choice items that have a fairly low level of cognitive demand (e.g., knowledge of simple facts and procedures as opposed to the application of knowledge in nonroutine problem-solving situations). Still, Linn does note that newer items increasingly are being included in cross-national achievement tests—particularly "constructed response" items that present a higher level of cognitive demand and a more "authentic" demonstration of what students know and are able to do. Nevertheless, as Linn points out, the use of newer item formats is inherently limited by restrictions on testing time in cross-national surveys and by the need to increase the sheer number of test items in particular content domains to enhance test reliability. This inherent tradeoff, Linn argues, explains why cross-national achievement tests still have a preponderance of conventional, multiple-choice test items pitched at lower levels of cognitive demand.

If Linn's comments about item formats and cognitive demand suggest that the achievement tests currently used in cross-national surveys don't fully reflect more ambitious views of academic standards for students, his comments about the curricular content included in such tests is even more eye opening. Earlier, I discussed the problems faced by test developers seeking to match the content of cross-national achievement tests to varying national curricula around the world. In discussing this problem, Linn notes two potential test construction strategies that can be used to build "fair" achievement tests in cross-national settings. One strategy is to include test items representing the union of curriculum objectives in all national curricula; an alternative is to include only items occurring at the intersection of national curricula. In point of fact, however, even the most current cross-national achievement tests are not based on either approach. Instead, for reasons having to do with the greater capacity of U.S. agencies to provide test items, and because of restrictions on test length, Linn reports that most of the achievement tests used in cross-national surveys have a distinctly American content and item-format bias.

In light of these arguments, it is worth revisiting the problem of how to use the cross-national surveys to set standards for American education. One thing should be clear from the discussion thus far. If we seek information about how American students are performing in relationship to *ambitious* standards for academic content and cognitive demand, the achievement tests used in most cross-national surveys don't provide the appropriate information. Instead, such tests continue to reflect American curriculum content as it now stands, and they continue to contain items that reflect a lower level of cognitive demand. From this perspective, comparisons of average student performance in the United States to average student performance in other nations are not—in and of themselves—an especially good yardstick for judging progress toward our most ambitious vision of educational standards. Instead, an appropriate *international* benchmarking process would more thoroughly investigate national curricula outside the United States and develop more challenging achievement tests.[2] From this perspective, the goal of bringing the average performance of American students on current tests up to the national averages found in "higher performing" countries serves only as a useful starting point in achieving higher educational standards in American schools, for even if we achieved this goal, we would still not know whether we had met our most ambitious goals for student learning.

Issues Related to Reporting Test Scores

Despite these caveats, many analysts and observers continue to treat cross-national comparisons of student performance as a reasonable standard for judging the performance of our education system. Moreover, many scholars (including myself) would argue that such comparisons, although limited, provide useful insights into how our education system functions, especially in comparison to others. But as the chapters in this volume suggest, there are ways in which these comparisons can be made even more informative.

Consider, for example, a frequently noted, but easily addressed, complaint about the use of achievement data in making cross-national comparisons. Many careful observers, including Raudenbush and Kim (this volume), argue that too much emphasis is placed on comparing country means on achievement. In this argument, a focus on mean differences in achievement across countries is seen as concealing as much as it reveals (see also Berliner & Biddle, 1995, and Bracey, 1997). It is my view that the focus on country means is largely a legacy of the relatively primitive scaling procedures used in the earliest cross-national surveys, for as Linn (this volume) reports, it was not until the use of more sophisticated scaling techniques that the possibility of detailed reporting of within-country variation in student achievement scores emerged. As a result, the focus on mean scores in cross-national comparisons could be seen as a simple case of cultural lag, that is, a phenomenon in which the average analyst has yet to catch up with the new possibilities for data analysis resulting from changes in test scaling procedures. If that is the case, more sophisticated reporting should begin to appear in the near future.

Issues Related to Sampling

The question, of course, is the form that such sophisticated reporting should take, for more complicated forms of data analysis abound. One obvious approach, appearing more and more frequently in publications originating in the United States, is to report not only mean achievement across countries, but also the dispersion of scores around national means and the uncertainty in estimates that results from this dispersion. Obviously, such statistics give a much better sense than do simple rankings of mean scores about whether, in fact, the differences in country means are statistically significant, and about how large such differences are in terms of the total dispersion in test scores (for a discussion, see Raudenbush and Kim, this volume).

Beyond that, it appears that cross-national comparisons of achievement also could be analyzed in ways that are more sensitive to differences in the composition of national samples. We know, for example, that the country-level samples in cross-national surveys conducted to date have varied in terms of the percentage of students participating in different curricular programs (or "tracks"), in terms of age and gender composition, in terms of socioeconomic and ethnic composition, and/or in terms of the percentage of students living in different residential locations (e.g., urban, rural). Raudenbush and Kim (this volume) argue that these differences can—and often do—affect student achievement and that reasonable comparisons of student achievement across nations need to: (a) demonstrate such effects and (b) adjust for differences in sample composition when reporting on cross-national differences in achievement (see also

Baker, 1993; Berliner & Biddle, 1995; Floden, this volume; and Westbury, 1992).

It should be noted that these recommendations involve more than just technical matters. The problem of whether or not to adjust country means for sample composition cuts to the very heart of setting standards for student learning in American society. For example, many critics of the cross-national surveys have argued that focusing on *mean* differences across nations obscures many of the unique challenges faced by the American educational system. In this view, cross-national comparisons need to take into account that the education system in the United States is called on to educate more children in poverty than the education systems in many of the "top-achieving" countries, that the United States has more ethnic and linguistic diversity than many countries, and that students in the United States live in more diverse residential locations than students in some of the "top-performing" countries. In this view, reporting unadjusted means does a real disservice to our nation's embattled educators, who are working against great odds to produce the results they do.

I believe this view should be treated with great caution, however. For one thing, a case can be made that a focus on unadjusted means represents what we truly desire—that *all* students in our country achieve at the highest levels. In fact, my own sympathies lie with this latter view, although I also favor more careful, disaggregated displays of achievement data for a number of reasons. For one, an examination of achievement among subpopulations in the United States gives us a much better sense about how American society currently distributes human capital among its members and about the pernicious patterns of inequality that still exist in our nation. Moreover, an examination of achievement patterns across subgroups need not undermine our concerns about educating *all* students well. In fact, a careful look at subgroup differences in achievement tells us precisely where we are succeeding and where we are not. Thus, although I favor disaggregated presentations of cross-national data, I do not favor this approach because I want to defend our educational system. Rather, I think such data are more informative and more telling in their description of educational outcomes in American society. In fact, I believe such analyses need to be extended beyond the analysis of U.S. data. Attention to the ways in which different educational systems in the world distribute human capital among members helps analysts in the United States reflect more thoughtfully on how our own system functions and on its consequences for academic learning across broad segments of the population.

There is one further way in which issues of sampling interact with the problem of setting standards for achievement in the United States. As Chromy (this volume) and Raudenbush and Kim (this volume) discuss, cross-national surveys have varied in how they define the samples to be selected for cross-national comparisons. In some studies, samples have been selected on the basis of students' locations in the graded educational system, but in others, students were selected to represent specified age cohorts. In particular, Raudenbush and Kim argue that sampling students who are in attendance at certain grade levels presents a host of problems, including the fact that patterns of promotion from grade to grade and patterns of school leaving (i.e., dropping out) vary across nations, presenting potentially intractable problems of selection bias in cross-national comparisons of student achievement. As a result, Raudenbush and Kim press for more consideration of age-based, household sampling.

Raudenbush and Kim's analysis of these issues is informative, and their advice is worth considering to the extent that it doesn't undermine researchers' ability to also examine school effects on student achievement outcomes. But again, the issue of what populations to sample in cross-national surveys is more than a technical issue and goes to the heart of the standards we want to hold for student achievement in American society. A number of observers, including Berliner and Biddle (1995), have argued that cross-national comparisons of achievement reflect on more than the simple efficiency of schools; they also reflect on the relative societal "press" for academic achievement at different stages of the life course in different societies. In this view, the performance of American students on cross-national surveys of achievement reflects not only the performance of schools in the United States, but also the very different strategies that parents and communities in the United States use to pass on human, social, and cultural capital to children, especially in comparison to the strategies used in many "high-performing" nations. In many countries around the world, emphasis is placed on school achievement *early* in the life course, especially when early achievement is required to advance in education systems that are more stratified and selective than our own, and that educate fewer students at higher system levels than we do. The United States, in contrast, maintains an education system that is very open—offering many "second chances" for slow starters—all of which allows for parenting strategies that emphasize early investments in human, social, and cultural capital that are only loosely related to the narrow goal of acquiring school knowledge.

To the extent that these observations are true, and they have been a stable feature of arguments about the American education system for decades in comparative sociology, cross-national comparisons of achievement among school-aged populations may not adequately reflect patterns of ultimate achievement in the United States. Following this argument, American society might have developed a pattern of education that promotes a slower pace of achievement. To the extent that we can tolerate (and afford) this educational strategy, a better way to think about educational standards in the United States would be to compare educational achievements at later ages, for example, at age 22 or so, after many American students have had an opportunity to complete postsecondary forms of education. Here, in fact, one could use household samples to great effect and also gain a much better sense of what American students (as well as students from other nations) end up knowing at a more realistic "school-leaving" age than the one most recently defined in the Third International Mathematics and Science Study (TIMSS).[3]

The bigger point, of course, is that we shouldn't let the age group comparisons available in current cross-national studies drive the standards-setting process in American education. Instead, we should use our own sense of desirable standards for learning at particular ages to define the strategy for selecting samples in cross-national studies, and this might involve sampling older students on a household basis. In this regard, the International Adult Literacy Survey, conducted by Statistics Canada, represents a welcome addition to the portfolio of cross-national surveys of educational achievement. One would hope, however, that future surveys of older populations—especially a realistic sample of "school leavers" suited to the American context—would include achievement assessments in more subject areas than just literacy.

All of this raises an interesting possibility for the design of future cross-national surveys. For one, cooperating agencies conducting this research might consider expanding the age groups sampled in such studies, including not only an older sample of school leavers, but also preschool populations.[4] In fact, an expansion of the age groups sampled in cross-national surveys would give us a much better picture of educational achievement across the life course in different societies, providing crucial information about patterns of achievement as these unfold prior to entry into schooling, at critical junctures during the school-age years, and at a more realistic end point than the one typically defined in current and past cross-national surveys. Moreover, analyses of achievement across the life course would give us a much better sense of how patterns of schooling in different countries affect the *distribution* of human capital in society, especially as people move across the life course. Currently, we get some sense of how human capital is distributed at various stages of the life course within the United States in the longitudinal studies program of the National Center for Education Statistics. But I know of no systematic program of cross-national research dealing with this critical question.

CROSS-NATIONAL SURVEYS AND
THE STUDY OF SCHOOL IMPROVEMENT

To this point, I have been discussing the use of cross-national surveys to set benchmarks for student achievement in the United States. In the discussion, I suggested that with additional developments in test design and with some changes in sampling design, international assessments would more usefully serve as benchmarks for student achievement in this country. But as we have seen, many educational researchers and policy analysts want cross-national surveys to be useful for more than setting benchmarks. First of all, they view the cross-national surveys as an opportunity to learn more about education systems around the world, especially how alternative systems are structured and how they function. In addition, many advocates want cross-national surveys to provide good information about how to improve our own education system. There is especially a notion—by no means universally held in the research community—that cross-national surveys might allow us to look at education systems in nations that do better than the United States in cross-national achievement comparisons, identify the practices in these countries that are leading to superior results, and then import these practices into our own system as a means of educational improvement.

Buried in all of this are many important questions about the cross-national surveys of achievement conducted to date and their promise for building sound knowledge about education systems. For one, we might ask what we have learned from three decades of investment in large-scale, cross-national surveys of student achievement, especially in comparison to the three-decade-old program of longitudinal studies supported by the National Center for Education Statistics (NCES).[5] But more importantly, we might ask how survey research can be used to study issues of educational improvement by probing more deeply into the idea that the world's varied education systems provide us with a "natural laboratory" allowing examination of the effects of alternative educational arrangements on student achievement and thereby informing education policy in the United States. Here, as Smith (this volume) notes, we confront sticky issues of causal inference from survey data, as well as issues related to how we might build theories of educational practice from cross-national research.

The Scholarly Yield of Cross-National Surveys of Achievement

One justification for conducting cross-national surveys of student achievement is that they will yield important insights about how education systems work, ideas that might or might not inform educational improvement, but that will move our basic understanding of educational processes forward. In fact, this justification figured centrally in a statement of the goals for cross-national research held by BICSE. As the Board noted, "A[n] . . . important purpose of cross-national research is the development of knowledge . . . [that] enriches and expands [our] understanding of the world and its complexities" (National Research Council, 1993, p. 14). BICSE also argued that achieving this goal would require the "collect[ion] of cross-national data at societal levels over reasonably long periods of time . . . to facilitate the identification of worldwide, regional, and national trends and permit the analysis of sources and effects of cross-national variation in education organization, policy, and practice" (p. 14). The question, then, is whether investments of research dollars in cross-national research have indeed contributed to the goal of building sound knowledge about education systems, and if so, what these insights have been.

My personal view on this question, which arises from interest and experience in conducting research on schooling in the United States, is that the cross-national surveys of achievement *have* led to a number of important insights that have relevance, not only to researchers in the field of comparative education, but also to those interested in educational processes in the United States. In fact, like the BICSE members who contributed to the 1993 monograph, I see an important "cross-walk" occurring between studies of educational achievement conducted solely in a U.S. setting and studies conducted cross-nationally.

One area where cross-national surveys have contributed important insights is in analyses of how socioeconomic origins and educational achievement are related. As Buchmann (this volume) points out, analyses of this issue have been central to educational research since publication of the Coleman Report (1966) in the United States and the Plowden Report in Great Britain (Central Advisory Council for Education, 1967). However, an important study by Heyneman and Loxley (1983) using cross-national surveys of student achievement added additional, and important, insights into the nature of this relationship. Using data from the early cross-national surveys of student achievement, Heyneman and Loxley suggested that the relationship of socioeconomic status and educational achievement was not uniform across societies. In fact, their analyses showed that the relationship among these variables was lower in less developed countries than in more developed countries. More recently, Baker, Goesling, and LeTendre (2000) used data from TIMSS to argue that this is no longer the case and that the relationship between socioeconomic status and achievement in less developed countries now approximates the relationship found in more developed countries. This is precisely the kind of progress in basic knowledge that BICSE (National Research Council, 1993) argued would result from repeated cross-national surveys in education. A major generalization derived from research in a particular kind of country (i.e., advanced industrial nations) is qualified by cross-national research, and then repeated cross-national surveys qualify these findings yet again, uncovering emerging trends in world societies.

An even more telling contribution of cross-national surveys to educational research can be found in Floden's discussion (this volume) of the concept of opportunity to learn (OTL). Although the origins of this concept can be traced to Carroll's (1963) studies of foreign language learning in the United States, the use of this concept in analyzing and explaining student achievement has been greatly advanced in repeated cross-national surveys of student achievement. In the cross-national studies, this concept first was used simply to control for differences in national curricula when comparing student achievement across nations, but in successive waves of the cross-national survey work, the concept of OTL figured more and more centrally as the single most important explanatory variable in the data. Moreover, the centrality of OTL in explaining student achievement has not gone unnoticed in studies of student achievement conducted exclusively in American settings. In fact, as Floden describes, conceptions of OTL now are being used to explain within- and among-school differences in student achievement in the United States.[6]

The evolution of this concept in repeated cross-national studies, coupled with the more careful curriculum analyses discussed by Linn (this volume), has had an added benefit for research on schooling. It is now leading to important conceptions of how curricula are organized and how this organization affects student learning—the kind of "synthetic" theories of education that Smith (this volume) discusses. In the latest TIMSS work, for example, Schmidt and colleagues (Schmidt, McKnight, & Raizen, 1997; Schmidt, McKnight, Cogan, Jakwerth, & Houng, 1999) have developed fascinating and important ideas about the fragmentation of the U.S. mathematics and science curricula and used these ideas to great effect as explanations for the performance of American students on TIMSS achievement tests. The importance of these ideas to the discussion here is that they gain credence—and power—precisely because they have been developed in a cross-national context where patterns of curricular organization other than our own can be glimpsed and where curriculum coverage can be viewed as a central determinant of student achievement. Despite the fact that Schmidt and colleagues' ideas about the American curriculum are still new, they have already begun to have an important influence on educational research and in debates about how to improve educational practice in the United States. They are, therefore, precisely the kinds of insights that BICSE sought to achieve in endorsing continued support for cross-national surveys in education.

Yet another example of the contributions of cross-national research to educational analysis resulted from the addition of videotaped case studies of teaching to the TIMSS portfolio. This work has been important both conceptually and methodologically. On the conceptual front, the video studies have pioneered a view of teaching as fundamentally a cultural activity, with its components composing a system of culturally embedded and interrelated practices (see Stigler and Hiebert, 1999). This insight takes us well beyond a mere mechanical vision of teaching as a set of technical procedures that can be easily packaged and repackaged toward a much more nuanced and realistic understanding of the constraints placed on instructional change by national culture. The TIMSS video studies also are a methodological advance, allowing teaching events to be studied and restudied by observers who are not physically present, using different coding schemes for understanding the events that transpire in a given setting. Already, the use of video studies of teaching is attracting the attention of NCES and the U.S. Department of Education's Planning and Evaluation Services, and we can expect to see more such studies conducted in American settings in the near future.

The larger point, of course, is that the cross-national studies are meeting one of the goals espoused for them by BICSE. These studies have become an important source of *defining* ideas about the nature of schooling in the United States, and about its consequences. In fact, the contributions made by this line of work—contributions that I would argue have been facilitated by the United States' repeated participation in such studies—rank alongside contributions made by, and make important contributions to, the national longitudinal studies and other large-scale evaluations conducted by the U.S. Department of Education. Thus, as a source of exciting scholarly ideas, continued support for the cross-national surveys of achievement seems warranted.

Cross-National Surveys and School Improvement

In many circles, the ambitions held for cross-national surveys go well beyond a contribution to basic knowledge. Many advocates of these surveys also hold that careful cross-national research will yield important insights about how to improve schools in the United States. The logic of this assertion is well stated by BICSE (National Research Council, 1993), where it is argued that the cross-national studies take advantage of "a natural worldwide laboratory of education systems" (p. 4) and that a "comparison of natural variation [across systems of education] is usually a feasible way to study the effects of differing [educational] policies and practices," especially given "that many people are reluctant to conduct controlled experiments with our children's education" (p. 3). Of course, these observations were offered with appropriate cautions, especially notation of the National Research Council's recommendation for greater use of controlled experiments in educational research (National Research Council, 1992). But the general thrust of the argument—and a position one suspects is widely shared in the educational research community—is that the cross-national surveys are a straightforward source of good ideas about school improvement in the United States (see, for example, Smith's discussion of this issue in this volume).

Two issues need to be addressed in thinking about this claim. The first has to do with how causal inferences can be made from nonexperimental data and the extent to which cross-national surveys are making progress in confronting this problem. Clearly, without good data on which to make causal inferences, the claim that we can identify why some education systems are more effective than others cannot be sustained. The second problem has to do with the theories of comparison that we bring to bear in cross-national research. As I will discuss, those who believe that we can use practices developed in other countries to the same effect in the United States are operating under an assumption that causal processes operate in the same way in all societies. As we shall see, however, this is only one of several possibilities.

Let's begin with the problem of making causal inferences from non-experimental data. By the typical standards of school effects research, one could argue that cross-national surveys took a real step *backward* with the design of TIMSS. For example, there is a large literature in this research area demonstrating how estimates from education production functions lead to faulty inferences in the absence of pretest data on achievement outcomes and good measures of home background and socioeconomic status. Yet, in contrast to the Second International Mathematics and Science Studies, TIMSS included no pretest measures of achievement and inadequate measures of home background (on the latter point, see Buchmann in this volume). The obvious recommendation for future cross-national studies, then, is to return to a design that includes achievement testing at two points in time and to take advantage of the advances in the measurement of home background and socioeconomic status described by Buchmann. With these steps, cross-national surveys at least will be able to yield credible education production functions, even if they cannot produce the kinds of sound causal inferences gained from randomized experiments.[7]

For our purposes, an even more telling discussion of how cross-national research can be used to inform issues of school improvement is provided by Raudenbush and Kim (this volume). Near the end of their commentary, Raudenbush and Kim caution readers not to assume that causal inferences about relationships among school characteristics and student achievement based on *between-nation* analyses apply to how such relationships might unfold in the U.S. setting. In their view, between-nation analyses can be used to form *hypotheses* about school improvement in the United States, but these hypotheses need to be tested explicitly through within-nation analyses of U.S. data. This is an extremely important point that requires further discussion, especially because it goes to the very heart of how to use cross-national data and findings to inform educational improvement decisions in the United States.

Consider, for example, one of the central findings from TIMSS—one that many researchers, policy makers, and practitioners think has immediate relevance to improving schooling in the United States. Schmidt and colleagues (1997, 1999) have argued that curriculum characteristics (especially curriculum coherence, focus, and rigor) account for much of the cross-national differences in student achievement in TIMSS data. But their analyses do *not* demonstrate that increased curricular coherence, focus, and rigor explain differences in student achievement within the United States, as Raudenbush and Kim (pp. 290-291) point out. Therefore, there is a need for analyses in which researchers first identify variations in curriculum coherence, focus, and rigor that are actually experienced by U.S. students and then estimate the effects of these real variations on variation in student achievement within the United States. The ways in which such analyses enhance causal inferences about educational processes in the United States are discussed in detail by Raudenbush and Kim, but suffice it to say that there is no *a priori* reason to expect that statistical relationships identified in between-nation analyses necessarily will be present in within-nation analyses.

There are, of course, several potential problems with the call for within-nation analyses of survey data to study the effects of educational practices appearing in other countries. One problem is that researchers might not be able to find sufficient variation in such practices in the U.S. education system, preventing a true test of hypotheses arising out of a cross-national context. For example, what would happen in the example above if no school system in the United States had a curriculum that even approximated the kind of curricular coherence, rigor, and focus characteristic of "high-performing" nations?[8] Under these conditions, we might be forced to actually *create* school conditions that approximate arrangements in other countries before testing their effects on student achievement in the United States, and from this perspective, the work of groups like the New Standards Project and the First in the World Consortium seem to be necessary first steps in translating at least some cross-national findings into practice in the United States, with sound causal inferences awaiting true randomized experiments.

This discussion raises another important issue in cross-national research—the approach to societal comparison being used by researchers in cross-national research and how that approach should be used to inform issues of study design in cross-national surveys. In the United States, discussions of the policy ramifications of cross-national surveys seem to be guided by two relatively simplistic, and related, assumptions. One is that education in all societies works in roughly equivalent ways, leading to a second assumption—that practices imported from other countries will work in the United States in ways that are equivalent to how they worked in other countries. The evidence from cross-national surveys, however, suggests that this will not necessarily be the case. Consider, once again, the findings of Schmidt and colleagues regarding curriculum effects on student achievement. The data presented in Schmidt et al. (1999) strongly suggest the presence of interactions, demonstrating the need for caution about these simplistic assumptions.

In light of this, there is a real need for policy analysts and researchers to think more explicitly about the assumptions they are making regarding comparative research. As Tilly (1984) shows in his short and insightful monograph on comparative cross-national research, we can make several assumptions when developing societal comparisons. One might be that all societies are unique and cannot easily be compared, implying that processes occurring in one society might not easily (or ever) be duplicated in others (this view is close to the one developed by Bempechat et al., this volume). Another assumption might be that there are certain "types" of societies, and that processes occurring within groups of similar societies can be duplicated, but relationships occurring in societies classified as being in one group cannot be duplicated in societies classified as being in other groups. This approach places a premium on measuring societal characteristics and on investigating how societal characteristics condition relationships among variables at constituent system levels. Yet another assumption would hold that national societies are embedded within a larger "world system" of societies (a system in which national societies increasingly are engaged in social relationships with and influenced by one another). In this view, processes occurring within societies often depend less on unique circumstances within societies than on a given society's location in a worldwide system of international relationships, where national societies hold unequal statuses in a dense network of international relationships and participate in an increasingly uniform, worldwide culture.

All three of these perspectives have figured centrally in cross-national research on education. The work of Heyneman and Loxley cited earlier, for example, is an instance of research that examines "types" of societies and that cautions against generalizing about educational processes across nations at different levels of economic development. Another example is the interesting work of Stevenson and Baker (1991) on the effects of educational governance regimes on consistency of content coverage in schools. In contrast, the TIMSS video studies, and the qualitative case studies recently included as companions to cross-national surveys (as discussed by LeTendre, this volume), are consistent with a more holistic form of cross-national analysis, in which societies are seen as relatively unique, and educational practices are seen as deeply embedded in national culture and therefore not easily transported across national boundaries. The work of Meyer, Ramirez, and colleagues exemplifies a third approach to comparison, one derived from a "world-systems" viewpoint on education, where educational developments within countries are seen as resulting not so much from internal social and cultural circumstances, but rather from a given society's position in a global cultural and social system (Meyer, Kamens, & Benavot, 1992; Ramirez & Boli, 1987).

The larger point is that judgments about the "validity" of data and findings from cross-national surveys depend to some extent on the assumptions one makes about appropriate forms of cross-societal comparisons. For example, to the extent that we believe there are "types" of societies, a key concern becomes the types of *societies* to include in the research, and how these societies differ on system-level properties—for example, governance regimes, economic development, ethnic homogeneity, school system types, and so on. In this view, the validity of cross-national studies, and the degree to which the results are informative, depends crucially on whether the types of societies one needs to compare in testing one's theory of societal processes are present in sufficient numbers in the sample to perform such a test and whether sufficient measures of societal properties have been developed for use in comparing system-level properties. In fact, attention to theory-driven thinking at this level of analysis, as well as discussions of how to measure societal-level properties critical to this research agenda, seem oddly lacking in this volume. As a result, readers of this volume would do well to revisit the arguments presented by BICSE (National Research Council, 1993, pp. 20-21), which explicitly attended to this issue.

More prevalent in this volume, but only barely so, is the attention paid to issues of research design and reporting arising from an assumption that national societies are unique and need to be understood on their own terms. This assumption has fostered the demand for qualitative case study research in cross-national comparisons of educational systems. As LeTendre discusses in this volume, well-conducted case studies can contribute in important ways to cross-national surveys by capturing the unique, culturally embedded nature of educational practices in nations. But LeTendre's discussion also shows that a great deal of ambiguity remains within the research community about how to use the information derived from case studies in relation to surveys, as well as the extent to which insights from case studies should drive issues of survey design, and how conclusions from case studies can be reported so that various members of the research and policy communities find them "valid." In fact, the simple contrast between LeTendre's discussion of the uncertainties and misunderstandings surrounding the use of qualitative data in the latest TIMSS work and BICSE's elegant statement of the role such work can play in cross-national survey research found in the National Research Council report (1993, pp. 22-23) is striking and shows that we have a long way to go before the use of qualitative research will be optimized in cross-national surveys of student achievement.

Thus, the papers in this volume suggest that we still need to make progress in articulating the theories of comparison we think should guide cross-national surveys of achievement. We might, for example, need to go beyond the simple assumption that all societies work in the same way, and in doing so, also develop a more realistic set of assumptions about how the findings from cross-national research can be applied to problems of school improvement. In this regard, it is interesting to note that the practitioner community in American education seems to be doing just this, carefully *recreating* practices imported from other nations and testing them in their own educational settings.[9] But this real progress in applying cross-national findings to problems of educational improvement is not much reflected in the current volume, except perhaps in Raudenbush and Kim's advice that hypotheses derived from cross-national comparisons should be carefully tested within the United States and in Smith's cautions about making inferences from cross-national studies to guide education policy. One hopes, therefore, that BICSE will pay more attention to this problem in its future discussions of the validity of large-scale cross-national research and articulate more clearly how cross-national findings can be used to stimulate school improvement in the United States.

CONCLUSION

Having considered the purposes that various constituencies hold for cross-national surveys of educational achievement, and some of the problems associated with achieving these purposes, I will now address directly the questions posed at the outset of this chapter. The first question is:

• **Looking at the history of large-scale, cross-national surveys of student achievement, what progress has been made in conducting studies that are increasingly valid and increasingly informative?**

The answer to this question, as I suggested at the outset, depends on the purposes one hopes to achieve through such studies. If the purpose is to use cross-national surveys to set standards for achievement in U.S. education, I would argue that a great deal of progress has been made in designing studies that are increasingly informative. Advances in test construction and scaling, coupled with better standardization of sampling procedures, have given us achievement tests that have better content validity with respect to national curricula and samples that are more standardized across nations. All of this helps produce comparisons that are fair. Moreover, because of these developments, we can now take better account of within-country variation in achievement, place confidence intervals around measures of central tendency, and do better analyses of subgroup performance, *all* at a more fine-grained level of curricular detail than in previous studies.

These technical advances are welcome and enhance the utility of cross-national comparisons. However, they do not guarantee that the tests of achievement used in the cross-national surveys are "valid" indicators of the educational standards to which we *aspire*, or that the cross-national comparisons based on these studies give us a valid picture of where the United States stands in terms of meeting these standards. As I argued in the body of this paper, despite advances, the cross-national achievement tests used most recently still do not reflect our most ambitious learning goals for students, and the ages at which students are tested in the cross-national surveys might not reflect the goals we actually hold for our education system.

Concerning the goal of using cross-national surveys to inform the process of school improvement in the United States, the picture is less clear. Cross-national studies certainly continue to make important contributions to our understanding of educational issues. The recent contributions of Schmidt and colleagues (1997, 1999) on the nature of curriculum organization in different countries, as well as the insights from the TIMSS video studies of teaching practice, represent two particularly stellar accomplishments in this area. Moreover, various segments of the practitioner community in American education seem to be developing interesting and sophisticated strategies for applying the findings of cross-national surveys to the school improvement process, as the efforts of the New Standards Project, the First in the World Consortium, and other groups suggest.

However, it is my view that the scientific community has yet to articulate a sound logic for how to link the findings from cross-national surveys to issues of school improvement. There are too few within-nation tests of hypotheses developed from cross-national comparisons, no clearly articulated perspectives on how to measure the features of national education systems in ways that guide cross-national comparative work or elucidate the sampling of societies for cross-national comparison, and too little clarity about what constitutes the valid use of qualitative case study data and how they can (or cannot) be used alongside survey data to improve our understanding of educational processes in different societies. In this sense, much more thinking is needed if we are to clearly articulate the role of cross-national studies in improving schools in the United States.

One thing is clear, however. Sound information about how to change American schooling in ways that improve student learning cannot be based on cross-national surveys alone, or even on surveys that seek to assess hypotheses drawn from cross-national analyses using within-nation analyses of survey data. Instead, to truly understand how practices imported from other countries might affect student achievement in the United States, it appears that we will have to recreate these practices in American settings through careful intervention and then investigate the effects of these practices in carefully controlled experimental work. That is a logical—and needed—addition to the cross-national research agenda, and one that I believe BICSE should support.

The second question is:

- **What opportunities lie ahead for improving the quality of such studies, both methodologically and in terms of information yield?**

This is a difficult question to answer in the absence of information about levels of funding for future cross-national research. Certainly, advances in the development of computerized adaptive testing are worth exploring as means of improving cross-national achievement tests, especially if this approach to achievement testing can be used to improve the information yielded per item in measures of achievement, thereby reducing the number of items required in testing. If that possibility exists, perhaps reductions in the required amount of time for testing resulting from this process can allow for the development of more items that assess "authentic" forms of academic performance and at higher levels of cognitive demand, bringing the tests used in cross-national surveys more in line with our most ambitious standards for student learning. The challenges here are enormous, however, and the resources required to make such advances could be beyond budgetary reach.

I would also like to see an expansion in age groups included in the cross-national surveys, not only to include an older population of school leavers, but also to include a group of preschool students. The inclusion of such populations could allow for the kinds of investigations into achievement across the life course that I believe are truly needed to understand the role of schooling in the distribution of human capital in societies, and to better understand how this distribution varies across nations with different educational ideals and/or systems of education. The absence of data on what students know before they enter schooling makes it particularly difficult to assess the true contribution of schooling to learning, as does the lack of pretest and posttest measures of achievement and adequate data on home background. At a minimum, one easy recommendation for improving cross-national surveys is to ensure that achievement is measured at two points in time in each age group under study and to ensure that state-of-the-art measures of home background are included. The inclusion of younger and older age groups, while desirable for a full analysis of the role of schooling in the distribution of cognitive development in societies, might confront too many budgetary and technical problems to prove feasible, although the use of household samples and a redefinition upward of the age at which we can consider individuals to be "school leavers" would be a welcome addition to cross-national comparisons of achievement.

Within the realm of achievable improvements, I would also encourage the continued use of qualitative case study research as a companion to survey work. I would, however, recommend that work on this front proceed slowly, starting first with a clarification (or at least a sustained discussion) of the approach to comparison that underlies the use of such research methods, and how data from these efforts will be used to inform issues of survey research design and to interpret survey results and be reported to the public.

I would also encourage more thought about ways to characterize societies—as entities worthy of study in and of themselves. Very little attention was given in this volume to how to improve the ways in which we conceptualize and measure properties of different education systems or the societies in which they are embedded, yet a clear understanding of these issues is the key to any good, comparative, cross-national theory of educational processes. Lacking good theories and explicit attention to the development of measures at the societal level of analysis, I fear that much of what passes as cross-national comparison will be based on hunch, myth, and uninformed secondary data analysis, rather than carefully crafted cross-national theories of education.

All of this leads to the third question:

- **How important is it to have international surveys of student achievement on a regular basis and with participation of a constant set of countries?**

The evidence on this point seems fairly clear. It is precisely because the cross-national surveys have been conducted continuously over a span of 30 years that this body of work has made the progress it has. Consider as examples of this point our changing understanding of the relationship of socioeconomic status and achievement, or the increasingly sophisticated conceptualization and measurement of opportunity to learn. These developments suggest the importance of continuing the cross-national surveys using samples of nations that at least approximate the kinds of nations used in prior studies.

As to whether cross-national studies strictly require a panel (that is, a constant set) of nations, I am uncertain, although for all intents and purposes, voluntary participation by societies around the world has been constant enough to result in a sample that comes close to being a panel of nations.[10] To argue for a panel of nations is to give weight to a goal of cross-national surveys that was not discussed much in this volume—looking at changes in educational processes over time and thinking about how and why educational processes change in different kinds of societies. To the extent that there are strong theories about this, I would urge that a panel be formed that includes the kinds of societies needed for testing those theories, but lacking such theories, voluntary participation in the cross-national surveys seems sufficient.

Finally, I am uncertain about how frequently cross-national surveys of student achievement should be conducted. On one hand, I think such studies should be mounted no more than once a decade, especially because this seems to be the amount of time the research community takes to fully digest the last round of studies and formulate new and better theories to test in the next wave. Too frequent a cycle of surveys, I fear, will simply routinize the work, leading to studies that gather the same data over and over again, and to data analyses that only partially digest any one set of findings. Still, I am mindful of the need to maintain a research infrastructure in nations that might otherwise lack it should funding for large-scale, cross-national surveys disappear; as a result, I can propose one alternative to a once-a-decade approach to cross-national surveys. That would be to conduct studies focused on one or a few academic subjects at intervals less than a decade—say every three years or so—rather than mounting one large, multisubject study each decade. In this design, there would be time for conceptual work between cycles of subject-matter testing, but there also would be a constant stream of work and data for the cross-national research community.

In closing, let me reiterate a point I hope I made clear throughout this essay. Despite the caveats I raised about cross-national surveys of student achievement, and despite my concerns about their validity for setting educational standards and informing the process of school improvement in the United States, I firmly believe that such studies meet many of the goals their advocates hold for them. The cross-national surveys have helped stimulate a national and public debate about educational standards in the United States, and have done so on a regular basis. They have also pointed the way to some very interesting designs for educational improvement in the United States that have given rise to some very interesting efforts at school improvement. What this line of work needs to improve, in my view, is no more or less than what any other well-conceived and well-conducted research program needs—more time to develop methods and theories that can be tested and revised on a regular basis. What the collection of papers in this volume contributes to this process is some very good insights into the theories and methods that can guide this development.

NOTES

1. Thanks to Larry Suter of the National Science Foundation for this insight.
2. In fact, this was precisely the approach used by the New Standards project described in National Research Council (1995).
3. The difficult problems of selection bias present in this age cohort in TIMSS are discussed in more detail in both Raudenbush and Kim (this volume) and Smith (this volume).
4. What would we conclude, for example, if it was found that the education system in the United States worked to reduce initial (preschool) dispersions in achievement among different social groups and led to "average" or above levels of achievement in international comparisons at age twenty-two? Would we not argue that our system was in fact achieving its main purposes, despite room for improvement? And would it not be interesting to compare dispersions in achievement, as these unfolded over the life course, as well as average levels of achievement at different time points, across a well-chosen sample of nations?
5. I am thinking here of the line of studies that originated in the 1970s with the National Longitudinal Survey, that progressed through High School and Beyond, and has continued with the National Educational Longitudinal Survey and the Early Childhood Longitudinal Study.
6. In fact, the development of carefully constructed measures of OTL were pioneered in the cross-national surveys, where elaborate lists of curricular content were prepared and where teachers were asked to report the extent to which they "covered" such content on self-administered questionnaires. Such elaborate measures of OTL (or content coverage) have begun to appear in large-scale surveys of student achievement in the United States, especially studies sponsored by the U.S. Department of Education's Planning and Evaluation Services (see, for example, the *Instructional Dimensions Study*, the *Sustaining Effects Study*, and *Prospects*), where the measures show statistically significant relationships with student achievement. Good measures of curriculum coverage in schools have not, however, been a hallmark of NCES-sponsored longitudinal studies.
7. Raudenbush and Kim (this volume) raise an additional set of concerns about the various strategies used by comparative educationists to make causal inferences about system-level change using cross-national surveys, including cautions about missing data problems and how these problems affect cross-national analyses of cohort differences in achievement and system-level analyses of changes in achievement over time. I do not discuss these forms of analysis or Raudenbush and Kim's critique of them in this chapter, except to note that these kinds of analyses, and the problems discussed by Raudenbush and Kim, are central to the important goal of cross-national work discussed by BICSE (National Research Council, 1993), namely, using repeated surveys to examine trends in schooling within and between nations of the world.
8. I thank Bill Schmidt for suggesting this as a real possibility.
9. I am thinking here again of the New Standards project and the work of the First in the World Consortium.
10. I thank David Baker for this insight.

REFERENCES

Baker, D. P. (1993). Compared to Japan, the U.S. is a low achiever . . . really: New evidence and comment on Westbury. *Educational Researcher, 22*(3), 18-20.

Baker, D. P., Goesling, B., & LeTendre, G. K. (2000). Social class, school quality, and national development: A cross-national analysis of the "Heyneman-Loxley" effect. Unpublished manuscript, Pennsylvania State University, College of Education.

Berliner, D. C., & Biddle, B. J. (1995). *The manufactured crisis: Myths, fraud and the attack on America's public schools.* Reading, MA: Addison Wesley.

Bracey, G. W. (1997). *Setting the record straight: Responses to misconceptions about public education in the United States.* Alexandria, VA: Association for Supervision and Curriculum Development.

Carroll, J. (1963). A model for school learning. *Teachers College Record, 64,* 723-733.

Central Advisory Council for Education. (1967). *Children and their primary schools. Vols. 1-2: The Plowden Report.* London: Her Majesty's Stationery Office.

Coleman, J. S., Campbell, E. Q., Hobson, C. J., McPartland, J., Mood A. M., Weinfeld, F. D., & York, R. L. (1966). *Equality of educational opportunity.* Washington, DC: U.S. Department of Health, Education, and Welfare.

Heyneman, S. P., & Loxley, W. A. (1983). The effect of primary school quality on academic achievement across twenty-nine high- and low-income countries. *American Journal of Sociology, 88,* 1162-1194.

Husen, T. (1987). Policy impact of IEA research. *Comparative Education Review, 31*(1), 129-136.

Meyer, J. W., Kamens, D., & Benavot, A. (1992). *School knowledge for the masses: World models and national primary curriculum categories in the twentieth century.* London: Falmer Press.

National Commission on Excellence in Education. (1983). *A nation at risk: The imperative for educational reform.* Washington, DC: U.S. Government Printing Office.

National Research Council (1992). *Assessing evaluation studies: The case of the bilingual education strategies.* Panel to Review Evaluation Studies of Bilingual Education, M. M. Meyer & S. E. Fienberg, eds. Committee on National Statistics, Commission on Behavioral and Social Sciences and Education. Washington, DC: National Academy Press.

National Research Council. (1993). *A collaborative agenda for improving international comparative studies in education.* Board on International Comparative Studies in Education, D. M. Gilford, ed. Commission on Behavioral and Social Sciences and Education. Washington, DC: National Academy Press.

National Research Council. (1995). *International comparative studies in education: Descriptions of selected large-scale assessments and case studies.* Board on International Comparative Studies in Education, Commission on Behavioral and Social Sciences and Education. Washington, D.C.: National Academy Press.

Ramirez, F. O., & Boli, J. (1987). The political construction of mass education: European origins and worldwide institutionalization. *Sociology of Education, 60,* 2-17.

Schmidt, W. H., McKnight, C. C., Cogan, L. S., Jakwerth, P. M., & Houng, R. T. (1999). *Facing the consequence: Using TIMSS for a closer look at U.S. mathematics and science education.* Boston: Kluwer Academic.

Schmidt, W. H., McKnight, C. C., & Raizen, S. A. (1997). *A splintered vision: An investigation of U.S. science and mathematics education.* Boston: Kluwer Academic.

Stevenson, D. & Baker, D. (1991). State control of the curriculum and classroom instruction. *Sociology of Education, 64,* 1-10.

Stigler, J., & Hiebert, J. (1999). Teaching is a cultural activity. *American Educator, Winter,* 4-11.

Tilly, C. (1984). *Big structures, large processes, huge comparisons.* New York: Russell Sage Foundation.

Westbury, I. (1992). Comparing American and Japanese achievement: Is the United States really a low achiever? *Educational Researcher, 22*(3), 18-24.

Appendixes

A

Symposium Agenda and Participants

**BOARD ON INTERNATIONAL
COMPARATIVE STUDIES IN EDUCATION**

**Methodological Advances in
Large-Scale Cross-National Education Surveys**

Symposium

November 1, 2000
The National Academies
National Academy of Sciences Building, entrance 2100 C Street, N.W.
Washington, D.C.

AGENDA

Lecture Room

8:00-8:30 a.m.   *Continental breakfast in meeting room*

8:30-9:00   Welcome and Introductions
        Andrew Porter (*Chair*), University of Wisconsin,
           Madison

9:00-10:30   *Panel #1: Study Design*
        Chair: Eugene Owen, U.S. Department of Education,
           National Center for Education Statistics

Commissioned authors:

Measuring achievement: Robert L. Linn, University of
   Colorado
Translation: Ronald K. Hambleton, University of
   Massachusetts
Sampling: James R. Chromy, Research Triangle Institute
Discussant: William H. Schmidt, Michigan State
   University

Author Response

10:30-10:45   *Break*

10:45-12:15   **Panel #2: Context and Culture**
                 Chair: Valena Plisko, U.S. Department of Education,
                      National Center for Education Statistics
                 Commissioned authors:
                 Cognition and culture: Janine Bempechat, Harvard
                      University
                 Family background: Claudia Buchmann, Duke
                      University
                 Cross-cultural issues: Gerald K. LeTendre,
                      Pennsylvania State University
                 Discussant: William C. Cummings, George Washington
                      University

                 Author Response

12:15-1:15 pm   *Lunch in Lecture Room, Executive Dining Room, Members
                 Room, and Room 150*

1:15-2:45   **Panel #3: Making Inferences**
                 Chair: Larry Suter, National Science Foundation,
                      Division of Research on Education, Policy and
                      Practice
                 Commissioned authors:
                 Measuring opportunity to learn: Robert Floden,
                      Michigan State University
                 Statistical methods: Stephen W. Raudenbush,
                      University of Michigan
                 Inferences for national policy: Marshall S. Smith,
                      Stanford University
                 Discussant: Senta Raizen, National Center for Improving
                      Science Education

                 Author Response

2:45-3:00	*Break*
3:00-4:00	**Roundtables**

Panels #1, 2, and 3 in three breakout groups
Executive Dining Room, Members Room, and Room
150
- Authors discuss cross-cutting issues and future
research directions
- Questions from the audience

4:00-5:00 **Rapporteur Review**
Chair: Adam Gamoran, University of Wisconsin,
Madison
Rapporteurs:
Gerald Bracey, Alexandria, Virginia
Brian Rowan, University of Michigan

5:00 *Adjourn*

PARTICIPANTS

Motoko Akiba, Pennsylvania State University
Naif al-Romi, Pennsylvania State University and Ministry of
Education, Saudi Arabia
David Baker, Pennsylvania State University
Janine Bempechat, Harvard University
L. Benveniste, The World Bank
David C. Berliner,* Arizona State University
Sue Berryman, The World Bank
Marilyn Binkley, U.S. Department of Education
Gerald Bracey, Writer, Alexandria, Virginia
Blanch Brownley, District of Columbia Public Schools
Claudia Buchmann, Duke University
Colette Chabbott, Board on International Comparative Studies in
Education, National Research Council
James R. Chromy, Research Triangle Institute
Yvan Clermont, Statistics Canada
William C. Cummings, George Washington University
Roseanne DeFabio, New York State Education Deptartment
Elizabeth Demarest, U.S. Department of Education
Sandra Dike, Virginia Technical University
Clea Fernandez,* Teachers College, Columbia University

---

*Member of BICSE in 2000

Robert Floden, Michigan State University
Mary Frase, National Science Foundation
Adam Gamoran,* University of Wisconsin, Madison
Lenore Garcia, U.S. Department of Education
Dorothy Gilford, Gilford Associates, Bethesda, Maryland
Alice Gill, American Federation of Teachers
Vincent Greaney, The World Bank
Ronald K. Hambleton, University of Massachusetts
Sandra Hanson, Catholic University
Richard Houang, Michigan State University
Marion Hoyda, Lockport District 205, Lockport, Illinois
Norma Jimenez, Harvard University
Jeremy Kilpatrick,* University of Georgia
Irwin Kirsch, Educational Testing Service
Archie LaPointe, Educational Testing Service
Michelle LaPointe, U.S. Department of Education
John Larson, Montgomery County Public Schools
Mariann Lemke, U.S. Department of Education
Gerald K. LeTendre, Pennsylvania State University
Robert L. Linn, University of Colorado
Marlaine E. Lockheed,* The World Bank
Giselle Lundy-Ponce, American Federation of Teachers
Kitty Mak, American Institutes for Research
James Maxwell, U.S. Department of Education
Sam McKee, U.S. Department of Education
Meredith Miller, U.S. Department of Education
Heinrich Mintrop, University of Maryland
Jena Mittelman, U.S. Department of Education
Jay Moskowitz, American Institutes for Research
Patricia Olmsted, High/Scope Educational Research Foundation
Martin Orland, U.S. Department of Education
Eugene H. Owen, U.S. Department of Education, National Center
    for Education Statistics
Lynn W. Paine, Michigan State University
Lois Peak,* U.S. Department of Education
Marianne Perie, American Institutes for Research
Gary Phillips, U.S. Department of Education
Valena W. Plisko, U.S. Department of Education, National Center
    for Education Statistics
Andrew C. Porter,* *(chair)* University of Wisconsin, Madison
Owen Power, Statistics Canada
Edys Quellmalz, SRI International
Francisco Ramirez, Stanford University

Senta A. Raizen, National Center for Improving Science Education
Stephen W. Raudenbush, University of Michigan
Iris Rotberg, George Washington University
Brian Rowan, University of Michigan
Laura Salganik, American Institutes for Research
Kathryn Scantlebury, National Science Foundation
William H. Schmidt, Michigan State University
Janet Ward Schofield,* University of Pittsburgh
Ramsay Selden, American Institutes for Research
Kusum Singh, Virginia Technical University
Marshall S. Smith, Stanford University
Thomas Smith, National Science Foundation
Ravay Snow-Renner, Mid-continent Research for Education and
Learning
Larry E. Suter, National Science Foundation, Division of Research
on Education, Policy and Practice
Maria Teresa Tatto, Michigan State University
William L. Taylor, Attorney at Law, Washington, D.C.
Joseph Tobin,* University of Hawaii
Judith Torney-Purta, University of Maryland
Monica Ulewicz, Board on International Comparative Studies in
Education, National Research Council
Arie van der Ploeg, North Central Regional Education Laboratory
Elizabeth VanderPutten, National Science Foundation
Hans Wagemaker, International Association for the Evaluation of
Educational Achievement
Myriam Waiser, The World Bank
Patsy Wang-Iverson, Research for Better Schools
Trevor Williams, WESTAT
Alex Wiseman, Pennsylvania State University
Shu Jing Yen, Maryland Department of Education

B

Biographical Sketches
of Board Members

Board on International Comparative Studies in Education

GORDON M. AMBACH *(ex-officio member until term ended November 2001)* most recently served as executive director of the Council of Chief State School Officers (CCSSO) before retiring in 2001. He also is a former New York State Commissioner of Education and served in the U.S. Office of Education in the 1950s and 1960s. His professional interests have centered on education policy making and legislation. His advisory roles include membership on commissions and panels on learning technology, job training, the arts, and education standards and assessment. His other National Research Council memberships have been the Mathematical Sciences Education Board and the National Summit on Mathematics Assessment Steering Committee. As executive director of CCSSO, he represents the United States in the International Association for the Evaluation of Education Achievement (IEA), and is a member of the IEA Standing Committee. Ambach received a C.A.S. in education administration and an M.A. in teaching from Harvard University, and a B.A. from Yale University.

DAVID C. BERLINER *(current member)* is Regents' Professor of Educational Leadership and Policy Studies and Professor of Psychology in Education and former dean of the College of Education at Arizona State University. His research has focused on the study of teaching, teacher education, and educational policy. He has taught at the University of Massachusetts, the University of Arizona, and universities abroad. His publications include *Educational Psychology* and *The Manufactured Crisis*. Among his many awards are the Friend of Education award from the National Education Association, the Distinguished Contributions award of the American Educational Research Association (AERA), and the E.L. Thorndike award of the Division of Educational Psychology of the American Psychological Association (APA). He has served as president of AERA and APA, and as a member of the National Research Council's Board on Testing and Assessment. He received a Ph.D. in educational psychology from Stanford University.

CHRISTOPHER T. CROSS *(member until term ended September 2001)* is a senior fellow with the Center on Education Policy and is the former president of the Council for Basic Education. In addition, he serves on the board of the American Institutes for Research, chairs the National Assessment of Title I Independent Review Panel for the U.S. Department of Education, and is chairman of the board of the Center for Education Policy. Previously, Mr. Cross served as president of the Maryland State Board of Education, assistant secretary for educational research and improvement at the U.S. Department of Education, and director of the education initiative of The Business Roundtable. He has written extensively in the education and public policy areas. Cross received an M.A. in government from California State University, Los Angeles.

EMERSON J. ELLIOTT *(current chair)* is a consultant, primarily with the National Council for Accreditation of Teacher Education, where he directs collaborative projects to develop performance-based standards and review processes for the program content element of accreditation. He has also consulted with the U.S. Department of Education National Educational Research Policy and Priorities Board and formerly served as the first Commissioner of Education Statistics with the U.S. Department of Education. He was elected American Statistical Association Fellow and has received Presidential Rank Awards for Meritorious and Distinguished Executive Service. His service with the National Research Council includes membership on the Committee on Strategic Education Research Program Feasibility Study. Elliott received an M.A. in public administration from the University of Michigan.

CLEA FERNANDEZ *(current member)* is an assistant professor of psychology and education in the Department of Human Development at Columbia University Teachers College. Her research interests are in the analysis of classroom processes, with a special emphasis on cross-cultural comparisons; the psychology of learning from instruction; and teachers' theories of instruction and teacher development. She has served as director of programs and research with Classroom, Inc., helping state school systems to implement computer-based simulations for use by teachers and students. She has also served as co-director of the videotape case studies project of the Third International Mathematics and Science Study, and has co-authored several journal articles and book chapters on Japanese and American mathematics education. She received a Ph.D. from the University of Chicago.

ADAM GAMORAN *(current member)* is a professor of sociology and educational policy studies at the University of Wisconsin, Madison. His research focuses on stratification and resource allocation in school systems. While a Fulbright Fellow at the University of Edinburgh, he studied curriculum change and educational inequality in Scotland. His publications include an article, "Student achievement in public magnet, public comprehensive, and private city high schools," in *Educational Evaluation and Policy Analysis*, as well as articles on student achievement, curriculum, and organizational analysis in *Sociology of Education, American Educational Research Journal*, and *American Sociological Review*. He received a Ph.D. in education from the University of Chicago.

LARRY V. HEDGES *(current member)* is Stella M. Rowley Professor at The University of Chicago in the Departments of Education, Psychology, and Sociology. His honors include Fellow of the American Statistical Association, Fellow of the American Psychological Association, and recipient of the Review of Research Award from the American Educational Research Association. He has authored and coauthored numerous books and articles on statistical methods for research and is editor of the *Journal of Educational and Behavioral Statistics*. His National Research Council service includes membership on the Committee on the Evaluation of National and State Assessments of Educational Progress, Forum on Educational Excellence and Testing Equity, and Panel on the Combination of Information. Hedges received a Ph.D. in mathematical methods in educational research from Stanford University.

HENRY W. HEIKKINEN *(current member)* is a professor of chemistry at the University of Northern Colorado, specializing in chemical education. His current interests focus on curriculum development in general chemistry, student preconceptions, and implications of standards-based education reforms in science. He has served as a member of the U.S. Steering Committee for the Third International Mathematics and Science Study. He has also served as a consultant to the American Association for the Advancement of Science Project 2061 and as a chemistry education consultant in numerous countries. His National Research Council service includes membership on the Commission on Life Sciences and the Committee on Development of an Addendum to the National Science Education Standards on Science and Technology. Heikkinen received a Ph.D. in chemical education from the University of Maryland.

JEREMY KILPATRICK (current member) is Regents Professor at the University of Georgia Department of Mathematics Education. He has served on advisory boards of the National Center for Research in Mathematical Sciences Education (chair); Project on Science, Mathematics and Technology Education in OECD Countries (Case Studies); and Core-Plus Mathematics Project. He has also served on the U.S. steering committee and subject matter advisory committee of the Third International Mathematics and Science Study, and as a researcher for the Mathematics Case Studies of U.S. Innovations in Science and Technology Education. His National Research Council service includes membership on the Mathematical Sciences Education Board and the Mathematics Learning Study Committee (chair). He received a Ph.D. in mathematics education from Stanford University.

MARLAINE E. LOCKHEED (member until term ended September 2001) is manager of evaluation at The World Bank Institute. She has served on the board of the Comparative International Education Society and as vice president of the American Educational Research Association (AERA) as well as president of the international studies special interest group of AERA. She serves on the research committee of the World Bank and as coeditor of Educational Evaluation and Policy Analysis. Her research focuses on school effectiveness in developing contexts. Her publications include National Assessment: Testing the System, Effective Schools in Developing Countries, and Improving Primary Education in Developing Countries. Lockheed received a Ph.D. in international development education from Stanford University.

LYNN W. PAINE (current vice chair) is an associate professor in the Department of Teacher Education at Michigan State University. Her research interests focus on understanding teaching and teacher education as contextualized practices. She currently serves as codirector of a study of mathematics and science new teacher induction in selected countries. She also has served as a researcher with a Spencer Foundation cross-national study of teacher education as a board member of the Comparative and International Education Study. Her publications include chapters in The Political Dimension of Teacher Education and Oxford Studies in Comparative Education. She also has served as a member of the National

Research Council Committee on Continuing to Learn from TIMSS. Paine received a Ph.D. in international development from Stanford University.

ANDREW C. PORTER *(chair until term ended September 2001)* is director of the Wisconsin Center for Education Research and professor of educational psychology, both at the University of Wisconsin, Madison. He currently directs the National Institute for Science Education, which is funded by the National Science Foundation. He has also served on the faculty at Michigan State University, where he was also associate dean for research and graduate study and codirector of the Institute for Research on Teaching. His research interests and numerous publications focus on psychometrics, student and teacher assessment, research on teaching, and education policy. His other National Research Council memberships include the Study Group on Fair Test Use, the Panel to Evaluate the National Center for Education Statistics, and the Committee on the Federal Role in Education Research. Porter received a Ph.D. in educational psychology from the University of Wisconsin.

JANET WARD SCHOFIELD *(current member)* is a professor of psychology and a senior scientist at the Learning Research and Development Center at the University of Pittsburgh. Her research interests focus on the impact of social and technological change on classroom processes. She has served as a consultant to the U.S. Office of Technology Assessment and to the Associate Commissioner for Equal Educational Opportunity at the U.S. Department of Education, as well as to state government bodies and local school districts. Her numerous publications include Computers and Classroom Culture and Black and White in School: Trust, Tension or Tolerance? She is a fellow of the American Psychological Association and the American Psychological Society. She received a Ph.D. in social psychology from Harvard University.

JOSEPH TOBIN *(current member)* is a professor of early childhood education in the College of Education at Arizona State University. He has formerly served as a professor in the College of Education at the University of Hawaii and as a visiting professor in human development at the University of Chicago. His research interests include educational ethnography, Japanese culture and education, visual anthropology, early childhood education, and children and the media. His publications include *Preschool in Three Cultures* and others on early childhood education, and classroom ethnography. He received a Ph.D. in human development from The University of Chicago.

Index